BELIEVE

LIVING THE STORY OF THE BIBLE
TO BECOME LIKE JESUS

SELECTIONS FROM THE NEW INTERNATIONAL VERSION

BELIEVE

LIVING THE STORY OF THE BIBLE
TO BECOME LIKE JESUS

GENERAL EDITOR
RANDY FRAZEE

ZONDERVAN®

ZONDERVAN
Believe, NIV
Copyright © 2014 by Zondervan

Requests for information should be addressed to:
Zondervan, 3900 *Sparks Drive SE, Grand Rapids, Michigan,* 49546

Library of Congress Cataloging-in-Publication Data

Believe : living the story of the Bible to become like Jesus / general editor, Randy Frazee.
    pages cm
  1. Bible — Criticism, interpretation, etc. — Miscellanea. 2. Christian life — Biblical teaching —
Miscellanea. I. Frazee, Randy, editor.
  BS511.3.B445 2014
  220.60 — dc23
                      2014023442

Cover design: Extra Credit Projects

Printed in the United States of America

14 15 16 17 18 19 20 21 22 23 24 25 /DCI/ 15 14 13 12 11 10 9 8 7 6 5 4 3 2 1

Table of Contents

Preface | 7

Preface

A distinguished sociologist embarked on a quest to answer this question, "How did the marginal Jesus movement become the dominant religious force in the Western world within just a few centuries?" By his estimates the number of Christians grew to 33,882,008 believers by AD 350.[1] A movement that started with Jesus and a handful of his followers grew at an amazing rate! This professor was not a personal follower of Jesus but was mesmerized by the influence of Jesus' life on the entire world.

What he discovered in his adventures through history was a group of very common, ordinary folks who ended up doing uncommon, extraordinary things. These people valued others who were looked down upon. When two devastating epidemics of measles and small pox wiped out one-fourth to one-third of the population of the Roman Empire, these Christ-followers not only nursed their own but also took in those whose family cast them out into the streets to die. People flocked to this new community founded on a rare expression of love. Anyone who said "yes" to Jesus' invitation of life was invited to belong.

At the end of the unbelieving social scientist's extensive search he wrote these words: "Therefore, as I conclude this study, I find it necessary to confront what appears to me to be *the ultimate factor* in the rise of Christianity ... I believe that it was the religion's particular doctrines that permitted Christianity to be among the most sweeping and successful revitalization movements in history. And it was the way these doctrines took on actual flesh, the way they directed organizational actions and individual behavior that led to the rise of Christianity."[2]

In a nutshell, the early Christians BELIEVED.

They simply, by faith, believed with their whole hearts the powerful truths taught in the Scriptures. It changed them from the inside out. Their loving and courageous actions toward their

---

1. Rodney Stark, *The Rise of Christianity: A Sociologist Reconsiders History* (New Jersey: Princeton University Press, 1996), 10.
2. Ibid, 211.

family, neighbors and even strangers were merely outpourings of what was flowing from the inside.

What are the core truths these followers believed that so radically changed their lives for the good? These truths make up the content of the book you now hold in your hands — *Believe*.

The first ten chapters of *Believe* detail the core Beliefs of the Christian life. Together they answer the question, "What do I believe?"

The second ten chapters discuss the core Practices of the Christian life. Together they answer the question, "What should I do?"

The final ten chapters contain the core Virtues of the Christian life. Together they answer the question, "Who am I becoming?"

Believe includes the actual, God-breathed words of the Bible, not one person or one denomination's words on these important, life-altering topics. *Believe* contains portions of Scripture that were thoughtfully and carefully excerpted from Genesis to Revelation because they speak directly to the core Belief, Practice or Virtue highlighted in each chapter. As you read, you will be bathed in what the Scriptures say about each of these key ideas. Transitions between Scripture text, which appear *in italic*, were written to give you an introduction, explanation and/or context to the Scripture you are about to read. After each section of Scripture, a reference is provided to let you know where to find it in the Bible.

The Scripture text used in *Believe* is taken from the New International Version (NIV). Helpful material placed at the end of *Believe* include an epilogue that gives you an idea of the global impact this story has had on the world and a discussion guide with questions for you to reflect on personally or with a group.

Also, *Believe* is a full Bible-engagement campaign with resources for an entire church, school or group of any kind to experience together. If you have experienced *The Story* and are wondering what is next and how to go deeper, then *Believe* is that next step for you. If you haven't experienced *The Story* and are looking for a tool that helps you and your church, organization or small group understand the Bible as one overarching narrative, then *The Story* will also be a useful resource for you to explore your faith. For more on *Believe* and *The Story*, check out www.thestory.com and www.believethestory.com.

As you turn the page and read the first core belief about God himself, remember *Believe* is an action word. God is personally watching over you as you embark on this journey. He doesn't want you to just believe in your head these truths; he wants you to believe with your whole heart his Word as the operating system for your life. He wants to transform your life and family for good and forever. He wants you to join the movement. He wants to put the "extra" in your "ordinary" so you can live an "extraordinary" life in Christ. What he did so radically in the beginning, he is doing again today if you will only BELIEVE.

Here is my prayer for you,

"Father, you fully know the reader who holds this book in their hands. You know them by name. You love them deeply — always have, always will. As they embark on this amazing journey, give them the faith to believe your truths with their whole heart. Work within them. Let that good work push out to their mouth, ears, hands and feet to positively affect the people you have placed around them. As they finish reading the last page, may they whisper to you and then shout to the world — I BELIEVE!"

— Randy Frazee
General Editor

What Do I Believe?

For where your treasure is,
there your heart will be also.
Matthew 6:21

What we believe in our hearts will define who we become. God wants you to become like Jesus. This is who God created you to be. It is the most truthful and powerful way to live. The journey to *becoming* like Jesus begins by *thinking* like Jesus.

The following ten chapters will introduce and expose you to the key beliefs of the Christian life. These beliefs were not only taught by Jesus but also modeled by Jesus when he walked this earth. Because we live from the heart, embracing these core truths in both our minds and our hearts is the first step to truly becoming like Jesus.

Each of the following chapters contains Scripture passages from Genesis to Revelation focused on a particular belief. You are about to discover what God wants you to know and believe about these important topics. Embark on each page with a passion to learn and understand. Then prayerfully ask, "What do *I* believe?"

Fully adopting these fantastic truths in your heart may not come at the end of reading the chapter. If you are honest, it may take a while, and that is okay. The Christian life is a journey. There are no shortcuts. As each of the key concepts takes up residence in your heart they, with the amazing help of God's presence in your life, will change your life for the good.

When you start thinking like Jesus, you are well on your way to becoming like Jesus.

CHAPTER

1

God

KEY IDEA

I believe the God of the Bible is the only true God—
Father, Son and Holy Spirit.

KEY VERSE

May the grace of the Lord Jesus Christ,
and the love of God, and the fellowship
of the Holy Spirit be with you all.
2 Corinthians 13:14

Everything begins with God. The Bible never seeks to defend the existence of God. It is assumed. God has revealed himself so powerfully through his creation—both at the macro and micro level—that at the end of the day, no one will have an excuse for not putting their trust in him.

GOD REVEALS HIMSELF

In the beginning God created the heavens and the earth.

GENESIS 1:1

> The heavens declare the glory of God;
>   the skies proclaim the work of his hands.
> Day after day they pour forth speech;
>   night after night they reveal knowledge.
> They have no speech, they use no words;
>   no sound is heard from them.
> Yet their voice goes out into all the earth,
>   their words to the ends of the world.
> In the heavens God has pitched a tent for the sun.

PSALM 19:1–4

For since the creation of the world God's invisible qualities—his eternal power and divine nature—have been clearly seen, being understood from what has been made, so that people are without excuse.

ROMANS 1:20

THE ONE TRUE GOD

From beginning to end, the Bible reveals that there is only one true God. But who is he? The book of Deuteronomy looks back after Moses had led the Israelites out of slavery in Egypt. During that time God had revealed himself as the one true, all-powerful God over Pharaoh through the ten plagues. Now a new generation had grown up in the wilderness and was poised to inherit the land God had promised Abraham. Moses offered the second generation a series of farewell speeches to remind them to choose, worship and follow the one true God—the God of Abraham, Isaac and Jacob. If they did, all would go well for them.

These are the commands, decrees and laws the LORD your God directed me to teach you to observe in the land that you are crossing the Jordan to possess, so that you, your children and their children after them may fear the LORD your God as long as you live by keeping all his decrees and commands that I give you, and so that you may enjoy long life. Hear, Israel, and be careful to obey so that it may go well with you and that you may increase greatly in a land flowing with milk and honey, just as the LORD, the God of your ancestors, promised you.

Hear, O Israel: The LORD our God, the LORD is one. Love the LORD your God with all your heart and with all your soul and with all your strength. These commandments that I give you today are to be on your hearts. Impress them on your children. Talk about them when you sit at home and when you walk along the road, when you lie down and when you get up. Tie them as symbols on your hands and bind them on your foreheads. Write them on the doorframes of your houses and on your gates. DEUTERONOMY 6:1–9

After Moses died, Joshua became the next great leader of the Israelites. He was charged with leading the people into the promised land. God was with them and fought for them as they began conquering the land. Under Joshua's leadership the Israelites remained steady in their devotion to God. Before Joshua died, he gathered the people together and issued them a stiff challenge to choose for themselves to serve the Lord, the one true God.

Then Joshua assembled all the tribes of Israel at Shechem. He summoned the elders, leaders, judges and officials of Israel, and they presented themselves before God.

Joshua said to all the people, "This is what the LORD, the God of Israel, says: 'Long ago your ancestors, including Terah the father of Abraham and Nahor, lived beyond the Euphrates River and worshiped other gods. But I took your father Abraham from the land beyond the Euphrates and led him throughout Canaan and gave him many descendants. I gave him Isaac, and to Isaac I gave Jacob and Esau. I assigned the hill country of Seir to Esau, but Jacob and his family went down to Egypt.

"'Then I sent Moses and Aaron, and I afflicted the Egyptians by what I did there, and I brought you out. When I brought your people out of Egypt, you came to the sea, and the Egyptians pursued them with chariots and horsemen as far as the Red Sea. But they cried to the LORD for help, and he put darkness between you and the Egyptians; he brought the sea over them and covered them. You saw with your own eyes what I did to the Egyptians. Then you lived in the wilderness for a long time.

" 'I brought you to the land of the Amorites who lived east of the Jordan. They fought against you, but I gave them into your hands. I destroyed them from before you, and you took possession of their land. When Balak son of Zippor, the king of Moab, prepared to fight against Israel, he sent for Balaam son of Beor to put a curse on you. But I would not listen to Balaam, so he blessed you again and again, and I delivered you out of his hand.

" 'Then you crossed the Jordan and came to Jericho. The citizens of Jericho fought against you, as did also the Amorites, Perizzites, Canaanites, Hittites, Girgashites, Hivites and Jebusites, but I gave them into your hands. I sent the hornet ahead of you, which drove them out before you — also the two Amorite kings. You did not do it with your own sword and bow. So I gave you a land on which you did not toil and cities you did not build; and you live in them and eat from vineyards and olive groves that you did not plant.'

"Now fear the LORD and serve him with all faithfulness. Throw away the gods your ancestors worshiped beyond the Euphrates River and in Egypt, and serve the LORD. But if serving the LORD seems undesirable to you, then choose for yourselves this day whom you will serve, whether the gods your ancestors served beyond the Euphrates, or the gods of the Amorites, in whose land you are living. But as for me and my household, we will serve the LORD."

Then the people answered, "Far be it from us to forsake the LORD to serve other gods! It was the LORD our God himself who brought us and our parents up out of Egypt, from that land of slavery, and performed those great signs before our eyes. He protected us on our entire journey and among all the nations through which we traveled. And the LORD drove out before us all the nations, including the Amorites, who lived in the land. We too will serve the LORD, because he is our God."

Joshua said to the people, "You are not able to serve the LORD. He is a holy God; he is a jealous God. He will not forgive your rebellion and your sins. If you forsake the LORD and serve foreign gods, he will turn and bring disaster on you and make an end of you, after he has been good to you."

But the people said to Joshua, "No! We will serve the LORD."

Then Joshua said, "You are witnesses against yourselves that you have chosen to serve the LORD."

"Yes, we are witnesses," they replied.

"Now then," said Joshua, "throw away the foreign gods that are among you and yield your hearts to the LORD, the God of Israel."

And the people said to Joshua, "We will serve the LORD our God and obey him."

On that day Joshua made a covenant for the people, and there at Shechem he reaffirmed for them decrees and laws. And Joshua recorded these things in the Book of the Law of God. Then he took a large stone and set it up there under the oak near the holy place of the LORD.

"See!" he said to all the people. "This stone will be a witness against us. It has heard all the words the LORD has said to us. It will be a witness against you if you are untrue to your God."

Then Joshua dismissed the people, each to their own inheritance.

After these things, Joshua son of Nun, the servant of the LORD, died at the age of a hundred and ten. And they buried him in the land of his inheritance, at Timnath Serah in the hill country of Ephraim, north of Mount Gaash.

Israel served the LORD throughout the lifetime of Joshua and of the elders who outlived him and who had experienced everything the LORD had done for Israel. JOSHUA 24:1–31

Unfortunately the Israelites failed to keep their promise to follow only God. Through the people's repeated disobedience, God weakened Israel's influence—445 years after Joshua died—by dividing them into two kingdoms: the northern kingdom of Israel and the southern kingdom of Judah. Israel did not have one good king during its more than 200 years of existence. King Ahab was particularly wicked, as he introduced the worship of the pagan god

Baal to Israel. But the Lord demonstrated through the prophet Elijah that he, not Baal or any other "god," is the one true God.

Ahab went to meet Elijah. When he saw Elijah, he said to him, "Is that you, you troubler of Israel?"

"I have not made trouble for Israel," Elijah replied. "But you and your father's family have. You have abandoned the LORD's commands and have followed the Baals. Now summon the people from all over Israel to meet me on Mount Carmel. And bring the four hundred and fifty prophets of Baal and the four hundred prophets of Asherah, who eat at Jezebel's table."

So Ahab sent word throughout all Israel and assembled the prophets on Mount Carmel. Elijah went before the people and said, "How long will you waver between two opinions? If the LORD is God, follow him; but if Baal is God, follow him."

But the people said nothing.

Then Elijah said to them, "I am the only one of the LORD's prophets left, but Baal has four hundred and fifty prophets. Get two bulls for us. Let Baal's prophets choose one for themselves, and let them cut it into pieces and put it on the wood but not set fire to it. I will prepare the other bull and put it on the wood but not set fire to it. Then you call on the name of your god, and I will call on the name of the LORD. The god who answers by fire — he is God."

Then all the people said, "What you say is good."

Elijah said to the prophets of Baal, "Choose one of the bulls and prepare it first, since there are so many of you. Call on the name of your god, but do not light the fire." So they took the bull given them and prepared it.

Then they called on the name of Baal from morning till noon. "Baal, answer us!" they shouted. But there was no response; no one answered. And they danced around the altar they had made.

At noon Elijah began to taunt them. "Shout louder!" he said. "Surely he is a god! Perhaps he is deep in thought, or busy, or traveling. Maybe he is sleeping and must be awakened." So they shouted louder and slashed themselves with swords and spears, as was their custom, until their blood flowed. Midday passed, and they continued their frantic prophesying until the time for the evening sacrifice. But there was no response, no one answered, no one paid attention.

Then Elijah said to all the people, "Come here to me." They came to him, and he repaired the altar of the LORD, which had been torn down. Elijah took twelve stones, one for each of the tribes descended from Jacob, to whom the word of the LORD had come, saying, "Your name shall be Israel." With the stones he built an altar in the name of the LORD, and he dug a trench around it large enough to hold two seahs of seed. He arranged the wood, cut the bull into pieces and laid it on the wood. Then he said to them, "Fill four large jars with water and pour it on the offering and on the wood."

"Do it again," he said, and they did it again.

"Do it a third time," he ordered, and they did it the third time. The water ran down around the altar and even filled the trench.

At the time of sacrifice, the prophet Elijah stepped forward and prayed: "LORD, the God of Abraham, Isaac and Israel, let it be known today that you are God in Israel and that I am your servant and have done all these things at your command. Answer me, LORD, answer me, so these people will know that you, LORD, are God, and that you are turning their hearts back again."

Then the fire of the LORD fell and burned up the sacrifice, the wood, the stones and the soil, and also licked up the water in the trench.

When all the people saw this, they fell prostrate and cried, "The LORD — he is God! The LORD — he is God!"

Then Elijah commanded them, "Seize the prophets of Baal. Don't let anyone get away!" They seized them, and Elijah had them brought down to the Kishon Valley and slaughtered there.

1 KINGS 18:16–40

GOD IN THREE PERSONS: THE FATHER, SON AND HOLY SPIRIT

Throughout the Old Testament, people were invited to worship the one true God, but what do we know about this amazing God, this God of miracles and creative wonder? Christians believe God is actually three Persons, a "Trinity." Though the word "Trinity" isn't found in the Bible, in the very beginning of God's story, the creation story, we see hints that God is plural. Genesis 1:26 says,

"Then God said, 'Let us make mankind in our image, in our like-ness.' " The creation story tells us we were created in the image of God, and Adam and Eve were two distinct persons who came together as one, just as God is three persons but one true God.

This is the account of the heavens and the earth when they were created, when the LORD God made the earth and the heavens.

Now no shrub had yet appeared on the earth and no plant had yet sprung up, for the LORD God had not sent rain on the earth and there was no one to work the ground, but streams came up from the earth and watered the whole surface of the ground. Then the LORD God formed a man from the dust of the ground and breathed into his nostrils the breath of life, and the man became a living being.

Now the LORD God had planted a garden in the east, in Eden; and there he put the man he had formed. The LORD God made all kinds of trees grow out of the ground — trees that were pleasing to the eye and good for food. In the middle of the garden were the tree of life and the tree of the knowledge of good and evil.   GENESIS 2:4–9

The LORD God took the man and put him in the Garden of Eden to work it and take care of it. And the LORD God command-ed the man, "You are free to eat from any tree in the garden; but you must not eat from the tree of the knowledge of good and evil, for when you eat from it you will certainly die."

The LORD God said, "It is not good for the man to be alone. I will make a helper suitable for him."

Now the LORD God had formed out of the ground all the wild animals and all the birds in the sky. He brought them to the man to see what he would name them; and whatever the man called each living creature, that was its name. So the man gave names to all the livestock, the birds in the sky and all the wild animals.

But for Adam no suitable helper was found. So the LORD God caused the man to fall into a deep sleep; and while he was sleeping, he took one of the man's ribs and then closed up the place with flesh. Then the LORD God made a woman from the rib he had taken out of the man, and he brought her to the man.

The man said,

> "This is now bone of my bones
> and flesh of my flesh;
> she shall be called 'woman,'
> for she was taken out of man."

That is why a man leaves his father and mother and is united to his wife, and they become one flesh. GENESIS 2:15–24

So what is the identity of these individual Persons of God, and how are they seen to be just one being? As we turn to the opening words of John's Gospel, the answer gets more and more clear.

In the beginning was the Word, and the Word was with God, and the Word was God. He was with God in the beginning. Through him all things were made; without him nothing was made that has been made. In him was life, and that life was the light of all mankind. The light shines in the darkness, and the darkness has not overcome it. JOHN 1:1–5

The "Word" here refers to Jesus, the one born of the Virgin Mary. John refers to him as "God," as divine. John also says Jesus was there in the beginning. Jesus was God, and yet he was with God. Jesus, the divine Word, partnered with God to create all that we see and all that we have yet to see.

Who was the other Person(s)? The second sentence of the Bible tells us that the Holy Spirit was also present at creation: "The earth was formless and empty, darkness was over the surface of the deep, and the Spirit of God was hovering over the waters" (Genesis 1:2). So Jesus and the Spirit were at the creation of the world; these two Persons are God. Is that it? Who else makes up the Person of God? Fast-forward to the baptism of Jesus at the age of 30 to discover the answer.

In the fifteenth year of the reign of Tiberius Caesar — when Pontius Pilate was governor of Judea, Herod tetrarch of Galilee, his brother Philip tetrarch of Iturea and Traconitis, and Lysanias tetrarch of Abilene — during the high-priesthood of Annas and

Caiaphas, the word of God came to John son of Zechariah in the wilderness. He went into all the country around the Jordan, preaching a baptism of repentance for the forgiveness of sins. As it is written in the book of the words of Isaiah the prophet:

"A voice of one calling in the wilderness,
'Prepare the way for the Lord,
    make straight paths for him.
Every valley shall be filled in,
    every mountain and hill made low.
The crooked roads shall become straight,
    the rough ways smooth.
And all people will see God's salvation.'" LUKE 3:1–6

The people were waiting expectantly and were all wondering in their hearts if John might possibly be the Messiah. John answered them all, "I baptize you with water. But one who is more powerful than I will come, the straps of whose sandals I am not worthy to untie. He will baptize you with the Holy Spirit and fire. His winnowing fork is in his hand to clear his threshing floor and to gather the wheat into his barn, but he will burn up the chaff with unquenchable fire." And with many other words John exhorted the people and proclaimed the good news to them. LUKE 3:15–18

When all the people were being baptized, Jesus was baptized too. And as he was praying, heaven was opened and the Holy Spirit descended on him in bodily form like a dove. And a voice came from heaven: "You are my Son, whom I love; with you I am well pleased."

Now Jesus himself was about thirty years old when he began his ministry. He was the son, so it was thought, of Joseph. LUKE 3:21–23

Three distinct Persons are fully revealed in Scripture to make up the identity of the one true God: the Father, the Son Jesus and the Spirit. And all three were involved at the baptism of Jesus—the Father spoke, the Son was baptized and the Holy Spirit descended on the Son. Throughout the centuries, followers of Jesus have come to call the one true God the "Trinity," three persons who share one being. As difficult as this concept is to understand, it is important to our lives.

THE TRINITY IN OUR LIVES

*This Good News about God, God's Son come to earth and
the work of the Holy Spirit spread throughout the known world
because of people like the apostle Paul, who experienced Jesus
on the road to Damascus and, in the spirit of Joshua before him,
traveled the world spreading the gospel. The Son of God, the
second person of the Trinity, came to earth as Jesus Christ to
live and die so we may be forgiven of our sins through faith in
him. People must hear this Good News and choose to believe for
themselves. During his travels Paul went to the great Areopagus
in Athens, Greece, and gave what some call his sermon at Mars
Hill.*

While Paul was waiting for [Silas and Timothy] in Athens, he
was greatly distressed to see that the city was full of idols. So he
reasoned in the synagogue with both Jews and God-fearing Greeks,
as well as in the marketplace day by day with those who happened
to be there. A group of Epicurean and Stoic philosophers began to
debate with him. Some of them asked, "What is this babbler trying to say?" Others remarked, "He seems to be advocating foreign
gods." They said this because Paul was preaching the good news
about Jesus and the resurrection. Then they took him and brought
him to a meeting of the Areopagus, where they said to him, "May
we know what this new teaching is that you are presenting? You
are bringing some strange ideas to our ears, and we would like to
know what they mean." (All the Athenians and the foreigners who
lived there spent their time doing nothing but talking about and
listening to the latest ideas.)

Paul then stood up in the meeting of the Areopagus and said:
"People of Athens! I see that in every way you are very religious.
For as I walked around and looked carefully at your objects of wor-
ship, I even found an altar with this inscription: TO AN UNKNOWN
GOD. So you are ignorant of the very thing you worship — and this
is what I am going to proclaim to you.

"The God who made the world and everything in it is the Lord
of heaven and earth and does not live in temples built by human
hands. And he is not served by human hands, as if he needed
anything. Rather, he himself gives everyone life and breath and

everything else. From one man he made all the nations, that they should inhabit the whole earth; and he marked out their appointed times in history and the boundaries of their lands. God did this so that they would seek him and perhaps reach out for him and find him, though he is not far from any one of us. 'For in him we live and move and have our being.' As some of your own poets have said, 'We are his offspring.'

"Therefore since we are God's offspring, we should not think that the divine being is like gold or silver or stone — an image made by human design and skill. In the past God overlooked such ignorance, but now he commands all people everywhere to repent. For he has set a day when he will judge the world with justice by the man he has appointed. He has given proof of this to everyone by raising him from the dead."

When they heard about the resurrection of the dead, some of them sneered, but others said, "We want to hear you again on this subject." At that, Paul left the Council. Some of the people became followers of Paul and believed. Among them was Dionysius, a member of the Areopagus, also a woman named Damaris, and a number of others. ACTS 17:16–34

The journey of faith begins with our belief in God. Like the early Christians, we too are called to make our own personal declaration. Do we believe in the one true God? Do we accept the Bible as it reveals that God exists in three Persons?

Even though we are weak and not fully able to understand the mysteries of God, he works mightily in and through those who believe. When we embrace God with our whole heart and worship him with our whole life, we experience the inner fruit of the Spirit that transforms our lives from the inside out. When we are growing, experiencing restoration in our relationships and doing the right thing, it is evident that God is in us and with us.

This was likely true for many of the new Christians in the churches Paul helped to establish and strengthen around the Mediterranean world. For example, the church at Corinth was a gifted church but struggled intensely. Paul wrapped up his final challenge and encouragement to them in the letter we know as 2 Corinthians. Take note in the last sentence that all three members of the Godhead are at work to produce this mighty outcome in our lives.

This will be my third visit to you. "Every matter must be established by the testimony of two or three witnesses." I already gave you a warning when I was with you the second time. I now repeat it while absent: On my return I will not spare those who sinned earlier or any of the others, since you are demanding proof that Christ is speaking through me. He is not weak in dealing with you, but is powerful among you. For to be sure, he was crucified in weakness, yet he lives by God's power. Likewise, we are weak in him, yet by God's power we will live with him in our dealing with you.

Examine yourselves to see whether you are in the faith; test yourselves. Do you not realize that Christ Jesus is in you — unless, of course, you fail the test? And I trust that you will discover that we have not failed the test. Now we pray to God that you will not do anything wrong — not so that people will see that we have stood the test but so that you will do what is right even though we may seem to have failed. For we cannot do anything against the truth, but only for the truth. We are glad whenever we are weak but you are strong; and our prayer is that you may be fully restored. This is why I write these things when I am absent, that when I come I may not have to be harsh in my use of authority — the authority the Lord gave me for building you up, not for tearing you down.

Finally, brothers and sisters, rejoice! Strive for full restoration, encourage one another, be of one mind, live in peace. And the God of love and peace will be with you.

Greet one another with a holy kiss. All God's people here send their greetings.

May the grace of the Lord Jesus Christ, and the love of God, and the fellowship of the Holy Spirit be with you all.

2 CORINTHIANS 13:1–14

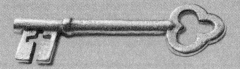

CHAPTER

2

Personal God

KEY IDEA

I believe God is involved in and cares
about my daily life.

KEY VERSE

I lift up my eyes to the mountains —
where does my help come from?
My help comes from the LORD,
the Maker of heaven and earth.
Psalm 121:1 – 2

The God of the Bible is the only true God—Father, Son and Holy Spirit. He is the one all-powerful, all-knowing eternal God. But is he good? Is he involved in his creation? Does he love us? Does he have a plan for us? Is he interceding and intervening to move the events of our life and world toward his intended purpose? Consider the following stories and decide for yourself.

God Is Good

Abraham and Sarah—the great patriarch and matriarch of the Israelite people—were first named Abram and Sarai. God had promised Abraham that he would be the father of a great nation, but how can you father a nation when you have no children?

Now Sarai, Abram's wife, had borne him no children. But she had an Egyptian slave named Hagar; so she said to Abram, "The LORD has kept me from having children. Go, sleep with my slave; perhaps I can build a family through her."

Abram agreed to what Sarai said. So after Abram had been living in Canaan ten years, Sarai his wife took her Egyptian slave Hagar and gave her to her husband to be his wife. He slept with Hagar, and she conceived.

When she knew she was pregnant, she began to despise her mistress. Then Sarai said to Abram, "You are responsible for the wrong I am suffering. I put my slave in your arms, and now that she knows she is pregnant, she despises me. May the LORD judge between you and me."

"Your slave is in your hands," Abram said. "Do with her whatever you think best." Then Sarai mistreated Hagar; so she fled from her.

The angel of the LORD found Hagar near a spring in the desert; it was the spring that is beside the road to Shur. And he said, "Hagar, slave of Sarai, where have you come from, and where are you going?"

"I'm running away from my mistress Sarai," she answered.

Then the angel of the LORD told her, "Go back to your mistress and submit to her." The angel added, "I will increase your descendants so much that they will be too numerous to count."

The angel of the LORD also said to her:

> "You are now pregnant
>   and you will give birth to a son.
> You shall name him Ishmael,
>   for the LORD has heard of your misery.
> He will be a wild donkey of a man;
>   his hand will be against everyone
>   and everyone's hand against him,
> and he will live in hostility
>   toward all his brothers."

She gave this name to the LORD who spoke to her: "You are the God who sees me," for she said, "I have now seen the One who sees me." That is why the well was called Beer Lahai Roi; it is still there, between Kadesh and Bered.

So Hagar bore Abram a son, and Abram gave the name Ishmael to the son she had borne. Abram was eighty-six years old when Hagar bore him Ishmael.   GENESIS 16:1–16

Abraham and Sarah had tried to "help God out" by having Abraham father a child with Hagar. What resulted was a debacle for everyone involved. But in this story, we see the beginning of a pattern—God takes our messes and turns them into something good. Hagar involuntarily became party to Abraham's and Sarah's lack of faith. Yet God heard her cries and helped her. The story continues . . .

Now the LORD was gracious to Sarah as he had said, and the LORD did for Sarah what he had promised. Sarah became pregnant and bore a son to Abraham in his old age, at the very time God had promised him. Abraham gave the name Isaac to the son Sarah bore him. When his son Isaac was eight days old, Abraham circumcised him, as God commanded him. Abraham was a hundred years old when his son Isaac was born to him.

Sarah said, "God has brought me laughter, and everyone who hears about this will laugh with me." And she added, "Who would have said to Abraham that Sarah would nurse children? Yet I have borne him a son in his old age."

The child grew and was weaned, and on the day Isaac was weaned Abraham held a great feast. But Sarah saw that the son whom Hagar the Egyptian had borne to Abraham was mocking, and she said to Abraham, "Get rid of that slave woman and her son, for that woman's son will never share in the inheritance with my son Isaac."

The matter distressed Abraham greatly because it concerned his son. But God said to him, "Do not be so distressed about the boy and your slave woman. Listen to whatever Sarah tells you, because it is through Isaac that your offspring will be reckoned. I will make the son of the slave into a nation also, because he is your offspring."

Early the next morning Abraham took some food and a skin of water and gave them to Hagar. He set them on her shoulders and then sent her off with the boy. She went on her way and wandered in the Desert of Beersheba.

When the water in the skin was gone, she put the boy under one of the bushes. Then she went off and sat down about a bow-shot away, for she thought, "I cannot watch the boy die." And as she sat there, she began to sob.

God heard the boy crying, and the angel of God called to Hagar from heaven and said to her, "What is the matter, Hagar? Do not be afraid; God has heard the boy crying as he lies there. Lift the boy up and take him by the hand, for I will make him into a great nation."

Then God opened her eyes and she saw a well of water. So she went and filled the skin with water and gave the boy a drink.

God was with the boy as he grew up. He lived in the desert and became an archer. While he was living in the Desert of Paran, his mother got a wife for him from Egypt. GENESIS 21:1–21

In the story of Hagar and Ishmael, even though they were on the wrong side of God's perfect plan, in his goodness, God provided for and blessed them (and even their descendants).

Another Biblical character in whose life we see how much God is involved and cares about his people is David, the poet, singer, shepherd, warrior and king, who wrote and sang from a deep well as he journeyed through life and encountered the one true God. David composed many of the psalms found in our Bible. David wrote as a shepherd boy while gazing at the billions of stars God created; he wrote while being chased down by King Saul; he wrote while he was king of Israel; and he wrote as he was coming to the end of his life on earth. The songs that David and the other psalmists wrote express their personal and intimate relationship with God.

LORD, our Lord,
    how majestic is your name in all the earth!

You have set your glory
    in the heavens.
Through the praise of children and infants
    you have established a stronghold against your enemies,
    to silence the foe and the avenger.
When I consider your heavens,
    the work of your fingers,
the moon and the stars,
    which you have set in place,
what is mankind that you are mindful of them,
    human beings that you care for them?

You have made them a little lower than the angels
    and crowned them with glory and honor.
You made them rulers over the works of your hands;
    you put everything under their feet:
all flocks and herds,
    and the animals of the wild,
the birds in the sky,
    and the fish in the sea,
    all that swim the paths of the seas.

LORD, our Lord,
    how majestic is your name in all the earth!   PSALM 8:1–9

The LORD is my shepherd, I lack nothing.
    He makes me lie down in green pastures,
he leads me beside quiet waters,
    he refreshes my soul.

He guides me along the right paths
    for his name's sake.
Even though I walk
    through the darkest valley,
I will fear no evil,
    for you are with me;
your rod and your staff,
    they comfort me.

You prepare a table before me
    in the presence of my enemies.
You anoint my head with oil;
    my cup overflows.
Surely your goodness and love will follow me
    all the days of my life,
and I will dwell in the house of the Lord
    forever.
                                     Psalm 23:1–6

You have searched me, Lord,
    and you know me.
You know when I sit and when I rise;
    you perceive my thoughts from afar.
You discern my going out and my lying down;
    you are familiar with all my ways.
Before a word is on my tongue
    you, Lord, know it completely.
You hem me in behind and before,
    and you lay your hand upon me.
Such knowledge is too wonderful for me,
    too lofty for me to attain.

Where can I go from your Spirit?
    Where can I flee from your presence?
If I go up to the heavens, you are there;
    if I make my bed in the depths, you are there.
If I rise on the wings of the dawn,
    if I settle on the far side of the sea,
even there your hand will guide me,
    your right hand will hold me fast.

If I say, "Surely the darkness will hide me
    and the light become night around me,"
even the darkness will not be dark to you;
    the night will shine like the day,
    for darkness is as light to you.

For you created my inmost being;
    you knit me together in my mother's womb.
I praise you because I am fearfully and wonderfully
        made;
    your works are wonderful,
    I know that full well.
My frame was not hidden from you
    when I was made in the secret place,
    when I was woven together in the depths of the earth.
Your eyes saw my unformed body;
    all the days ordained for me were written in your book
    before one of them came to be.
How precious to me are your thoughts, God!
    How vast is the sum of them!
Were I to count them,
    they would outnumber the grains of sand—
    when I awake, I am still with you.

If only you, God, would slay the wicked!
    Away from me, you who are bloodthirsty!
They speak of you with evil intent;
    your adversaries misuse your name.
Do I not hate those who hate you, LORD,
    and abhor those who are in rebellion against you?
I have nothing but hatred for them;
    I count them my enemies.
Search me, God, and know my heart;
    test me and know my anxious thoughts.
See if there is any offensive way in me,
    and lead me in the way everlasting.   PSALM 139:1–24

I will exalt you, my God the King;
    I will praise your name for ever and ever.

Every day I will praise you
    and extol your name for ever and ever.

Great is the LORD and most worthy of praise;
    his greatness no one can fathom.
One generation commends your works to another;
    they tell of your mighty acts.
They speak of the glorious splendor of your majesty —
    and I will meditate on your wonderful works.
They tell of the power of your awesome works —
    and I will proclaim your great deeds.
They celebrate your abundant goodness
    and joyfully sing of your righteousness.

The LORD is gracious and compassionate,
    slow to anger and rich in love.

The LORD is good to all;
    he has compassion on all he has made.
All your works praise you, LORD;
    your faithful people extol you.
They tell of the glory of your kingdom
    and speak of your might,
so that all people may know of your mighty acts
    and the glorious splendor of your kingdom.
Your kingdom is an everlasting kingdom,
    and your dominion endures through all
        generations.

The LORD is trustworthy in all he promises
    and faithful in all he does.
The LORD upholds all who fall
    and lifts up all who are bowed down.
The eyes of all look to you,
    and you give them their food at the proper time.
You open your hand
    and satisfy the desires of every living thing.

The LORD is righteous in all his ways
    and faithful in all he does.

The Lord is near to all who call on him,
    to all who call on him in truth.
He fulfills the desires of those who fear him;
    he hears their cry and saves them.
The Lord watches over all who love him,
    but all the wicked he will destroy.

My mouth will speak in praise of the Lord.
    Let every creature praise his holy name
for ever and ever.   Psalm 145:1–21

God Has a Plan

Forty years after the death of David, the nation of Israel was torn in two, and what resulted were two nations: the northern kingdom of Israel and the southern kingdom of Judah. All the kings of Israel did evil in the eyes of the Lord. In Judah, only a handful of kings were good. One of them was Hezekiah. He courageously served the Lord in perilous times.

Then when he was about 38 years old, Hezekiah became ill and was about to die. He was devastated and pleaded with the Lord for mercy. In response, the Lord sent him a shocking message and a tender change of plan. We know from the Bible that God has a plan for our individual lives and has our days numbered. This story shows how God will hear our prayers and see our tears. He may not answer us in the way we desire, but he will sometimes alter the plan he has for us at the request of his children.

In those days Hezekiah became ill and was at the point of death. The prophet Isaiah son of Amoz went to him and said, "This is what the Lord says: Put your house in order, because you are going to die; you will not recover."

Hezekiah turned his face to the wall and prayed to the Lord, "Remember, Lord, how I have walked before you faithfully and with wholehearted devotion and have done what is good in your eyes." And Hezekiah wept bitterly.

Before Isaiah had left the middle court, the word of the Lord came to him: "Go back and tell Hezekiah, the ruler of my people, 'This is what the Lord, the God of your father David, says: I have heard your prayer and seen your tears; I will heal you. On the third day from now you will go up to the temple of the LORD. I will add fifteen years to your life. And I will deliver you and this city from the hand of the king of Assyria. I will defend this city for my sake and for the sake of my servant David.' "

Then Isaiah said, "Prepare a poultice of figs." They did so and applied it to the boil, and he recovered. 2 KINGS 20:1–7

While Hezekiah's story focuses on the length of his life, Jeremiah's story goes all the way back before he was born. Jeremiah was a prophet who lived in the time of the divided kingdom. He lived in the southern kingdom of Judah and prophesied to the people there of their coming conquest and exile by the Babylonians. In both Hezekiah's life and Jeremiah's, God is not distant or ambivalent, but near and loving.

The words of Jeremiah son of Hilkiah, one of the priests at Anathoth in the territory of Benjamin. The word of the LORD came to him in the thirteenth year of the reign of Josiah son of Amon king of Judah, and through the reign of Jehoiakim son of Josiah king of Judah, down to the fifth month of the eleventh year of Zedekiah son of Josiah king of Judah, when the people of Jerusalem went into exile.

The word of the LORD came to me, saying,

> "Before I formed you in the womb I knew you,
>   before you were born I set you apart;
>   I appointed you as a prophet to the nations."

"Alas, Sovereign LORD," I said, "I do not know how to speak; I am too young."

But the LORD said to me, "Do not say, 'I am too young.' You must go to everyone I send you to and say whatever I command you. Do not be afraid of them, for I am with you and will rescue you," declares the LORD.

Then the LORD reached out his hand and touched my mouth and said to me, "I have put my words in your mouth. See, today I appoint you over nations and kingdoms to uproot and tear down, to destroy and overthrow, to build and to plant."

The word of the LORD came to me: "What do you see, Jeremiah?"

"I see the branch of an almond tree," I replied.

The LORD said to me, "You have seen correctly, for I am watching to see that my word is fulfilled."

The word of the LORD came to me again: "What do you see?"

"I see a pot that is boiling," I answered. "It is tilting toward us from the north."

The LORD said to me, "From the north disaster will be poured out on all who live in the land. I am about to summon all the peoples of the northern kingdoms," declares the LORD.

> "Their kings will come and set up their thrones
>   in the entrance of the gates of Jerusalem;
> they will come against all her surrounding walls
>   and against all the towns of Judah.
> I will pronounce my judgments on my people
>   because of their wickedness in forsaking me,
> in burning incense to other gods
>   and in worshiping what their hands have made.

"Get yourself ready! Stand up and say to them whatever I command you. Do not be terrified by them, or I will terrify you before them. Today I have made you a fortified city, an iron pillar and a bronze wall to stand against the whole land — against the kings of Judah, its officials, its priests and the people of the land. They will fight against you but will not overcome you, for I am with you and will rescue you," declares the LORD.   JEREMIAH 1:1–19

Jeremiah's calling was very specific to the overall plan God was revealing through Israel. He faithfully warned the southern kingdom of Judah about their unfaithfulness and God's pending discipline. He knew up front that they would not listen, but his task was simply to be faithful and courageous and to deliver the message from God. Three times the dreaded Babylonians attacked Jerusalem and carried away some of the people to Babylon. In 597, after the second deportation, God gave Jeremiah the assignment of writing a letter to those exiles to remind them that, as Jeremiah had experienced personally, God has a grand and good plan for their lives.

This is the text of the letter that the prophet Jeremiah sent from Jerusalem to the surviving elders among the exiles and to the priests, the prophets and all the other people Nebuchadnezzar had carried into exile from Jerusalem to Babylon. (This was after King Jehoiachin and the queen mother, the court officials and the leaders of Judah and Jerusalem, the skilled workers and the artisans had gone into exile from Jerusalem.) He entrusted the letter to Elasah son of Shaphan and to Gemariah son of Hilkiah, whom Zedekiah king of Judah sent to King Nebuchadnezzar in Babylon. It said:

This is what the LORD Almighty, the God of Israel, says to all those I carried into exile from Jerusalem to Babylon: "Build houses and settle down; plant gardens and eat what they produce. Marry and have sons and daughters; find wives for your sons and give your daughters in marriage, so that they too may have sons and daughters. Increase in number there; do not decrease. Also, seek the peace and prosperity of the city to which I have carried you into exile. Pray to the LORD for it, because if it prospers, you too will prosper." Yes, this is what the LORD Almighty, the God of Israel, says: "Do not let the prophets and diviners among you deceive you. Do not listen to the dreams you encourage them to have. They are prophesying lies to you in my name. I have not sent them," declares the LORD.

This is what the LORD says: "When seventy years are completed for Babylon, I will come to you and fulfill my good promise to bring you back to this place. For I know the plans I have for you," declares the LORD, "plans to prosper you and not to harm you, plans to give you hope and a future. Then you will call on me and come and pray to me, and I will listen to you. You will seek me and find me when you seek me with all your heart. I will be found by you," declares the LORD, "and will bring you back from captivity. I will gather you from all the nations and places where I have banished you," declares the LORD, "and will bring you back to the place from which I carried you into exile."   JEREMIAH 29:1–14

GOD CARES FOR US

Jesus, the Son of God, came to earth. He was born as a human baby and lived among us. His arrival removes any doubt about the nearness of God in our lives. Jesus is Immanuel, "God with us."

When a large crowd assembled on a hillside by the Sea of Galilee, Jesus taught this weary and worn bunch about the intricate involvement of God in their lives.

"Therefore I tell you, do not worry about your life, what you will eat or drink; or about your body, what you will wear. Is not life more than food, and the body more than clothes? Look at the birds of the air; they do not sow or reap or store away in barns, and yet your heavenly Father feeds them. Are you not much more valuable than they? Can any one of you by worrying add a single hour to your life?

"And why do you worry about clothes? See how the flowers of the field grow. They do not labor or spin. Yet I tell you that not even Solomon in all his splendor was dressed like one of these. If that is how God clothes the grass of the field, which is here today and tomorrow is thrown into the fire, will he not much more clothe you — you of little faith? So do not worry, saying, 'What shall we eat?' or 'What shall we drink?' or 'What shall we wear?' For the pagans run after all these things, and your heavenly Father knows that you need them. But seek first his kingdom and his righteousness, and all these things will be given to you as well. Therefore do not worry about tomorrow, for tomorrow will worry about itself. Each day has enough trouble of its own." MATTHEW 6:25–34

After Jesus' death on the cross, he ascended back to the Father in heaven. Then God the Holy Spirit descended on all who believed in Jesus. The dwelling place for God was no longer in temples built by human hands but in the very inner spirits of his people. From the inside out the Holy Spirit speaks to us, ministers to us, affirms us, directs us, challenges us and empowers us. With pen in hand, the apostle Paul instructed the church that gathered in Rome of this great truth.

Therefore, brothers and sisters, we have an obligation — but it is not to the flesh, to live according to it. For if you live according to the flesh, you will die; but if by the Spirit you put to death the misdeeds of the body, you will live.

For those who are led by the Spirit of God are the children of

God. The Spirit you received does not make you slaves, so that you live in fear again; rather, the Spirit you received brought about your adoption to sonship. And by him we cry, *"Abba,* Father." The Spirit himself testifies with our spirit that we are God's children. Now if we are children, then we are heirs — heirs of God and co-heirs with Christ, if indeed we share in his sufferings in order that we may also share in his glory.

I consider that our present sufferings are not worth comparing with the glory that will be revealed in us. For the creation waits in eager expectation for the children of God to be revealed. For the creation was subjected to frustration, not by its own choice, but by the will of the one who subjected it, in hope that the creation itself will be liberated from its bondage to decay and brought into the freedom and glory of the children of God.

We know that the whole creation has been groaning as in the pains of childbirth right up to the present time. Not only so, but we ourselves, who have the firstfruits of the Spirit, groan inwardly as we wait eagerly for our adoption to sonship, the redemption of our bodies. For in this hope we were saved. But hope that is seen is no hope at all. Who hopes for what they already have? But if we hope for what we do not yet have, we wait for it patiently.

In the same way, the Spirit helps us in our weakness. We do not know what we ought to pray for, but the Spirit himself intercedes for us through wordless groans. And he who searches our hearts knows the mind of the Spirit, because the Spirit intercedes for God's people in accordance with the will of God.

And we know that in all things God works for the good of those who love him, who have been called according to his purpose. For those God foreknew he also predestined to be conformed to the image of his Son, that he might be the firstborn among many brothers and sisters. And those he predestined, he also called; those he called, he also justified; those he justified, he also glorified.

What, then, shall we say in response to these things? If God is for us, who can be against us? He who did not spare his own Son, but gave him up for us all — how will he not also, along with him, graciously give us all things? Who will bring any charge against those whom God has chosen? It is God who justifies. Who then is the one who condemns? No one. Christ Jesus who died — more than that, who was raised to life—is at the right hand of God and is also interceding for us. Who shall separate us from the love of Christ? Shall trouble or hardship or persecution or famine or nakedness or danger or sword? As it is written:

> "For your sake we face death all day long;
>> we are considered as sheep to be slaughtered."

No, in all these things we are more than conquerors through him who loved us. For I am convinced that neither death nor life, neither angels nor demons, neither the present nor the future, nor any powers, neither height nor depth, nor anything else in all creation, will be able to separate us from the love of God that is in Christ Jesus our Lord.   ROMANS 8:12–39

What amazing love God has for his people! In the spirit of this love, James, the half brother of Jesus, wrote a practical letter to Jesus' early disciples. He reminded them that God is involved in and cares about their daily lives—although they too had a role to play. As believers, we can acknowledge God's involvement in our lives, even during seasons of trial. We can seek God and ask him for wisdom. We must also be careful not to blame God for our trials and temptations and realize that every good gift comes from his hand.

James, a servant of God and of the Lord Jesus Christ,

To the twelve tribes scattered among the nations:

Greetings.

Consider it pure joy, my brothers and sisters, whenever you face trials of many kinds, because you know that the testing of your faith produces perseverance. Let perseverance finish its work so that you may be mature and complete, not lacking anything. If any of you lacks wisdom, you should ask God, who gives generously to all without finding fault, and it will be given to you. But when you ask, you must believe and not doubt, because the one who doubts is like a wave of the sea, blown and tossed by the wind. That person should not expect to receive anything from the Lord. Such a person is double-minded and unstable in all they do.

Believers in humble circumstances ought to take pride in their high position. But the rich should take pride in their humiliation — since they will pass away like a wild flower. For the sun rises with scorching heat and withers the plant; its blossom falls and its beauty is destroyed. In the same way, the rich will fade away even while they go about their business.

Blessed is the one who perseveres under trial because, having stood the test, that person will receive the crown of life that the Lord has promised to those who love him.

When tempted, no one should say, "God is tempting me." For God cannot be tempted by evil, nor does he tempt anyone; but each person is tempted when they are dragged away by their own evil desire and enticed. Then, after desire has conceived, it gives birth to sin; and sin, when it is full-grown, gives birth to death.

Don't be deceived, my dear brothers and sisters. Every good and perfect gift is from above, coming down from the Father of the heavenly lights, who does not change like shifting shadows. He chose to give us birth through the word of truth, that we might be a kind of firstfruits of all he created.   James 1:1–18

THINK

CHAPTER

3

Salvation

------------------------------- KEY IDEA -------------------------------

I believe a person comes into a right relationship
with God by God's grace through faith in Jesus Christ.

------------------------------- KEY VERSE -------------------------------

For it is by grace you have been saved, through faith —
and this is not from yourselves, it is the gift of God —
not by works, so that no one can boast.
Ephesians 2:8 – 9

THE PROBLEM

Satan, the great deceiver, clothed himself as a serpent, one of God's good creatures, and set out to trick Adam and Eve into disobeying their good and gracious God. After creating Adam and Eve, God had told them not to eat of the fruit of a certain tree in the Garden of Eden. But Satan suggested that God wasn't being honest when he warned of the results of eating the forbidden fruit. The great deceiver's ploy succeeded, and Adam and Eve willfully rejected God and his promise of life together in the garden.

The consequences of Adam and Eve's rebellion were passed on to their offspring and then again and again to every generation since. Every human born receives this "virus" at conception and then acts out of this nature throughout their life. The Bible calls it sin. It creates death — both the physical death of our bodies and the spiritual death of separation from God.

Now the LORD God had planted a garden in the east, in Eden; and there he put the man he had formed. The LORD God made all kinds of trees grow out of the ground — trees that were pleasing to the eye and good for food. In the middle of the garden were the tree of life and the tree of the knowledge of good and evil.   GENESIS 2:8–9

The LORD God took the man and put him in the Garden of Eden to work it and take care of it. And the LORD God commanded the man, "You are free to eat from any tree in the garden; but you must not eat from the tree of the knowledge of good and evil, for when you eat from it you will certainly die."   GENESIS 2:15–17

Now the serpent was more crafty than any of the wild animals the LORD God had made. He said to the woman, "Did God really say, 'You must not eat from any tree in the garden'?"

The woman said to the serpent, "We may eat fruit from the trees in the garden, but God did say, 'You must not eat fruit from the tree that is in the middle of the garden, and you must not touch it, or you will die.'"

"You will not certainly die," the serpent said to the woman. "For God knows that when you eat from it your eyes will be opened, and you will be like God, knowing good and evil."

When the woman saw that the fruit of the tree was good for food and pleasing to the eye, and also desirable for gaining wisdom, she took some and ate it. She also gave some to her husband, who was with her, and he ate it. Then the eyes of both of them were opened, and they realized they were naked; so they sewed fig leaves together and made coverings for themselves.

Then the man and his wife heard the sound of the LORD God as he was walking in the garden in the cool of the day, and they hid from the LORD God among the trees of the garden. But the LORD God called to the man, "Where are you?"

He answered, "I heard you in the garden, and I was afraid because I was naked; so I hid."

And he said, "Who told you that you were naked? Have you eaten from the tree that I commanded you not to eat from?"

The man said, "The woman you put here with me — she gave me some fruit from the tree, and I ate it."

Then the LORD God said to the woman, "What is this you have done?"

The woman said, "The serpent deceived me, and I ate."

So the LORD God said to the serpent, "Because you have done this,

> "Cursed are you above all livestock
>   and all wild animals!
> You will crawl on your belly
>   and you will eat dust
>   all the days of your life.
> And I will put enmity
>   between you and the woman,
>   and between your offspring and hers;
> he will crush your head,
>   and you will strike his heel."

To the woman he said,

> "I will make your pains in childbearing very severe;
>   with painful labor you will give birth to children.
> Your desire will be for your husband,
>   and he will rule over you."

To Adam he said, "Because you listened to your wife and ate fruit from the tree about which I commanded you, 'You must not eat from it,'

> "Cursed is the ground because of you;
>> through painful toil you will eat food from it
>> all the days of your life.
> It will produce thorns and thistles for you,
>> and you will eat the plants of the field.
> By the sweat of your brow
>> you will eat your food
> until you return to the ground,
>> since from it you were taken;
> for dust you are
>> and to dust you will return."

Adam named his wife Eve, because she would become the mother of all the living.

The LORD God made garments of skin for Adam and his wife and clothed them. And the LORD God said, "The man has now become like one of us, knowing good and evil. He must not be allowed to reach out his hand and take also from the tree of life and eat, and live forever." So the LORD God banished him from the Garden of Eden to work the ground from which he had been taken. After he drove the man out, he placed on the east side of the Garden of Eden cherubim and a flaming sword flashing back and forth to guard the way to the tree of life. GENESIS 3:1–24

THE SOLUTION

Even before Adam and Eve sinned, God had a plan to get people back into a relationship with him. When he replaced their clothes of fig leaves with the skins of animals, he signaled something important—it would take the blood of another to cover the sins of humankind. God's plan began with the founding of a brand-new nation through which he would reveal himself and his plan to restore humankind. For more than 1,600 years, every Biblical story of the chosen people of Israel would point to the coming of the solution.

Abraham and Sarah, the founders of the Israelites, were unable to have children. God miraculously intervened and provided

Abraham and Sarah with a child named Isaac. When Isaac was
likely in his adolescent years, God visited Abraham and asked him
to do the unthinkable. This story, which takes place on the site of
the future temple in Jerusalem, foreshadows the position God the
Father would be in with his own Son.

Some time later God tested Abraham. He said to him, "Abraham!"

"Here I am," he replied.

Then God said, "Take your son, your only son, whom you love — Isaac — and go to the region of Moriah. Sacrifice him there as a burnt offering on a mountain I will show you."

Early the next morning Abraham got up and loaded his donkey. He took with him two of his servants and his son Isaac. When he had cut enough wood for the burnt offering, he set out for the place God had told him about. On the third day Abraham looked up and saw the place in the distance. He said to his servants, "Stay here with the donkey while I and the boy go over there. We will worship and then we will come back to you."

Abraham took the wood for the burnt offering and placed it on his son Isaac, and he himself carried the fire and the knife. As the two of them went on together, Isaac spoke up and said to his father Abraham, "Father?"

"Yes, my son?" Abraham replied.

"The fire and wood are here," Isaac said, "but where is the lamb for the burnt offering?"

Abraham answered, "God himself will provide the lamb for the burnt offering, my son." And the two of them went on together.

When they reached the place God had told him about, Abraham built an altar there and arranged the wood on it. He bound his son Isaac and laid him on the altar, on top of the wood. Then he reached out his hand and took the knife to slay his son. But the angel of the LORD called out to him from heaven, "Abraham! Abraham!"

"Here I am," he replied.

"Do not lay a hand on the boy," he said. "Do not do anything to him. Now I know that you fear God, because you have not withheld from me your son, your only son."

Abraham looked up and there in a thicket he saw a ram caught by its horns. He went over and took the ram and sacrificed it as a burnt offering instead of his son. So Abraham called that place The Lord Will Provide. And to this day it is said, "On the mountain of the Lord it will be provided."

The angel of the Lord called to Abraham from heaven a second time and said, "I swear by myself, declares the Lord, that because you have done this and have not withheld your son, your only son, I will surely bless you and make your descendants as numerous as the stars in the sky and as the sand on the seashore. Your descendants will take possession of the cities of their enemies, and through your offspring all nations on earth will be blessed, because you have obeyed me." GENESIS 22:1–18

God pledged to Abraham and his descendants a special place in the world, a land for them. But when a famine occurred, Abraham's and Sarah's grandson Jacob—along with all Jacob's children and their families—left the land and went to Egypt. But God promised that the nation of Israel would return to the promised land 400 years later.

While in Egypt the people of Israel were made slaves under Pharaoh. When it was time for Israel to occupy the land of Canaan, God raised up Moses to deliver his people out of slavery and move them into the promised land. But Pharaoh was hard-hearted and would not let the people leave. To make Pharaoh understand and believe in God's power, God issued ten brutal plagues on Egypt and its people. The tenth and final one foretells of the ultimate solution of humankind's deliverance from the slavery of sin.

Now the Lord had said to Moses, "I will bring one more plague on Pharaoh and on Egypt. After that, he will let you go from here, and when he does, he will drive you out completely. Tell the people that men and women alike are to ask their neighbors for articles of silver and gold." (The Lord made the Egyptians favorably disposed toward the people, and Moses himself was highly regarded in Egypt by Pharaoh's officials and by the people.)

So Moses said, "This is what the Lord says: 'About midnight I will go throughout Egypt. Every firstborn son in Egypt will die, from the firstborn son of Pharaoh, who sits on the throne, to the firstborn son of the female slave, who is at her hand mill, and all the firstborn of the cattle as well. There will be loud wailing throughout Egypt — worse than there has ever been or ever will be again. But among the Israelites not a dog will bark at any person or animal.' Then you will know that the LORD makes a distinction between Egypt and Israel. All these officials of yours will come to me, bowing down before me and saying, 'Go, you and all the people who follow you!' After that I will leave." Then Moses, hot with anger, left Pharaoh.

The LORD had said to Moses, "Pharaoh will refuse to listen to you — so that my wonders may be multiplied in Egypt." Moses and Aaron performed all these wonders before Pharaoh, but the LORD hardened Pharaoh's heart, and he would not let the Israelites go out of his country.

The LORD said to Moses and Aaron in Egypt, "This month is to be for you the first month, the first month of your year. Tell the whole community of Israel that on the tenth day of this month each man is to take a lamb for his family, one for each household. If any household is too small for a whole lamb, they must share one with their nearest neighbor, having taken into account the number of people there are. You are to determine the amount of lamb needed in accordance with what each person will eat. The animals you choose must be year-old males without defect, and you may take them from the sheep or the goats. Take care of them until the fourteenth day of the month, when all the members of the community of Israel must slaughter them at twilight. Then they are to take some of the blood and put it on the sides and tops of the doorframes of the houses where they eat the lambs. That same night they are to eat the meat roasted over the fire, along with bitter herbs, and bread made without yeast. Do not eat the meat raw or boiled in water, but roast it over a fire — with the head, legs and internal organs. Do not leave any of it till morning; if some is left till morning, you must burn it. This is how you are to eat it: with your cloak tucked into your belt, your sandals on your feet and your staff in your hand. Eat it in haste; it is the LORD's Passover.

"On that same night I will pass through Egypt and strike down every firstborn of both people and animals, and I will bring judgment on all the gods of Egypt. I am the LORD. The blood will be a sign for you on the houses where you are, and when I see the blood, I will pass over you. No destructive plague will touch you when I strike Egypt.

"This is a day you are to commemorate; for the generations to come you shall celebrate it as a festival to the LORD — a lasting ordinance. For seven days you are to eat bread made without yeast. On the first day remove the yeast from your houses, for whoever eats anything with yeast in it from the first day through the seventh must be cut off from Israel. On the first day hold a sacred assembly, and another one on the seventh day. Do no work at all on these days, except to prepare food for everyone to eat; that is all you may do.

"Celebrate the Festival of Unleavened Bread, because it was on this very day that I brought your divisions out of Egypt. Celebrate this day as a lasting ordinance for the generations to come. In the first month you are to eat bread made without yeast, from the evening of the fourteenth day until the evening of the twenty-first day. For seven days no yeast is to be found in your houses. And anyone, whether foreigner or native-born, who eats anything with yeast in it must be cut off from the community of Israel. Eat nothing made with yeast. Wherever you live, you must eat unleavened bread."

Then Moses summoned all the elders of Israel and said to them, "Go at once and select the animals for your families and slaughter the Passover lamb. Take a bunch of hyssop, dip it into the blood in the basin and put some of the blood on the top and on both sides of the doorframe. None of you shall go out of the door of your house until morning. When the LORD goes through the land to strike down the Egyptians, he will see the blood on the top and sides of the doorframe and will pass over that doorway, and he will not permit the destroyer to enter your houses and strike you down.

"Obey these instructions as a lasting ordinance for you and your descendants. When you enter the land that the LORD will give you as he promised, observe this ceremony. And when your children ask you, 'What does this ceremony mean to you?' then tell them, 'It is the Passover sacrifice to the LORD, who passed over the houses of the Israelites in Egypt and spared our homes when he struck down the Egyptians.'" Then the people bowed down and worshiped. The Israelites did just what the LORD commanded Moses and Aaron.

At midnight the LORD struck down all the firstborn in Egypt, from the firstborn of Pharaoh, who sat on the throne, to the firstborn of the prisoner, who was in the dungeon, and the firstborn of all the livestock as well. Pharaoh and all his officials and all the Egyptians got up during the night, and there was loud wailing in Egypt, for there was not a house without someone dead.

During the night Pharaoh summoned Moses and Aaron and said, "Up! Leave my people, you and the Israelites! Go, worship the LORD as you have requested." EXODUS 11:1—12:31

About 1,300 years after the time of Abraham and 700 years before the birth of Jesus, God inspired the prophet Isaiah to speak on his behalf. The following prophecy about the Lord's "suffering servant" takes the concept of blood sacrifice, or substitutionary atonement, to a new level; like the Passover lamb described in the previous passage, this servant will suffer for the sake of others. This Scripture, which is quoted more often in the New Testament than any other Old Testament passage, also foretells the mission of the One who will provide the way for our sins to be forgiven.

See, my servant will act wisely;
    he will be raised and lifted up and highly exalted.
Just as there were many who were appalled at him —
    his appearance was so disfigured beyond that of any
        human being
    and his form marred beyond human likeness —
so he will sprinkle many nations,
    and kings will shut their mouths because of him.
For what they were not told, they will see,
    and what they have not heard, they will understand.

Who has believed our message
    and to whom has the arm of the LORD been revealed?
He grew up before him like a tender shoot,
    and like a root out of dry ground.
He had no beauty or majesty to attract us to him,
    nothing in his appearance that we should desire him.

He was despised and rejected by mankind,
    a man of suffering, and familiar with pain.
Like one from whom people hide their faces
    he was despised, and we held him in low esteem.

Surely he took up our pain
    and bore our suffering,
yet we considered him punished by God,
    stricken by him, and afflicted.
But he was pierced for our transgressions,
    he was crushed for our iniquities;
the punishment that brought us peace was on him,
    and by his wounds we are healed.
We all, like sheep, have gone astray,
    each of us has turned to our own way;
and the Lord has laid on him
    the iniquity of us all.

He was oppressed and afflicted,
    yet he did not open his mouth;
he was led like a lamb to the slaughter,
    and as a sheep before its shearers is silent,
    so he did not open his mouth.
By oppression and judgment he was taken away.
    Yet who of his generation protested?
For he was cut off from the land of the living;
    for the transgression of my people he was punished.
He was assigned a grave with the wicked,
    and with the rich in his death,
though he had done no violence,
    nor was any deceit in his mouth.

Yet it was the Lord's will to crush him and cause him
        to suffer,
    and though the Lord makes his life an offering for sin,
he will see his offspring and prolong his days,
    and the will of the Lord will prosper in his hand.
After he has suffered,
    he will see the light of life and be satisfied;

by his knowledge my righteous servant will justify many,
and he will bear their iniquities.
Therefore I will give him a portion among the great,
and he will divide the spoils with the strong,
because he poured out his life unto death,
and was numbered with the transgressors.
For he bore the sin of many,
and made intercession for the transgressors.

ISAIAH 52:13—53:12

About 2,000 years after God provided "the lamb for the burnt offering" in place of Abraham's son Isaac, 1,500 years after God spared the Israelites through the sacrifice of their Passover lambs, and 700 years after Isaiah foresaw the suffering servant who would be "pierced for our transgressions" and "crushed for our iniquities," the Messiah Jesus was crucified on a cross for the sins of humankind. God's solution to the problem of sin was made complete through the sacrifice of his Son.

[Jesus] said to his disciples, "As you know, the Passover is two days away — and the Son of Man will be handed over to be crucified."

Then the chief priests and the elders of the people assembled in the palace of the high priest, whose name was Caiaphas, and they schemed to arrest Jesus secretly and kill him.   MATTHEW 26:1–4

Then the governor's soldiers took Jesus into the Praetorium and gathered the whole company of soldiers around him. They stripped him and put a scarlet robe on him, and then twisted together a crown of thorns and set it on his head. They put a staff in his right hand. Then they knelt in front of him and mocked him. "Hail, king of the Jews!" they said. They spit on him, and took the staff and struck him on the head again and again. After they had mocked him, they took off the robe and put his own clothes on him. Then they led him away to crucify him.

As they were going out, they met a man from Cyrene, named Simon, and they forced him to carry the cross. They came to a place called Golgotha (which means "the place of the skull"). There they offered Jesus wine to drink, mixed with gall; but after tasting it, he refused to drink it. When they had crucified him, they divided up his clothes by casting lots. And sitting down, they kept watch over him there. Above his head they placed the written charge against him: THIS IS JESUS, THE KING OF THE JEWS.

Two rebels were crucified with him, one on his right and one on his left. Those who passed by hurled insults at him, shaking their heads and saying, "You who are going to destroy the temple and build it in three days, save yourself! Come down from the cross, if you are the Son of God!" In the same way the chief priests, the teachers of the law and the elders mocked him. "He saved others," they said, "but he can't save himself! He's the king of Israel! Let him come down now from the cross, and we will believe in him. He trusts in God. Let God rescue him now if he wants him, for he said, 'I am the Son of God.'" In the same way the rebels who were crucified with him also heaped insults on him.

From noon until three in the afternoon darkness came over all the land. About three in the afternoon Jesus cried out in a loud voice, *"Eli, Eli, lema sabachthani?"* (which means "My God, my God, why have you forsaken me?").

When some of those standing there heard this, they said, "He's calling Elijah."

Immediately one of them ran and got a sponge. He filled it with wine vinegar, put it on a staff, and offered it to Jesus to drink. The rest said, "Now leave him alone. Let's see if Elijah comes to save him."

And when Jesus had cried out again in a loud voice, he gave up his spirit.

At that moment the curtain of the temple was torn in two from top to bottom. The earth shook, the rocks split and the tombs broke open. The bodies of many holy people who had died were raised to life. They came out of the tombs after Jesus' resurrection and went into the holy city and appeared to many people.

When the centurion and those with him who were guarding Jesus saw the earthquake and all that had happened, they were terrified, and exclaimed, "Surely he was the Son of God!"

Many women were there, watching from a distance. They had followed Jesus from Galilee to care for his needs. Among them were Mary Magdalene, Mary the mother of James and Joseph, and the mother of Zebedee's sons.

As evening approached, there came a rich man from Arimathea, named Joseph, who had himself become a disciple of Jesus. Going to Pilate, he asked for Jesus' body, and Pilate ordered that it be given to him. Joseph took the body, wrapped it in a clean linen cloth, and placed it in his own new tomb that he had cut out of the rock. He rolled a big stone in front of the entrance to the tomb and went away. Mary Magdalene and the other Mary were sitting there opposite the tomb.

The next day, the one after Preparation Day, the chief priests and the Pharisees went to Pilate. "Sir," they said, "we remember that while he was still alive that deceiver said, 'After three days I will rise again.' So give the order for the tomb to be made secure until the third day. Otherwise, his disciples may come and steal the body and tell the people that he has been raised from the dead. This last deception will be worse than the first."

"Take a guard," Pilate answered. "Go, make the tomb as secure as you know how." So they went and made the tomb secure by putting a seal on the stone and posting the guard.

After the Sabbath, at dawn on the first day of the week, Mary Magdalene and the other Mary went to look at the tomb.

There was a violent earthquake, for an angel of the Lord came down from heaven and, going to the tomb, rolled back the stone and sat on it. His appearance was like lightning, and his clothes were white as snow. The guards were so afraid of him that they shook and became like dead men.

The angel said to the women, "Do not be afraid, for I know that you are looking for Jesus, who was crucified. He is not here; he has risen, just as he said. Come and see the place where he lay. Then go quickly and tell his disciples: 'He has risen from the dead and is going ahead of you into Galilee. There you will see him.' Now I have told you."

So the women hurried away from the tomb, afraid yet filled with joy, and ran to tell his disciples. Suddenly Jesus met them. "Greetings," he said. They came to him, clasped his feet and worshiped him. Then Jesus said to them, "Do not be afraid. Go and tell my brothers to go to Galilee; there they will see me." MATTHEW 27:27—28:10

THE OUTCOME

Even with all the incredible stories connecting the dots from the promised Messiah to the person Jesus, most members of this blessed nation of Israel didn't recognize or accept Jesus as the Savior of the world. They didn't recognize the One who would provide the way for our sin to be eliminated so we could enter into a personal relationship with God, overcome death and have eternal life. John tells the story of one Jewish religious leader who approached Jesus at night to probe his true identity and mission.

Now there was a Pharisee, a man named Nicodemus who was a member of the Jewish ruling council. He came to Jesus at night and said, "Rabbi, we know that you are a teacher who has come from God. For no one could perform the signs you are doing if God were not with him."

Jesus replied, "Very truly I tell you, no one can see the kingdom of God unless they are born again."

"How can someone be born when they are old?" Nicodemus asked. "Surely they cannot enter a second time into their mother's womb to be born!"

Jesus answered, "Very truly I tell you, no one can enter the kingdom of God unless they are born of water and the Spirit. Flesh gives birth to flesh, but the Spirit gives birth to spirit. You should not be surprised at my saying, 'You must be born again.' The wind blows wherever it pleases. You hear its sound, but you cannot tell where it comes from or where it is going. So it is with everyone born of the Spirit."

"How can this be?" Nicodemus asked.

"You are Israel's teacher," said Jesus, "and do you not understand these things? Very truly I tell you, we speak of what we know, and we testify to what we have seen, but still you people do not accept our testimony. I have spoken to you of earthly things and you do not believe; how then will you believe if I speak of heavenly things? No one has ever gone into heaven except the one who came from heaven — the Son of Man. Just as Moses lifted up the snake in the wilderness, so the Son of Man must be lifted up, that everyone who believes may have eternal life in him."

For God so loved the world that he gave his one and only Son, that whoever believes in him shall not perish but have eternal life. For God did not send his Son into the world to condemn the world, but to save the world through him. Whoever believes in him is not condemned, but whoever does not believe stands condemned already because they have not believed in the name of God's one and only Son. This is the verdict: Light has come into the world, but people loved darkness instead of light because their deeds were evil. Everyone who does evil hates the light, and will not come into the light for fear that their deeds will be exposed. But whoever lives by the truth comes into the light, so that it may be seen plainly that what they have done has been done in the sight of God.

JOHN 3:1–21

In his letter to the church at Rome, the apostle Paul—who was called by God to tell this Good News to the rest of the world— further reinforces what we must do to receive this gift of grace.

Therefore, just as sin entered the world through one man, and death through sin, and in this way death came to all people, because all sinned—

To be sure, sin was in the world before the law was given, but sin is not charged against anyone's account where there is no law. Nevertheless, death reigned from the time of Adam to the time of Moses, even over those who did not sin by breaking a command, as did Adam, who is a pattern of the one to come.

But the gift is not like the trespass. For if the many died by the trespass of the one man, how much more did God's grace and the gift that came by the grace of the one man, Jesus Christ, overflow to the many! Nor can the gift of God be compared with the result of one man's sin: The judgment followed one sin and brought condemnation, but the gift followed many trespasses and brought justification. For if, by the trespass of the one man, death reigned through that one man, how much more will those who receive God's abundant provision of grace and of the gift of righteousness reign in life through the one man, Jesus Christ!

Consequently, just as one trespass resulted in condemnation for all people, so also one righteous act resulted in justification and life for all people. For just as through the disobedience of the one man the many were made sinners, so also through the obedience of the one man the many will be made righteous.

The law was brought in so that the trespass might increase. But where sin increased, grace increased all the more, so that, just as sin reigned in death, so also grace might reign through righteousness to bring eternal life through Jesus Christ our Lord.

ROMANS 5:12–21

Brothers and sisters, my heart's desire and prayer to God for the Israelites is that they may be saved. For I can testify about them that they are zealous for God, but their zeal is not based on knowledge. Since they did not know the righteousness of God and sought to establish their own, they did not submit to God's righteousness. Christ is the culmination of the law so that there may be righteousness for everyone who believes.

Moses writes this about the righteousness that is by the law: "The person who does these things will live by them." But the righteousness that is by faith says: "Do not say in your heart, 'Who will ascend into heaven?'" (that is, to bring Christ down) "or 'Who will descend into the deep?'" (that is, to bring Christ up from the dead). But what does it say? "The word is near you; it is in your mouth and in your heart," that is, the message concerning faith that we proclaim: If you declare with your mouth, "Jesus is Lord," and believe in your heart that God raised him from the dead, you will be saved. For it is with your heart that you believe and are justified, and it is with your mouth that you profess your faith and are saved. As Scripture says, "Anyone who believes in him will never be put to shame." For there is no difference between Jew and Gentile — the same Lord is Lord of all and richly blesses all who call on him, for, "Everyone who calls on the name of the Lord will be saved."

ROMANS 10:1–13

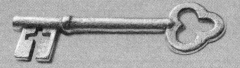

CHAPTER

4

The Bible

KEY IDEA

I believe the Bible is the inspired Word of God
that guides my beliefs and actions.

KEY VERSE

All Scripture is God-breathed and is useful for teaching,
rebuking, correcting and training in righteousness,
so that the servant of God may be thoroughly
equipped for every good work.
2 Timothy 3:16 – 17

How do we know God? How do we understand and see the world we live in? How do we grasp where we came from and why we are here? How do we know where this story is ultimately heading? The answer is profound—God reveals himself and his grand plan to us. Our role is to listen and believe.

By simply looking at nature and the world around us, we can conclude there is a God. But how do we learn about this God? How do we come into a full relationship with God? What are his plans and purposes for us? What are the principles he wants us to live by to guide us into his truth? The answer to all of these questions is found in God's revelation to us—the Bible.

The Bible repeatedly records that God communicated to his people at specific times with specific messages. In some cases, such as with Moses at the burning bush, he spoke audibly. In other instances he spoke through dreams or visions or less direct impressions. But the words of the Lord were always given to his people to reveal his plan for them and for all humanity. God revealed his story because he loves us.

GOD SPEAKS

Now Moses was tending the flock of Jethro his father-in-law, the priest of Midian, and he led the flock to the far side of the wilderness and came to Horeb, the mountain of God. There the angel of the LORD appeared to him in flames of fire from within a bush. Moses saw that though the bush was on fire it did not burn up. So Moses thought, "I will go over and see this strange sight — why the bush does not burn up."

When the LORD saw that he had gone over to look, God called to him from within the bush, "Moses! Moses!"

And Moses said, "Here I am."

"Do not come any closer," God said. "Take off your sandals, for the place where you are standing is holy ground." Then he said, "I am the God of your father, the God of Abraham, the God of Isaac and the God of Jacob." At this, Moses hid his face, because he was afraid to look at God.

The LORD said, "I have indeed seen the misery of my people in Egypt. I have heard them crying out because of their slave drivers, and I am concerned about their suffering. So I have come down to rescue them from the hand of the Egyptians and to bring them up out of that land into a good and spacious land, a land flowing with milk and honey — the home of the Canaanites, Hittites, Amorites, Perizzites, Hivites and Jebusites. And now the cry of the Israelites has reached me, and I have seen the way the Egyptians are oppressing them. So now, go. I am sending you to Pharaoh to bring my people the Israelites out of Egypt."

But Moses said to God, "Who am I that I should go to Pharaoh and bring the Israelites out of Egypt?"

And God said, "I will be with you. And this will be the sign to you that it is I who have sent you: When you have brought the people out of Egypt, you will worship God on this mountain."

Moses said to God, "Suppose I go to the Israelites and say to them, 'The God of your fathers has sent me to you,' and they ask me, 'What is his name?' Then what shall I tell them?"

God said to Moses, "I AM WHO I AM. This is what you are to say to the Israelites: 'I AM has sent me to you.'"

God also said to Moses, "Say to the Israelites, 'The LORD, the God of your fathers — the God of Abraham, the God of Isaac and the God of Jacob — has sent me to you.'

"This is my name forever,
      the name you shall call me
      from generation to generation.

"Go, assemble the elders of Israel and say to them, 'The LORD, the God of your fathers — the God of Abraham, Isaac and Jacob — appeared to me and said: I have watched over you and have seen what has been done to you in Egypt. And I have promised to bring you up out of your misery in Egypt into the land of the Canaanites, Hittites, Amorites, Perizzites, Hivites and Jebusites — a land flowing with milk and honey.'

"The elders of Israel will listen to you. Then you and the elders are to go to the king of Egypt and say to him, 'The LORD, the God of the Hebrews, has met with us. Let us take a three-day journey into the wilderness to offer sacrifices to the LORD our God.' But I know that the king of Egypt will not let you go unless a mighty hand compels him. So I will stretch out my hand and strike the Egyptians with all the wonders that I will perform among them. After that, he will let you go.

"And I will make the Egyptians favorably disposed toward this people, so that when you leave you will not go empty-handed. Every woman is to ask her neighbor and any woman living in her house for articles of silver and gold and for clothing, which you will put on your sons and daughters. And so you will plunder the Egyptians."

Moses answered, "What if they do not believe me or listen to me and say, 'The LORD did not appear to you'?"

Then the LORD said to him, "What is that in your hand?"

"A staff," he replied.

The LORD said, "Throw it on the ground."

Moses threw it on the ground and it became a snake, and he ran from it. Then the LORD said to him, "Reach out your hand and take it by the tail." So Moses reached out and took hold of the snake and it turned back into a staff in his hand. "This," said the LORD, "is so that they may believe that the LORD, the God of their fathers — the God of Abraham, the God of Isaac and the God of Jacob — has appeared to you."

Then the LORD said, "Put your hand inside your cloak." So Moses put his hand into his cloak, and when he took it out, the skin was leprous — it had become as white as snow.

"Now put it back into your cloak," he said. So Moses put his hand back into his cloak, and when he took it out, it was restored, like the rest of his flesh.

Then the LORD said, "If they do not believe you or pay attention to the first sign, they may believe the second. But if they do not believe these two signs or listen to you, take some water from the Nile and pour it on the dry ground. The water you take from the river will become blood on the ground."

Moses said to the LORD, "Pardon your servant, Lord. I have never been eloquent, neither in the past nor since you have spoken to your servant. I am slow of speech and tongue."

The LORD said to him, "Who gave human beings their mouths? Who makes them deaf or mute? Who gives them sight or makes them blind? Is it not I, the LORD? Now go; I will help you speak and will teach you what to say."

But Moses said, "Pardon your servant, Lord. Please send someone else."

Then the LORD's anger burned against Moses and he said, "What about your brother, Aaron the Levite? I know he can speak well. He is already on his way to meet you, and he will be glad to see you. You shall speak to him and put words in his mouth; I will help both of you speak and will teach you what to do. He will speak to the people for you, and it will be as if he were your mouth and as if you were God to him. But take this staff in your hand so you can perform the signs with it."   EXODUS 3:1—4:17

The Lord spoke mostly through prophets in the Old Testament and through Jesus and the apostles in the New Testament. After Jesus' death on the cross and his miraculous resurrection, two of his followers (who were not part of the "Eleven"—Jesus' close circle of disciples, now minus Judas Iscariot) were walking on the road from Jerusalem to Emmaus. Jesus came up and started walking and talking with them, though they were kept from recognizing him at first. He told stories from the Old Testament books he called Scripture, which means Jesus understood these writings were inspired by God.

Beginning with Moses and all the Prophets, [Jesus] explained to them what was said in all the Scriptures concerning himself.

As they approached the village to which they were going, Jesus continued on as if he were going farther. But they urged him strongly, "Stay with us, for it is nearly evening; the day is almost over." So he went in to stay with them.

When he was at the table with them, he took bread, gave thanks, broke it and began to give it to them. Then their eyes were opened and they recognized him, and he disappeared from their sight. They asked each other, "Were not our hearts burning within us while he talked with us on the road and opened the Scriptures to us?"

They got up and returned at once to Jerusalem. There they found the Eleven and those with them, assembled together and saying, "It is true! The Lord has risen and has appeared to Simon." Then the two told what had happened on the way, and how Jesus was recognized by them when he broke the bread.

While they were still talking about this, Jesus himself stood among them and said to them, "Peace be with you."

They were startled and frightened, thinking they saw a ghost. He said to them, "Why are you troubled, and why do doubts rise in your minds? Look at my hands and my feet. It is I myself! Touch me and see; a ghost does not have flesh and bones, as you see I have."

When he had said this, he showed them his hands and feet. And while they still did not believe it because of joy and amazement, he asked them, "Do you have anything here to eat?" They gave him a piece of broiled fish, and he took it and ate it in their presence.

He said to them, "This is what I told you while I was still with you: Everything must be fulfilled that is written about me in the Law of Moses, the Prophets and the Psalms."

Then he opened their minds so they could understand the Scriptures. He told them, "This is what is written: The Messiah will suffer and rise from the dead on the third day, and repentance for the forgiveness of sins will be preached in his name to all nations, beginning at Jerusalem. You are witnesses of these things. I am going to send you what my Father has promised; but stay in the city until you have been clothed with power from on high." LUKE 24:27–49

Before appearing to the Eleven in Jerusalem, Jesus also appeared to Peter, also known as Simon, who, after denying Jesus, went on to become a faithful follower of Christ and a key leader in the early church.

Like other leaders of the church, Peter sent letters to those early believers; those letters are preserved in the Bible in the New Testament. The situation for the writing of this letter to one of the churches is that false teaching was infiltrating the church and causing followers to stray from God's Word. Peter wrote to them to shepherd them back toward the truth. In the process, he provided insight into the origin of Scripture and how followers can use it to guide their lives.

Simon Peter, a servant and apostle of Jesus Christ,

To those who through the righteousness of our God and Savior Jesus Christ have received a faith as precious as ours:

Grace and peace be yours in abundance through the knowledge of God and of Jesus our Lord.

His divine power has given us everything we need for a godly life through our knowledge of him who called us by his own glory and goodness. Through these he has given us his very great and precious promises, so that through them you may participate in the divine nature, having escaped the corruption in the world caused by evil desires.

For this very reason, make every effort to add to your faith goodness; and to goodness, knowledge; and to knowledge, self-control; and to self-control, perseverance; and to perseverance, godliness; and to godliness, mutual affection; and to mutual affection, love. For if you possess these qualities in increasing measure, they will keep you from being ineffective and unproductive in your knowledge of our Lord Jesus Christ. But whoever does not have them is nearsighted and blind, forgetting that they have been cleansed from their past sins.

Therefore, my brothers and sisters, make every effort to confirm your calling and election. For if you do these things, you will never stumble, and you will receive a rich welcome into the eternal kingdom of our Lord and Savior Jesus Christ.

So I will always remind you of these things, even though you know them and are firmly established in the truth you now have. I think it is right to refresh your memory as long as I live in the tent of this body, because I know that I will soon put it aside, as our Lord Jesus Christ has made clear to me. And I will make every effort to see that after my departure you will always be able to remember these things.

For we did not follow cleverly devised stories when we told you about the coming of our Lord Jesus Christ in power, but we were eyewitnesses of his majesty. He received honor and glory from God the Father when the voice came to him from the Majestic Glory, saying, "This is my Son, whom I love; with him I am well pleased." We ourselves heard this voice that came from heaven when we were with him on the sacred mountain.

We also have the prophetic message as something completely reliable, and you will do well to pay attention to it, as to a light shining in a dark place, until the day dawns and the morning star rises in your hearts. Above all, you must understand that no prophecy of Scripture came about by the prophet's own interpretation of things. For prophecy never had its origin in the human will, but prophets, though human, spoke from God as they were carried along by the Holy Spirit.   2 PETER 1:1–21

THE AUTHORITY OF SCRIPTURE

To understand the power of the authority of Scripture, we must go back to the early days of Israel. With a mighty hand God led the Israelites out of slavery in Egypt. In the wilderness God made preparations for them to enter into the land of Canaan that he had promised to Abraham 600 years earlier. Soon God descended from the heavens to Mount Sinai to meet with his servant Moses and the people and proclaim to them the Ten Commandments. These laws spoken directly by God to Moses to write down and give to the people guided the values and behavior of the Israelites.

On the first day of the third month after the Israelites left Egypt — on that very day — they came to the Desert of Sinai. After they set out from Rephidim, they entered the Desert of Sinai, and Israel camped there in the desert in front of the mountain.

Then Moses went up to God, and the LORD called to him from the mountain and said, "This is what you are to say to the descendants of Jacob and what you are to tell the people of Israel: 'You yourselves have seen what I did to Egypt, and how I carried you on eagles' wings and brought you to myself. Now if you obey me fully and keep my covenant, then out of all nations you will be my treasured possession. Although the whole earth is mine, you will be for me a kingdom of priests and a holy nation.' These are the words you are to speak to the Israelites."

So Moses went back and summoned the elders of the people and set before them all the words the LORD had commanded him to speak. The people all responded together, "We will do everything the LORD has said." So Moses brought their answer back to the LORD.

The LORD said to Moses, "I am going to come to you in a dense cloud, so that the people will hear me speaking with you and will always put their trust in you." Then Moses told the LORD what the people had said. EXODUS 19:1–9

On the morning of the third day there was thunder and lightning, with a thick cloud over the mountain, and a very loud trumpet blast. Everyone in the camp trembled. Then Moses led the people out of the camp to meet with God, and they stood at the foot of the mountain. Mount Sinai was covered with smoke, because the LORD descended on it in fire. The smoke billowed up from it like smoke from a furnace, and the whole mountain trembled violently. As the sound of the trumpet grew louder and louder, Moses spoke and the voice of God answered him. EXODUS 19:16–19

And God spoke all these words:

"I am the LORD your God, who brought you out of Egypt, out of the land of slavery.

"You shall have no other gods before me.

"You shall not make for yourself an image in the form of anything in heaven above or on the earth beneath or in the waters below. You shall not bow down to them or worship them; for I, the LORD your God, am a jealous God, punishing the children for the sin of the parents to the third and fourth generation of those who hate me, but showing love to a thousand generations of those who love me and keep my commandments.

"You shall not misuse the name of the LORD your God, for the LORD will not hold anyone guiltless who misuses his name.

"Remember the Sabbath day by keeping it holy. Six days you shall labor and do all your work, but the seventh day is a sabbath to the LORD your God. On it you shall not do any work, neither you, nor your son or daughter, nor your male or female servant, nor your animals, nor any foreigner residing in your towns. For in six days the LORD made the heavens and the earth, the sea, and all that is in them, but he rested on the seventh day. Therefore the LORD blessed the Sabbath day and made it holy.

"Honor your father and your mother, so that you may live long in the land the LORD your God is giving you.

"You shall not murder.

"You shall not commit adultery.

"You shall not steal.

"You shall not give false testimony against your neighbor.

"You shall not covet your neighbor's house. You shall not covet your neighbor's wife, or his male or female servant, his ox or donkey, or anything that belongs to your neighbor."

When the people saw the thunder and lightning and heard the trumpet and saw the mountain in smoke, they trembled with fear. They stayed at a distance and said to Moses, "Speak to us yourself and we will listen. But do not have God speak to us or we will die."

Moses said to the people, "Do not be afraid. God has come to test you, so that the fear of God will be with you to keep you from sinning."

The people remained at a distance, while Moses approached the thick darkness where God was.   EXODUS 20:1–21

God's words carry the authority of the one who speaks them. Throughout the Bible, in the Old Testament and the New, examples of the authority of Scripture are presented. For instance, immediately after John baptized Jesus, the Spirit led Jesus into the wilderness where Satan sought to take advantage of Jesus' isolation, hunger and physical exhaustion. But God's power was revealed in Jesus' interactions with Satan; Jesus quoted Scripture three times — twice from Deuteronomy and once from Psalms — as his authority to overcome each temptation. Despite facing genuine temptations at a time when he was vulnerable, Jesus remained rooted in the principles recorded in God's Word.

Then Jesus was led by the Spirit into the wilderness to be tempted by the devil. After fasting forty days and forty nights, he was hungry. The tempter came to him and said, "If you are the Son of God, tell these stones to become bread."

Jesus answered, "It is written: 'Man shall not live on bread alone, but on every word that comes from the mouth of God.'"

Then the devil took him to the holy city and had him stand on the highest point of the temple. "If you are the Son of God," he said, "throw yourself down. For it is written:

> " 'He will command his angels concerning you,
>   and they will lift you up in their hands,
>   so that you will not strike your foot against a stone.' "

Jesus answered him, "It is also written: 'Do not put the Lord your God to the test.' "

Again, the devil took him to a very high mountain and showed him all the kingdoms of the world and their splendor. "All this I will give you," he said, "if you will bow down and worship me."

Jesus said to him, "Away from me, Satan! For it is written: 'Worship the Lord your God, and serve him only.' "

Then the devil left him, and angels came and attended him.

MATTHEW 4:1–11

One of Jesus' faithful followers, the apostle Paul, was languishing in a dungeon in Rome. The end of his life was drawing near, yet one of his main priorities was passing the mantle of leadership to young pastors like Timothy. In Paul's final charge to Timothy, he encouraged him to continue to follow the Scriptures, God's Word, as his sole authority.

You, however, know all about my teaching, my way of life, my purpose, faith, patience, love, endurance, persecutions, sufferings — what kinds of things happened to me in Antioch, Iconium and Lystra, the persecutions I endured. Yet the Lord rescued me from all of them. In fact, everyone who wants to live a godly life in Christ Jesus will be persecuted, while evildoers and impostors will go from bad to worse, deceiving and being deceived. But as for you, continue in what you have learned and have become convinced of, because you know those from whom you learned it, and how from infancy you have known the Holy Scriptures, which are able to make you wise for salvation through faith in Christ Jesus. All Scripture is God-breathed and is useful for teaching, rebuking, correcting and training in righteousness, so that the servant of God may be thoroughly equipped for every good work. 2 TIMOTHY 3:10–17

THE PURPOSE OF SCRIPTURE

Because the collection of sacred writings, or Scriptures, came from God, it is referred to as the Word of God. In the Old Testa-

ment, Isaiah spoke for the Lord during a difficult season in Israel's history. Because the people of the northern kingdom of Israel had perpetually disregarded God and his Word, Isaiah lived to see that nation's destruction at the hands of the Assyrians. The Lord revealed to Isaiah that his own nation, the southern kingdom of Judah, would likewise be conquered—by the Babylonians. But God's prophet, under the inspiration of the Holy Spirit, also looked many years ahead and foretold Judah's restoration following the Babylonian exile. He reminded the Israelites that God's Word is eternal and always accomplishes God's purposes.

> A voice says, "Cry out."
> And I said, "What shall I cry?"
>
> "All people are like grass,
>   and all their faithfulness is like the flowers of the
>   field.
> The grass withers and the flowers fall,
>   because the breath of the LORD blows on them.
>   Surely the people are grass.
> The grass withers and the flowers fall,
>   but the word of our God endures forever."   ISAIAH 40:6–8

> Seek the LORD while he may be found;
>   call on him while he is near.
> Let the wicked forsake their ways
>   and the unrighteous their thoughts.
> Let them turn to the LORD, and he will have mercy
>   on them,
>   and to our God, for he will freely pardon.
>
> "For my thoughts are not your thoughts,
>   neither are your ways my ways,"
>   declares the LORD.
> "As the heavens are higher than the earth,
>   so are my ways higher than your ways
>   and my thoughts than your thoughts.
> As the rain and the snow
>   come down from heaven,

and do not return to it
    without watering the earth
and making it bud and flourish,
    so that it yields seed for the sower and bread for the eater,
so is my word that goes out from my mouth:
    It will not return to me empty,
but will accomplish what I desire
    and achieve the purpose for which I sent it.
You will go out in joy
    and be led forth in peace;
the mountains and hills
    will burst into song before you,
and all the trees of the field
    will clap their hands.
Instead of the thornbush will grow the juniper,
    and instead of briers the myrtle will grow.
This will be for the Lord's renown,
    for an everlasting sign,
    that will endure forever." ISAIAH 55:6–13

The writer of the book of Hebrews builds on the idea that God breathed life into the words of the Bible. The Scriptures are a live organism that has a way of "getting under our skin."

For the word of God is alive and active. Sharper than any double-edged sword, it penetrates even to dividing soul and spirit, joints and marrow; it judges the thoughts and attitudes of the heart. Nothing in all creation is hidden from God's sight. Everything is uncovered and laid bare before the eyes of him to whom we must give account. HEBREWS 4:12–13

Throughout the Bible the writers warned readers that they should not add or take away from God's Word. God has given and preserved his Word for us so we can rely on it to guide our lives into all truth and according to God's good plan. Therefore, Christians revere the Bible and affirm its right to command our beliefs and actions.
Moses writes,

Now, Israel, hear the decrees and laws I am about to teach you. Follow them so that you may live and may go in and take possession of the land the LORD, the God of your ancestors, is giving you. Do not add to what I command you and do not subtract from it, but keep the commands of the LORD your God that I give you.

DEUTERONOMY 4:1–2

In the book of Proverbs, Agur declares,

> "Every word of God is flawless;
>   he is a shield to those who take refuge in him.
> Do not add to his words,
>   or he will rebuke you and prove you a liar."   PROVERBS 30:5-6

John, the author of Revelation, writes,

I warn everyone who hears the words of the prophecy of this scroll: If anyone adds anything to them, God will add to that person the plagues described in this scroll. And if anyone takes words away from this scroll of prophecy, God will take away from that person any share in the tree of life and in the Holy City, which are described in this scroll.   REVELATION 22:18–19

CHAPTER

5

Identity in Christ

--- KEY IDEA ---

I believe I am significant because of
my position as a child of God.

--- KEY VERSE ---

Yet to all who did receive him, to those
who believed in his name, he gave the right
to become children of God.
John 1:12

A NEW NAME

During Bible times, a person's name was more than simply a reference to one's family or a way to uniquely identify someone; typically it characterized something about them. There are several instances recorded in the Bible of God giving a person a new name. When God would rename a person, he was establishing for them a new identity and marking that he was changing their mission or place in life. This was the case with Abram (meaning "exalted father"), whose name God changed to Abraham (meaning "father of many"). The meaning of the name Abraham represented God's plan to make Abraham's offspring into the great nation of Israel—and eventually into the body of Christ through Abraham's spiritual descendants.

When Abram was ninety-nine years old, the LORD appeared to him and said, "I am God Almighty; walk before me faithfully and be blameless. Then I will make my covenant between me and you and will greatly increase your numbers."

Abram fell facedown, and God said to him, "As for me, this is my covenant with you: You will be the father of many nations. No longer will you be called Abram; your name will be Abraham, for I have made you a father of many nations. I will make you very fruitful; I will make nations of you, and kings will come from you. I will establish my covenant as an everlasting covenant between me and you and your descendants after you for the generations to come, to be your God and the God of your descendants after you." GENESIS 17:1–7

God's promise to make Abraham a great nation seemed laughable, given the ages of Abraham and Sarah. But God followed through on his promise and gave them a son when Abraham was 100 years old and Sarah was 90. God gave him the name Isaac, which means "he laughs."

Abraham fell facedown; he laughed and said to himself, "Will a son be born to a man a hundred years old? Will Sarah bear a child at the age of ninety?" GENESIS 17:17

Then God said, "Yes, but your wife Sarah will bear you a son, and you will call him Isaac. I will establish my covenant with him as an everlasting covenant for his descendants after him."

GENESIS 17:19

Now the LORD was gracious to Sarah as he had said, and the LORD did for Sarah what he had promised. Sarah became pregnant and bore a son to Abraham in his old age, at the very time God had promised him. Abraham gave the name Isaac to the son Sarah bore him. When his son Isaac was eight days old, Abraham circumcised him, as God commanded him. Abraham was a hundred years old when his son Isaac was born to him.

Sarah said, "God has brought me laughter, and everyone who hears about this will laugh with me." And she added, "Who would have said to Abraham that Sarah would nurse children? Yet I have borne him a son in his old age."

GENESIS 21:1–7

A NEW COVENANT

In Old Testament times, God provided his people with a promise under what is termed the old covenant, which included his directions to his people under Moses' leadership. A covenant is a binding agreement between two parties, in this case God and Israel, that lays out what each side promises to do. The prophet Jeremiah, however, foretold of a new covenant—a new deal God had in the works—that would redefine the identity of God's people. This time it involved more than just a name change.

"The days are coming," declares the LORD,
  "when I will make a new covenant
with the people of Israel
  and with the people of Judah.
It will not be like the covenant
  I made with their ancestors
when I took them by the hand
  to lead them out of Egypt,
because they broke my covenant,
  though I was a husband to them,"
declares the LORD.

"This is the covenant I will make with the people of Israel
   after that time," declares the LORD.
"I will put my law in their minds
   and write it on their hearts.
I will be their God,
   and they will be my people.
No longer will they teach their neighbor,
   or say to one another, 'Know the LORD,'
because they will all know me,
   from the least of them to the greatest,"
                                                declares the LORD.
"For I will forgive their wickedness
   and will remember their sins no more."   JEREMIAH 31:31–34

What an amazing promise of restoration for a people who were wondering if God had forgotten them. The promise of hope was manifested in the person of Jesus Christ, the Son of God come to earth. Jesus is the Deliverer of this new covenant—the ultimate sacrifice, the Lamb who was slain to make this new identity possible. Jesus was fully prepared to pay this price for us.

In this passage from the New Testament, Jesus knew he would soon be crucified for the sins of the world. He knew the excruciating pain he would endure would make it possible to restore what God had envisioned at the beginning in the Garden of Eden—Jesus' death and resurrection would make it possible for people to have a personal and abiding relationship with God. People would be restored to the position of oneness with God that God envisioned for us in the beginning. Jesus expressed his passionate love for us in one of the last prayers he prayed before his death.

"Father, the hour has come. Glorify your Son, that your Son may glorify you. For you granted him authority over all people that he might give eternal life to all those you have given him. Now this is eternal life: that they know you, the only true God, and Jesus Christ, whom you have sent. I have brought you glory on earth by finishing the work you gave me to do. And now, Father, glorify me in your presence with the glory I had with you before the world began.

"I have revealed you to those whom you gave me out of the world. They were yours; you gave them to me and they have obeyed your word. Now they know that everything you have given me comes from you. For I gave them the words you gave me and they accepted them. They knew with certainty that I came from you, and they believed that you sent me. I pray for them. I am not praying for the world, but for those you have given me, for they are yours. All I have is yours, and all you have is mine. And glory has come to me through them. I will remain in the world no longer, but they are still in the world, and I am coming to you. Holy Father, protect them by the power of your name, the name you gave me, so that they may be one as we are one. While I was with them, I protected them and kept them safe by that name you gave me. None has been lost except the one doomed to destruction so that Scripture would be fulfilled.

"I am coming to you now, but I say these things while I am still in the world, so that they may have the full measure of my joy within them. I have given them your word and the world has hated them, for they are not of the world any more than I am of the world. My prayer is not that you take them out of the world but that you protect them from the evil one. They are not of the world, even as I am not of it. Sanctify them by the truth; your word is truth. As you sent me into the world, I have sent them into the world. For them I sanctify myself, that they too may be truly sanctified.

"My prayer is not for them alone. I pray also for those who will believe in me through their message, that all of them may be one, Father, just as you are in me and I am in you. May they also be in us so that the world may believe that you have sent me. I have given them the glory that you gave me, that they may be one as we are one — I in them and you in me — so that they may be brought to complete unity. Then the world will know that you sent me and have loved them even as you have loved me.

"Father, I want those you have given me to be with me where I am, and to see my glory, the glory you have given me because you loved me before the creation of the world.

"Righteous Father, though the world does not know you, I know you, and they know that you have sent me. I have made you known to them, and will continue to make you known in order that the love you have for me may be in them and that I myself may be in them." JOHN 17:1–26

Jesus Christ fulfilled the requirements of the old covenant God made with Moses and ushered in a new season of amazing grace. Those who embrace this new covenant and turn from their sins will have their sins wiped away and receive a new identity.

The true light that gives light to everyone was coming into the world. He was in the world, and though the world was made through him, the world did not recognize him. He came to that which was his own, but his own did not receive him. Yet to all who did receive him, to those who believed in his name, he gave the right to become children of God—children born not of natural descent, nor of human decision or a husband's will, but born of God. JOHN 1:9–13

The law is only a shadow of the good things that are coming—not the realities themselves. For this reason it can never, by the same sacrifices repeated endlessly year after year, make perfect those who draw near to worship. Otherwise, would they not have stopped being offered? For the worshipers would have been cleansed once for all, and would no longer have felt guilty for their sins. But those sacrifices are an annual reminder of sins. It is impossible for the blood of bulls and goats to take away sins.

Therefore, when Christ came into the world, he said:

> "Sacrifice and offering you did not desire,
>> but a body you prepared for me;
> with burnt offerings and sin offerings
>> you were not pleased.
> Then I said, 'Here I am—it is written about me in the
>> scroll—
> I have come to do your will, my God.'"

First he said, "Sacrifices and offerings, burnt offerings and sin offerings you did not desire, nor were you pleased with them"—though they were offered in accordance with the law. Then he said,

"Here I am, I have come to do your will." He sets aside the first to establish the second. And by that will, we have been made holy through the sacrifice of the body of Jesus Christ once for all.

Day after day every priest stands and performs his religious duties; again and again he offers the same sacrifices, which can never take away sins. But when this priest had offered for all time one sacrifice for sins, he sat down at the right hand of God, and since that time he waits for his enemies to be made his footstool. For by one sacrifice he has made perfect forever those who are being made holy.

The Holy Spirit also testifies to us about this. First he says:

> "This is the covenant I will make with them
>   after that time, says the Lord.
> I will put my laws in their hearts,
>   and I will write them on their minds."

Then he adds:

> "Their sins and lawless acts
>   I will remember no more."

And where these have been forgiven, sacrifice for sin is no longer necessary.   HEBREWS 10:1–18

ADOPTION

The beautiful thing about God's kingdom is that all those who welcome Jesus as their Lord are given the opportunity to accept a new identity through him. This is illustrated poignantly through the story of a crooked tax collector named Zacchaeus. Tax collectors were among the most despised people in Israel because they chose to work for Rome and were making themselves rich by gouging their fellow Jews. But Zacchaeus shows that even the lost can be adopted and made new.

Jesus entered Jericho and was passing through. A man was there by the name of Zacchaeus; he was a chief tax collector and was wealthy. He wanted to see who Jesus was, but because he was short he could not see over the crowd. So he ran ahead and climbed a sycamore-fig tree to see him, since Jesus was coming that way.

When Jesus reached the spot, he looked up and said to him, "Zacchaeus, come down immediately. I must stay at your house today." So he came down at once and welcomed him gladly.

All the people saw this and began to mutter, "He has gone to be the guest of a sinner."

But Zacchaeus stood up and said to the Lord, "Look, Lord! Here and now I give half of my possessions to the poor, and if I have cheated anybody out of anything, I will pay back four times the amount."

Jesus said to him, "Today salvation has come to this house, because this man, too, is a son of Abraham."   Luke 19:1–9

The early church was richly invested in the changes that resulted from following Jesus. The letter to the Romans was written by the apostle Paul to present the full picture of the new covenant, starting with our position in sin and moving to a graphic and overwhelming description of our new identity in Christ.

As it is written:

> "There is no one righteous, not even one;
>   there is no one who understands;
>   there is no one who seeks God.
> All have turned away,
>   they have together become worthless;
> there is no one who does good,
>   not even one."
> "Their throats are open graves;
>   their tongues practice deceit."
> "The poison of vipers is on their lips."
>   "Their mouths are full of cursing and bitterness."
> "Their feet are swift to shed blood;
>   ruin and misery mark their ways,
> and the way of peace they do not know."
>   "There is no fear of God before their eyes."

Now we know that whatever the law says, it says to those who are under the law, so that every mouth may be silenced and the whole world held accountable to God. Therefore no one will be declared righteous in God's sight by the works of the law; rather, through the law we become conscious of our sin.

But now apart from the law the righteousness of God has been made known, to which the Law and the Prophets testify. This righteousness is given through faith in Jesus Christ to all who believe. There is no difference between Jew and Gentile, for all have sinned and fall short of the glory of God, and all are justified freely by his grace through the redemption that came by Christ Jesus. God presented Christ as a sacrifice of atonement, through the shedding of his blood — to be received by faith. He did this to demonstrate his righteousness, because in his forbearance he had left the sins committed beforehand unpunished — he did it to demonstrate his righteousness at the present time, so as to be just and the one who justifies those who have faith in Jesus. ROMANS 3:10–26

Therefore, since we have been justified through faith, we have peace with God through our Lord Jesus Christ, through whom we have gained access by faith into this grace in which we now stand. And we boast in the hope of the glory of God. ROMANS 5:1–2

You see, at just the right time, when we were still powerless, Christ died for the ungodly. Very rarely will anyone die for a righteous person, though for a good person someone might possibly dare to die. But God demonstrates his own love for us in this: While we were still sinners, Christ died for us.

Since we have now been justified by his blood, how much more shall we be saved from God's wrath through him! For if, while we were God's enemies, we were reconciled to him through the death of his Son, how much more, having been reconciled, shall we be saved through his life! Not only is this so, but we also boast in God through our Lord Jesus Christ, through whom we have now received reconciliation. ROMANS 5:6–11

What shall we say, then? Shall we go on sinning so that grace may increase? By no means! We are those who have died to sin; how can we live in it any longer? Or don't you know that all of us who were baptized into Christ Jesus were baptized into his death? We were therefore buried with him through baptism into death in order that, just as Christ was raised from the dead through the glory of the Father, we too may live a new life.

For if we have been united with him in a death like his, we will certainly also be united with him in a resurrection like his. For we know that our old self was crucified with him so that the body ruled by sin might be done away with, that we should no longer be slaves to sin — because anyone who has died has been set free from sin.   ROMANS 6:1–7

Therefore, there is now no condemnation for those who are in Christ Jesus, because through Christ Jesus the law of the Spirit who gives life has set you free from the law of sin and death. For what the law was powerless to do because it was weakened by the flesh, God did by sending his own Son in the likeness of sinful flesh to be a sin offering. And so he condemned sin in the flesh, in order that the righteous requirement of the law might be fully met in us, who do not live according to the flesh but according to the Spirit.

Those who live according to the flesh have their minds set on what the flesh desires; but those who live in accordance with the Spirit have their minds set on what the Spirit desires. The mind governed by the flesh is death, but the mind governed by the Spirit is life and peace. The mind governed by the flesh is hostile to God; it does not submit to God's law, nor can it do so. Those who are in the realm of the flesh cannot please God.

You, however, are not in the realm of the flesh but are in the realm of the Spirit, if indeed the Spirit of God lives in you. And if anyone does not have the Spirit of Christ, they do not belong to Christ. But if Christ is in you, then even though your body is subject to death because of sin, the Spirit gives life because of righteousness. And if the Spirit of him who raised Jesus from the dead is living in you, he who raised Christ from the dead will also give life to your mortal bodies because of his Spirit who lives in you.

Therefore, brothers and sisters, we have an obligation — but it is not to the flesh, to live according to it. For if you live according to the flesh, you will die; but if by the Spirit you put to death the misdeeds of the body, you will live.

For those who are led by the Spirit of God are the children of God. The Spirit you received does not make you slaves, so that you live in fear again; rather, the Spirit you received brought about your adoption to sonship. And by him we cry, *"Abba,* Father." The Spirit himself testifies with our spirit that we are God's children. Now if we are children, then we are heirs — heirs of God and co-heirs with Christ, if indeed we share in his sufferings in order that we may also share in his glory.

I consider that our present sufferings are not worth comparing with the glory that will be revealed in us. For the creation waits in eager expectation for the children of God to be revealed. For the creation was subjected to frustration, not by its own choice, but by the will of the one who subjected it, in hope that the creation itself will be liberated from its bondage to decay and brought into the freedom and glory of the children of God.

We know that the whole creation has been groaning as in the pains of childbirth right up to the present time. Not only so, but we ourselves, who have the firstfruits of the Spirit, groan inwardly as we wait eagerly for our adoption to sonship, the redemption of our bodies. For in this hope we were saved. But hope that is seen is no hope at all. Who hopes for what they already have? But if we hope for what we do not yet have, we wait for it patiently.

In the same way, the Spirit helps us in our weakness. We do not know what we ought to pray for, but the Spirit himself intercedes for us through wordless groans. And he who searches our hearts knows the mind of the Spirit, because the Spirit intercedes for God's people in accordance with the will of God.

And we know that in all things God works for the good of those who love him, who have been called according to his purpose. For those God foreknew he also predestined to be conformed to the image of his Son, that he might be the firstborn among many brothers and sisters. And those he predestined, he also called; those he called, he also justified; those he justified, he also glorified.

What, then, shall we say in response to these things? If God is for us, who can be against us? He who did not spare his own Son, but gave him up for us all — how will he not also, along with him, graciously give us all things? Who will bring any charge against those whom God has chosen? It is God who justifies. Who then is the one who condemns? No one. Christ Jesus who died — more than that, who was raised to life — is at the right hand of God and is also interceding for us. Who shall separate us from the love of Christ? Shall trouble or hardship or persecution or famine or nakedness or danger or sword? As it is written:

"For your sake we face death all day long;
　　we are considered as sheep to be slaughtered."

No, in all these things we are more than conquerors through him who loved us. For I am convinced that neither death nor life, neither angels nor demons, neither the present nor the future, nor any powers, neither height nor depth, nor anything else in all creation, will be able to separate us from the love of God that is in Christ Jesus our Lord. ROMANS 8:1–39

HEIRS OF GOD

Paul not only wrote to the Romans about their significance due to their new identity in Christ, but he also laid out eloquently to the believers in Ephesus this magnificent heritage. Note all the incredible things God has done to make our status as his children possible.

Paul, an apostle of Christ Jesus by the will of God,

To God's holy people in Ephesus, the faithful in Christ Jesus:

Grace and peace to you from God our Father and the Lord Jesus Christ.

Praise be to the God and Father of our Lord Jesus Christ, who has blessed us in the heavenly realms with every spiritual blessing in Christ. For he chose us in him before the creation of the world to be holy and blameless in his sight. In love he predestined us for adoption to sonship through Jesus Christ, in accordance with his pleasure and will — to the praise of his glorious grace, which he has freely given us in the One he loves. In him we have redemption through his blood, the forgiveness of sins, in accordance with the riches of God's grace that he lavished on us. With all wisdom and understanding, he made known to us the mystery of his will according to his good pleasure, which he purposed in Christ, to be put into effect when the times reach their fulfillment — to bring unity to all things in heaven and on earth under Christ.

In him we were also chosen, having been predestined according to the plan of him who works out everything in conformity with the purpose of his will, in order that we, who were the first to put our hope in Christ, might be for the praise of his glory. And you also were included in Christ when you heard the message of truth, the gospel of your salvation. When you believed, you were marked in him with a seal, the promised Holy Spirit, who is a deposit guaranteeing our inheritance until the redemption of those who are God's possession — to the praise of his glory.

For this reason, ever since I heard about your faith in the Lord Jesus and your love for all God's people, I have not stopped giving thanks for you, remembering you in my prayers. I keep asking that the God of our Lord Jesus Christ, the glorious Father, may give you the Spirit of wisdom and revelation, so that you may know him better. I pray that the eyes of your heart may be enlightened in order that you may know the hope to which he has called you, the riches of his glorious inheritance in his holy people, and his incomparably great power for us who believe. That power is the same as the mighty strength he exerted when he raised Christ from the dead and seated him at his right hand in the heavenly realms, far above all rule and authority, power and dominion, and every name that is invoked, not only in the present age but also in the one to come. And God placed all things under his feet and appointed him to be head over everything for the church, which is his body, the fullness of him who fills everything in every way.

As for you, you were dead in your transgressions and sins, in which you used to live when you followed the ways of this world and of the ruler of the kingdom of the air, the spirit who is now at work in those who are disobedient. All of us also lived among them at one time, gratifying the cravings of our flesh and following its desires and thoughts. Like the rest, we were by nature deserving of wrath. But because of his great love for us, God, who is rich in mercy, made us alive with Christ even when we were dead in transgressions — it is by grace you have been saved. And God raised us up with Christ and seated us with him in the heavenly realms in Christ Jesus, in order that in the coming ages he might show the incomparable riches of his grace, expressed in his kindness to us in Christ Jesus. For it is by grace you have been saved, through faith — and this is not from yourselves, it is the gift of God — not by works, so that no one can boast. For we are God's handiwork, created in Christ Jesus to do good works, which God prepared in advance for us to do.

Therefore, remember that formerly you who are Gentiles by birth and called "uncircumcised" by those who call themselves "the circumcision" (which is done in the body by human hands) — remember that at that time you were separate from Christ, excluded from citizenship in Israel and foreigners to the covenants of the promise, without hope and without God in the world. But now in Christ Jesus you who once were far away have been brought near by the blood of Christ.

For he himself is our peace, who has made the two groups one and has destroyed the barrier, the dividing wall of hostility, by setting aside in his flesh the law with its commands and regulations. His purpose was to create in himself one new humanity out of the two, thus making peace, and in one body to reconcile both of them to God through the cross, by which he put to death their hostility. He came and preached peace to you who were far away and peace to those who were near. For through him we both have access to the Father by one Spirit.

Consequently, you are no longer foreigners and strangers, but fellow citizens with God's people and also members of his household, built on the foundation of the apostles and prophets, with Christ Jesus himself as the chief cornerstone. In him the whole building is joined together and rises to become a holy temple in the Lord. And in him you too are being built together to become a dwelling in which God lives by his Spirit.

For this reason I, Paul, the prisoner of Christ Jesus for the sake of you Gentiles —

Surely you have heard about the administration of God's grace that was given to me for you, that is, the mystery made known to me by revelation, as I have already written briefly. In reading this, then, you will be able to understand my insight into the mystery of Christ, which was not made known to people in other generations as it has now been revealed by the Spirit to God's holy apostles and prophets. This mystery is that through the gospel the Gentiles are heirs together with Israel, members together of one body, and sharers together in the promise in Christ Jesus.

I became a servant of this gospel by the gift of God's grace given me through the working of his power. Although I am less than the least of all the Lord's people, this grace was given me: to preach to the Gentiles the boundless riches of Christ, and to make plain to everyone the administration of this mystery, which for ages past was kept hidden in God, who created all things. His intent was that now, through the church, the manifold wisdom of God should be made known to the rulers and authorities in the heavenly realms, according to his eternal purpose that he accomplished in Christ Jesus our Lord. In him and through faith in him we may approach God with freedom and confidence. I ask you, therefore, not to be discouraged because of my sufferings for you, which are your glory.

For this reason I kneel before the Father, from whom every family in heaven and on earth derives its name. I pray that out of his glorious riches he may strengthen you with power through his Spirit in your inner being, so that Christ may dwell in your hearts through faith. And I pray that you, being rooted and established in love, may have power, together with all the Lord's holy people, to grasp how wide and long and high and deep is the love of Christ, and to know this love that surpasses knowledge — that you may be filled to the measure of all the fullness of God.

Now to him who is able to do immeasurably more than all we ask or imagine, according to his power that is at work within us, to him be glory in the church and in Christ Jesus throughout all generations, for ever and ever! Amen.   EPHESIANS 1:1—3:21

The church at Corinth in Greece was blessed with spiritual gifts but struggled to grasp the full meaning and freedom of being heirs with Christ. Paul wrote passionately to help them understand their new identity and to call them to live up to it in their daily lives. And as he did in his letter to the Ephesians, he also exalted the reality and importance of their life together as the body of Christ.

Don't you know that you yourselves are God's temple and that God's Spirit dwells in your midst? If anyone destroys God's temple, God will destroy that person; for God's temple is sacred, and you together are that temple. 1 Corinthians 3:16–17

Do you not know that your bodies are temples of the Holy Spirit, who is in you, whom you have received from God? You are not your own. 1 Corinthians 6:19

Just as a body, though one, has many parts, but all its many parts form one body, so it is with Christ. For we were all baptized by one Spirit so as to form one body—whether Jews or Gentiles, slave or free—and we were all given the one Spirit to drink. Even so the body is not made up of one part but of many.

1 Corinthians 12:12–14

The apostle Peter felt as deeply about these new realities as the apostle Paul. He wrote to believers scattered throughout Asia Minor (in modern-day Turkey), reinforcing the new identity they had in Christ. Though his readers consisted of both Jewish and Gentile Christians, Peter used lofty words like "chosen" and "holy" that had previously been reserved only for the people of Israel.

Peter, an apostle of Jesus Christ,

To God's elect, exiles scattered throughout the provinces of Pontus, Galatia, Cappadocia, Asia and Bithynia, who have been chosen according to the foreknowledge of God the Father, through the sanctifying work of the Spirit, to be obedient to Jesus Christ and sprinkled with his blood:

Grace and peace be yours in abundance.

Praise be to the God and Father of our Lord Jesus Christ! In his great mercy he has given us new birth into a living hope through the resurrection of Jesus Christ from the dead, and into an inheritance that can never perish, spoil or fade. This inheritance is kept in heaven for you, who through faith are shielded by God's power until the coming of the salvation that is ready to be revealed in the last time. 1 Peter 1:1–5

Now that you have purified yourselves by obeying the truth so that you have sincere love for each other, love one another deeply, from the heart. For you have been born again, not of perishable seed, but of imperishable, through the living and enduring word of God.   1 PETER 1:22–23

As you come to him, the living Stone — rejected by humans but chosen by God and precious to him — you also, like living stones, are being built into a spiritual house to be a holy priesthood, offering spiritual sacrifices acceptable to God through Jesus Christ. For in Scripture it says:

> "See, I lay a stone in Zion,
>   a chosen and precious cornerstone,
> and the one who trusts in him
>   will never be put to shame."

Now to you who believe, this stone is precious. But to those who do not believe,

> "The stone the builders rejected
>   has become the cornerstone,"

and,

> "A stone that causes people to stumble
>   and a rock that makes them fall."

They stumble because they disobey the message — which is also what they were destined for.

But you are a chosen people, a royal priesthood, a holy nation, God's special possession, that you may declare the praises of him who called you out of darkness into his wonderful light. Once you were not a people, but now you are the people of God; once you had not received mercy, but now you have received mercy.

1 PETER 2:4–10

CHAPTER

6

Church

KEY IDEA

I believe the church is God's primary way
to accomplish his purposes on earth.

KEY VERSE

Speaking the truth in love, we will grow
to become in every respect the mature body of him
who is the head, that is, Christ.
Ephesians 4:15

FOUNDING

From the very beginning God has had a vision to be with his people in perfect community. When the first two humans—Adam and Eve—rejected this vision and were escorted from the Garden of Eden, God began to unveil a plan to provide the way back.

God's plan consisted of making Abraham's offspring into a great nation and then into the body of Christ through Abraham's descendants. Thus the story of Israel pointed people of all nations to the first coming of Christ—and through him to God's plan to restore a relationship with his people.

Again we return to the story of Abraham (Abram) to observe the beginnings of God's covenant with a people who came to be known as Israel. It starts with God's call to Abram and Abram's amazing response of complete faith and trust.

The LORD had said to Abram, "Go from your country, your people and your father's household to the land I will show you.

"I will make you into a great nation,
  and I will bless you;
I will make your name great,
  and you will be a blessing.
I will bless those who bless you,
  and whoever curses you I will curse;
and all peoples on earth
  will be blessed through you."

So Abram went, as the LORD had told him; and Lot went with him. Abram was seventy-five years old when he set out from Harran. He took his wife Sarai, his nephew Lot, all the possessions they had accumulated and the people they had acquired in Harran, and they set out for the land of Canaan, and they arrived there.

Abram traveled through the land as far as the site of the great tree of Moreh at Shechem. At that time the Canaanites were in the land. The LORD appeared to Abram and said, "To your offspring I will give this land." So he built an altar there to the LORD, who had appeared to him.

From there he went on toward the hills east of Bethel and

pitched his tent, with Bethel on the west and Ai on the east. There he built an altar to the Lᴏʀᴅ and called on the name of the Lᴏʀᴅ.

Then Abram set out and continued toward the Negev.

Gᴇɴᴇsɪs 12:1–9

After this, the word of the Lᴏʀᴅ came to Abram in a vision:

> "Do not be afraid, Abram.
> I am your shield,
> your very great reward."

But Abram said, "Sovereign Lᴏʀᴅ, what can you give me since I remain childless and the one who will inherit my estate is Eliezer of Damascus?" And Abram said, "You have given me no children; so a servant in my household will be my heir."

Then the word of the Lᴏʀᴅ came to him: "This man will not be your heir, but a son who is your own flesh and blood will be your heir." He took him outside and said, "Look up at the sky and count the stars — if indeed you can count them." Then he said to him, "So shall your offspring be."

Abram believed the Lᴏʀᴅ, and he credited it to him as righteousness.

Gᴇɴᴇsɪs 15:1–6

At this time and place in history, a covenant was a type of promise. The covenant described in the following verses is a covenant that would have been made between a king and a subject. The narrative describes the establishment of a covenant between God and Abram, initiated by God himself.

[The Lᴏʀᴅ] also said to him, "I am the Lᴏʀᴅ, who brought you out of Ur of the Chaldeans to give you this land to take possession of it."

But Abram said, "Sovereign Lᴏʀᴅ, how can I know that I will gain possession of it?"

So the Lᴏʀᴅ said to him, "Bring me a heifer, a goat and a ram, each three years old, along with a dove and a young pigeon."

Abram brought all these to him, cut them in two and arranged the halves opposite each other; the birds, however, he did not cut in half. Then birds of prey came down on the carcasses, but Abram drove them away.

As the sun was setting, Abram fell into a deep sleep, and a thick and dreadful darkness came over him. Then the LORD said to him, "Know for certain that for four hundred years your descendants will be strangers in a country not their own and that they will be enslaved and mistreated there. But I will punish the nation they serve as slaves, and afterward they will come out with great possessions. You, however, will go to your ancestors in peace and be buried at a good old age. In the fourth generation your descendants will come back here, for the sin of the Amorites has not yet reached its full measure."

When the sun had set and darkness had fallen, a smoking firepot with a blazing torch appeared and passed between the pieces. On that day the LORD made a covenant with Abram and said, "To your descendants I give this land, from the Wadi of Egypt to the great river, the Euphrates — the land of the Kenites, Kenizzites, Kadmonites, Hittites, Perizzites, Rephaites, Amorites, Canaanites, Girgashites and Jebusites."   GENESIS 15:7–21

The covenant with Abram resulted in God's long and complicated relationship with the nation of Israel. The Old Testament of the Bible contains the details of this relationship, but as we have read in previous chapters, a new covenant was instituted in the person of Jesus.

As Jesus was nearing his crucifixion, he told the disciples about what was ahead and about their role in accomplishing God's ultimate vision for the coming kingdom. This exchange highlights that God's plan for believers is still in force; the vision is for believers to come together in a community that continues to this day. And here Jesus speaks of the founding of that community.

When Jesus came to the region of Caesarea Philippi, he asked his disciples, "Who do people say the Son of Man is?"

They replied, "Some say John the Baptist; others say Elijah; and still others, Jeremiah or one of the prophets."

"But what about you?" he asked. "Who do you say I am?"

Simon Peter answered, "You are the Messiah, the Son of the living God."

Jesus replied, "Blessed are you, Simon son of Jonah, for this was not revealed to you by flesh and blood, but by my Father in heaven. And I tell you that you are Peter, and on this rock I will build my church, and the gates of Hades will not overcome it. I will give you the keys of the kingdom of heaven; whatever you bind on earth will be bound in heaven, and whatever you loose on earth will be loosed in heaven." MATTHEW 16:13–19

After the resurrection and ascension of Jesus, God formed this community, called the church, led by his disciples. The story of the church points people of all nations to the second coming of Christ when he will fully restore the original vision of God.

Forty days after Jesus' resurrection and right before his ascension back to the Father, Jesus visited with his disciples and gave them his final instructions. Luke, who also wrote the Gospel bearing his name, recorded the incident in the book of Acts. The result? The church was born!

In my former book, Theophilus, I wrote about all that Jesus began to do and to teach until the day he was taken up to heaven, after giving instructions through the Holy Spirit to the apostles he had chosen. After his suffering, he presented himself to them and gave many convincing proofs that he was alive. He appeared to them over a period of forty days and spoke about the kingdom of God. On one occasion, while he was eating with them, he gave them this command: "Do not leave Jerusalem, but wait for the gift my Father promised, which you have heard me speak about. For John baptized with water, but in a few days you will be baptized with the Holy Spirit."

Then they gathered around him and asked him, "Lord, are you at this time going to restore the kingdom to Israel?"

He said to them: "It is not for you to know the times or dates the Father has set by his own authority. But you will receive power when the Holy Spirit comes on you; and you will be my witnesses in Jerusalem, and in all Judea and Samaria, and to the ends of the earth."

After he said this, he was taken up before their very eyes, and a cloud hid him from their sight.

They were looking intently up into the sky as he was going,

when suddenly two men dressed in white stood beside them. "Men of Galilee," they said, "why do you stand here looking into the sky? This same Jesus, who has been taken from you into heaven, will come back in the same way you have seen him go into heaven."

ACTS 1:1–11

For the next ten days, Jesus' followers—about 120 men and women—met together. They joined together constantly in prayer in anticipation of what was about to happen. After they became filled with the Holy Spirit, Peter used the "keys of the kingdom" that Jesus had mentioned earlier. Peter announced that the door of the kingdom had been unlocked.

When the day of Pentecost came, they were all together in one place. Suddenly a sound like the blowing of a violent wind came from heaven and filled the whole house where they were sitting. They saw what seemed to be tongues of fire that separated and came to rest on each of them. All of them were filled with the Holy Spirit and began to speak in other tongues as the Spirit enabled them.

Now there were staying in Jerusalem God-fearing Jews from every nation under heaven. When they heard this sound, a crowd came together in bewilderment, because each one heard their own language being spoken. Utterly amazed, they asked: "Aren't all these who are speaking Galileans? Then how is it that each of us hears them in our native language? Parthians, Medes and Elamites; residents of Mesopotamia, Judea and Cappadocia, Pontus and Asia, Phrygia and Pamphylia, Egypt and the parts of Libya near Cyrene; visitors from Rome (both Jews and converts to Judaism); Cretans and Arabs—we hear them declaring the wonders of God in our own tongues!" Amazed and perplexed, they asked one another, "What does this mean?"

Some, however, made fun of them and said, "They have had too much wine."

Then Peter stood up with the Eleven, raised his voice and addressed the crowd: "Fellow Jews and all of you who live in Jerusalem, let me explain this to you; listen carefully to what I say. These people are not drunk, as you suppose. It's only nine in the morning! No, this is what was spoken by the prophet Joel:

" 'In the last days, God says,
　　I will pour out my Spirit on all people.
Your sons and daughters will prophesy,
　　your young men will see visions,
　　your old men will dream dreams.
Even on my servants, both men and women,
　　I will pour out my Spirit in those days,
　　and they will prophesy.
I will show wonders in the heavens above
　　and signs on the earth below,
　　blood and fire and billows of smoke.
The sun will be turned to darkness
　　and the moon to blood
　　before the coming of the great and glorious
　　　　day of the Lord.
And everyone who calls
　　on the name of the Lord will be saved.'

"Fellow Israelites, listen to this: Jesus of Nazareth was a man accredited by God to you by miracles, wonders and signs, which God did among you through him, as you yourselves know. This man was handed over to you by God's deliberate plan and foreknowledge; and you, with the help of wicked men, put him to death by nailing him to the cross. But God raised him from the dead, freeing him from the agony of death, because it was impossible for death to keep its hold on him. David said about him:

" 'I saw the Lord always before me.
　　Because he is at my right hand,
　　I will not be shaken.
Therefore my heart is glad and my tongue rejoices;
　　my body also will rest in hope,
because you will not abandon me to the realm of the dead,
　　you will not let your holy one see decay.
You have made known to me the paths of life;
　　you will fill me with joy in your presence.'

"Fellow Israelites, I can tell you confidently that the patriarch David died and was buried, and his tomb is here to this day. But he was a prophet and knew that God had promised him on oath that he would place one of his descendants on his throne. Seeing what was to come, he spoke of the resurrection of the Messiah, that he was not abandoned to the realm of the dead, nor did his body see decay. God has raised this Jesus to life, and we are all witnesses of it. Exalted to the right hand of God, he has received from the Father the promised Holy Spirit and has poured out what you now see and hear. For David did not ascend to heaven, and yet he said,

> "'The Lord said to my Lord:
> "Sit at my right hand
> until I make your enemies
> a footstool for your feet."'

"Therefore let all Israel be assured of this: God has made this Jesus, whom you crucified, both Lord and Messiah."

When the people heard this, they were cut to the heart and said to Peter and the other apostles, "Brothers, what shall we do?"

Peter replied, "Repent and be baptized, every one of you, in the name of Jesus Christ for the forgiveness of your sins. And you will receive the gift of the Holy Spirit. The promise is for you and your children and for all who are far off — for all whom the Lord our God will call."

With many other words he warned them; and he pleaded with them, "Save yourselves from this corrupt generation." Those who accepted his message were baptized, and about three thousand were added to their number that day.   ACTS 2:1–41

EXPANSION

Jesus' commission to the first disciples in AD 30 was to spread the Good News and to build his church beyond Jerusalem to all of Judea and Samaria, and ultimately to the ends of the earth. The book of Acts records the fulfillment of that mission by chronicling the miraculous journey and exponential development of the church community. The story of the expansion of the church out of Jerusalem comes on the heels of the stoning of the disciple Stephen for his bold faith amid a hostile crowd of Jews.

On that day a great persecution broke out against the church in Jerusalem, and all except the apostles were scattered throughout Judea and Samaria. Godly men buried Stephen and mourned deeply for him. But Saul began to destroy the church. Going from house to house, he dragged off both men and women and put them in prison.

Those who had been scattered preached the word wherever they went. Philip went down to a city in Samaria and proclaimed the Messiah there. When the crowds heard Philip and saw the signs he performed, they all paid close attention to what he said. For with shrieks, impure spirits came out of many, and many who were paralyzed or lame were healed. So there was great joy in that city.

Now for some time a man named Simon had practiced sorcery in the city and amazed all the people of Samaria. He boasted that he was someone great, and all the people, both high and low, gave him their attention and exclaimed, "This man is rightly called the Great Power of God." They followed him because he had amazed them for a long time with his sorcery. But when they believed Philip as he proclaimed the good news of the kingdom of God and the name of Jesus Christ, they were baptized, both men and women. Simon himself believed and was baptized. And he followed Philip everywhere, astonished by the great signs and miracles he saw.

When the apostles in Jerusalem heard that Samaria had accepted the word of God, they sent Peter and John to Samaria. When they arrived, they prayed for the new believers there that they might receive the Holy Spirit, because the Holy Spirit had not yet come on any of them; they had simply been baptized in the name of the Lord Jesus. Then Peter and John placed their hands on them, and they received the Holy Spirit.

When Simon saw that the Spirit was given at the laying on of the apostles' hands, he offered them money and said, "Give me also this ability so that everyone on whom I lay my hands may receive the Holy Spirit."

Peter answered: "May your money perish with you, because you thought you could buy the gift of God with money! You have no part or share in this ministry, because your heart is not right before God. Repent of this wickedness and pray to the Lord in the hope that he may forgive you for having such a thought in your heart. For I see that you are full of bitterness and captive to sin."

Then Simon answered, "Pray to the Lord for me so that nothing you have said may happen to me."

After they had further proclaimed the word of the Lord and testified about Jesus, Peter and John returned to Jerusalem, preaching the gospel in many Samaritan villages.   ACTS 8:1–25

Then the church throughout Judea, Galilee and Samaria enjoyed a time of peace and was strengthened. Living in the fear of the Lord and encouraged by the Holy Spirit, it increased in numbers.   ACTS 9:31

As Peter had used the "keys of the kingdom" on the day of Pentecost to announce to the Jews in Jerusalem that the door of the kingdom had been unlocked, he also used those keys to open the door to the Gentiles. God supernaturally led both Peter and a Roman centurion named Cornelius to meet at Cornelius's house. When Peter told Cornelius and his relatives and close friends the Good News about Jesus, they believed, were filled with the Holy Spirit and were baptized.

The apostles and the believers throughout Judea heard that the Gentiles also had received the word of God. So when Peter went up to Jerusalem, the circumcised believers criticized him and said, "You went into the house of uncircumcised men and ate with them."

Starting from the beginning, Peter told them the whole story: "I was in the city of Joppa praying, and in a trance I saw a vision. I saw something like a large sheet being let down from heaven by its four corners, and it came down to where I was. I looked into it and saw four-footed animals of the earth, wild beasts, reptiles and birds. Then I heard a voice telling me, 'Get up, Peter. Kill and eat.'

"I replied, 'Surely not, Lord! Nothing impure or unclean has ever entered my mouth.'

"The voice spoke from heaven a second time, 'Do not call anything impure that God has made clean.' This happened three times, and then it was all pulled up to heaven again.

"Right then three men who had been sent to me from Caesarea stopped at the house where I was staying. The Spirit told me to have no hesitation about going with them. These six brothers also went with me, and we entered the man's house. He told us how he had seen an angel appear in his house and say, 'Send to Joppa for Simon who is called Peter. He will bring you a message through which you and all your household will be saved.'

"As I began to speak, the Holy Spirit came on them as he had come on us at the beginning. Then I remembered what the Lord had said: 'John baptized with water, but you will be baptized with the Holy Spirit.' So if God gave them the same gift he gave us who believed in the Lord Jesus Christ, who was I to think that I could stand in God's way?"

When they heard this, they had no further objections and praised God, saying, "So then, even to Gentiles God has granted repentance that leads to life." Acts 11:1–18

But Saul, the very man who was among those persecuting the church, causing it to spread beyond Jerusalem to all of Judea and Samaria, is the man God would use to take the gospel and the church to the Gentiles. Around AD 35, Saul encountered the risen Jesus in a vision on the road to Damascus. Saul surrendered his life to Christ and from then on devoted the rest of his days on earth to building Christ's church. His home base was the church at Antioch.

Now those who had been scattered by the persecution that broke out when Stephen was killed traveled as far as Phoenicia, Cyprus and Antioch, spreading the word only among Jews. Some of them, however, men from Cyprus and Cyrene, went to Antioch and began to speak to Greeks also, telling them the good news about the Lord Jesus. The Lord's hand was with them, and a great number of people believed and turned to the Lord.

News of this reached the church in Jerusalem, and they sent Barnabas to Antioch. When he arrived and saw what the grace of God had done, he was glad and encouraged them all to remain true to the Lord with all their hearts. He was a good man, full of the Holy Spirit and faith, and a great number of people were brought to the Lord.

Then Barnabas went to Tarsus to look for Saul, and when he found him, he brought him to Antioch. So for a whole year Barnabas and Saul met with the church and taught great numbers of people. The disciples were called Christians first at Antioch.   ACTS 11:19–26

Now in the church at Antioch there were prophets and teachers: Barnabas, Simeon called Niger, Lucius of Cyrene, Manaen (who had been brought up with Herod the tetrarch) and Saul. While they were worshiping the Lord and fasting, the Holy Spirit said, "Set apart for me Barnabas and Saul for the work to which I have called them." So after they had fasted and prayed, they placed their hands on them and sent them off.   ACTS 13:1–3

Saul, soon to be known as Paul, would embark on numerous journeys for approximately the next 20 years to spread the gospel and strengthen and build the church as it stretched toward the ends of the earth, just as Jesus had envisioned. Paul's first missionary trip began around AD 46, and in each city he visited, he used a skillful blend of history, theology and philosophy to declare the Good News to both Jews and Gentiles, who responded and joined the expanding church.

[Paul and Barnabas], sent on their way by the Holy Spirit, went down to Seleucia and sailed from there to Cyprus. When they arrived at Salamis, they proclaimed the word of God in the Jewish synagogues. John was with them as their helper.

They traveled through the whole island until they came to Paphos.   ACTS 13:4–6

From Paphos, Paul and his companions sailed to Perga in Pamphylia, where John left them to return to Jerusalem. From Perga they went on to Pisidian Antioch. On the Sabbath they entered the synagogue and sat down. After the reading from the Law and the Prophets, the leaders of the synagogue sent word to them, saying, "Brothers, if you have a word of exhortation for the people, please speak."

Standing up, Paul motioned with his hand and said: "Fellow Israelites and you Gentiles who worship God, listen to me! The God of the people of Israel chose our ancestors; he made the people prosper during their stay in Egypt; with mighty power he led them out of that country; for about forty years he endured their conduct in the wilderness; and he overthrew seven nations in Canaan, giving their land to his people as their inheritance. All this took about 450 years.

"After this, God gave them judges until the time of Samuel the prophet. Then the people asked for a king, and he gave them Saul son of Kish, of the tribe of Benjamin, who ruled forty years. After removing Saul, he made David their king. God testified concerning him: 'I have found David son of Jesse, a man after my own heart; he will do everything I want him to do.'

"From this man's descendants God has brought to Israel the Savior Jesus, as he promised. Before the coming of Jesus, John preached repentance and baptism to all the people of Israel. As John was completing his work, he said: 'Who do you suppose I am? I am not the one you are looking for. But there is one coming after me whose sandals I am not worthy to untie.'

"Fellow children of Abraham and you God-fearing Gentiles, it is to us that this message of salvation has been sent. The people of Jerusalem and their rulers did not recognize Jesus, yet in condemning him they fulfilled the words of the prophets that are read every Sabbath. Though they found no proper ground for a death sentence, they asked Pilate to have him executed. When they had carried out all that was written about him, they took him down from the cross and laid him in a tomb. But God raised him from the dead, and for many days he was seen by those who had traveled with him from Galilee to Jerusalem. They are now his witnesses to our people.

"We tell you the good news: What God promised our ancestors he has fulfilled for us, their children, by raising up Jesus. As it is written in the second Psalm:

> " 'You are my son;
>   today I have become your father.'

God raised him from the dead so that he will never be subject to decay. As God has said,

> " 'I will give you the holy and sure blessings promised
>   to David.'

So it is also stated elsewhere:

> "'You will not let your holy one see decay.'

"Now when David had served God's purpose in his own generation, he fell asleep; he was buried with his ancestors and his body decayed. But the one whom God raised from the dead did not see decay.

"Therefore, my friends, I want you to know that through Jesus the forgiveness of sins is proclaimed to you. Through him everyone who believes is set free from every sin, a justification you were not able to obtain under the law of Moses. Take care that what the prophets have said does not happen to you:

> "'Look, you scoffers,
>   wonder and perish,
> for I am going to do something in your days
>   that you would never believe,
>   even if someone told you.'"

As Paul and Barnabas were leaving the synagogue, the people invited them to speak further about these things on the next Sabbath. When the congregation was dismissed, many of the Jews and devout converts to Judaism followed Paul and Barnabas, who talked with them and urged them to continue in the grace of God.

On the next Sabbath almost the whole city gathered to hear the word of the Lord. When the Jews saw the crowds, they were filled with jealousy. They began to contradict what Paul was saying and heaped abuse on him.

Then Paul and Barnabas answered them boldly: "We had to speak the word of God to you first. Since you reject it and do not consider yourselves worthy of eternal life, we now turn to the Gentiles. For this is what the Lord has commanded us:

> "'I have made you a light for the Gentiles,
>   that you may bring salvation to the ends of the earth.'"

When the Gentiles heard this, they were glad and honored the word of the Lord; and all who were appointed for eternal life believed.

The word of the Lord spread through the whole region. But

the Jewish leaders incited the God-fearing women of high standing and the leading men of the city. They stirred up persecution against Paul and Barnabas, and expelled them from their region. So they shook the dust off their feet as a warning to them and went to Iconium. And the disciples were filled with joy and with the Holy Spirit.   ACTS 13:13–52

Paul's attention turned to the spreading of the gospel and the building of the church in a world dominated by Gentiles. One of the churches dear to Paul's heart was the one at Ephesus. During his third missionary journey, he spent between two and three years there building the church and its leadership. A couple of years later, around AD 57, Paul was in a hurry to get to Jerusalem before Pentecost. Concerned that he might not ever return to Ephesus, he called for the elders of the church to meet him on his way to Jerusalem. He wanted to have one last meeting with them to build them up and solidify the fledgling church he sacrificed so much to launch.

From Miletus, Paul sent to Ephesus for the elders of the church. When they arrived, he said to them: "You know how I lived the whole time I was with you, from the first day I came into the province of Asia. I served the Lord with great humility and with tears and in the midst of severe testing by the plots of my Jewish opponents. You know that I have not hesitated to preach anything that would be helpful to you but have taught you publicly and from house to house. I have declared to both Jews and Greeks that they must turn to God in repentance and have faith in our Lord Jesus.

"And now, compelled by the Spirit, I am going to Jerusalem, not knowing what will happen to me there. I only know that in every city the Holy Spirit warns me that prison and hardships are facing me. However, I consider my life worth nothing to me; my only aim is to finish the race and complete the task the Lord Jesus has given me — the task of testifying to the good news of God's grace.

"Now I know that none of you among whom I have gone about preaching the kingdom will ever see me again. Therefore, I declare to you today that I am innocent of the blood of any of you. For I have not hesitated to proclaim to you the whole will of God. Keep watch over yourselves and all the flock of which the Holy Spirit has made you overseers. Be shepherds of the church of God, which he bought with his own blood. I know that after I leave, savage wolves will come in among you and will not spare the flock. Even from your own number men will arise and distort the truth in order to draw away disciples after them. So be on your guard! Remember that for three years I never stopped warning each of you night and day with tears.

"Now I commit you to God and to the word of his grace, which can build you up and give you an inheritance among all those who are sanctified. I have not coveted anyone's silver or gold or clothing. You yourselves know that these hands of mine have supplied my own needs and the needs of my companions. In everything I did, I showed you that by this kind of hard work we must help the weak, remembering the words the Lord Jesus himself said: 'It is more blessed to give than to receive.'"

When Paul had finished speaking, he knelt down with all of them and prayed. They all wept as they embraced him and kissed him. What grieved them most was his statement that they would never see his face again. Then they accompanied him to the ship.

After we had torn ourselves away from them, we put out to sea and sailed straight to Kos.   ACTS 20:17—21:1

PLAN AND PURPOSE

As Paul had anticipated, prison and hardships awaited him when he arrived in Jerusalem. While under house arrest in Rome a few years later, around AD 60, Paul penned a letter to the church at Ephesus. Paul explained God's great plan for the church, the new community of Christ. Along with reconciling individuals to himself as an act of grace, God has reconciled these saved individuals to each other. Through his death, Christ has broken down the barriers, uniting believers in one body—the church.

Remember that formerly you who are Gentiles by birth and called "uncircumcised" by those who call themselves "the circumcision" (which is done in the body by human hands) — remember that at that time you were separate from Christ, excluded from citizenship in Israel and foreigners to the covenants of the promise, without hope and without God in the world. But now in Christ Jesus you who once were far away have been brought near by the blood of Christ.

For he himself is our peace, who has made the two groups one and has destroyed the barrier, the dividing wall of hostility, by setting aside in his flesh the law with its commands and regulations. His purpose was to create in himself one new humanity out of the two, thus making peace, and in one body to reconcile both of them to God through the cross, by which he put to death their hostility. He came and preached peace to you who were far away and peace to those who were near. For through him we both have access to the Father by one Spirit.

Consequently, you are no longer foreigners and strangers, but fellow citizens with God's people and also members of his household, built on the foundation of the apostles and prophets, with Christ Jesus himself as the chief cornerstone. In him the whole building is joined together and rises to become a holy temple in the Lord. And in him you too are being built together to become a dwelling in which God lives by his Spirit.

For this reason I, Paul, the prisoner of Christ Jesus for the sake of you Gentiles —

Surely you have heard about the administration of God's grace that was given to me for you, that is, the mystery made known to me by revelation, as I have already written briefly. In reading this, then, you will be able to understand my insight into the mystery of Christ, which was not made known to people in other generations as it has now been revealed by the Spirit to God's holy apostles and prophets. This mystery is that through the gospel the Gentiles are heirs together with Israel, members together of one body, and sharers together in the promise in Christ Jesus.

I became a servant of this gospel by the gift of God's grace given me through the working of his power. Although I am less than the least of all the Lord's people, this grace was given me: to preach to the Gentiles the boundless riches of Christ, and to make plain to everyone the administration of this mystery, which for ages past was kept hidden in God, who created all things. His intent was that now, through the church, the manifold wisdom of God should be made known to the rulers and authorities in the heavenly realms, according to his eternal purpose that he accomplished in Christ Jesus our Lord. In him and through faith in him we may approach God with freedom and confidence.   EPHESIANS 2:11—3:12

As a prisoner for the Lord, then, I urge you to live a life worthy of the calling you have received. Be completely humble and gentle; be patient, bearing with one another in love. Make every effort to keep the unity of the Spirit through the bond of peace. There is one body and one Spirit, just as you were called to one hope when you were called; one Lord, one faith, one baptism; one God and Father of all, who is over all and through all and in all.

But to each one of us grace has been given as Christ apportioned it. This is why it says:

> "When he ascended on high,
>   he took many captives
>   and gave gifts to his people."

(What does "he ascended" mean except that he also descended to the lower, earthly regions? He who descended is the very one who ascended higher than all the heavens, in order to fill the whole universe.) So Christ himself gave the apostles, the prophets, the evangelists, the pastors and teachers, to equip his people for works of service, so that the body of Christ may be built up until we all reach unity in the faith and in the knowledge of the Son of God and become mature, attaining to the whole measure of the fullness of Christ.

Then we will no longer be infants, tossed back and forth by the waves, and blown here and there by every wind of teaching and by the cunning and craftiness of people in their deceitful scheming. Instead, speaking the truth in love, we will grow to become in every respect the mature body of him who is the head, that is, Christ. From him the whole body, joined and held together by every supporting ligament, grows and builds itself up in love, as each part does its work.   EPHESIANS 4:1—16

Likely near the end of the first century, around AD 95, the apostle John received the amazing visions from God contained in the book of Revelation. He addresses the book to seven churches in the Roman province of Asia (in modern-day Turkey), one of them being the church in Ephesus. As part of the book, John records letters from the risen Christ to those seven churches, in which he typically issues words of commendation, complaint and correction. Some 45 years after Paul penned his letter to the church in Ephesus, Christ's message to them represents a report card on their progress. May it be both a word of encouragement and a challenge to the church today.

"To the angel of the church in Ephesus write:

These are the words of him who holds the seven stars in his right hand and walks among the seven golden lampstands. I know your deeds, your hard work and your perseverance. I know that you cannot tolerate wicked people, that you have tested those who claim to be apostles but are not, and have found them false. You have persevered and have endured hardships for my name, and have not grown weary.

Yet I hold this against you: You have forsaken the love you had at first. Consider how far you have fallen! Repent and do the things you did at first. If you do not repent, I will come to you and remove your lampstand from its place. But you have this in your favor: You hate the practices of the Nicolaitans, which I also hate.

Whoever has ears, let them hear what the Spirit says to the churches. To the one who is victorious, I will give the right to eat from the tree of life, which is in the paradise of God."

REVELATION 2:1–7

CHAPTER

7

Humanity

KEY IDEA

I believe all people are loved by God
and need Jesus Christ as their Savior.

KEY VERSE

For God so loved the world
that he gave his one and only Son,
that whoever believes in him shall not perish
but have eternal life.
John 3:16

God created everything, but the pinnacle of creation was the creation of human beings—beings made in the image of God. Humanity is special, and the Bible is the record of the love story between Creator and created, between God and humans. From the very beginning of time to the modern-day church, God has loved and pursued his people.

ORIGINS
God is the origin of all life.

In the beginning God created the heavens and the earth. Now the earth was formless and empty, darkness was over the surface of the deep, and the Spirit of God was hovering over the waters.

And God said, "Let there be light," and there was light. God saw that the light was good, and he separated the light from the darkness. God called the light "day," and the darkness he called "night." And there was evening, and there was morning—the first day.

And God said, "Let there be a vault between the waters to separate water from water." So God made the vault and separated the water under the vault from the water above it. And it was so. God called the vault "sky." And there was evening, and there was morning—the second day.

And God said, "Let the water under the sky be gathered to one place, and let dry ground appear." And it was so. God called the dry ground "land," and the gathered waters he called "seas." And God saw that it was good.

Then God said, "Let the land produce vegetation: seed-bearing plants and trees on the land that bear fruit with seed in it, according to their various kinds." And it was so. The land produced vegetation: plants bearing seed according to their kinds and trees bearing fruit with seed in it according to their kinds. And God saw that it was good. And there was evening, and there was morning—the third day.

And God said, "Let there be lights in the vault of the sky to separate the day from the night, and let them serve as signs to mark sacred times, and days and years, and let them be lights in the vault of the sky to give light on the earth." And it was so. God made two great lights—the greater light to govern the day and the lesser light to govern the night. He also made the stars. God set them in the vault of the sky to give light on the earth, to govern the day and the night, and to separate light from darkness. And God saw that it was good. And there was evening, and there was morning — the fourth day.

And God said, "Let the water teem with living creatures, and let birds fly above the earth across the vault of the sky." So God created the great creatures of the sea and every living thing with which the water teems and that moves about in it, according to their kinds, and every winged bird according to its kind. And God saw that it was good. God blessed them and said, "Be fruitful and increase in number and fill the water in the seas, and let the birds increase on the earth." And there was evening, and there was morning — the fifth day.

And God said, "Let the land produce living creatures according to their kinds: the livestock, the creatures that move along the ground, and the wild animals, each according to its kind." And it was so. God made the wild animals according to their kinds, the livestock according to their kinds, and all the creatures that move along the ground according to their kinds. And God saw that it was good.

Then God said, "Let us make mankind in our image, in our likeness, so that they may rule over the fish in the sea and the birds in the sky, over the livestock and all the wild animals, and over all the creatures that move along the ground."

> So God created mankind in his own image,
>> in the image of God he created them;
>> male and female he created them.

God blessed them and said to them, "Be fruitful and increase in number; fill the earth and subdue it. Rule over the fish in the sea and the birds in the sky and over every living creature that moves on the ground."

Then God said, "I give you every seed-bearing plant on the face of the whole earth and every tree that has fruit with seed in it. They will be yours for food. And to all the beasts of the earth and all the birds in the sky and all the creatures that move along the ground — everything that has the breath of life in it — I give every green plant for food." And it was so.

God saw all that he had made, and it was very good. And there was evening, and there was morning — the sixth day.   Genesis 1:1–31

The Devastating Human Condition

God created the cosmos and everything in it. He created the earth so that he could be with the people he created. Unfortunately, the first two people — Adam and Eve — rejected God's vision for his creation, causing sin to enter into their nature and thereby making them unfit for community with a holy God. The greatest pandemic ever experienced by humanity is the transference of this sin "DNA" to every generation.

Adam made love to his wife Eve, and she became pregnant and gave birth to Cain. She said, "With the help of the Lord I have brought forth a man." Later she gave birth to his brother Abel.

Now Abel kept flocks, and Cain worked the soil. In the course of time Cain brought some of the fruits of the soil as an offering to the Lord. And Abel also brought an offering — fat portions from some of the firstborn of his flock. The Lord looked with favor on Abel and his offering, but on Cain and his offering he did not look with favor. So Cain was very angry, and his face was downcast.

Genesis 4:1–5

Here we see the results of Adam and Eve's choices. We know from other Scriptures that God rejected Cain's offering and accepted Abel's offering because of the faith of the two men. The Bible doesn't tell us explicitly why God rejected Cain's offering, but it had something to do with Cain's attitude toward God.

Then the Lord said to Cain, "Why are you angry? Why is your face downcast? If you do what is right, will you not be accepted? But if you do not do what is right, sin is crouching at your door; it desires to have you, but you must rule over it."

Now Cain said to his brother Abel, "Let's go out to the field." While they were in the field, Cain attacked his brother Abel and killed him.

Then the Lord said to Cain, "Where is your brother Abel?"

"I don't know," he replied. "Am I my brother's keeper?"

The LORD said, "What have you done? Listen! Your brother's blood cries out to me from the ground. Now you are under a curse and driven from the ground, which opened its mouth to receive your brother's blood from your hand. When you work the ground, it will no longer yield its crops for you. You will be a restless wanderer on the earth."

Cain said to the LORD, "My punishment is more than I can bear. Today you are driving me from the land, and I will be hidden from your presence; I will be a restless wanderer on the earth, and whoever finds me will kill me."

But the LORD said to him, "Not so; anyone who kills Cain will suffer vengeance seven times over." Then the LORD put a mark on Cain so that no one who found him would kill him. So Cain went out from the LORD's presence and lived in the land of Nod, east of Eden.   GENESIS 4:6–16

> *Adam and Eve had more children, but those offspring continued inheriting and passing on a fallen, sinful nature. In the New Testament era, Jude, who was both a half brother and a follower of Jesus, wrote a letter to warn Christians about false teachers who were trying to convince believers that salvation by grace gave them license to sin. Jude notes that these dangerous teachers had "taken the way of Cain," meaning the way of selfishness and greed—demonstrated by Cain's careless, thoughtless offering— and the way of hatred and murder—demonstrated by Cain's slaying of Abel.*

Jude, a servant of Jesus Christ and a brother of James,

To those who have been called, who are loved in God the Father and kept for Jesus Christ:

Mercy, peace and love be yours in abundance.

Dear friends, although I was very eager to write to you about the salvation we share, I felt compelled to write and urge you to contend for the faith that was once for all entrusted to God's holy people. For certain individuals whose condemnation was written about long ago have secretly slipped in among you. They are ungodly people, who pervert the grace of our God into a license for immorality and deny Jesus Christ our only Sovereign and Lord.

Though you already know all this, I want to remind you that the Lord at one time delivered his people out of Egypt, but later destroyed those who did not believe. And the angels who did not keep their positions of authority but abandoned their proper dwelling — these he has kept in darkness, bound with everlasting chains for judgment on the great Day. In a similar way, Sodom and Gomorrah and the surrounding towns gave themselves up to sexual immorality and perversion. They serve as an example of those who suffer the punishment of eternal fire.

In the very same way, on the strength of their dreams these ungodly people pollute their own bodies, reject authority and heap abuse on celestial beings. But even the archangel Michael, when he was disputing with the devil about the body of Moses, did not himself dare to condemn him for slander but said, "The Lord rebuke you!" Yet these people slander whatever they do not understand, and the very things they do understand by instinct — as irrational animals do — will destroy them.

Woe to them! They have taken the way of Cain; they have rushed for profit into Balaam's error; they have been destroyed in Korah's rebellion.

These people are blemishes at your love feasts, eating with you without the slightest qualm — shepherds who feed only themselves. They are clouds without rain, blown along by the wind; autumn trees, without fruit and uprooted — twice dead. They are wild waves of the sea, foaming up their shame; wandering stars, for whom blackest darkness has been reserved forever.

Enoch, the seventh from Adam, prophesied about them: "See, the Lord is coming with thousands upon thousands of his holy ones to judge everyone, and to convict all of them of all the ungodly acts they have committed in their ungodliness, and of all the defiant words ungodly sinners have spoken against him." These people are grumblers and faultfinders; they follow their own evil desires; they boast about themselves and flatter others for their own advantage. Jude 1–16

Paul's letter to the Christians in Rome contains a chilling declaration of the extent and consequences of the sin nature that has permeated the entire human race beginning with Adam and

*Eve and their offspring. First, Paul indicts the sinfulness of the
Gentiles and then, perhaps surprising his readers, shows the
sinfulness of the Jews. He makes it clear that no one is righteous.*

The wrath of God is being revealed from heaven against all the
godlessness and wickedness of people, who suppress the truth by
their wickedness, since what may be known about God is plain to
them, because God has made it plain to them. For since the creation
of the world God's invisible qualities — his eternal power and
divine nature — have been clearly seen, being understood from
what has been made, so that people are without excuse.

For although they knew God, they neither glorified him as God
nor gave thanks to him, but their thinking became futile and their
foolish hearts were darkened. Although they claimed to be wise,
they became fools and exchanged the glory of the immortal God
for images made to look like a mortal human being and birds and
animals and reptiles.

Therefore God gave them over in the sinful desires of their
hearts to sexual impurity for the degrading of their bodies with
one another. They exchanged the truth about God for a lie, and
worshiped and served created things rather than the Creator —
who is forever praised. Amen.

Because of this, God gave them over to shameful lusts. Even
their women exchanged natural sexual relations for unnatural
ones. In the same way the men also abandoned natural relations
with women and were inflamed with lust for one another. Men
committed shameful acts with other men, and received in themselves
the due penalty for their error.

Furthermore, just as they did not think it worthwhile to retain
the knowledge of God, so God gave them over to a depraved
mind, so that they do what ought not to be done. They have become
filled with every kind of wickedness, evil, greed and depravity.
They are full of envy, murder, strife, deceit and malice. They
are gossips, slanderers, God-haters, insolent, arrogant and boastful;
they invent ways of doing evil; they disobey their parents; they
have no understanding, no fidelity, no love, no mercy. Although
they know God's righteous decree that those who do such things

deserve death, they not only continue to do these very things but also approve of those who practice them. Romans 1:18–32

Now you, if you call yourself a Jew; if you rely on the law and boast in God; if you know his will and approve of what is superior because you are instructed by the law; if you are convinced that you are a guide for the blind, a light for those who are in the dark, an instructor of the foolish, a teacher of little children, because you have in the law the embodiment of knowledge and truth — you, then, who teach others, do you not teach yourself? You who preach against stealing, do you steal? You who say that people should not commit adultery, do you commit adultery? You who abhor idols, do you rob temples? You who boast in the law, do you dishonor God by breaking the law? As it is written: "God's name is blasphemed among the Gentiles because of you." Romans 2:17–24

What shall we conclude then? Do we have any advantage? Not at all! For we have already made the charge that Jews and Gentiles alike are all under the power of sin. As it is written:

> "There is no one righteous, not even one;
>> there is no one who understands;
>> there is no one who seeks God.
> All have turned away,
>> they have together become worthless;
> there is no one who does good,
>> not even one."
> "Their throats are open graves;
>> their tongues practice deceit."
> "The poison of vipers is on their lips."
>> "Their mouths are full of cursing and bitterness."
> "Their feet are swift to shed blood;
>> ruin and misery mark their ways,
> and the way of peace they do not know."
>> "There is no fear of God before their eyes."

Now we know that whatever the law says, it says to those who are under the law, so that every mouth may be silenced and the whole world held accountable to God. Therefore no one will be declared righteous in God's sight by the works of the law; rather, through the law we become conscious of our sin.   Romans 3:9–20

God's Love

Despite the sin that has permeated his creation, God remains faithful to his people. In the Old Testament God modeled his love for humankind through his special relationship with Israel. God used a profound and unusual object lesson to illustrate how much he loved the Israelites despite their unfaithfulness. He asked Hosea, a prophet to the northern kingdom of Israel, to marry an immoral woman named Gomer. Hosea would play the part of God; Gomer would play the part of Israel.

The word of the Lord that came to Hosea son of Beeri during the reigns of Uzziah, Jotham, Ahaz and Hezekiah, kings of Judah, and during the reign of Jeroboam son of Jehoash king of Israel:

When the Lord began to speak through Hosea, the Lord said to him, "Go, marry a promiscuous woman and have children with her, for like an adulterous wife this land is guilty of unfaithfulness to the Lord." So he married Gomer daughter of Diblaim, and she conceived and bore him a son.   Hosea 1:1–3

Hosea provided Gomer with a wonderful life of love and provision. But she chose to spurn his love; Gomer left Hosea and returned to her immoral lifestyle. And she evidently became a slave. God told Hosea to track down his wife, purchase her, take her back in and love her. What Hosea did for Gomer, God did for the people of Israel.

The Lord said to me, "Go, show your love to your wife again, though she is loved by another man and is an adulteress. Love her as the Lord loves the Israelites, though they turn to other gods and love the sacred raisin cakes."

So I bought her for fifteen shekels of silver and about a homer and a lethek of barley. Then I told her, "You are to live with me many days; you must not be a prostitute or be intimate with any man, and I will behave the same way toward you."   Hosea 3:1–3

*In the book of Hosea, God also reflected on his relationship with
Israel in terms of a wayward son rather than an unfaithful wife.
He intervened for the Israelites even when they didn't recognize
his presence. Out of love he rescued them from slavery in Egypt.
Now Israel, referred to as Ephraim after Israel's largest tribe, was
about to go into slavery again. This time the mighty nation of
Assyria was going to take the people captive. They would experience the blows of discipline for walking away from God, but he
declared yet again that he would redeem them. This is the same
kind of unending, undeserved love God has for us.*

> "When Israel was a child, I loved him,
>   and out of Egypt I called my son.
> But the more they were called,
>   the more they went away from me.
> They sacrificed to the Baals
>   and they burned incense to images.
> It was I who taught Ephraim to walk,
>   taking them by the arms;
> but they did not realize
>   it was I who healed them.
> I led them with cords of human kindness,
>   with ties of love.
> To them I was like one who lifts
>   a little child to the cheek,
>   and I bent down to feed them.
>
> "Will they not return to Egypt
>   and will not Assyria rule over them
>   because they refuse to repent?
> A sword will flash in their cities;
>   it will devour their false prophets
>   and put an end to their plans.
> My people are determined to turn from me.
>   Even though they call me God Most High,
>   I will by no means exalt them.
>
> "How can I give you up, Ephraim?
>   How can I hand you over, Israel?

How can I treat you like Admah?
How can I make you like Zeboyim?
My heart is changed within me;
all my compassion is aroused.
I will not carry out my fierce anger,
nor will I devastate Ephraim again.
For I am God, and not a man —
the Holy One among you.
I will not come against their cities.
They will follow the LORD;
he will roar like a lion.
When he roars,
his children will come trembling from the
west.
They will come from Egypt,
trembling like sparrows,
from Assyria, fluttering like doves.
I will settle them in their homes,"
declares the LORD.   HOSEA 11:1–11

ALL AND WHOEVER

One of the special assignments John took on in his Gospel was to share that Jesus' offer of forgiveness and restoration to God for eternity is for everyone. Throughout his Gospel John uses the words "all" and "whoever." We are included in the "all" and "whoever"; therefore God extends his offer of love to us. He "so loves us."

In [the Word, Jesus Christ] was life, and that life was the light of **all** mankind.   JOHN 1:4

[John the Baptist] came as a witness to testify concerning that light, so that through him **all** might believe.   JOHN 1:7

[The Word, Jesus Christ] came to that which was his own, but his own did not receive him. Yet to **all** who did receive him, to those who believed in his name, he gave the right to become children of God.   JOHN 1:11–12

For God so loved the world that he gave his one and only Son, that **whoever** believes in him shall not perish but have eternal life.

JOHN 3:16

Whoever believes in the Son has eternal life, but **whoever** rejects the Son will not see life, for God's wrath remains on them.

JOHN 3:36

"**Whoever** drinks the water I give them will never thirst. Indeed, the water I give them will become in them a spring of water welling up to eternal life."

JOHN 4:14

"Very truly I tell you, **whoever** hears my word and believes him who sent me has eternal life and will not be judged but has crossed over from death to life."

JOHN 5:24

Then Jesus declared, "I am the bread of life. **Whoever** comes to me will never go hungry, and **whoever** believes in me will never be thirsty."

JOHN 6:35

"**All** those the Father gives me will come to me, and **whoever** comes to me I will never drive away."

JOHN 6:37

"I am the living bread that came down from heaven. **Whoever** eats this bread will live forever. This bread is my flesh, which I will give for the life of the world."

JOHN 6:51

"**Whoever** eats my flesh and drinks my blood has eternal life, and I will raise them up at the last day."

JOHN 6:54

"**Whoever** believes in me, as Scripture has said, rivers of living water will flow from within them."

JOHN 7:38

When Jesus spoke again to the people, he said, "I am the light of the world. **Whoever** follows me will never walk in darkness, but will have the light of life."

JOHN 8:12

"Very truly I tell you, **whoever** obeys my word will never see death."

JOHN 8:51

"I am the gate; **whoever** enters through me will be saved. They will come in and go out, and find pasture." John 10:9

"**Whoever** lives by believing in me will never die." John 11:26

"Now is the time for judgment on this world; now the prince of this world will be driven out. And I, when I am lifted up from the earth, will draw **all** people to myself." John 12:31–32

SEEING PEOPLE AS GOD SEES THEM

At that time the disciples came to Jesus and asked, "Who, then, is the greatest in the kingdom of heaven?"

He called a little child to him, and placed the child among them. And he said: "Truly I tell you, unless you change and become like little children, you will never enter the kingdom of heaven. Therefore, whoever takes the lowly position of this child is the greatest in the kingdom of heaven. And whoever welcomes one such child in my name welcomes me.

"If anyone causes one of these little ones — those who believe in me — to stumble, it would be better for them to have a large millstone hung around their neck and to be drowned in the depths of the sea. Woe to the world because of the things that cause people to stumble! Such things must come, but woe to the person through whom they come! If your hand or your foot causes you to stumble, cut it off and throw it away. It is better for you to enter life maimed or crippled than to have two hands or two feet and be thrown into eternal fire. And if your eye causes you to stumble, gouge it out and throw it away. It is better for you to enter life with one eye than to have two eyes and be thrown into the fire of hell.

"See that you do not despise one of these little ones. For I tell you that their angels in heaven always see the face of my Father in heaven.

"What do you think? If a man owns a hundred sheep, and one of them wanders away, will he not leave the ninety-nine on the hills and go to look for the one that wandered off? And if he finds it, truly I tell you, he is happier about that one sheep than about the ninety-nine that did not wander off. In the same way your Father in heaven is not willing that any of these little ones should perish." Matthew 18:1–14

As the parable of the wandering sheep illustrates, God loves us deeply. He also wants us to follow his example in how we treat each other. In the early season of his ministry Jesus spoke to a large crowd of people who gathered to be healed by him and to hear what he had to say. Jesus taught that we are to see and treat people the way God sees and treats us. Our heavenly Father provides the supreme example that we are to follow.

"But to you who are listening I say: Love your enemies, do good to those who hate you, bless those who curse you, pray for those who mistreat you. If someone slaps you on one cheek, turn to them the other also. If someone takes your coat, do not withhold your shirt from them. Give to everyone who asks you, and if anyone takes what belongs to you, do not demand it back. Do to others as you would have them do to you.

"If you love those who love you, what credit is that to you? Even sinners love those who love them. And if you do good to those who are good to you, what credit is that to you? Even sinners do that. And if you lend to those from whom you expect repayment, what credit is that to you? Even sinners lend to sinners, expecting to be repaid in full. But love your enemies, do good to them, and lend to them without expecting to get anything back. Then your reward will be great, and you will be children of the Most High, because he is kind to the ungrateful and wicked. Be merciful, just as your Father is merciful."   LUKE 6:27–36

The new reality in Christ is this: There is no more division between Jews and Gentiles, men and women, masters and slaves. We all belong to Christ equally. The apostle Paul had a grand opportunity to demonstrate this in the latter years of his life. His good friend Philemon had a slave — Onesimus — who may have stolen from Philemon and then ran away (a crime punishable by death). Amazingly, while Paul was in Rome he met Onesimus, and Onesimus became a Christian. Paul wrote Philemon a letter with the personal appeal to welcome Onesimus back, not as a slave but as a brother in Christ. God lays before us today the same challenge to embrace every believer as a precious family member.

Paul, a prisoner of Christ Jesus, and Timothy our brother,

To Philemon our dear friend and fellow worker — also to Apphia our sister and Archippus our fellow soldier — and to the church that meets in your home:

Grace and peace to you from God our Father and the Lord Jesus Christ.

I always thank my God as I remember you in my prayers, because I hear about your love for all his holy people and your faith in the Lord Jesus. I pray that your partnership with us in the faith may be effective in deepening your understanding of every good thing we share for the sake of Christ. Your love has given me great joy and encouragement, because you, brother, have refreshed the hearts of the Lord's people.

Therefore, although in Christ I could be bold and order you to do what you ought to do, yet I prefer to appeal to you on the basis of love. It is as none other than Paul — an old man and now also a prisoner of Christ Jesus — that I appeal to you for my son Onesimus, who became my son while I was in chains. Formerly he was useless to you, but now he has become useful both to you and to me.

I am sending him — who is my very heart — back to you. I would have liked to keep him with me so that he could take your place in helping me while I am in chains for the gospel. But I did not want to do anything without your consent, so that any favor you do would not seem forced but would be voluntary. Perhaps the reason he was separated from you for a little while was that you might have him back forever — no longer as a slave, but better than a slave, as a dear brother. He is very dear to me but even dearer to you, both as a fellow man and as a brother in the Lord.

So if you consider me a partner, welcome him as you would welcome me. If he has done you any wrong or owes you anything, charge it to me. I, Paul, am writing this with my own hand. I will pay it back — not to mention that you owe me your very self. I do wish, brother, that I may have some benefit from you in the Lord; refresh my heart in Christ. Confident of your obedience, I write to you, knowing that you will do even more than I ask.

And one thing more: Prepare a guest room for me, because I hope to be restored to you in answer to your prayers.

Epaphras, my fellow prisoner in Christ Jesus, sends you greetings. And so do Mark, Aristarchus, Demas and Luke, my fellow workers.

The grace of the Lord Jesus Christ be with your spirit.

PHILEMON 1–25

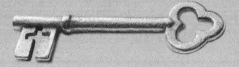

CHAPTER

8

Compassion

KEY IDEA

I believe God calls all Christians to show
compassion to people in need.

KEY VERSE

Defend the weak and the fatherless;
uphold the cause of the poor and the oppressed.
Rescue the weak and the needy;
deliver them from the hand of the wicked.

Psalm 82:3 – 4

Compassion literally means "suffer with." God calls us to come alongside of people who are suffering and suffer with them so they are not alone. It doesn't mean we can fix the problem, but it does mean we can enter into their pain. Before we act on or practice this belief, we must believe it is God's call on the life of all Christ followers. When we believe this in our heart, we will show compassion to all people, especially to those in need. This is not a "do as I say, not as I do" command from the Lord. God himself is merciful and full of compassion.

GOD: FULL OF JUSTICE AND COMPASSION

Throughout their history, the Israelites struggled to stay true to God. Sometimes they followed God, but those periods of faithfulness were followed by times of sin and rebellion. But God's love for his people was always evident. His compassion was constant as he offered the people relief from the misery caused by their own sin. In this passage, the Israelites are back in the promised land after suffering years of exile and hardship.

The Israelites gathered together, fasting and wearing sackcloth and putting dust on their heads. Those of Israelite descent had separated themselves from all foreigners. They stood in their places and confessed their sins and the sins of their ancestors. They stood where they were and read from the Book of the Law of the LORD their God for a quarter of the day, and spent another quarter in confession and in worshiping the LORD their God. Standing on the stairs of the Levites were Jeshua, Bani, Kadmiel, Shebaniah, Bunni, Sherebiah, Bani and Kenani. They cried out with loud voices to the LORD their God. And the Levites — Jeshua, Kadmiel, Bani, Hashabneiah, Sherebiah, Hodiah, Shebaniah and Pethahiah — said: "Stand up and praise the LORD your God, who is from everlasting to everlasting."

"Blessed be your glorious name, and may it be exalted above all blessing and praise. You alone are the LORD. You made the heavens, even the highest heavens, and all their starry host, the earth and all that is on it, the seas and all that is in them. You give life to everything, and the multitudes of heaven worship you.

"You are the LORD God, who chose Abram and brought him

out of Ur of the Chaldeans and named him Abraham. You found his heart faithful to you, and you made a covenant with him to give to his descendants the land of the Canaanites, Hittites, Amorites, Perizzites, Jebusites and Girgashites. You have kept your promise because you are righteous.

"You saw the suffering of our ancestors in Egypt; you heard their cry at the Red Sea. You sent signs and wonders against Pharaoh, against all his officials and all the people of his land, for you knew how arrogantly the Egyptians treated them. You made a name for yourself, which remains to this day. You divided the sea before them, so that they passed through it on dry ground, but you hurled their pursuers into the depths, like a stone into mighty waters. By day you led them with a pillar of cloud, and by night with a pillar of fire to give them light on the way they were to take.

"You came down on Mount Sinai; you spoke to them from heaven. You gave them regulations and laws that are just and right, and decrees and commands that are good. You made known to them your holy Sabbath and gave them commands, decrees and laws through your servant Moses. In their hunger you gave them bread from heaven and in their thirst you brought them water from the rock; you told them to go in and take possession of the land you had sworn with uplifted hand to give them.

"But they, our ancestors, became arrogant and stiff-necked, and they did not obey your commands. They refused to listen and failed to remember the miracles you performed among them. They became stiff-necked and in their rebellion appointed a leader in order to return to their slavery. But you are a forgiving God, gracious and compassionate, slow to anger and abounding in love. Therefore you did not desert them, even when they cast for themselves an image of a calf and said, 'This is your god, who brought you up out of Egypt,' or when they committed awful blasphemies.

"Because of your great compassion you did not abandon them in the wilderness. By day the pillar of cloud did not fail to guide them on their path, nor the pillar of fire by night to shine on the way they were to take. You gave your good Spirit to instruct them. You did not withhold your manna from their mouths, and you gave them water for their thirst. For forty years you sustained them in the wilderness; they lacked nothing, their clothes did not wear out nor did their feet become swollen.

"You gave them kingdoms and nations, allotting to them even the remotest frontiers. They took over the country of Sihon king of Heshbon and the country of Og king of Bashan. You made their children as numerous as the stars in the sky, and you brought them into the land that you told their parents to enter and possess. Their children went in and took possession of the land. You subdued before them the Canaanites, who lived in the land; you gave the Canaanites into their hands, along with their kings and the peoples of the land, to deal with them as they pleased. They captured fortified cities and fertile land; they took possession of houses filled with all kinds of good things, wells already dug, vineyards, olive groves and fruit trees in abundance. They ate to the full and were well-nourished; they reveled in your great goodness.

"But they were disobedient and rebelled against you; they turned their backs on your law. They killed your prophets, who had warned them in order to turn them back to you; they committed awful blasphemies. So you delivered them into the hands of their enemies, who oppressed them. But when they were oppressed they cried out to you. From heaven you heard them, and in your great compassion you gave them deliverers, who rescued them from the hand of their enemies.

"But as soon as they were at rest, they again did what was evil in your sight. Then you abandoned them to the hand of their enemies so that they ruled over them. And when they cried out to you again, you heard from heaven, and in your compassion you delivered them time after time.

"You warned them in order to turn them back to your law, but they became arrogant and disobeyed your commands. They sinned against your ordinances, of which you said, 'The person who obeys them will live by them.' Stubbornly they turned their backs on you, became stiff-necked and refused to listen. For many years you were patient with them. By your Spirit you warned them through your prophets. Yet they paid no attention, so you gave them into the hands of the neighboring peoples. But in your great mercy you did not put an end to them or abandon them, for you are a gracious and merciful God.

"Now therefore, our God, the great God, mighty and awesome, who keeps his covenant of love, do not let all this hardship seem trifling in your eyes — the hardship that has come on us, on our kings and leaders, on our priests and prophets, on our ancestors and all your people, from the days of the kings of Assyria until today. In all that has happened to us, you have remained righteous; you have acted faithfully, while we acted wickedly. Our kings, our leaders, our priests and our ancestors did not follow your law; they did not pay attention to your commands or the statutes you warned them to keep. Even while they were in their kingdom, enjoying your great goodness to them in the spacious and fertile land you gave them, they did not serve you or turn from their evil ways.

"But see, we are slaves today, slaves in the land you gave our ancestors so they could eat its fruit and the other good things it produces. Because of our sins, its abundant harvest goes to the kings you have placed over us. They rule over our bodies and our cattle as they please. We are in great distress.

"In view of all this, we are making a binding agreement, putting it in writing, and our leaders, our Levites and our priests are affixing their seals to it."   NEHEMIAH 9:1–38

Throughout history God has graciously shown compassion for his people, with the ultimate demonstration being the sacrifice of his only Son, Jesus Christ. Because the only just response to the sins of humankind was death, our just God, according to his righteousness, issued the death penalty on us. Then, out of his grand compassion, he offered Jesus as a "substitutionary atonement" — that is, Jesus took humanity's place. Through this one act God demonstrated his complete compassion without budging an inch on his complete justice. We who are guilty are made just by the sacrifice of the only person who was completely righteous.

Apart from the law the righteousness of God has been made known, to which the Law and the Prophets testify. This righteousness is given through faith in Jesus Christ to all who believe. There is no difference between Jew and Gentile, for all have sinned and fall short of the glory of God, and all are justified freely by his grace through the redemption that came by Christ Jesus. God presented Christ as a sacrifice of atonement, through the shedding of his blood — to be received by faith. He did this to demonstrate his righteousness, because in his forbearance he had left the sins committed beforehand unpunished — he did it to demonstrate his righteousness at the present time, so as to be just and the one who justifies those who have faith in Jesus. ROMANS 3:21–26

Dear friends, let us love one another, for love comes from God. Everyone who loves has been born of God and knows God. Whoever does not love does not know God, because God is love. This is how God showed his love among us: He sent his one and only Son into the world that we might live through him. This is love: not that we loved God, but that he loved us and sent his Son as an atoning sacrifice for our sins. 1 JOHN 4:7–10

ISRAEL: CALLED TO COMPASSION

Compassion was an important aspect of the testimony of the people of Israel to the world. When God set up the foundational laws for his people, he revealed through Moses specific guidelines for helping the poor and those in need.

When you make a loan of any kind to your neighbor, do not go into their house to get what is offered to you as a pledge. Stay outside and let the neighbor to whom you are making the loan bring the pledge out to you. If the neighbor is poor, do not go to sleep with their pledge in your possession. Return their cloak by sunset so that your neighbor may sleep in it. Then they will thank you, and it will be regarded as a righteous act in the sight of the LORD your God.

Do not take advantage of a hired worker who is poor and needy, whether that worker is a fellow Israelite or a foreigner residing in one of your towns. Pay them their wages each day before sunset, because they are poor and are counting on it. Otherwise they may cry to the LORD against you, and you will be guilty of sin. DEUTERONOMY 24:10–15

Do not deprive the foreigner or the fatherless of justice, or take the cloak of the widow as a pledge. Remember that you were slaves in Egypt and the LORD your God redeemed you from there. That is why I command you to do this.

When you are harvesting in your field and you overlook a sheaf, do not go back to get it. Leave it for the foreigner, the fatherless and the widow, so that the LORD your God may bless you in all the work of your hands. When you beat the olives from your trees, do not go over the branches a second time. Leave what remains for the foreigner, the fatherless and the widow. When you harvest the grapes in your vineyard, do not go over the vines again. Leave what remains for the foreigner, the fatherless and the widow. Remember that you were slaves in Egypt. That is why I command you to do this.   DEUTERONOMY 24:17–22

> In the promised land, the continuity of each family and its allotment of land was of considerable importance. Though it may seem strange to us today, God led Moses to lay out for Israel the custom known as "levirate marriage," by which a brother (or nearest relative by marriage) would marry a widow without children and produce descendants in the dead relative's name, ensuring a lineage and inheritance for that family. Although the brother-in-law (or more distantly related "guardian-redeemer") wasn't strictly obligated to marry his brother's wife, social shame would have discouraged him from failing to do so.

If brothers are living together and one of them dies without a son, his widow must not marry outside the family. Her husband's brother shall take her and marry her and fulfill the duty of a brother-in-law to her. The first son she bears shall carry on the name of the dead brother so that his name will not be blotted out from Israel.

However, if a man does not want to marry his brother's wife, she shall go to the elders at the town gate and say, "My husband's brother refuses to carry on his brother's name in Israel. He will not fulfill the duty of a brother-in-law to me." Then the elders of his town shall summon him and talk to him. If he persists in saying, "I do not want to marry her," his brother's widow shall go up to him in the presence of the elders, take off one of his sandals, spit in his face and say, "This is what is done to the man who will not build up his brother's family line." That man's line shall be known in Israel as The Family of the Unsandaled.   DEUTERONOMY 25:5–10

Moses issued the laws above in the 1400s BC while the Israelites were wandering in the wilderness. A couple of hundred years later, during the time of the judges, a beautiful application of the principle of levirate marriage unfolded. Because of famine, Naomi and Elimelek and their two children left for the land of Moab. While there, the two sons married Moabite women, but over the years the father and the two sons died. Naomi and one of her daughters-in-law, Ruth, made their way back to Naomi's hometown of Bethlehem. Without husbands or children, Naomi and Ruth were forced to live a life of poverty.

One day, Ruth decided to go out and glean after the harvesters in order to provide food for herself and Naomi. When Ruth came home after a successful day of gleaning, her mother-in-law asked her in whose field she had gleaned. The rest of the story shows the power and provision of the principle of the guardian-redeemer Moses put in place years earlier.

Now Naomi had a relative on her husband's side, a man of standing from the clan of Elimelek, whose name was Boaz.

And Ruth the Moabite said to Naomi, "Let me go to the fields and pick up the leftover grain behind anyone in whose eyes I find favor."

Naomi said to her, "Go ahead, my daughter." So she went out, entered a field and began to glean behind the harvesters. As it turned out, she was working in a field belonging to Boaz, who was from the clan of Elimelek.

Just then Boaz arrived from Bethlehem and greeted the harvesters, "The LORD be with you!"

"The LORD bless you!" they answered.

Boaz asked the overseer of his harvesters, "Who does that young woman belong to?"

The overseer replied, "She is the Moabite who came back from Moab with Naomi. She said, 'Please let me glean and gather among the sheaves behind the harvesters.' She came into the field and has remained here from morning till now, except for a short rest in the shelter."

So Boaz said to Ruth, "My daughter, listen to me. Don't go and glean in another field and don't go away from here. Stay here with the women who work for me. Watch the field where the men are harvesting, and follow along after the women. I have told the men not to lay a hand on you. And whenever you are thirsty, go and get a drink from the water jars the men have filled."

At this, she bowed down with her face to the ground. She asked him, "Why have I found such favor in your eyes that you notice me — a foreigner?"

Boaz replied, "I've been told all about what you have done for your mother-in-law since the death of your husband — how you left your father and mother and your homeland and came to live with a people you did not know before. May the LORD repay you for what you have done. May you be richly rewarded by the LORD, the God of Israel, under whose wings you have come to take refuge."

"May I continue to find favor in your eyes, my lord," she said. "You have put me at ease by speaking kindly to your servant — though I do not have the standing of one of your servants."

At mealtime Boaz said to her, "Come over here. Have some bread and dip it in the wine vinegar."

When she sat down with the harvesters, he offered her some roasted grain. She ate all she wanted and had some left over. As she got up to glean, Boaz gave orders to his men, "Let her gather among the sheaves and don't reprimand her. Even pull out some stalks for her from the bundles and leave them for her to pick up, and don't rebuke her."

So Ruth gleaned in the field until evening. Then she threshed the barley she had gathered, and it amounted to about an ephah. She carried it back to town, and her mother-in-law saw how much she had gathered. Ruth also brought out and gave her what she had left over after she had eaten enough.

Her mother-in-law asked her, "Where did you glean today? Where did you work? Blessed be the man who took notice of you!"

Then Ruth told her mother-in-law about the one at whose place she had been working. "The name of the man I worked with today is Boaz," she said.

"The LORD bless him!" Naomi said to her daughter-in-law. "He has not stopped showing his kindness to the living and the dead."

She added, "That man is our close relative; he is one of our guardian-redeemers."

Then Ruth the Moabite said, "He even said to me, 'Stay with my workers until they finish harvesting all my grain.'"

Naomi said to Ruth her daughter-in-law, "It will be good for you, my daughter, to go with the women who work for him, because in someone else's field you might be harmed."

So Ruth stayed close to the women of Boaz to glean until the barley and wheat harvests were finished. And she lived with her mother-in-law.

One day Ruth's mother-in-law Naomi said to her, "My daughter, I must find a home for you, where you will be well provided for. Now Boaz, with whose women you have worked, is a relative of ours. Tonight he will be winnowing barley on the threshing floor. Wash, put on perfume, and get dressed in your best clothes. Then go down to the threshing floor, but don't let him know you are there until he has finished eating and drinking. When he lies down, note the place where he is lying. Then go and uncover his feet and lie down. He will tell you what to do."

"I will do whatever you say," Ruth answered. So she went down to the threshing floor and did everything her mother-in-law told her to do.

When Boaz had finished eating and drinking and was in good spirits, he went over to lie down at the far end of the grain pile. Ruth approached quietly, uncovered his feet and lay down. In the middle of the night something startled the man; he turned — and there was a woman lying at his feet!

"Who are you?" he asked.

"I am your servant Ruth," she said. "Spread the corner of your garment over me, since you are a guardian-redeemer of our family."

"The LORD bless you, my daughter," he replied. "This kindness is greater than that which you showed earlier: You have not run after the younger men, whether rich or poor. And now, my daughter, don't be afraid. I will do for you all you ask. All the people of my town know that you are a woman of noble character. Although it is true that I am a guardian-redeemer of our family, there is another who is more closely related than I. Stay here for the night, and in the morning if he wants to do his duty as your guardian-redeemer, good; let him redeem you. But if he is not willing, as surely as the LORD lives I will do it. Lie here until morning."

So she lay at his feet until morning, but got up before anyone could be recognized; and he said, "No one must know that a woman came to the threshing floor."

He also said, "Bring me the shawl you are wearing and hold it out." When she did so, he poured into it six measures of barley and placed the bundle on her. Then he went back to town.

When Ruth came to her mother-in-law, Naomi asked, "How did it go, my daughter?"

Then she told her everything Boaz had done for her and added, "He gave me these six measures of barley, saying, 'Don't go back to your mother-in-law empty-handed.'"

Then Naomi said, "Wait, my daughter, until you find out what happens. For the man will not rest until the matter is settled today."

Meanwhile Boaz went up to the town gate and sat down there just as the guardian-redeemer he had mentioned came along. Boaz said, "Come over here, my friend, and sit down." So he went over and sat down.

Boaz took ten of the elders of the town and said, "Sit here," and they did so. Then he said to the guardian-redeemer, "Naomi, who has come back from Moab, is selling the piece of land that belonged to our relative Elimelek. I thought I should bring the matter to your attention and suggest that you buy it in the presence of these seated here and in the presence of the elders of my people. If you will redeem it, do so. But if you will not, tell me, so I will know. For no one has the right to do it except you, and I am next in line."

"I will redeem it," he said.

Then Boaz said, "On the day you buy the land from Naomi, you also acquire Ruth the Moabite, the dead man's widow, in order to maintain the name of the dead with his property."

At this, the guardian-redeemer said, "Then I cannot redeem it because I might endanger my own estate. You redeem it yourself. I cannot do it."

(Now in earlier times in Israel, for the redemption and transfer of property to become final, one party took off his sandal and gave it to the other. This was the method of legalizing transactions in Israel.)

So the guardian-redeemer said to Boaz, "Buy it yourself." And he removed his sandal.

Then Boaz announced to the elders and all the people, "Today you are witnesses that I have bought from Naomi all the property of Elimelek, Kilion and Mahlon. I have also acquired Ruth the Moabite, Mahlon's widow, as my wife, in order to maintain the name of the dead with his property, so that his name will not disappear from among his family or from his hometown. Today you are witnesses!"

Then the elders and all the people at the gate said, "We are witnesses. May the LORD make the woman who is coming into your home like Rachel and Leah, who together built up the family of Israel. May you have standing in Ephrathah and be famous in Bethlehem. Through the offspring the LORD gives you by this young woman, may your family be like that of Perez, whom Tamar bore to Judah."

So Boaz took Ruth and she became his wife. When he made love to her, the LORD enabled her to conceive, and she gave birth to a son. The women said to Naomi: "Praise be to the LORD, who this day has not left you without a guardian-redeemer. May he become famous throughout Israel! He will renew your life and sustain you in your old age. For your daughter-in-law, who loves you and who is better to you than seven sons, has given him birth."

Then Naomi took the child in her arms and cared for him. The women living there said, "Naomi has a son!" And they named him Obed. He was the father of Jesse, the father of David.   RUTH 2:1—4:17

The Israelites were given laws to ensure their compassion to others. Here, a king is urged to be compassionate. Note the source of the compassion is the great King, God himself.

Endow the king with your justice, O God,
    the royal son with your righteousness.
May he judge your people in righteousness,
    your afflicted ones with justice.

May the mountains bring prosperity to the people,
    the hills the fruit of righteousness.

May he defend the afflicted among the people
   and save the children of the needy;
   may he crush the oppressor.
May he endure as long as the sun,
   as long as the moon, through all generations.
May he be like rain falling on a mown field,
   like showers watering the earth.
In his days may the righteous flourish
   and prosperity abound till the moon is no more.

May he rule from sea to sea
   and from the River to the ends of the earth.
May the desert tribes bow before him
   and his enemies lick the dust.
May the kings of Tarshish and of distant shores
   bring tribute to him.
May the kings of Sheba and Seba
   present him gifts.
May all kings bow down to him
   and all nations serve him.

For he will deliver the needy who cry out,
   the afflicted who have no one to help.
He will take pity on the weak and the needy
   and save the needy from death.
He will rescue them from oppression and violence,
   for precious is their blood in his sight.   PSALM 72:1–14

JESUS: MODEL OF COMPASSION

On one occasion an expert in the law stood up to test Jesus. "Teacher," he asked, "what must I do to inherit eternal life?"

"What is written in the Law?" he replied. "How do you read it?"

He answered, "'Love the Lord your God with all your heart and with all your soul and with all your strength and with all your mind'; and, 'Love your neighbor as yourself.'"

"You have answered correctly," Jesus replied. "Do this and you will live."

But he wanted to justify himself, so he asked Jesus, "And who is my neighbor?"

In reply Jesus said: "A man was going down from Jerusalem to Jericho, when he was attacked by robbers. They stripped him of his clothes, beat him and went away, leaving him half dead. A priest happened to be going down the same road, and when he saw the man, he passed by on the other side. So too, a Levite, when he came to the place and saw him, passed by on the other side. But a Samaritan, as he traveled, came where the man was; and when he saw him, he took pity on him. He went to him and bandaged his wounds, pouring on oil and wine. Then he put the man on his own donkey, brought him to an inn and took care of him. The next day he took out two denarii and gave them to the innkeeper. 'Look after him,' he said, 'and when I return, I will reimburse you for any extra expense you may have.'

"Which of these three do you think was a neighbor to the man who fell into the hands of robbers?"

The expert in the law replied, "The one who had mercy on him."

Jesus told him, "Go and do likewise."   LUKE 10:25–37

Throughout his teaching ministry, Jesus masterfully instructed his followers to show compassion to people in need as the ultimate fulfillment of the Law of Moses. Toward the very end of his life on earth, Jesus provided his disciples with divine insight into the ministry of compassion to the poor and needy. He tells them their acts of compassion now have eternal consequences. When Jesus returns he will separate the obedient followers from the unbelievers. How we treat others should make it clear into which of the two groups we fall. After all, our behavior has results that reach far beyond our time on this earth.

"When the Son of Man comes in his glory, and all the angels with him, he will sit on his glorious throne. All the nations will be gathered before him, and he will separate the people one from another as a shepherd separates the sheep from the goats. He will put the sheep on his right and the goats on his left.

"Then the King will say to those on his right, 'Come, you who are blessed by my Father; take your inheritance, the kingdom prepared for you since the creation of the world. For I was hungry and you gave me something to eat, I was thirsty and you gave me something to drink, I was a stranger and you invited me in, I needed clothes and you clothed me, I was sick and you looked after me, I was in prison and you came to visit me.'

"Then the righteous will answer him, 'Lord, when did we see you hungry and feed you, or thirsty and give you something to drink? When did we see you a stranger and invite you in, or needing clothes and clothe you? When did we see you sick or in prison and go to visit you?'

"The King will reply, 'Truly I tell you, whatever you did for one of the least of these brothers and sisters of mine, you did for me.'

"Then he will say to those on his left, 'Depart from me, you who are cursed, into the eternal fire prepared for the devil and his angels. For I was hungry and you gave me nothing to eat, I was thirsty and you gave me nothing to drink, I was a stranger and you did not invite me in, I needed clothes and you did not clothe me, I was sick and in prison and you did not look after me.'

"They also will answer, 'Lord, when did we see you hungry or thirsty or a stranger or needing clothes or sick or in prison, and did not help you?'

"He will reply, 'Truly I tell you, whatever you did not do for one of the least of these, you did not do for me.'

"Then they will go away to eternal punishment, but the righteous to eternal life."   MATTHEW 25:31–46

BELIEVERS: THE ONGOING CALL TO COMPASSION

The same challenge given to the people of Israel to live a life of compassion was also issued to the newly formed Christian church after Jesus' death and resurrection. James, who became the leader of the church in Jerusalem and was likely the half brother of Jesus, wrote what may have been the first book of the New Testament. In his letter, James instructs new believers on the practical how-tos of living this new life in Christ. These same charges apply to believers today.

My dear brothers and sisters, take note of this: Everyone should be quick to listen, slow to speak and slow to become angry, because human anger does not produce the righteousness that God desires. Therefore, get rid of all moral filth and the evil that is so prevalent and humbly accept the word planted in you, which can save you.

Do not merely listen to the word, and so deceive yourselves. Do what it says. Anyone who listens to the word but does not do what it says is like someone who looks at his face in a mirror and, after looking at himself, goes away and immediately forgets what he looks like. But whoever looks intently into the perfect law that gives freedom, and continues in it — not forgetting what they have heard, but doing it — they will be blessed in what they do.

Those who consider themselves religious and yet do not keep a tight rein on their tongues deceive themselves, and their religion is worthless. Religion that God our Father accepts as pure and faultless is this: to look after orphans and widows in their distress and to keep oneself from being polluted by the world.

My brothers and sisters, believers in our glorious Lord Jesus Christ must not show favoritism. Suppose a man comes into your meeting wearing a gold ring and fine clothes, and a poor man in filthy old clothes also comes in. If you show special attention to the man wearing fine clothes and say, "Here's a good seat for you," but say to the poor man, "You stand there" or "Sit on the floor by my feet," have you not discriminated among yourselves and become judges with evil thoughts?

Listen, my dear brothers and sisters: Has not God chosen those who are poor in the eyes of the world to be rich in faith and to inherit the kingdom he promised those who love him? But you have dishonored the poor. Is it not the rich who are exploiting you? Are they not the ones who are dragging you into court? Are they not the ones who are blaspheming the noble name of him to whom you belong?

If you really keep the royal law found in Scripture, "Love your neighbor as yourself," you are doing right. But if you show favoritism, you sin and are convicted by the law as lawbreakers. For whoever keeps the whole law and yet stumbles at just one point is guilty of breaking all of it. For he who said, "You shall not commit adultery," also said, "You shall not murder." If you do not commit adultery but do commit murder, you have become a lawbreaker.

Speak and act as those who are going to be judged by the law that gives freedom, because judgment without mercy will be shown to anyone who has not been merciful. Mercy triumphs over judgment.

JAMES 1:19—2:13

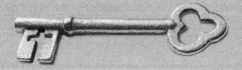

THINK

CHAPTER

9

Stewardship

KEY IDEA

I believe everything I am and
everything I own belong to God.

KEY VERSE

The earth is the LORD's, and everything in it,
the world, and all who live in it;
for he founded it on the seas and
established it on the waters.

Psalm 24:1 – 2

God created the earth and the cosmos. Everything belongs to him. But people are given a special role to play in creation. It is both an honor and a great responsibility. This chapter on stewardship helps us understand the reason for God's mandate to us and how we are to live.

GOD IS OWNER

Psalm 24 was a processional psalm used by the ancient Israelites to celebrate the entrance of the ark of the covenant, the symbol of the Lord's presence, into Jerusalem and into God's sanctuary. Whether or not the psalm was written for the occasion when King David brought the ark to Jerusalem, it was likely used at later commemorations of that event. The psalm begins by praising God as the owner of the earth and everything in it—a reality that consequently makes us, in turn, the stewards of the world and its resources.

> The earth is the LORD's, and everything in it,
>   the world, and all who live in it;
> for he founded it on the seas
>   and established it on the waters.
>
> Who may ascend the mountain of the LORD?
>   Who may stand in his holy place?
> The one who has clean hands and a pure heart,
>   who does not trust in an idol
>   or swear by a false god.
>
> They will receive blessing from the LORD
>   and vindication from God their Savior.
> Such is the generation of those who seek him,
>   who seek your face, God of Jacob.
>
> Lift up your heads, you gates;
>   be lifted up, you ancient doors,
>   that the King of glory may come in.
> Who is this King of glory?
>   The LORD strong and mighty,
>   the LORD mighty in battle.

Lift up your heads, you gates;
    lift them up, you ancient doors,
    that the King of glory may come in.
Who is he, this King of glory?
    The LORD Almighty —
    he is the King of glory.   PSALM 24:1–10

One way that the Lord wanted his people to honor him was through thank offerings, overflowing out of a heart of gratitude for all God has given. But too often the Israelites offered sacrifices but then lived however they wanted, with no sincere thanksgiving behind their actions. They were just going through the motions — like a person today who goes to church on Sunday and then ignores God's commands for living on the other six days of the week. Though God commanded his people to offer sacrifices, and their offerings were pleasing to him, what he was most looking for was their wholehearted obedience in every aspect of their lives.

The Mighty One, God, the LORD,
    speaks and summons the earth
    from the rising of the sun to where it sets.
From Zion, perfect in beauty,
    God shines forth.
Our God comes
    and will not be silent;
a fire devours before him,
    and around him a tempest rages.
He summons the heavens above,
    and the earth, that he may judge his people:
"Gather to me this consecrated people,
    who made a covenant with me by sacrifice."
And the heavens proclaim his righteousness,
    for he is a God of justice.

"Listen, my people, and I will speak;
    I will testify against you, Israel:
    I am God, your God.

I bring no charges against you concerning your sacrifices
    or concerning your burnt offerings, which are ever
        before me.
I have no need of a bull from your stall
    or of goats from your pens,
for every animal of the forest is mine,
    and the cattle on a thousand hills.
I know every bird in the mountains,
    and the insects in the fields are mine.
If I were hungry I would not tell you,
    for the world is mine, and all that is in it.
Do I eat the flesh of bulls
    or drink the blood of goats?

"Sacrifice thank offerings to God,
    fulfill your vows to the Most High,
and call on me in the day of trouble;
    I will deliver you, and you will honor me."

But to the wicked person, God says:

"What right have you to recite my laws
    or take my covenant on your lips?
You hate my instruction
    and cast my words behind you.
When you see a thief, you join with him;
    you throw in your lot with adulterers.
You use your mouth for evil
    and harness your tongue to deceit.
You sit and testify against your brother
    and slander your own mother's son.
When you did these things and I kept silent,
    you thought I was exactly like you.
But I now arraign you
    and set my accusations before you.

"Consider this, you who forget God,
    or I will tear you to pieces, with no one to rescue you:
Those who sacrifice thank offerings honor me,
    and to the blameless I will show my salvation."

Psalm 50:1–23

GOD'S PEOPLE ARE MANAGERS ...

Since God created everything, including humans, how do we fit into the created order? What is our role in this reality? The parable below instructs us on the importance of seeing ourselves not as owners but as managers of our lives and gifts. The bags of gold represent any resource God, the master, gives us. He ultimately owns the resource, but we are charged with caring for it and investing it in ways that yield results for the sake of the kingdom of God.

"Again, it will be like a man going on a journey, who called his servants and entrusted his wealth to them. To one he gave five bags of gold, to another two bags, and to another one bag, each according to his ability. Then he went on his journey. The man who had received five bags of gold went at once and put his money to work and gained five bags more. So also, the one with two bags of gold gained two more. But the man who had received one bag went off, dug a hole in the ground and hid his master's money.

"After a long time the master of those servants returned and settled accounts with them. The man who had received five bags of gold brought the other five. 'Master,' he said, 'you entrusted me with five bags of gold. See, I have gained five more.'

"His master replied, 'Well done, good and faithful servant! You have been faithful with a few things; I will put you in charge of many things. Come and share your master's happiness!'

"The man with two bags of gold also came. 'Master,' he said, 'you entrusted me with two bags of gold; see, I have gained two more.'

"His master replied, 'Well done, good and faithful servant! You have been faithful with a few things; I will put you in charge of many things. Come and share your master's happiness!'

"Then the man who had received one bag of gold came. 'Master,' he said, 'I knew that you are a hard man, harvesting where you have not sown and gathering where you have not scattered seed. So I was afraid and went out and hid your gold in the ground. See, here is what belongs to you.'

"His master replied, 'You wicked, lazy servant! So you knew that I harvest where I have not sown and gather where I have not scattered seed? Well then, you should have put my money on deposit with the bankers, so that when I returned I would have received it back with interest.

"'So take the bag of gold from him and give it to the one who has ten bags. For whoever has will be given more, and they will have an abundance. Whoever does not have, even what they have will be taken from them. And throw that worthless servant outside, into the darkness, where there will be weeping and gnashing of teeth.'" MATTHEW 25:14–30

... OF GOD'S CREATION

God showed great attentiveness in creating the earth, which he entrusted to humankind to care for. Being created in his likeness, we are responsible to be respectful stewards of his precious design and the creatures that are a part of it.

Then God said, "Let us make mankind in our image, in our likeness, so that they may rule over the fish in the sea and the birds in the sky, over the livestock and all the wild animals, and over all the creatures that move along the ground."

So God created mankind in his own image,
in the image of God he created them;
male and female he created them.

God blessed them and said to them, "Be fruitful and increase in number; fill the earth and subdue it. Rule over the fish in the sea and the birds in the sky and over every living creature that moves on the ground."

Then God said, "I give you every seed-bearing plant on the face of the whole earth and every tree that has fruit with seed in it. They will be yours for food. And to all the beasts of the earth and all the birds in the sky and all the creatures that move along the ground — everything that has the breath of life in it — I give every green plant for food." And it was so. GENESIS 1:26–30

... OF THEIR CHILDREN

During the period in which Israel transitioned from being led by judges to being ruled by kings, the book of 1 Samuel tells the story of a woman named Hannah who could not have children. She pleaded earnestly with the Lord for a child, and he granted her request. Hannah's story highlights that our children belong to the Lord. He gives them to us to raise according to his instructions and purposes, but ultimately, they belong to him.

There was a certain man from Ramathaim, a Zuphite from the hill country of Ephraim, whose name was Elkanah son of Jeroham, the son of Elihu, the son of Tohu, the son of Zuph, an Ephraimite. He had two wives; one was called Hannah and the other Peninnah. Peninnah had children, but Hannah had none.

Year after year this man went up from his town to worship and sacrifice to the LORD Almighty at Shiloh, where Hophni and Phinehas, the two sons of Eli, were priests of the LORD. Whenever the day came for Elkanah to sacrifice, he would give portions of the meat to his wife Peninnah and to all her sons and daughters. But to Hannah he gave a double portion because he loved her, and the LORD had closed her womb. Because the LORD had closed Hannah's womb, her rival kept provoking her in order to irritate her. This went on year after year. Whenever Hannah went up to the house of the LORD, her rival provoked her till she wept and would not eat. Her husband Elkanah would say to her, "Hannah, why are you weeping? Why don't you eat? Why are you downhearted? Don't I mean more to you than ten sons?"

Once when they had finished eating and drinking in Shiloh, Hannah stood up. Now Eli the priest was sitting on his chair by the doorpost of the LORD's house. In her deep anguish Hannah prayed to the LORD, weeping bitterly. And she made a vow, saying, "LORD Almighty, if you will only look on your servant's misery and remember me, and not forget your servant but give her a son, then I will give him to the LORD for all the days of his life, and no razor will ever be used on his head."

As she kept on praying to the LORD, Eli observed her mouth. Hannah was praying in her heart, and her lips were moving but her voice was not heard. Eli thought she was drunk and said to her, "How long are you going to stay drunk? Put away your wine."

"Not so, my lord," Hannah replied, "I am a woman who is deeply troubled. I have not been drinking wine or beer; I was pouring out my soul to the LORD. Do not take your servant for a wicked woman; I have been praying here out of my great anguish and grief."

Eli answered, "Go in peace, and may the God of Israel grant you what you have asked of him."

She said, "May your servant find favor in your eyes." Then she went her way and ate something, and her face was no longer downcast.

Early the next morning they arose and worshiped before the LORD and then went back to their home at Ramah. Elkanah made love to his wife Hannah, and the LORD remembered her. So in the course of time Hannah became pregnant and gave birth to a son. She named him Samuel, saying, "Because I asked the LORD for him."

When her husband Elkanah went up with all his family to offer the annual sacrifice to the LORD and to fulfill his vow, Hannah did not go. She said to her husband, "After the boy is weaned, I will take him and present him before the LORD, and he will live there always."

"Do what seems best to you," her husband Elkanah told her. "Stay here until you have weaned him; only may the LORD make good his word." So the woman stayed at home and nursed her son until she had weaned him.

After he was weaned, she took the boy with her, young as he was, along with a three-year-old bull, an ephah of flour and a skin of wine, and brought him to the house of the LORD at Shiloh. When the bull had been sacrificed, they brought the boy to Eli, and she said to him, "Pardon me, my lord. As surely as you live, I am the woman who stood here beside you praying to the LORD. I prayed for this child, and the LORD has granted me what I asked of him. So now I give him to the LORD. For his whole life he will be given over to the LORD." And he worshiped the LORD there.

1 SAMUEL 1:1–28

Samuel was ministering before the LORD — a boy wearing a linen ephod. Each year his mother made him a little robe and took it to him when she went up with her husband to offer the annual sacrifice. Eli would bless Elkanah and his wife, saying, "May the LORD give you children by this woman to take the place of the one she prayed for and gave to the LORD." Then they would go home. And the LORD was gracious to Hannah; she gave birth to three sons and two daughters. Meanwhile, the boy Samuel grew up in the presence of the LORD.   1 SAMUEL 2:18–21

... OF THEIR CALLING

Because the people of Judah chose not to trust in God, he disciplined them with 70 years of captivity in Babylon. While many Jews returned to Jerusalem after the exile, a number of them remained east in the heart of the Babylonian Empire, which had now been conquered by the Persians. Esther, along with her cousin Mordecai, was among the latter group. After catching the eye of King Xerxes, the beautiful young Esther became queen, although her Jewish heritage remained secret. While God's name is not mentioned in the book of Esther, when an edict was issued condemning the Jews to be destroyed, Esther's role in God's plan for his people became evident. She had a job to do and did not shy away from it.

When Mordecai learned of all that had been done, he tore his clothes, put on sackcloth and ashes, and went out into the city, wailing loudly and bitterly. But he went only as far as the king's gate, because no one clothed in sackcloth was allowed to enter it. In every province to which the edict and order of the king came, there was great mourning among the Jews, with fasting, weeping and wailing. Many lay in sackcloth and ashes.

When Esther's eunuchs and female attendants came and told her about Mordecai, she was in great distress. She sent clothes for him to put on instead of his sackcloth, but he would not accept them. Then Esther summoned Hathak, one of the king's eunuchs assigned to attend her, and ordered him to find out what was troubling Mordecai and why.

So Hathak went out to Mordecai in the open square of the city in front of the king's gate. Mordecai told him everything that had happened to him, including the exact amount of money Haman had promised to pay into the royal treasury for the destruction of the Jews. He also gave him a copy of the text of the edict for their annihilation, which had been published in Susa, to show to Esther and explain it to her, and he told him to instruct her to go into the king's presence to beg for mercy and plead with him for her people.

Hathak went back and reported to Esther what Mordecai had said. Then she instructed him to say to Mordecai, "All the king's officials and the people of the royal provinces know that for any man or woman who approaches the king in the inner court without being summoned the king has but one law: that they be put to death unless the king extends the gold scepter to them and spares their lives. But thirty days have passed since I was called to go to the king."

When Esther's words were reported to Mordecai, he sent back this answer: "Do not think that because you are in the king's house you alone of all the Jews will escape. For if you remain silent at this time, relief and deliverance for the Jews will arise from another place, but you and your father's family will perish. And who knows but that you have come to your royal position for such a time as this?"

Then Esther sent this reply to Mordecai: "Go, gather together all the Jews who are in Susa, and fast for me. Do not eat or drink for three days, night or day. I and my attendants will fast as you do. When this is done, I will go to the king, even though it is against the law. And if I perish, I perish."

So Mordecai went away and carried out all of Esther's instructions. ESTHER 4:1–17

... OF THEIR MONEY

You are to seek the place the LORD your God will choose from among all your tribes to put his Name there for his dwelling. To that place you must go; there bring your burnt offerings and sacrifices, your tithes and special gifts, what you have vowed to give and your freewill offerings, and the firstborn of your herds and flocks. There, in the presence of the LORD your God, you and your families shall eat and shall rejoice in everything you have put your hand to, because the LORD your God has blessed you. DEUTERONOMY 12:5–7

During the prophet Malachi's day, at the end of the Old Testament era, the Israelites were failing to follow the requirements for offerings and gifts outlined for them. God, through Malachi,

*challenged the people to honor him with their material resources
as they were commanded.*

"I the LORD do not change. So you, the descendants of Jacob,
are not destroyed. Ever since the time of your ancestors you have
turned away from my decrees and have not kept them. Return to
me, and I will return to you," says the LORD Almighty.

"But you ask, 'How are we to return?'

"Will a mere mortal rob God? Yet you rob me.

"But you ask, 'How are we robbing you?'

"In tithes and offerings. You are under a curse — your whole
nation — because you are robbing me. Bring the whole tithe into
the storehouse, that there may be food in my house. Test me in
this," says the LORD Almighty, "and see if I will not throw open the
floodgates of heaven and pour out so much blessing that there will
not be room enough to store it. I will prevent pests from devouring
your crops, and the vines in your fields will not drop their fruit before it is ripe," says the LORD Almighty. "Then all the nations will
call you blessed, for yours will be a delightful land," says the LORD
Almighty.   MALACHI 3:6–12

> *Because everything we have is ultimately from the Lord, when we
> fail to return to him a portion of what he has provided for us, we
> rob him. In a rather unusual parable, Jesus explained a powerful
> principle regarding how we are to manage the money God has
> entrusted to us. Money has a lot of power and can be used for
> good or for evil. We are to look for "shrewd" ways to use God's
> resources, not to help ourselves, but to help others and serve
> God.*

Jesus told his disciples: "There was a rich man whose manager
was accused of wasting his possessions. So he called him in and
asked him, 'What is this I hear about you? Give an account of your
management, because you cannot be manager any longer.'

"The manager said to himself, 'What shall I do now? My master is taking away my job. I'm not strong enough to dig, and I'm
ashamed to beg — I know what I'll do so that, when I lose my job
here, people will welcome me into their houses.'

"So he called in each one of his master's debtors. He asked the first, 'How much do you owe my master?'

"'Nine hundred gallons of olive oil,' he replied.

"The manager told him, 'Take your bill, sit down quickly, and make it four hundred and fifty.'

"Then he asked the second, 'And how much do you owe?'

"'A thousand bushels of wheat,' he replied.

"He told him, 'Take your bill and make it eight hundred.'

"The master commended the dishonest manager because he had acted shrewdly. For the people of this world are more shrewd in dealing with their own kind than are the people of the light. I tell you, use worldly wealth to gain friends for yourselves, so that when it is gone, you will be welcomed into eternal dwellings.

"Whoever can be trusted with very little can also be trusted with much, and whoever is dishonest with very little will also be dishonest with much. So if you have not been trustworthy in handling worldly wealth, who will trust you with true riches? And if you have not been trustworthy with someone else's property, who will give you property of your own?

"No one can serve two masters. Either you will hate the one and love the other, or you will be devoted to the one and despise the other. You cannot serve both God and money."

The Pharisees, who loved money, heard all this and were sneering at Jesus. He said to them, "You are the ones who justify yourselves in the eyes of others, but God knows your hearts. What people value highly is detestable in God's sight."   LUKE 16:1–15

In sharp contrast to the Pharisees, one poor widow Jesus encountered outside the temple used the money in her possession, though it was very little, not for herself but for God's kingdom. Unlike many others, she gave not to be noticed but to give back to God.

Jesus sat down opposite the place where the offerings were put and watched the crowd putting their money into the temple treasury. Many rich people threw in large amounts. But a poor widow came and put in two very small copper coins, worth only a few cents.

Calling his disciples to him, Jesus said, "Truly I tell you, this poor widow has put more into the treasury than all the others. They all gave out of their wealth; but she, out of her poverty, put in everything — all she had to live on." MARK 12:41–44

... OF THEIR HOMES

Hospitality was highly valued during Old Testament times, by the Israelites as well as by other peoples. Elijah was a mighty prophet of God who announced an impending drought in Israel brought on by the spiritual unfaithfulness of the king and the people. God sent Elijah outside Israel's borders, to the home of a destitute Gentile widow. Their story exemplifies the power of both human hospitality and divine provision.

Now Elijah the Tishbite, from Tishbe in Gilead, said to Ahab, "As the LORD, the God of Israel, lives, whom I serve, there will be neither dew nor rain in the next few years except at my word."

Then the word of the LORD came to Elijah: "Leave here, turn eastward and hide in the Kerith Ravine, east of the Jordan. You will drink from the brook, and I have directed the ravens to supply you with food there."

So he did what the LORD had told him. He went to the Kerith Ravine, east of the Jordan, and stayed there. The ravens brought him bread and meat in the morning and bread and meat in the evening, and he drank from the brook.

Some time later the brook dried up because there had been no rain in the land. Then the word of the LORD came to him: "Go at once to Zarephath in the region of Sidon and stay there. I have directed a widow there to supply you with food." So he went to Zarephath. When he came to the town gate, a widow was there gathering sticks. He called to her and asked, "Would you bring me a little water in a jar so I may have a drink?" As she was going to get it, he called, "And bring me, please, a piece of bread."

"As surely as the LORD your God lives," she replied, "I don't have any bread — only a handful of flour in a jar and a little olive oil in a jug. I am gathering a few sticks to take home and make a meal for myself and my son, that we may eat it — and die."

Elijah said to her, "Don't be afraid. Go home and do as you have said. But first make a small loaf of bread for me from what you have and bring it to me, and then make something for yourself and your son. For this is what the LORD, the God of Israel, says: 'The jar of flour will not be used up and the jug of oil will not run dry until the day the LORD sends rain on the land.'"

She went away and did as Elijah had told her. So there was food every day for Elijah and for the woman and her family. For the jar of flour was not used up and the jug of oil did not run dry, in keeping with the word of the LORD spoken by Elijah.

Some time later the son of the woman who owned the house became ill. He grew worse and worse, and finally stopped breathing. She said to Elijah, "What do you have against me, man of God? Did you come to remind me of my sin and kill my son?"

"Give me your son," Elijah replied. He took him from her arms, carried him to the upper room where he was staying, and laid him on his bed. Then he cried out to the LORD, "LORD my God, have you brought tragedy even on this widow I am staying with, by causing her son to die?" Then he stretched himself out on the boy three times and cried out to the LORD, "LORD my God, let this boy's life return to him!"

The LORD heard Elijah's cry, and the boy's life returned to him, and he lived. Elijah picked up the child and carried him down from the room into the house. He gave him to his mother and said, "Look, your son is alive!"

Then the woman said to Elijah, "Now I know that you are a man of God and that the word of the LORD from your mouth is the truth." 1 KINGS 17:1–24

Our homes—no matter how large or small, how simple or fancy—belong to God and can be used by us to accomplish his purposes. The importance of hospitality portrayed in the Old Testament is intensified in the New Testament, as believers are instructed, commanded and commended in regard to practicing hospitality.

Paul's challenge:

Share with the Lord's people who are in need. Practice hospitality. ROMANS 12:13

Instruction from the writer of Hebrews:

Do not forget to show hospitality to strangers, for by so doing some people have shown hospitality to angels without knowing it.

HEBREWS 13:2

Peter's charge:

Offer hospitality to one another without grumbling.   1 PETER 4:9

John's commendation:

Dear friend, I pray that you may enjoy good health and that all may go well with you, even as your soul is getting along well. It gave me great joy when some believers came and testified about your faithfulness to the truth, telling how you continue to walk in it. I have no greater joy than to hear that my children are walking in the truth.

Dear friend, you are faithful in what you are doing for the brothers and sisters, even though they are strangers to you. They have told the church about your love. Please send them on their way in a manner that honors God. It was for the sake of the Name that they went out, receiving no help from the pagans. We ought therefore to show hospitality to such people so that we may work together for the truth.   3 JOHN 2–8

... OF THEIR BODIES

Paul challenged the members of the church at Corinth to honor God with their bodies. Why? Because, like our resources, our bodies belong to God. We are mere managers.

"I have the right to do anything," you say — but not every-thing is beneficial. "I have the right to do anything" — but I will not be mastered by anything. You say, "Food for the stomach and the stomach for food, and God will destroy them both." The body, however, is not meant for sexual immorality but for the Lord, and the Lord for the body. By his power God raised the Lord from the dead, and he will raise us also. Do you not know that your bodies are members of Christ himself? Shall I then take the members of

Christ and unite them with a prostitute? Never! Do you not know that he who unites himself with a prostitute is one with her in body? For it is said, "The two will become one flesh." But whoever is united with the Lord is one with him in spirit.

Flee from sexual immorality. All other sins a person commits are outside the body, but whoever sins sexually, sins against their own body. Do you not know that your bodies are temples of the Holy Spirit, who is in you, whom you have received from God? You are not your own; you were bought at a price. Therefore honor God with your bodies. 1 CORINTHIANS 6:12–20

... OVER ALL THEY DO

Paul brings us full circle by quoting from Psalm 24, which declares God's ownership over everything. We are managers, and absolutely everything we do is for his glory.

"I have the right to do anything," you say — but not everything is beneficial. "I have the right to do anything" — but not everything is constructive. No one should seek their own good, but the good of others.

Eat anything sold in the meat market without raising questions of conscience, for, "The earth is the Lord's, and everything in it."

If an unbeliever invites you to a meal and you want to go, eat whatever is put before you without raising questions of conscience. But if someone says to you, "This has been offered in sacrifice," then do not eat it, both for the sake of the one who told you and for the sake of conscience. I am referring to the other person's conscience, not yours. For why is my freedom being judged by another's conscience? If I take part in the meal with thankfulness, why am I denounced because of something I thank God for?

So whether you eat or drink or whatever you do, do it all for the glory of God. Do not cause anyone to stumble, whether Jews, Greeks or the church of God — even as I try to please everyone in every way. For I am not seeking my own good but the good of many, so that they may be saved. Follow my example, as I follow the example of Christ. 1 CORINTHIANS 10:23—11:1

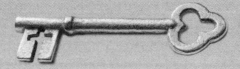

CHAPTER

10

Eternity

KEY IDEA

I believe there is a heaven and a hell
and that Jesus will return to judge all people
and to establish his eternal kingdom.

KEY VERSE

Do not let your hearts be troubled. You believe in God;
believe also in me. My Father's house has many rooms;
if that were not so, would I have told you that
I am going there to prepare a place for you?
John 14:1 – 2

While the Old Testament writers don't address the afterlife in as much detail as the New Testament writers, the Old Testament does contain the magnificent description of the prophet Elijah being taken up to heaven without dying. Elijah is one of only three people taken to heaven in bodily form, the other two being Enoch (you can read about him in Genesis 5:21–24) and, of course, Jesus.

THE ENDING OF A LIFE

When the LORD was about to take Elijah up to heaven in a whirlwind, Elijah and Elisha were on their way from Gilgal. Elijah said to Elisha, "Stay here; the LORD has sent me to Bethel."

But Elisha said, "As surely as the LORD lives and as you live, I will not leave you." So they went down to Bethel.

The company of the prophets at Bethel came out to Elisha and asked, "Do you know that the LORD is going to take your master from you today?"

"Yes, I know," Elisha replied, "so be quiet."

Then Elijah said to him, "Stay here, Elisha; the LORD has sent me to Jericho."

And he replied, "As surely as the LORD lives and as you live, I will not leave you." So they went to Jericho.

The company of the prophets at Jericho went up to Elisha and asked him, "Do you know that the LORD is going to take your master from you today?"

"Yes, I know," he replied, "so be quiet."

Then Elijah said to him, "Stay here; the LORD has sent me to the Jordan."

And he replied, "As surely as the LORD lives and as you live, I will not leave you." So the two of them walked on.

Fifty men from the company of the prophets went and stood at a distance, facing the place where Elijah and Elisha had stopped at the Jordan. Elijah took his cloak, rolled it up and struck the water with it. The water divided to the right and to the left, and the two of them crossed over on dry ground.

When they had crossed, Elijah said to Elisha, "Tell me, what can I do for you before I am taken from you?"

"Let me inherit a double portion of your spirit," Elisha replied.

"You have asked a difficult thing," Elijah said, "yet if you see me when I am taken from you, it will be yours — otherwise, it will not."

As they were walking along and talking together, suddenly a chariot of fire and horses of fire appeared and separated the two of them, and Elijah went up to heaven in a whirlwind. Elisha saw this and cried out, "My father! My father! The chariots and horsemen of Israel!" And Elisha saw him no more. Then he took hold of his garment and tore it in two.

Elisha then picked up Elijah's cloak that had fallen from him and went back and stood on the bank of the Jordan. He took the cloak that had fallen from Elijah and struck the water with it. "Where now is the LORD, the God of Elijah?" he asked. When he struck the water, it divided to the right and to the left, and he crossed over.

The company of the prophets from Jericho, who were watching, said, "The spirit of Elijah is resting on Elisha." And they went to meet him and bowed to the ground before him. "Look," they said, "we your servants have fifty able men. Let them go and look for your master. Perhaps the Spirit of the LORD has picked him up and set him down on some mountain or in some valley."

"No," Elisha replied, "do not send them."

But they persisted until he was too embarrassed to refuse. So he said, "Send them." And they sent fifty men, who searched for three days but did not find him. When they returned to Elisha, who was staying in Jericho, he said to them, "Didn't I tell you not to go?"

2 KINGS 2:1–18

THE INTERMEDIATE STATE

What happens when we die? The New Testament indicates that people experience an "intermediate state," which refers to a person's existence between their time of death and the promised resurrection of their new body. Their earthly body goes into the grave; their spirit lives on in one of two places — in God's presence where they enjoy a time of peace until they receive their resurrected bodies or in a place of torment where they await final judgment. Jesus talked about this vividly in the story about a rich man and Lazarus (not the Lazarus Jesus raised from the dead). Jesus depicted the place of blessedness for the righteous as Abraham's side and the place of torment for the wicked as Hades.

"There was a rich man who was dressed in purple and fine linen and lived in luxury every day. At his gate was laid a beggar named Lazarus, covered with sores and longing to eat what fell from the rich man's table. Even the dogs came and licked his sores.

"The time came when the beggar died and the angels carried him to Abraham's side. The rich man also died and was buried. In Hades, where he was in torment, he looked up and saw Abraham far away, with Lazarus by his side. So he called to him, 'Father Abraham, have pity on me and send Lazarus to dip the tip of his finger in water and cool my tongue, because I am in agony in this fire.'

"But Abraham replied, 'Son, remember that in your lifetime you received your good things, while Lazarus received bad things, but now he is comforted here and you are in agony. And besides all this, between us and you a great chasm has been set in place, so that those who want to go from here to you cannot, nor can anyone cross over from there to us.'

"He answered, 'Then I beg you, father, send Lazarus to my family, for I have five brothers. Let him warn them, so that they will not also come to this place of torment.'

"Abraham replied, 'They have Moses and the Prophets; let them listen to them.'

"'No, father Abraham,' he said, 'but if someone from the dead goes to them, they will repent.'

"He said to him, 'If they do not listen to Moses and the Prophets, they will not be convinced even if someone rises from the dead.'"

LUKE 16:19–31

THE RESURRECTION

The grand promise of God and the ultimate hope for all Christians is the resurrection. Just as Christ was raised from the dead and received an imperishable body, so will all those who believe in Christ. Paul, writing to the church at Corinth, details this major truth.

Now, brothers and sisters, I want to remind you of the gospel I preached to you, which you received and on which you have taken your stand. By this gospel you are saved, if you hold firmly to the word I preached to you. Otherwise, you have believed in vain.

For what I received I passed on to you as of first importance: that Christ died for our sins according to the Scriptures, that he was buried, that he was raised on the third day according to the Scriptures, and that he appeared to Cephas [Peter], and then to the Twelve. After that, he appeared to more than five hundred of the brothers and sisters at the same time, most of whom are still living, though some have fallen asleep. Then he appeared to James, then to all the apostles, and last of all he appeared to me also, as to one abnormally born.

For I am the least of the apostles and do not even deserve to be called an apostle, because I persecuted the church of God. But by the grace of God I am what I am, and his grace to me was not without effect. No, I worked harder than all of them — yet not I, but the grace of God that was with me. Whether, then, it is I or they, this is what we preach, and this is what you believed.

But if it is preached that Christ has been raised from the dead, how can some of you say that there is no resurrection of the dead? If there is no resurrection of the dead, then not even Christ has been raised. And if Christ has not been raised, our preaching is useless and so is your faith. More than that, we are then found to be false witnesses about God, for we have testified about God that he raised Christ from the dead. But he did not raise him if in fact the dead are not raised. For if the dead are not raised, then Christ has not been raised either. And if Christ has not been raised, your faith is futile; you are still in your sins. Then those also who have fallen asleep in Christ are lost. If only for this life we have hope in Christ, we are of all people most to be pitied.

But Christ has indeed been raised from the dead, the first-fruits of those who have fallen asleep. For since death came through a man, the resurrection of the dead comes also through a man. For as in Adam all die, so in Christ all will be made alive. But each in turn: Christ, the firstfruits; then, when he comes, those who belong to him. Then the end will come, when he hands over the kingdom to God the Father after he has destroyed all dominion, authority and power. For he must reign until he has put all his enemies under his feet. The last enemy to be destroyed is death. For he "has put everything under his feet." Now when it says that "everything" has been put under him, it is clear that this does not include God himself, who put everything under Christ. When he has done this, then the Son himself will be made subject to him who put everything under him, so that God may be all in all.   1 CORINTHIANS 15:1–28

But someone will ask, "How are the dead raised? With what kind of body will they come?" How foolish! What you sow does not come to life unless it dies. When you sow, you do not plant the body that will be, but just a seed, perhaps of wheat or of something else. But God gives it a body as he has determined, and to each kind of seed he gives its own body. Not all flesh is the same: People have one kind of flesh, animals have another, birds another and fish another. There are also heavenly bodies and there are earthly bodies; but the splendor of the heavenly bodies is one kind, and the splendor of the earthly bodies is another. The sun has one kind of splendor, the moon another and the stars another; and star differs from star in splendor.

So will it be with the resurrection of the dead. The body that is sown is perishable, it is raised imperishable; it is sown in dishonor, it is raised in glory; it is sown in weakness, it is raised in power; it is sown a natural body, it is raised a spiritual body.

If there is a natural body, there is also a spiritual body. So it is written: "The first man Adam became a living being"; the last Adam, a life-giving spirit. The spiritual did not come first, but the natural, and after that the spiritual. The first man was of the dust of the earth; the second man is of heaven. As was the earthly man, so are those who are of the earth; and as is the heavenly man, so also are those who are of heaven. And just as we have borne the image of the earthly man, so shall we bear the image of the heavenly man.

I declare to you, brothers and sisters, that flesh and blood cannot inherit the kingdom of God, nor does the perishable inherit the imperishable. Listen, I tell you a mystery: We will not all sleep, but we will all be changed — in a flash, in the twinkling of an eye, at the last trumpet. For the trumpet will sound, the dead will be raised imperishable, and we will be changed. For the perishable must clothe itself with the imperishable, and the mortal with immortality. When the perishable has been clothed with the imperishable, and the mortal with immortality, then the saying that is written will come true: "Death has been swallowed up in victory."

> "Where, O death, is your victory?
> Where, O death, is your sting?"

The sting of death is sin, and the power of sin is the law. But thanks be to God! He gives us the victory through our Lord Jesus Christ.

Therefore, my dear brothers and sisters, stand firm. Let nothing move you. Always give yourselves fully to the work of the Lord, because you know that your labor in the Lord is not in vain.

1 CORINTHIANS 15:35–58

It is written: "I believed; therefore I have spoken." Since we have that same spirit of faith, we also believe and therefore speak, because we know that the one who raised the Lord Jesus from the dead will also raise us with Jesus and present us with you to himself. All this is for your benefit, so that the grace that is reaching more and more people may cause thanksgiving to overflow to the glory of God.

Therefore we do not lose heart. Though outwardly we are wasting away, yet inwardly we are being renewed day by day. For our light and momentary troubles are achieving for us an eternal glory that far outweighs them all. So we fix our eyes not on what is seen, but on what is unseen, since what is seen is temporary, but what is unseen is eternal.

For we know that if the earthly tent we live in is destroyed, we have a building from God, an eternal house in heaven, not built by human hands. Meanwhile we groan, longing to be clothed instead with our heavenly dwelling, because when we are clothed, we will not be found naked. For while we are in this tent, we groan and are burdened, because we do not wish to be unclothed but to be clothed instead with our heavenly dwelling, so that what is mortal may be swallowed up by life. Now the one who has fashioned us for this very purpose is God, who has given us the Spirit as a deposit, guaranteeing what is to come.

Therefore we are always confident and know that as long as we are at home in the body we are away from the Lord. For we live by faith, not by sight. We are confident, I say, and would prefer to be away from the body and at home with the Lord. So we make it our goal to please him, whether we are at home in the body or away from it. For we must all appear before the judgment seat of Christ, so that each of us may receive what is due us for the things done while in the body, whether good or bad.   2 Corinthians 4:13—5:10

THE RETURN OF CHRIST

The event that will trigger this promised resurrection is the second coming of Christ. There are varied beliefs about the details leading up to this grand occasion, but all followers of Jesus embrace its truth and significance. Often the Bible refers to the return of Christ as the "day of the Lord." Paul uses this phrase in an important letter addressed to the church at Thessalonica. Some of the believers there thought all Christians would be alive at the return of Christ, causing them to be concerned about fellow believers who had died. Paul explains that on the great day of Christ's return God will resurrect those who have died and then all believers will be brought together and will be with the Lord Jesus forever.

Brothers and sisters, we do not want you to be uninformed about those who sleep in death, so that you do not grieve like the rest of mankind, who have no hope. For we believe that Jesus died and rose again, and so we believe that God will bring with Jesus those who have fallen asleep in him. According to the Lord's word, we tell you that we who are still alive, who are left until the coming of the Lord, will certainly not precede those who have fallen asleep. For the Lord himself will come down from heaven, with a loud command, with the voice of the archangel and with the trumpet call of God, and the dead in Christ will rise first. After that, we who are still alive and are left will be caught up together with them in the clouds to meet the Lord in the air. And so we will be with the Lord forever. Therefore encourage one another with these words.

Now, brothers and sisters, about times and dates we do not need to write to you, for you know very well that the day of the Lord will come like a thief in the night. While people are saying, "Peace and safety," destruction will come on them suddenly, as labor pains on a pregnant woman, and they will not escape.

But you, brothers and sisters, are not in darkness so that this day should surprise you like a thief. You are all children of the light and children of the day. We do not belong to the night or to the darkness. So then, let us not be like others, who are asleep, but let us be awake and sober. For those who sleep, sleep at night, and those who get drunk, get drunk at night. But since we belong to the day, let us be sober, putting on faith and love as a breastplate, and the hope of salvation as a helmet. For God did not appoint us to suffer wrath but to receive salvation through our Lord Jesus Christ. He died for us so that, whether we are awake or asleep, we may live together with him. Therefore encourage one another and build each other up, just as in fact you are doing.

1 THESSALONIANS 4:13—5:11

The apostle Peter also writes in great detail about "the day of the Lord," adding further clarification and admonition regarding how believers should live their lives in light of this future reality.

Dear friends, this is now my second letter to you. I have written both of them as reminders to stimulate you to wholesome thinking. I want you to recall the words spoken in the past by the holy prophets and the command given by our Lord and Savior through your apostles.

Above all, you must understand that in the last days scoffers will come, scoffing and following their own evil desires. They will say, "Where is this 'coming' he promised? Ever since our ancestors died, everything goes on as it has since the beginning of creation." But they deliberately forget that long ago by God's word the heavens came into being and the earth was formed out of water and by water. By these waters also the world of that time was deluged and destroyed. By the same word the present heavens and earth are reserved for fire, being kept for the day of judgment and destruction of the ungodly.

But do not forget this one thing, dear friends: With the Lord a day is like a thousand years, and a thousand years are like a day. The Lord is not slow in keeping his promise, as some understand slowness. Instead he is patient with you, not wanting anyone to perish, but everyone to come to repentance.

But the day of the Lord will come like a thief. The heavens will disappear with a roar; the elements will be destroyed by fire, and the earth and everything done in it will be laid bare.

Since everything will be destroyed in this way, what kind of people ought you to be? You ought to live holy and godly lives as you look forward to the day of God and speed its coming. That day will bring about the destruction of the heavens by fire, and the elements will melt in the heat. But in keeping with his promise we are looking forward to a new heaven and a new earth, where righteousness dwells.

So then, dear friends, since you are looking forward to this, make every effort to be found spotless, blameless and at peace with him. Bear in mind that our Lord's patience means salvation, just as our dear brother Paul also wrote you with the wisdom that God gave him. He writes the same way in all his letters, speaking in them of these matters. His letters contain some things that are hard to understand, which ignorant and unstable people distort, as they do the other Scriptures, to their own destruction.

Therefore, dear friends, since you have been forewarned, be on your guard so that you may not be carried away by the error of the lawless and fall from your secure position. But grow in the grace and knowledge of our Lord and Savior Jesus Christ. To him be glory both now and forever! Amen.   2 PETER 3:1–18

NEW HEAVEN AND NEW EARTH

After Jesus returns and we are resurrected into our imperishable bodies, there will be a final judgment by God of every nation. John saw and recorded a vision from God about what will happen at this time of judgment. John wrote down the final movement in God's grand story—the restoration of what was lost in the beginning. What we read in the opening creation story of Genesis we see again in Revelation—a re-creation—but on a grander scale to accommodate all the people over the centuries who have embraced Christ and received eternal life.

I saw a great white throne and him who was seated on it. The earth and the heavens fled from his presence, and there was no place for them. And I saw the dead, great and small, standing before the throne, and books were opened. Another book was opened, which is the book of life. The dead were judged according to what they had done as recorded in the books. The sea gave up the dead that were in it, and death and Hades gave up the dead that were in them, and each person was judged according to what they had done. Then death and Hades were thrown into the lake of fire. The lake of fire is the second death. Anyone whose name was not found written in the book of life was thrown into the lake of fire.

Then I saw "a new heaven and a new earth," for the first heaven and the first earth had passed away, and there was no longer any sea. I saw the Holy City, the new Jerusalem, coming down out of heaven from God, prepared as a bride beautifully dressed for her husband. And I heard a loud voice from the throne saying, "Look! God's dwelling place is now among the people, and he will dwell with them. They will be his people, and God himself will be with them and be their God. 'He will wipe every tear from their eyes. There will be no more death' or mourning or crying or pain, for the old order of things has passed away."

He who was seated on the throne said, "I am making everything new!" Then he said, "Write this down, for these words are trustworthy and true."

He said to me: "It is done. I am the Alpha and the Omega, the Beginning and the End. To the thirsty I will give water without cost from the spring of the water of life. Those who are victorious will inherit all this, and I will be their God and they will be my children. But the cowardly, the unbelieving, the vile, the murderers, the sexually immoral, those who practice magic arts, the idolaters and all liars — they will be consigned to the fiery lake of burning sulfur. This is the second death."

One of the seven angels who had the seven bowls full of the seven last plagues came and said to me, "Come, I will show you the bride, the wife of the Lamb." And he carried me away in the Spirit to a mountain great and high, and showed me the Holy City, Jerusalem, coming down out of heaven from God. It shone with the glory of God, and its brilliance was like that of a very precious jewel, like a jasper, clear as crystal. It had a great, high wall with twelve gates, and with twelve angels at the gates. On the gates were written the names of the twelve tribes of Israel. There were three gates on the east, three on the north, three on the south and three on the west. The wall of the city had twelve foundations, and on them were the names of the twelve apostles of the Lamb.

The angel who talked with me had a measuring rod of gold to measure the city, its gates and its walls. The city was laid out like a square, as long as it was wide. He measured the city with the rod and found it to be 12,000 stadia in length, and as wide and high as it is long. The angel measured the wall using human measurement, and it was 144 cubits thick. The wall was made of jasper, and the city of pure gold, as pure as glass. The foundations of the city walls were decorated with every kind of precious stone. The first foundation was jasper, the second sapphire, the third agate, the fourth emerald, the fifth onyx, the sixth ruby, the seventh chrysolite, the eighth beryl, the ninth topaz, the tenth turquoise, the eleventh jacinth, and the twelfth amethyst. The twelve gates were twelve pearls, each gate made of a single pearl. The great street of the city was of gold, as pure as transparent glass.

I did not see a temple in the city, because the Lord God Almighty and the Lamb are its temple. The city does not need the sun or the moon to shine on it, for the glory of God gives it light, and the Lamb is its lamp. The nations will walk by its light, and the kings of the earth will bring their splendor into it. On no day will its gates ever be shut, for there will be no night there. The glory and honor of the nations will be brought into it. Nothing impure will ever enter it, nor will anyone who does what is shameful or deceitful, but only those whose names are written in the Lamb's book of life.

Then the angel showed me the river of the water of life, as clear as crystal, flowing from the throne of God and of the Lamb down the middle of the great street of the city. On each side of the river stood the tree of life, bearing twelve crops of fruit, yielding its fruit every month. And the leaves of the tree are for the healing of the nations. No longer will there be any curse. The throne of God and of the Lamb will be in the city, and his servants will serve him. They will see his face, and his name will be on their foreheads. There will be no more night. They will not need the light of a lamp or the light of the sun, for the Lord God will give them light. And they will reign for ever and ever.

The angel said to me, "These words are trustworthy and true. The Lord, the God who inspires the prophets, sent his angel to show his servants the things that must soon take place."

"Look, I am coming soon! Blessed is the one who keeps the words of the prophecy written in this scroll."

I, John, am the one who heard and saw these things. And when I had heard and seen them, I fell down to worship at the feet of the angel who had been showing them to me. But he said to me, "Don't do that! I am a fellow servant with you and with your fellow prophets and with all who keep the words of this scroll. Worship God!"

Then he told me, "Do not seal up the words of the prophecy of this scroll, because the time is near. Let the one who does wrong continue to do wrong; let the vile person continue to be vile; let the one who does right continue to do right; and let the holy person continue to be holy."

"Look, I am coming soon! My reward is with me, and I will give to each person according to what they have done. I am the Alpha and the Omega, the First and the Last, the Beginning and the End.

"Blessed are those who wash their robes, that they may have the right to the tree of life and may go through the gates into the city. Outside are the dogs, those who practice magic arts, the sexually immoral, the murderers, the idolaters and everyone who loves and practices falsehood.

"I, Jesus, have sent my angel to give you this testimony for the churches. I am the Root and the Offspring of David, and the bright Morning Star."

The Spirit and the bride say, "Come!" And let the one who hears say, "Come!" Let the one who is thirsty come; and let the one who wishes take the free gift of the water of life.

I warn everyone who hears the words of the prophecy of this scroll: If anyone adds anything to them, God will add to that person the plagues described in this scroll. And if anyone takes words away from this scroll of prophecy, God will take away from that person any share in the tree of life and in the Holy City, which are described in this scroll.

He who testifies to these things says, "Yes, I am coming soon."
Amen. Come, Lord Jesus.

The grace of the Lord Jesus be with God's people. Amen.

REVELATION 20:11—22:21

In Jesus' last week on earth before he returned to the Father, he comforted the disciples concerning the future. He informed them that he was leaving, but he also promised that he would be overseeing the construction of a place for each of them in heaven — the New Jerusalem John saw and described. As you read these words, please know that Jesus' message to the disciples applies to you as well. He has prepared an eternal home for all those who believe.

"Do not let your hearts be troubled. You believe in God; believe also in me. My Father's house has many rooms; if that were not so, would I have told you that I am going there to prepare a place for you? And if I go and prepare a place for you, I will come back and take you to be with me that you also may be where I am. You know the way to the place where I am going."

Thomas said to him, "Lord, we don't know where you are going, so how can we know the way?"

Jesus answered, "I am the way and the truth and the life. No one comes to the Father except through me. If you really know me, you will know my Father as well. From now on, you do know him and have seen him." JOHN 14:1–7

What Should I Do?

Do you not know that in a race all the runners run, but only one gets the prize? Run in such a way as to get the prize. Everyone who competes in the games goes into strict training. They do it to get a crown that will not last, but we do it to get a crown that will last forever. Therefore I do not run like someone running aimlessly; I do not fight like a boxer beating the air. No, I strike a blow to my body and make it my slave so that after I have preached to others, I myself will not be disqualified for the prize.
1 Corinthians 9:24 – 27

When you study the life of Jesus you will notice a distinct pattern. Jesus faithfully lived in a purposeful way. Once again, Jesus was modeling for us the Christian life. We would do well to simply follow his pattern — to *act* like Jesus.

The following ten chapters are going to introduce you to the key spiritual practices of Christian life. You will encounter axioms to guide you and real life stories to inspire you.

As you read each chapter and come to understand what God wants you to do, prayerfully ask yourself, "Will I do what God is inviting me to do?" In the passage above the apostle Paul invites us to think of the Christian life like an athlete. If an Olympic runner wants to cross the finish line first, they must commit to a life of strict training. Essentially, Paul is saying that if we want to win at life, we too need to be disciplined in the way we approach each day.

If you resolve to practice what you are about to learn, remember you will not be alone. God's Spirit can give you the internal strength, silence the voices of dissenters and blow wind at your back.

These practices will not only aid you in understanding the key beliefs, they will also catalyze you in fulfilling your mission to love God and to love your neighbor better.

On your mark ... get set ... GO!

ACT

CHAPTER

11

Worship

KEY IDEA

I worship God for who he is
and what he has done for me.

KEY VERSE

Come, let us sing for joy to the LORD;
let us shout aloud to the Rock of our salvation.
Let us come before him with thanksgiving
and extol him with music and song.

Psalm 95:1 – 2

173

Worshiping God for who he is and what he has done for us can be expressed in many different forms and diverse environments, but it's the heart behind the actions that matters to God. Throughout Scripture we see how God's people worshiped him on towering mountaintops, inside homes with dirt floors, at a lavishly adorned temple and in dark prisons. They demonstrated their devotion to God with singing, dancing, sacrifices and public and private prayer. What's most important to God is not the way that we choose to worship him, but the motivation that directs our actions.

THE HEART'S INTENT

Come, let us sing for joy to the LORD;
    let us shout aloud to the Rock of our salvation.
Let us come before him with thanksgiving
    and extol him with music and song.

For the LORD is the great God,
    the great King above all gods.
In his hand are the depths of the earth,
    and the mountain peaks belong to him.
The sea is his, for he made it,
    and his hands formed the dry land.

Come, let us bow down in worship,
    let us kneel before the LORD our Maker;
for he is our God
    and we are the people of his pasture,
    the flock under his care.   PSALM 95:1–7

During Old Testament times, worship involved animal sacrifices. Instead of leaving his people with no recourse except to face their punishment for sin, God, in his mercy, allowed his people to sacrifice the best animal from their herd as a payment for their disobedience. The animal had to be without defect, since a defective sacrifice could not be a substitute for a defective people. This practice was intended to be accompanied by repentance. The worshiper confessed their sin and laid hands on the animal; then the sin was symbolically transferred away from the sinner to the sacrifice.

Unfortunately, over time the Israelites' sacrifices became meaningless rituals. God was angry and heartbroken. The people brought him an abundance of sacrifices, yet their character and conduct were anything but pleasing to him.

"The multitude of your sacrifices—
    what are they to me?" says the LORD.
"I have more than enough of burnt offerings,
    of rams and the fat of fattened animals;
I have no pleasure
    in the blood of bulls and lambs and goats.
When you come to appear before me,
    who has asked this of you,
    this trampling of my courts?
Stop bringing meaningless offerings!
    Your incense is detestable to me.
New Moons, Sabbaths and convocations—
    I cannot bear your worthless assemblies.
Your New Moon feasts and your appointed festivals
    I hate with all my being.
They have become a burden to me;
    I am weary of bearing them.
When you spread out your hands in prayer,
    I hide my eyes from you;
even when you offer many prayers,
    I am not listening.

Your hands are full of blood!

Wash and make yourselves clean.
    Take your evil deeds out of my sight;
    stop doing wrong.
Learn to do right; seek justice.
    Defend the oppressed.
Take up the cause of the fatherless;
    plead the case of the widow.

"Come now, let us settle the matter,"
    says the LORD.

"Though your sins are like scarlet,
    they shall be as white as snow;
though they are red as crimson,
    they shall be like wool.
If you are willing and obedient,
    you will eat the good things of the land;
but if you resist and rebel,
    you will be devoured by the sword."
                    For the mouth of the LORD has spoken.

                                                ISAIAH 1:11–20

In the New Testament, those who failed to worship and honor God properly received some harsh words from Jesus. This was especially true for the religious leaders whose layers of religious exercises and rituals hid a weak and shallow faith. As a crowd gathered to listen to Jesus' teachings, he warned them about the influence of these hollow religious leaders.

Then Jesus said to the crowds and to his disciples: "The teachers of the law and the Pharisees sit in Moses' seat. So you must be careful to do everything they tell you. But do not do what they do, for they do not practice what they preach. They tie up heavy, cumbersome loads and put them on other people's shoulders, but they themselves are not willing to lift a finger to move them.

"Everything they do is done for people to see: They make their phylacteries wide and the tassels on their garments long; they love the place of honor at banquets and the most important seats in the synagogues; they love to be greeted with respect in the marketplaces and to be called 'Rabbi' by others.

"But you are not to be called 'Rabbi,' for you have one Teacher, and you are all brothers. And do not call anyone on earth 'father,' for you have one Father, and he is in heaven. Nor are you to be called instructors, for you have one Instructor, the Messiah. The greatest among you will be your servant. For those who exalt themselves will be humbled, and those who humble themselves will be exalted.

"Woe to you, teachers of the law and Pharisees, you hypocrites! You shut the door of the kingdom of heaven in people's faces. You yourselves do not enter, nor will you let those enter who are trying to.

"Woe to you, teachers of the law and Pharisees, you hypocrites! You travel over land and sea to win a single convert, and when you have succeeded, you make them twice as much a child of hell as you are.

"Woe to you, blind guides! You say, 'If anyone swears by the temple, it means nothing; but anyone who swears by the gold of the temple is bound by that oath.' You blind fools! Which is greater: the gold, or the temple that makes the gold sacred? You also say, 'If anyone swears by the altar, it means nothing; but anyone who swears by the gift on the altar is bound by that oath.' You blind men! Which is greater: the gift, or the altar that makes the gift sacred? Therefore, anyone who swears by the altar swears by it and by everything on it. And anyone who swears by the temple swears by it and by the one who dwells in it. And anyone who swears by heaven swears by God's throne and by the one who sits on it.

"Woe to you, teachers of the law and Pharisees, you hypocrites! You give a tenth of your spices — mint, dill and cumin. But you have neglected the more important matters of the law — justice, mercy and faithfulness. You should have practiced the latter, without neglecting the former. You blind guides! You strain out a gnat but swallow a camel.

"Woe to you, teachers of the law and Pharisees, you hypocrites! You clean the outside of the cup and dish, but inside they are full of greed and self-indulgence. Blind Pharisee! First clean the inside of the cup and dish, and then the outside also will be clean.

"Woe to you, teachers of the law and Pharisees, you hypocrites! You are like whitewashed tombs, which look beautiful on the outside but on the inside are full of the bones of the dead and everything unclean. In the same way, on the outside you appear to people as righteous but on the inside you are full of hypocrisy and wickedness." MATTHEW 23:1–28

UNASHAMED WORSHIPERS

When God calls us to love him with all our heart, soul, mind and strength, he is demanding that we hold nothing back from him. A commitment to worship God is a vow to be bold and unashamed of our love and devotion to him. With great power, God rescued the Israelites when the army of Egypt had them backed against the Red Sea. After their escape, Moses and his sister Miriam led the Israelites in an unapologetic song of celebration and blessing, praising God for who he is and what he had done for them.

Then Moses and the Israelites sang this song to the LORD:

> "I will sing to the LORD,
>   for he is highly exalted.
> Both horse and driver
>   he has hurled into the sea.
>
> "The LORD is my strength and my defense;
>   he has become my salvation.
> He is my God, and I will praise him,
>   my father's God, and I will exalt him.
> The LORD is a warrior;
>   the LORD is his name.
> Pharaoh's chariots and his army
>   he has hurled into the sea.
> The best of Pharaoh's officers
>   are drowned in the Red Sea.
> The deep waters have covered them;
>   they sank to the depths like a stone.
> Your right hand, LORD,
>   was majestic in power.
> Your right hand, LORD,
>   shattered the enemy.
>
> "In the greatness of your majesty
>   you threw down those who opposed you.
> You unleashed your burning anger;
>   it consumed them like stubble.
> By the blast of your nostrils
>   the waters piled up.
> The surging waters stood up like a wall;
>   the deep waters congealed in the heart of the sea.
> The enemy boasted,
>   'I will pursue, I will overtake them.

I will divide the spoils;
    I will gorge myself on them.
I will draw my sword
    and my hand will destroy them.'
But you blew with your breath,
    and the sea covered them.
They sank like lead
    in the mighty waters.
Who among the gods
    is like you, LORD?
Who is like you —
    majestic in holiness,
awesome in glory,
    working wonders?

"You stretch out your right hand,
    and the earth swallows your enemies.
In your unfailing love you will lead
    the people you have redeemed.
In your strength you will guide them
    to your holy dwelling.
The nations will hear and tremble;
    anguish will grip the people of Philistia.
The chiefs of Edom will be terrified,
    the leaders of Moab will be seized with
        trembling,
the people of Canaan will melt away;
    terror and dread will fall on them.
By the power of your arm
    they will be as still as a stone —
until your people pass by, LORD,
    until the people you bought pass by.
You will bring them in and plant them
    on the mountain of your inheritance —
the place, LORD, you made for your dwelling,
    the sanctuary, Lord, your hands established.

"The LORD reigns
    for ever and ever."

When Pharaoh's horses, chariots and horsemen went into the sea, the LORD brought the waters of the sea back over them, but the Israelites walked through the sea on dry ground. Then Miriam the prophet, Aaron's sister, took a timbrel in her hand, and all the women followed her, with timbrels and dancing. Miriam sang to them:

> "Sing to the LORD,
>   for he is highly exalted.
> Both horse and driver
>   he has hurled into the sea."   EXODUS 15:1–21

While Moses and Miriam expressed their praise vocally, bold worship can also be displayed with very few words. Take Daniel, for example. His quiet refusal to worship anyone or anything but the one true God was a risky decision because King Darius dealt harshly with disobedience in his kingdom. Unlike the songs of Moses and Miriam, it was Daniel's actions that did all the talking.

It pleased Darius to appoint 120 satraps to rule throughout the kingdom, with three administrators over them, one of whom was Daniel. The satraps were made accountable to them so that the king might not suffer loss. Now Daniel so distinguished himself among the administrators and the satraps by his exceptional qualities that the king planned to set him over the whole kingdom. At this, the administrators and the satraps tried to find grounds for charges against Daniel in his conduct of government affairs, but they were unable to do so. They could find no corruption in him, because he was trustworthy and neither corrupt nor negligent. Finally these men said, "We will never find any basis for charges against this man Daniel unless it has something to do with the law of his God."

So these administrators and satraps went as a group to the king and said: "May King Darius live forever! The royal administrators, prefects, satraps, advisers and governors have all agreed that the king should issue an edict and enforce the decree that anyone who prays to any god or human being during the next thirty days, except to you, Your Majesty, shall be thrown into the lions' den. Now,

Your Majesty, issue the decree and put it in writing so that it cannot be altered — in accordance with the law of the Medes and Persians, which cannot be repealed." So King Darius put the decree in writing.

Now when Daniel learned that the decree had been published, he went home to his upstairs room where the windows opened toward Jerusalem. Three times a day he got down on his knees and prayed, giving thanks to his God, just as he had done before. Then these men went as a group and found Daniel praying and asking God for help. So they went to the king and spoke to him about his royal decree: "Did you not publish a decree that during the next thirty days anyone who prays to any god or human being except to you, Your Majesty, would be thrown into the lions' den?"

The king answered, "The decree stands — in accordance with the law of the Medes and Persians, which cannot be repealed."

Then they said to the king, "Daniel, who is one of the exiles from Judah, pays no attention to you, Your Majesty, or to the decree you put in writing. He still prays three times a day." When the king heard this, he was greatly distressed; he was determined to rescue Daniel and made every effort until sundown to save him.

Then the men went as a group to King Darius and said to him, "Remember, Your Majesty, that according to the law of the Medes and Persians no decree or edict that the king issues can be changed."

So the king gave the order, and they brought Daniel and threw him into the lions' den. The king said to Daniel, "May your God, whom you serve continually, rescue you!"

A stone was brought and placed over the mouth of the den, and the king sealed it with his own signet ring and with the rings of his nobles, so that Daniel's situation might not be changed. Then the king returned to his palace and spent the night without eating and without any entertainment being brought to him. And he could not sleep.

At the first light of dawn, the king got up and hurried to the lions' den. When he came near the den, he called to Daniel in an anguished voice, "Daniel, servant of the living God, has your God, whom you serve continually, been able to rescue you from the lions?"

Daniel answered, "May the king live forever! My God sent his angel, and he shut the mouths of the lions. They have not hurt me, because I was found innocent in his sight. Nor have I ever done any wrong before you, Your Majesty."

The king was overjoyed and gave orders to lift Daniel out of the den. And when Daniel was lifted from the den, no wound was found on him, because he had trusted in his God.

At the king's command, the men who had falsely accused Daniel were brought in and thrown into the lions' den, along with their wives and children. And before they reached the floor of the den, the lions overpowered them and crushed all their bones.

Then King Darius wrote to all the nations and peoples of every language in all the earth:

"May you prosper greatly!

"I issue a decree that in every part of my kingdom people must fear and reverence the God of Daniel.

"For he is the living God
    and he endures forever;
his kingdom will not be destroyed,
    his dominion will never end.
He rescues and he saves;
    he performs signs and wonders
    in the heavens and on the earth.
He has rescued Daniel
    from the power of the lions."   DANIEL 6:1–27

God's signs and wonders are undeniably awe-inspiring. In the book of Acts, Paul's and Silas's boldness got them thrown into jail; then as they lifted their voices in prayers and singing hymns of worship during the night, a sudden earthquake resulted in their release.

Once when we were going to the place of prayer, we were met by a female slave who had a spirit by which she predicted the future. She earned a great deal of money for her owners by fortune-telling. She followed Paul and the rest of us, shouting, "These men are servants of the Most High God, who are telling you the way to be saved." She kept this up for many days. Finally Paul became so annoyed that he turned around and said to the spirit, "In the name of Jesus Christ I command you to come out of her!" At that moment the spirit left her.

When her owners realized that their hope of making money was gone, they seized Paul and Silas and dragged them into the marketplace to face the authorities. They brought them before the magistrates and said, "These men are Jews, and are throwing our city into an uproar by advocating customs unlawful for us Romans to accept or practice."

The crowd joined in the attack against Paul and Silas, and the magistrates ordered them to be stripped and beaten with rods. After they had been severely flogged, they were thrown into prison, and the jailer was commanded to guard them carefully. When he received these orders, he put them in the inner cell and fastened their feet in the stocks.

About midnight Paul and Silas were praying and singing hymns to God, and the other prisoners were listening to them. Suddenly there was such a violent earthquake that the foundations of the prison were shaken. At once all the prison doors flew open, and everyone's chains came loose. The jailer woke up, and when he saw the prison doors open, he drew his sword and was about to kill himself because he thought the prisoners had escaped. But Paul shouted, "Don't harm yourself! We are all here!"

The jailer called for lights, rushed in and fell trembling before Paul and Silas. He then brought them out and asked, "Sirs, what must I do to be saved?"

They replied, "Believe in the Lord Jesus, and you will be saved — you and your household." Then they spoke the word of the Lord to him and to all the others in his house. At that hour of the night the jailer took them and washed their wounds; then immediately he and all his household were baptized. The jailer brought them into his house and set a meal before them; he was filled with joy because he had come to believe in God — he and his whole household.

When it was daylight, the magistrates sent their officers to the jailer with the order: "Release those men." ACTS 16:16–35

Worshiping Together

A relationship with God can be both a private and a personal experience, but much of worship is meant to be practiced in community. God is a community within himself (Father, Son and Holy Spirit), and his Word encourages us to gather with other believers to encourage one another, pray together and remember God's love for us. After the crucifixion, death and resurrection of Jesus, the dynamics of communal worship changed drastically. Animal sacrifices are no longer required to restore a relationship with God. Instead, through Jesus' blood, shed as a voluntary sacrifice, those who repent and accept Jesus as their Savior will have their sins forgiven.

The law is only a shadow of the good things that are coming — not the realities themselves. For this reason it can never, by the same sacrifices repeated endlessly year after year, make perfect those who draw near to worship. Otherwise, would they not have stopped being offered? For the worshipers would have been cleansed once for all, and would no longer have felt guilty for their sins. But those sacrifices are an annual reminder of sins. It is impossible for the blood of bulls and goats to take away sins.

Therefore, when Christ came into the world, he said:

> "Sacrifice and offering you did not desire,
>   but a body you prepared for me;
> with burnt offerings and sin offerings
>   you were not pleased.
> Then I said, 'Here I am — it is written about me
>   in the scroll —
> I have come to do your will, my God.'"

First he said, "Sacrifices and offerings, burnt offerings and sin offerings you did not desire, nor were you pleased with them" — though they were offered in accordance with the law. Then he said, "Here I am, I have come to do your will." He sets aside the first to establish the second. And by that will, we have been made holy through the sacrifice of the body of Jesus Christ once for all.

Day after day every priest stands and performs his religious duties; again and again he offers the same sacrifices, which can never take away sins. But when this priest had offered for all time one sacrifice for sins, he sat down at the right hand of God, and since that time he waits for his enemies to be made his footstool. For by one sacrifice he has made perfect forever those who are being made holy.

The Holy Spirit also testifies to us about this. First he says:

> "This is the covenant I will make with them
>   after that time, says the Lord.
> I will put my laws in their hearts,
>   and I will write them on their minds."

Then he adds:

> "Their sins and lawless acts
>   I will remember no more."

And where these have been forgiven, sacrifice for sin is no longer necessary.

Therefore, brothers and sisters, since we have confidence to enter the Most Holy Place by the blood of Jesus, by a new and living way opened for us through the curtain, that is, his body, and since we have a great priest [Jesus] over the house of God, let us draw near to God with a sincere heart and with the full assurance that faith brings, having our hearts sprinkled to cleanse us from a guilty conscience and having our bodies washed with pure water. Let us hold unswervingly to the hope we profess, for he who promised is faithful. And let us consider how we may spur one another on toward love and good deeds, not giving up meeting together, as some are in the habit of doing, but encouraging one another — and all the more as you see the Day approaching.   Hᴇʙʀᴇᴡs 10:1–25

The Lord's Supper essentially replaced the practice of animal sacrifice in the New Testament church. When believers gather to pray, sing and learn, they break bread and share a cup of wine as a way of remembering Christ's love for them. Jesus introduced this new practice to his disciples the night before his crucifixion.

Then came the day of Unleavened Bread on which the Passover lamb had to be sacrificed. Jesus sent Peter and John, saying, "Go and make preparations for us to eat the Passover."

"Where do you want us to prepare for it?" they asked.

He replied, "As you enter the city, a man carrying a jar of water will meet you. Follow him to the house that he enters, and say to the owner of the house, 'The Teacher asks: Where is the guest room, where I may eat the Passover with my disciples?' He will show you a large room upstairs, all furnished. Make preparations there."

They left and found things just as Jesus had told them. So they prepared the Passover.

When the hour came, Jesus and his apostles reclined at the table. And he said to them, "I have eagerly desired to eat this Passover with you before I suffer. For I tell you, I will not eat it again until it finds fulfillment in the kingdom of God."

After taking the cup, he gave thanks and said, "Take this and divide it among you. For I tell you I will not drink again from the fruit of the vine until the kingdom of God comes."

And he took bread, gave thanks and broke it, and gave it to them, saying, "This is my body given for you; do this in remembrance of me."

In the same way, after the supper he took the cup, saying, "This cup is the new covenant in my blood, which is poured out for you. But the hand of him who is going to betray me is with mine on the table. The Son of Man will go as it has been decreed. But woe to that man who betrays him!" They began to question among themselves which of them it might be who would do this.

A dispute also arose among them as to which of them was considered to be greatest. Jesus said to them, "The kings of the Gentiles lord it over them; and those who exercise authority over them call themselves Benefactors. But you are not to be like that. Instead, the greatest among you should be like the youngest, and the one who rules like the one who serves. For who is greater, the one who is at the table or the one who serves? Is it not the one who is at the table? But I am among you as one who serves. You are those who have stood by me in my trials. And I confer on you a kingdom, just as my Father conferred one on me, so that you may eat and drink at my table in my kingdom and sit on thrones, judging the twelve tribes of Israel."   LUKE 22:7–30

Of course, believers can also honor Jesus' sacrifice every day in the way that they choose to live. While under house arrest in Rome, the apostle Paul wrote to the Christians in the city of Colossae. He encouraged them to throw off their old self-centered way of living and commit to live their new lives solely for the purpose of worshiping and serving God. Paul's instructions were not addressed to individual worshipers, but to the worship community as a whole.

Since, then, you have been raised with Christ, set your hearts on things above, where Christ is, seated at the right hand of God. Set your minds on things above, not on earthly things. For you died, and your life is now hidden with Christ in God. When Christ, who is your life, appears, then you also will appear with him in glory.

Put to death, therefore, whatever belongs to your earthly nature: sexual immorality, impurity, lust, evil desires and greed, which is idolatry. Because of these, the wrath of God is coming. You used to walk in these ways, in the life you once lived. But now you must also rid yourselves of all such things as these: anger, rage, malice, slander, and filthy language from your lips. Do not lie to each other, since you have taken off your old self with its practices and have put on the new self, which is being renewed in knowledge in the image of its Creator. Here there is no Gentile or Jew, circumcised or uncircumcised, barbarian, Scythian, slave or free, but Christ is all, and is in all.

Therefore, as God's chosen people, holy and dearly loved, clothe yourselves with compassion, kindness, humility, gentleness and patience. Bear with each other and forgive one another if any of you has a grievance against someone. Forgive as the Lord forgave you. And over all these virtues put on love, which binds them all together in perfect unity.

Let the peace of Christ rule in your hearts, since as members of one body you were called to peace. And be thankful. Let the message of Christ dwell among you richly as you teach and admonish one another with all wisdom through psalms, hymns, and songs from the Spirit, singing to God with gratitude in your hearts. And whatever you do, whether in word or deed, do it all in the name of the Lord Jesus, giving thanks to God the Father through him.

COLOSSIANS 3:1–17

ACT

CHAPTER

12

Prayer

KEY IDEA

I pray to God to know him,
to find direction for my life and
to lay my requests before him.

KEY VERSE

If I had cherished sin in my heart,
the Lord would not have listened;
but God has surely listened and has heard my prayer.
Praise be to God, who has not rejected my prayer
or withheld his love from me!

Psalm 66:18 – 20

Our God is a personal God who desires a real relationship with us. He is not a distant, cosmic being, but a good father who longs to interact with his children. Prayer is a conversation between God and his people. We serve a God who is not threatened by our questions and doubts. We don't have to put on a false persona to please him. He permits us to be honest about our fears, our feelings of isolation and our disappointments. When we rehearse our story before him, we see his good involvement in our lives.

> Come and hear, all you who fear God;
>   let me tell you what he has done for me.
> I cried out to him with my mouth;
>   his praise was on my tongue.
> If I had cherished sin in my heart,
>   the Lord would not have listened;
> but God has surely listened
>   and has heard my prayer.
> Praise be to God,
>   who has not rejected my prayer
>   or withheld his love from me!   PSALM 66:16–20

THE MODEL PRAYER LIFE

Scripture contains many examples of men and women who demonstrated a healthy prayer life, but there is a no more perfect model than Jesus. Spending time in prayer with the Father gave him the strength and guidance he needed to fulfill his purpose in coming to earth. Jesus consistently sought direction and support from his Father, as we see on two occasions from early in his ministry.

After sunset the people brought to Jesus all the sick and demon-possessed. The whole town gathered at the door, and Jesus healed many who had various diseases. He also drove out many demons, but he would not let the demons speak because they knew who he was.

Very early in the morning, while it was still dark, Jesus got up, left the house and went off to a solitary place, where he prayed.

MARK 1:32–35

And also ...

Jesus went out to a mountainside to pray, and spent the night praying to God. When morning came, he called his disciples to him and chose twelve of them, whom he also designated apostles: Simon (whom he named Peter), his brother Andrew, James, John, Philip, Bartholomew, Matthew, Thomas, James son of Alphaeus, Simon who was called the Zealot, Judas son of James, and Judas Iscariot, who became a traitor. LUKE 6:12–16

Sometime after choosing his disciples, Jesus received news that Herod had cruelly beheaded Jesus' cousin John the Baptist. Upon hearing the news and to avoid the threat of Herod, Jesus went by boat with his disciples to a solitary place. However, thousands of followers got ahead of the group and met them when they landed ashore. Despite the interruption to his plans, Jesus took compassion on the people and taught them about the kingdom of God. At the end of the day, when the people were hungry, the disciples told Jesus to send them away. But Jesus miraculously turned five loaves and two fish into a meal that would feed five thousand people. On the heels of the emotional loss of John and a long day of ministering, Jesus retreated to a secluded place to spend time with the Father.

Jesus directed [the disciples] to have all the people sit down in groups on the green grass. So they sat down in groups of hundreds and fifties. Taking the five loaves and the two fish and looking up to heaven, he gave thanks and broke the loaves. Then he gave them to his disciples to distribute to the people. He also divided the two fish among them all. They all ate and were satisfied, and the disciples picked up twelve basketfuls of broken pieces of bread and fish. The number of the men who had eaten was five thousand.

Immediately Jesus made his disciples get into the boat and go on ahead of him to Bethsaida, while he dismissed the crowd. After leaving them, he went up on a mountainside to pray. MARK 6:39–46

As Jesus approached the conclusion of his ministry, he knew it would culminate on a cross, which typically meant a slow and excruciatingly painful death. Knowing what he was about to endure, Jesus appealed to God for a way around the torture, though he remained unflinching in his resolve to accomplish his Father's will.

Jesus went with his disciples to a place called Gethsemane, and he said to them, "Sit here while I go over there and pray." He took Peter and the two sons of Zebedee along with him, and he began to be sorrowful and troubled. Then he said to them, "My soul is overwhelmed with sorrow to the point of death. Stay here and keep watch with me."

Going a little farther, he fell with his face to the ground and prayed, "My Father, if it is possible, may this cup be taken from me. Yet not as I will, but as you will."

Then he returned to his disciples and found them sleeping. "Couldn't you men keep watch with me for one hour?" he asked Peter. "Watch and pray so that you will not fall into temptation. The spirit is willing, but the flesh is weak."

He went away a second time and prayed, "My Father, if it is not possible for this cup to be taken away unless I drink it, may your will be done."

When he came back, he again found them sleeping, because their eyes were heavy. So he left them and went away once more and prayed the third time, saying the same thing.

Then he returned to the disciples and said to them, "Are you still sleeping and resting? Look, the hour has come, and the Son of Man is delivered into the hands of sinners. Rise! Let us go! Here comes my betrayer!"
                                            MATTHEW 26:36–46

A WAY TO KNOW GOD

The book of Psalms is a collection of songs and prayers to God composed by many different authors over many years. These prayers reveal that people in the times of the Bible are very much like people today: they had hopes, fears, joy and pain. What is remarkable is that these writers spilled out what was on their hearts to the powerful God of the universe. They believed God wanted to know what they were experiencing and feeling. That same God longs to hear from us today as well.

How long, LORD? Will you forget me forever?
   How long will you hide your face from me?
How long must I wrestle with my thoughts
   and day after day have sorrow in my heart?
   How long will my enemy triumph over me?

Look on me and answer, LORD my God.
   Give light to my eyes, or I will sleep in death,
and my enemy will say, "I have overcome him,"
   and my foes will rejoice when I fall.

But I trust in your unfailing love;
   my heart rejoices in your salvation.
I will sing the LORD's praise,
   for he has been good to me.   PSALM 13:1–6

There is something therapeutic about an honest, lamenting prayer. Most laments start with anguish and pain, but as we remember who God is and what he has done for us, our lamentations become declarations of hope and trust. Please remember, prayer is not an eloquent performance. It's a personal conversation with the one true God who loves us and cares deeply for us.

I cried out to God for help;
   I cried out to God to hear me.
When I was in distress, I sought the Lord;
   at night I stretched out untiring hands,
   and I would not be comforted.

I remembered you, God, and I groaned;
   I meditated, and my spirit grew faint.
You kept my eyes from closing;
   I was too troubled to speak.
I thought about the former days,
   the years of long ago;
I remembered my songs in the night.
   My heart meditated and my spirit asked:

"Will the Lord reject forever?
   Will he never show his favor again?

Has his unfailing love vanished forever?
   Has his promise failed for all time?
Has God forgotten to be merciful?
   Has he in anger withheld his compassion?"

Then I thought, "To this I will appeal:
   the years when the Most High stretched out his right hand.
I will remember the deeds of the LORD;
   yes, I will remember your miracles of long ago.
I will consider all your works
   and meditate on all your mighty deeds."

Your ways, God, are holy.
   What god is as great as our God?
You are the God who performs miracles;
   you display your power among the peoples.
With your mighty arm you redeemed your people,
   the descendants of Jacob and Joseph.

The waters saw you, God,
   the waters saw you and writhed;
   the very depths were convulsed.
The clouds poured down water,
   the heavens resounded with thunder;
   your arrows flashed back and forth.
Your thunder was heard in the whirlwind,
   your lightning lit up the world;
   the earth trembled and quaked.
Your path led through the sea,
   your way through the mighty waters,
   though your footprints were not seen.

You led your people like a flock
   by the hand of Moses and Aaron.   PSALM 77:1–20

Perhaps it's because God leads his people like a flock that Solomon wrote that we should approach prayer with a priority to listen. In the Old Testament times, vows were of importance to the people. They represented trust and honor between two individuals. This only intensifies with our relationship with the great God of the universe. He gives us access to him, but we should not approach him with hollow words, frivolous or rote prayers, or promises made lightly.

Guard your steps when you go to the house of God. Go near to listen rather than to offer the sacrifice of fools, who do not know that they do wrong.

> Do not be quick with your mouth,
>> do not be hasty in your heart
>> to utter anything before God.
> God is in heaven
>> and you are on earth,
>> so let your words be few.
> A dream comes when there are many cares,
>> and many words mark the speech of a fool.

When you make a vow to God, do not delay to fulfill it. He has no pleasure in fools; fulfill your vow. It is better not to make a vow than to make one and not fulfill it. Do not let your mouth lead you into sin. And do not protest to the temple messenger, "My vow was a mistake." Why should God be angry at what you say and destroy the work of your hands? Much dreaming and many words are meaningless. Therefore fear God. ECCLESIASTES 5:1–7

A WAY TO FIND THE DIRECTION WE NEED

Like a needle on a compass, prayer helps us navigate life's toughest obstacles. Heroes of the faith from the beginning to the end of the Bible used prayer to determine their actions. Often the directions they received seemed a bit odd. For example, Gideon, who was by no means fearless, was asked to lead the Israelites into battle against an army that greatly outnumbered his own. God's clear directions allowed him to triumph. But before he set out, Gideon asked God to give him clarity on this overwhelming assignment. This is a good practice for all of us today. When we take our concerns and questions to God, he will provide the clarity we need.

The Israelites did evil in the eyes of the LORD, and for seven years he gave them into the hands of the Midianites. Because the power of Midian was so oppressive, the Israelites prepared shelters for themselves in mountain clefts, caves and strongholds. Whenever the Israelites planted their crops, the Midianites, Amalekites and other eastern peoples invaded the country. They camped on the land and ruined the crops all the way to Gaza and did not spare a living thing for Israel, neither sheep nor cattle nor donkeys. They came up with their livestock and their tents like swarms of locusts. It was impossible to count them or their camels; they invaded the land to ravage it. Midian so impoverished the Israelites that they cried out to the LORD for help.

When the Israelites cried out to the LORD because of Midian, he sent them a prophet, who said, "This is what the LORD, the God of Israel, says: I brought you up out of Egypt, out of the land of slavery. I rescued you from the hand of the Egyptians. And I delivered you from the hand of all your oppressors; I drove them out before you and gave you their land. I said to you, 'I am the LORD your God; do not worship the gods of the Amorites, in whose land you live.' But you have not listened to me."

The angel of the LORD came and sat down under the oak in Ophrah that belonged to Joash the Abiezrite, where his son Gideon was threshing wheat in a winepress to keep it from the Midianites. When the angel of the LORD appeared to Gideon, he said, "The LORD is with you, mighty warrior."

"Pardon me, my lord," Gideon replied, "but if the LORD is with us, why has all this happened to us? Where are all his wonders that our ancestors told us about when they said, 'Did not the LORD bring us up out of Egypt?' But now the LORD has abandoned us and given us into the hand of Midian."

The LORD turned to him and said, "Go in the strength you have and save Israel out of Midian's hand. Am I not sending you?"

"Pardon me, my lord," Gideon replied, "but how can I save Israel? My clan is the weakest in Manasseh, and I am the least in my family."

The LORD answered, "I will be with you, and you will strike down all the Midianites, leaving none alive."

Gideon replied, "If now I have found favor in your eyes, give me a sign that it is really you talking to me. Please do not go away until I come back and bring my offering and set it before you."

And the LORD said, "I will wait until you return."

Gideon went inside, prepared a young goat, and from an ephah of flour he made bread without yeast. Putting the meat in a basket and its broth in a pot, he brought them out and offered them to him under the oak.

The angel of God said to him, "Take the meat and the unleavened bread, place them on this rock, and pour out the broth." And Gideon did so. Then the angel of the LORD touched the meat and the unleavened bread with the tip of the staff that was in his hand. Fire flared from the rock, consuming the meat and the bread. And the angel of the LORD disappeared. When Gideon realized that it was the angel of the LORD, he exclaimed, "Alas, Sovereign LORD! I have seen the angel of the LORD face to face!"

But the LORD said to him, "Peace! Do not be afraid. You are not going to die."

So Gideon built an altar to the LORD there and called it The LORD Is Peace. To this day it stands in Ophrah of the Abiezrites.

That same night the LORD said to him, "Take the second bull from your father's herd, the one seven years old. Tear down your father's altar to Baal and cut down the Asherah pole beside it. Then build a proper kind of altar to the LORD your God on the top of this height. Using the wood of the Asherah pole that you cut down, offer the second bull as a burnt offering."

So Gideon took ten of his servants and did as the LORD told him. But because he was afraid of his family and the townspeople, he did it at night rather than in the daytime.

In the morning when the people of the town got up, there was Baal's altar, demolished, with the Asherah pole beside it cut down and the second bull sacrificed on the newly built altar!

They asked each other, "Who did this?"

When they carefully investigated, they were told, "Gideon son of Joash did it."

The people of the town demanded of Joash, "Bring out your son. He must die, because he has broken down Baal's altar and cut down the Asherah pole beside it."

But Joash replied to the hostile crowd around him, "Are you going to plead Baal's cause? Are you trying to save him? Whoever fights for him shall be put to death by morning! If Baal really is a god, he can defend himself when someone breaks down his altar." So because Gideon broke down Baal's altar, they gave him the name Jerub-Baal that day, saying, "Let Baal contend with him."

Now all the Midianites, Amalekites and other eastern peoples joined forces and crossed over the Jordan and camped in the Valley of Jezreel. Then the Spirit of the LORD came on Gideon, and he blew a trumpet, summoning the Abiezrites to follow him. He sent messengers throughout Manasseh, calling them to arms, and also into Asher, Zebulun and Naphtali, so that they too went up to meet them.

Gideon said to God, "If you will save Israel by my hand as you have promised — look, I will place a wool fleece on the threshing floor. If there is dew only on the fleece and all the ground is dry, then I will know that you will save Israel by my hand, as you said." And that is what happened. Gideon rose early the next day; he squeezed the fleece and wrung out the dew — a bowlful of water.

Then Gideon said to God, "Do not be angry with me. Let me make just one more request. Allow me one more test with the fleece, but this time make the fleece dry and let the ground be covered with dew." That night God did so. Only the fleece was dry; all the ground was covered with dew.

Early in the morning, Jerub-Baal (that is, Gideon) and all his men camped at the spring of Harod. The camp of Midian was north of them in the valley near the hill of Moreh. The LORD said to Gideon, "You have too many men. I cannot deliver Midian into their hands, or Israel would boast against me, 'My own strength has saved me.' Now announce to the army, 'Anyone who trembles with fear may turn back and leave Mount Gilead.'" So twenty-two thousand men left, while ten thousand remained.

But the LORD said to Gideon, "There are still too many men. Take them down to the water, and I will thin them out for you there. If I say, 'This one shall go with you,' he shall go; but if I say, 'This one shall not go with you,' he shall not go."

So Gideon took the men down to the water. There the LORD told him, "Separate those who lap the water with their tongues as a dog laps from those who kneel down to drink." Three hundred of them drank from cupped hands, lapping like dogs. All the rest got down on their knees to drink.

The LORD said to Gideon, "With the three hundred men that lapped I will save you and give the Midianites into your hands. Let all the others go home." So Gideon sent the rest of the Israelites home but kept the three hundred, who took over the provisions and trumpets of the others.

Now the camp of Midian lay below him in the valley. During that night the LORD said to Gideon, "Get up, go down against the camp, because I am going to give it into your hands. If you are afraid to attack, go down to the camp with your servant Purah and listen to what they are saying. Afterward, you will be encouraged to attack the camp." So he and Purah his servant went down to the outposts of the camp. The Midianites, the Amalekites and all the other eastern peoples had settled in the valley, thick as locusts. Their camels could no more be counted than the sand on the seashore.

Gideon arrived just as a man was telling a friend his dream. "I had a dream," he was saying. "A round loaf of barley bread came tumbling into the Midianite camp. It struck the tent with such force that the tent overturned and collapsed."

His friend responded, "This can be nothing other than the sword of Gideon son of Joash, the Israelite. God has given the Midianites and the whole camp into his hands."

When Gideon heard the dream and its interpretation, he bowed down and worshiped. He returned to the camp of Israel and called out, "Get up! The LORD has given the Midianite camp into your hands." Dividing the three hundred men into three companies, he placed trumpets and empty jars in the hands of all of them, with torches inside.

"Watch me," he told them. "Follow my lead. When I get to the edge of the camp, do exactly as I do. When I and all who are with me blow our trumpets, then from all around the camp blow yours and shout, 'For the LORD and for Gideon.'"

Gideon and the hundred men with him reached the edge of the camp at the beginning of the middle watch, just after they had changed the guard. They blew their trumpets and broke the jars that were in their hands. The three companies blew the trumpets and smashed the jars. Grasping the torches in their left hands and holding in their right hands the trumpets they were to blow, they shouted, "A sword for the LORD and for Gideon!" While each man held his position around the camp, all the Midianites ran, crying out as they fled.

When the three hundred trumpets sounded, the Lord caused the men throughout the camp to turn on each other with their swords. The army fled to Beth Shittah toward Zererah as far as the border of Abel Meholah near Tabbath. Israelites from Naphtali, Asher and all Manasseh were called out, and they pursued the Midianites. Gideon sent messengers throughout the hill country of Ephraim, saying, "Come down against the Midianites and seize the waters of the Jordan ahead of them as far as Beth Barah."

So all the men of Ephraim were called out and they seized the waters of the Jordan as far as Beth Barah. They also captured two of the Midianite leaders, Oreb and Zeeb. They killed Oreb at the rock of Oreb, and Zeeb at the winepress of Zeeb. They pursued the Midianites and brought the heads of Oreb and Zeeb to Gideon, who was by the Jordan. JUDGES 6:1—7:25

Like Gideon, shepherd-turned-king David experienced God's leading throughout his life. Psalm 25 captures David's passion for his Father God. Notice how David sought to know God personally by truthfully laying out his requests and seeking God's direction. It's an example we would be wise to follow.

In you, Lord my God,
 I put my trust.

I trust in you;
 do not let me be put to shame,
 nor let my enemies triumph over me.
No one who hopes in you
 will ever be put to shame,
but shame will come on those
 who are treacherous without cause.

Show me your ways, Lord,
 teach me your paths.
Guide me in your truth and teach me,
 for you are God my Savior,
 and my hope is in you all day long.

Remember, LORD, your great mercy and love,
for they are from of old.
Do not remember the sins of my youth
and my rebellious ways;
according to your love remember me,
for you, LORD, are good.

Good and upright is the LORD;
therefore he instructs sinners in his ways.
He guides the humble in what is right
and teaches them his way.
All the ways of the LORD are loving and faithful
toward those who keep the demands of his covenant.
For the sake of your name, LORD,
forgive my iniquity, though it is great.

Who, then, are those who fear the LORD?
He will instruct them in the ways they should
choose.
They will spend their days in prosperity,
and their descendants will inherit the land.
The LORD confides in those who fear him;
he makes his covenant known to them.
My eyes are ever on the LORD,
for only he will release my feet from the snare.

Turn to me and be gracious to me,
for I am lonely and afflicted.
Relieve the troubles of my heart
and free me from my anguish.
Look on my affliction and my distress
and take away all my sins.
See how numerous are my enemies
and how fiercely they hate me!

Guard my life and rescue me;
do not let me be put to shame,
for I take refuge in you.
May integrity and uprightness protect me,
because my hope, LORD, is in you.

Deliver Israel, O God,
  from all their troubles!   PSALM 25:1-22

A WAY TO LAY OUR REQUESTS BEFORE GOD

Because we are God's most prized creation, he wants to know the desires of our hearts. Scripture encourages us to, without hesitation, lay our requests before him. The Bible includes many stories in which God's people express their needs, wants and desires to God. For example, after God issued the order to destroy the sin-filled cities of Sodom and Gomorrah, where Abraham's nephew Lot and his family were living, Abraham engaged in a conversation with God that displays the freedom we have to talk honestly with him.

The LORD said, "The outcry against Sodom and Gomorrah is so great and their sin so grievous that I will go down and see if what they have done is as bad as the outcry that has reached me. If not, I will know."

The men turned away and went toward Sodom, but Abraham remained standing before the LORD. Then Abraham approached him and said: "Will you sweep away the righteous with the wicked? What if there are fifty righteous people in the city? Will you really sweep it away and not spare the place for the sake of the fifty righteous people in it? Far be it from you to do such a thing—to kill the righteous with the wicked, treating the righteous and the wicked alike. Far be it from you! Will not the Judge of all the earth do right?"

The LORD said, "If I find fifty righteous people in the city of Sodom, I will spare the whole place for their sake."

Then Abraham spoke up again: "Now that I have been so bold as to speak to the Lord, though I am nothing but dust and ashes, what if the number of the righteous is five less than fifty? Will you destroy the whole city for lack of five people?"

"If I find forty-five there," he said, "I will not destroy it."

Once again he spoke to him, "What if only forty are found there?"

He said, "For the sake of forty, I will not do it."

Then he said, "May the Lord not be angry, but let me speak. What if only thirty can be found there?"

He answered, "I will not do it if I find thirty there."

Abraham said, "Now that I have been so bold as to speak to the Lord, what if only twenty can be found there?"

He said, "For the sake of twenty, I will not destroy it."

Then he said, "May the Lord not be angry, but let me speak just once more. What if only ten can be found there?"

He answered, "For the sake of ten, I will not destroy it."

When the LORD had finished speaking with Abraham, he left, and Abraham returned home.   GENESIS 18:20–33

In addition to Abraham, King Hezekiah also spoke honestly before the Lord. Hezekiah was one of the few good kings in Judah during the era of the divided kingdom. He laid a personal request before God, and God answered with a powerful "yes."

In those days Hezekiah became ill and was at the point of death. The prophet Isaiah son of Amoz went to him and said, "This is what the LORD says: Put your house in order, because you are going to die; you will not recover."

Hezekiah turned his face to the wall and prayed to the LORD, "Remember, LORD, how I have walked before you faithfully and with wholehearted devotion and have done what is good in your eyes." And Hezekiah wept bitterly.

Before Isaiah had left the middle court, the word of the LORD came to him: "Go back and tell Hezekiah, the ruler of my people, 'This is what the LORD, the God of your father David, says: I have heard your prayer and seen your tears; I will heal you. On the third day from now you will go up to the temple of the LORD. I will add fifteen years to your life. And I will deliver you and this city from the hand of the king of Assyria. I will defend this city for my sake and for the sake of my servant David.'"

Then Isaiah said, "Prepare a poultice of figs." They did so and applied it to the boil, and he recovered.

Hezekiah had asked Isaiah, "What will be the sign that the LORD will heal me and that I will go up to the temple of the LORD on the third day from now?"

Isaiah answered, "This is the LORD's sign to you that the LORD will do what he has promised: Shall the shadow go forward ten steps, or shall it go back ten steps?"

"It is a simple matter for the shadow to go forward ten steps," said Hezekiah. "Rather, have it go back ten steps."

Then the prophet Isaiah called on the LORD, and the LORD made the shadow go back the ten steps it had gone down on the stairway of Ahaz.

2 KINGS 20:1–11

And our ultimate prayer model, Jesus, using tangible illustrations, encouraged his followers to be bold in their prayers.

One day Jesus was praying in a certain place. When he finished, one of his disciples said to him, "Lord, teach us to pray, just as John taught his disciples."

He said to them, "When you pray, say:

> "'Father,
> hallowed be your name,
> your kingdom come.
> Give us each day our daily bread.
> Forgive us our sins,
>   for we also forgive everyone who sins against us.
> And lead us not into temptation.'"

Then Jesus said to them, "Suppose you have a friend, and you go to him at midnight and say, 'Friend, lend me three loaves of bread; a friend of mine on a journey has come to me, and I have no food to offer him.' And suppose the one inside answers, 'Don't bother me. The door is already locked, and my children and I are in bed. I can't get up and give you anything.' I tell you, even though he will not get up and give you the bread because of friendship, yet because of your shameless audacity he will surely get up and give you as much as you need.

"So I say to you: Ask and it will be given to you; seek and you will find; knock and the door will be opened to you. For everyone who asks receives; the one who seeks finds; and to the one who knocks, the door will be opened.

"Which of you fathers, if your son asks for a fish, will give him a snake instead? Or if he asks for an egg, will give him a scorpion? If you then, though you are evil, know how to give good gifts to your children, how much more will your Father in heaven give the Holy Spirit to those who ask him!"

LUKE 11:1–13

The result of laying our requests before God is peace. The apostle Paul experienced this firsthand. He endured incredible hardships, including religious persecution, wrongful imprisonment and a catastrophic shipwreck. Paul wrote letters (the books of Galatians, Ephesians, Philippians, Colossians, 1 and 2 Thessalonians) to the churches he started throughout the Mediterranean, encouraging them to find peace in God through prayer.

Do not be anxious about anything, but in every situation, by prayer and petition, with thanksgiving, present your requests to God. And the peace of God, which transcends all understanding, will guard your hearts and your minds in Christ Jesus.

Finally, brothers and sisters, whatever is true, whatever is noble, whatever is right, whatever is pure, whatever is lovely, whatever is admirable — if anything is excellent or praiseworthy — think about such things. Whatever you have learned or received or heard from me, or seen in me — put it into practice. And the God of peace will be with you.   PHILIPPIANS 4:6–9

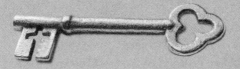

CHAPTER

13

Bible Study

KEY IDEA

I study the Bible to know God and his truth
and to find direction for my daily life.

KEY VERSE

For the word of God is alive and active.
Sharper than any double-edged sword, it penetrates
even to dividing soul and spirit, joints and marrow;
it judges the thoughts and attitudes of the heart.
Hebrews 4:12

The Bible is the actual Word of God, given to us by our good God. The ancient stories and words are "alive and active" and totally capable of leading us down the right path. But like a trust-worthy map, we must be diligent in studying it in order for it to help us get to where God wants to take us.

THE FIRST SCRIPTURES

Both Jews and Christians have traditionally regarded Moses as the author of the first five books of the Old Testament. Until the time of Moses, the words of God and the stories of his people were communicated orally from generation to generation. And even after Moses wrote these first portions of Scripture, the people didn't have access to their own complete copy. Before Moses died, the Lord led him to deliver farewell messages to the people—which are recorded in Deuteronomy. Parents were charged with the responsibility to share with their children God's principles and commandments. Moses also made a provision to ensure that everyone living in Israel would regularly and faithfully hear God's Word.

These are the commands, decrees and laws the LORD your God directed me to teach you to observe in the land that you are crossing the Jordan to possess, so that you, your children and their children after them may fear the LORD your God as long as you live by keeping all his decrees and commands that I give you, and so that you may enjoy long life. Hear, Israel, and be careful to obey so that it may go well with you and that you may increase greatly in a land flowing with milk and honey, just as the LORD, the God of your ancestors, promised you.

Hear, O Israel: The LORD our God, the LORD is one. Love the LORD your God with all your heart and with all your soul and with all your strength. These commandments that I give you today are to be on your hearts. Impress them on your children. Talk about them when you sit at home and when you walk along the road, when you lie down and when you get up. Tie them as symbols on your hands and bind them on your foreheads. Write them on the doorframes of your houses and on your gates.

When the LORD your God brings you into the land he swore to your fathers, to Abraham, Isaac and Jacob, to give you — a land with large, flourishing cities you did not build, houses filled with all kinds of good things you did not provide, wells you did not dig, and vineyards and olive groves you did not plant — then when you eat and are satisfied, be careful that you do not forget the LORD, who brought you out of Egypt, out of the land of slavery.

Fear the LORD your God, serve him only and take your oaths in his name. Do not follow other gods, the gods of the peoples around you; for the LORD your God, who is among you, is a jealous God and his anger will burn against you, and he will destroy you from the face of the land. Do not put the LORD your God to the test as you did at Massah. Be sure to keep the commands of the LORD your God and the stipulations and decrees he has given you. Do what is right and good in the LORD's sight, so that it may go well with you and you may go in and take over the good land the LORD promised on oath to your ancestors, thrusting out all your enemies before you, as the LORD said.

In the future, when your son asks you, "What is the meaning of the stipulations, decrees and laws the LORD our God has commanded you?" tell him: "We were slaves of Pharaoh in Egypt, but the LORD brought us out of Egypt with a mighty hand. Before our eyes the LORD sent signs and wonders — great and terrible — on Egypt and Pharaoh and his whole household. But he brought us out from there to bring us in and give us the land he promised on oath to our ancestors. The LORD commanded us to obey all these decrees and to fear the LORD our God, so that we might always prosper and be kept alive, as is the case today. And if we are careful to obey all this law before the LORD our God, as he has commanded us, that will be our righteousness." DEUTERONOMY 6:1–25

So Moses wrote down this law and gave it to the Levitical priests, who carried the ark of the covenant of the LORD, and to all the elders of Israel. Then Moses commanded them: "At the end of every seven years, in the year for canceling debts, during the Festival of Tabernacles, when all Israel comes to appear before the LORD your God at the place he will choose, you shall read this law before them in their hearing. Assemble the people — men, women and children, and the foreigners residing in your towns — so they can listen and learn to fear the LORD your God and follow carefully all the words of this law. Their children, who do not know this law, must hear it and learn to fear the LORD your God as long as you live in the land you are crossing the Jordan to possess."

DEUTERONOMY 31:9–13

After Moses' death, the mantle of leadership passed to Joshua. God visited Joshua to remind him of the importance of not only reading God's Word but also following it.

After the death of Moses the servant of the LORD, the LORD said to Joshua son of Nun, Moses' aide: "Moses my servant is dead. Now then, you and all these people, get ready to cross the Jordan River into the land I am about to give to them — to the Israelites. I will give you every place where you set your foot, as I promised Moses. Your territory will extend from the desert to Lebanon, and from the great river, the Euphrates — all the Hittite country — to the Mediterranean Sea in the west. No one will be able to stand against you all the days of your life. As I was with Moses, so I will be with you; I will never leave you nor forsake you. Be strong and courageous, because you will lead these people to inherit the land I swore to their ancestors to give them.

"Be strong and very courageous. Be careful to obey all the law my servant Moses gave you; do not turn from it to the right or to the left, that you may be successful wherever you go. Keep this Book of the Law always on your lips; meditate on it day and night, so that you may be careful to do everything written in it. Then you will be prosperous and successful. Have I not commanded you? Be strong and courageous. Do not be afraid; do not be discouraged, for the LORD your God will be with you wherever you go."

JOSHUA 1:1–9

The value of reflecting on God's Word was not lost on God's people. In 586 BC, Jerusalem was destroyed and the people of Judah went into exile in Babylon. In 537, the Jews began returning home. In 444, the restored community came together in Jerusalem to hear the proclamation of God's Word. Revival broke out as the people were filled with great emotion and resolve. With an insatiable appetite for Scripture, they discovered the Lord's desire for them to observe the Festival of Tabernacles. The great joy with which the people celebrated had not been seen since the days of Joshua nearly a thousand years earlier.

When the seventh month came and the Israelites had settled in their towns, all the people came together as one in the square before the Water Gate. They told Ezra the teacher of the Law to bring out the Book of the Law of Moses, which the LORD had commanded for Israel.

So on the first day of the seventh month Ezra the priest brought the Law before the assembly, which was made up of men and women and all who were able to understand. He read it aloud from daybreak till noon as he faced the square before the Water Gate in the presence of the men, women and others who could understand. And all the people listened attentively to the Book of the Law.

Ezra the teacher of the Law stood on a high wooden platform built for the occasion. Beside him on his right stood Mattithiah, Shema, Anaiah, Uriah, Hilkiah and Maaseiah; and on his left were Pedaiah, Mishael, Malkijah, Hashum, Hashbaddanah, Zechariah and Meshullam.

Ezra opened the book. All the people could see him because he was standing above them; and as he opened it, the people all stood up. Ezra praised the LORD, the great God; and all the people lifted their hands and responded, "Amen! Amen!" Then they bowed down and worshiped the LORD with their faces to the ground.

The Levites — Jeshua, Bani, Sherebiah, Jamin, Akkub, Shabbethai, Hodiah, Maaseiah, Kelita, Azariah, Jozabad, Hanan and Pelaiah — instructed the people in the Law while the people were standing there. They read from the Book of the Law of God, making it clear and giving the meaning so that the people understood what was being read.

Then Nehemiah the governor, Ezra the priest and teacher of the Law, and the Levites who were instructing the people said to them all, "This day is holy to the LORD your God. Do not mourn or weep." For all the people had been weeping as they listened to the words of the Law.

Nehemiah said, "Go and enjoy choice food and sweet drinks, and send some to those who have nothing prepared. This day is holy to our Lord. Do not grieve, for the joy of the LORD is your strength."

The Levites calmed all the people, saying, "Be still, for this is a holy day. Do not grieve."

Then all the people went away to eat and drink, to send portions of food and to celebrate with great joy, because they now understood the words that had been made known to them.

On the second day of the month, the heads of all the families, along with the priests and the Levites, gathered around Ezra the teacher to give attention to the words of the Law. They found written in the Law, which the LORD had commanded through Moses, that the Israelites were to live in temporary shelters during the festival of the seventh month and that they should proclaim this word and spread it throughout their towns and in Jerusalem: "Go out into the hill country and bring back branches from olive and wild olive trees, and from myrtles, palms and shade trees, to make temporary shelters" — as it is written.

So the people went out and brought back branches and built themselves temporary shelters on their own roofs, in their courtyards, in the courts of the house of God and in the square by the Water Gate and the one by the Gate of Ephraim. The whole company that had returned from exile built temporary shelters and lived in them. From the days of Joshua son of Nun until that day, the Israelites had not celebrated it like this. And their joy was very great.

Day after day, from the first day to the last, Ezra read from the Book of the Law of God. They celebrated the festival for seven days, and on the eighth day, in accordance with the regulation, there was an assembly.

On the twenty-fourth day of the same month, the Israelites gathered together, fasting and wearing sackcloth and putting dust on their heads. Those of Israelite descent had separated themselves from all foreigners. They stood in their places and confessed their sins and the sins of their ancestors. They stood where they were and read from the Book of the Law of the LORD their God for a quarter of the day, and spent another quarter in confession and in worshiping the LORD their God. NEHEMIAH 7:73—9:3

THE ROAD MAP FOR LIVING

God's instructions to Joshua included meditating on God's Word continually so that he might "do everything written in it." Like Joshua, the author of Psalm 19 seemed to know God's Word intimately. He relied on it to guide him, to help him in crisis, to gain understanding in confusing times, and to refresh him and give him joy.

> The law of the LORD is perfect,
>   refreshing the soul.
> The statutes of the LORD are trustworthy,
>   making wise the simple.
> The precepts of the LORD are right,
>   giving joy to the heart.
> The commands of the LORD are radiant,
>   giving light to the eyes.
> The fear of the LORD is pure,
>   enduring forever.
> The decrees of the LORD are firm,
>   and all of them are righteous.
>
> They are more precious than gold,
>   than much pure gold;
> they are sweeter than honey,
>   than honey from the honeycomb.
> By them your servant is warned;
>   in keeping them there is great reward.
> But who can discern their own errors?
>   Forgive my hidden faults.
> Keep your servant also from willful sins;
>   may they not rule over me.
> Then I will be blameless,
>   innocent of great transgression.
>
> May these words of my mouth and this meditation of
>   my heart
>   be pleasing in your sight,
>   LORD, my Rock and my Redeemer. PSALM 19:7–14

An unknown psalmist wrote Psalm 119, the longest chapter in the Bible, which centers on the value of reading and studying God's Word.

How can a young person stay on the path of
     purity?
   By living according to your word.
I seek you with all my heart;
   do not let me stray from your commands.
I have hidden your word in my heart
   that I might not sin against you.
Praise be to you, Lord;
   teach me your decrees.
With my lips I recount
   all the laws that come from your mouth.
I rejoice in following your statutes
   as one rejoices in great riches.
I meditate on your precepts
   and consider your ways.
I delight in your decrees;
   I will not neglect your word.

Be good to your servant while I live,
   that I may obey your word.
Open my eyes that I may see
   wonderful things in your law.
I am a stranger on earth;
   do not hide your commands from me.
My soul is consumed with longing
   for your laws at all times.
You rebuke the arrogant, who are accursed,
   those who stray from your commands.
Remove from me their scorn and contempt,
   for I keep your statutes.
Though rulers sit together and slander me,
   your servant will meditate on your decrees.
Your statutes are my delight;
   they are my counselors. Psalm 119:9–24

Teach me, Lord, the way of your decrees,
    that I may follow it to the end.
Give me understanding, so that I may keep your law
    and obey it with all my heart.
Direct me in the path of your commands,
    for there I find delight.
Turn my heart toward your statutes
    and not toward selfish gain.
Turn my eyes away from worthless things;
    preserve my life according to your word.
Fulfill your promise to your servant,
    so that you may be feared.
Take away the disgrace I dread,
    for your laws are good.
How I long for your precepts!
    In your righteousness preserve my life.   Psalm 119:33–40

Oh, how I love your law!
    I meditate on it all day long.
Your commands are always with me
    and make me wiser than my enemies.
I have more insight than all my teachers,
    for I meditate on your statutes.
I have more understanding than the elders,
    for I obey your precepts.
I have kept my feet from every evil path
    so that I might obey your word.
I have not departed from your laws,
    for you yourself have taught me.
How sweet are your words to my taste,
    sweeter than honey to my mouth!
I gain understanding from your precepts;
    therefore I hate every wrong path.

Your word is a lamp for my feet,
    a light on my path.
I have taken an oath and confirmed it,
    that I will follow your righteous laws.

I have suffered much;
    preserve my life, LORD, according to your word.
Accept, LORD, the willing praise of my mouth,
    and teach me your laws.
Though I constantly take my life in my hands,
    I will not forget your law.
The wicked have set a snare for me,
    but I have not strayed from your precepts.
Your statutes are my heritage forever;
    they are the joy of my heart.
My heart is set on keeping your decrees
    to the very end.   PSALM 119:97–112

AIDS TO UNDERSTANDING

The Bible is unlike any other narrative. It is God's story chock-full of amazing depth and application for our lives. Jesus reminds us that the condition of our heart is important when we hear or read God's Word. If we are open and receptive to God's words, they will take root in our lives and transform us.

Jesus went out of the house and sat by the lake. Such large crowds gathered around him that he got into a boat and sat in it, while all the people stood on the shore. Then he told them many things in parables, saying: "A farmer went out to sow his seed. As he was scattering the seed, some fell along the path, and the birds came and ate it up. Some fell on rocky places, where it did not have much soil. It sprang up quickly, because the soil was shallow. But when the sun came up, the plants were scorched, and they withered because they had no root. Other seed fell among thorns, which grew up and choked the plants. Still other seed fell on good soil, where it produced a crop — a hundred, sixty or thirty times what was sown. Whoever has ears, let them hear."

The disciples came to him and asked, "Why do you speak to the people in parables?"

He replied, "Because the knowledge of the secrets of the kingdom of heaven has been given to you, but not to them. Whoever has will be given more, and they will have an abundance. Whoever does not have, even what they have will be taken from them. This is why I speak to them in parables:

> "Though seeing, they do not see;
>> though hearing, they do not hear or understand.

In them is fulfilled the prophecy of Isaiah:

> " 'You will be ever hearing but never understanding;
>> you will be ever seeing but never perceiving.
> For this people's heart has become calloused;
>> they hardly hear with their ears,
>> and they have closed their eyes.
> Otherwise they might see with their eyes,
>> hear with their ears,
>> understand with their hearts
> and turn, and I would heal them.'

But blessed are your eyes because they see, and your ears because they hear. For truly I tell you, many prophets and righteous people longed to see what you see but did not see it, and to hear what you hear but did not hear it.

"Listen then to what the parable of the sower means: When anyone hears the message about the kingdom and does not understand it, the evil one comes and snatches away what was sown in their heart. This is the seed sown along the path. The seed falling on rocky ground refers to someone who hears the word and at once receives it with joy. But since they have no root, they last only a short time. When trouble or persecution comes because of the word, they quickly fall away. The seed falling among the thorns refers to someone who hears the word, but the worries of this life and the deceitfulness of wealth choke the word, making it unfruitful. But the seed falling on good soil refers to someone who hears the word and understands it. This is the one who produces a crop, yielding a hundred, sixty or thirty times what was sown." MATTHEW 13:1–23

But how does our heart open up to God in order to be receptive to his words? Jesus told his disciples that after he returned to heaven, the Holy Spirit would come to reside in them and to remind them of everything he had said. This same Spirit lives in all believers today.

"If you love me, keep my commands. And I will ask the Father, and he will give you another advocate to help you and be with you forever — the Spirit of truth. The world cannot accept him, because it neither sees him nor knows him. But you know him, for he lives with you and will be in you. I will not leave you as orphans; I will come to you. Before long, the world will not see me anymore, but you will see me. Because I live, you also will live. On that day you will realize that I am in my Father, and you are in me, and I am in you. Whoever has my commands and keeps them is the one who loves me. The one who loves me will be loved by my Father, and I too will love them and show myself to them."

Then Judas (not Judas Iscariot) said, "But, Lord, why do you intend to show yourself to us and not to the world?"

Jesus replied, "Anyone who loves me will obey my teaching. My Father will love them, and we will come to them and make our home with them. Anyone who does not love me will not obey my teaching. These words you hear are not my own; they belong to the Father who sent me.

"All this I have spoken while still with you. But the Advocate, the Holy Spirit, whom the Father will send in my name, will teach you all things and will remind you of everything I have said to you. Peace I leave with you; my peace I give you. I do not give to you as the world gives. Do not let your hearts be troubled and do not be afraid."

JOHN 14:15–27

The early church was devoted to the Word of God. However, at that time individuals did not have their own personal copies of the books of the Bible, so they had to rely heavily on the public reading of Scripture during their meetings. As promised by Jesus, the Holy Spirit came down to indwell believers.

One of the roles of the Holy Spirit is to illuminate the message of Scripture. It is through the Holy Spirit that we are able to understand the Bible's full meaning, accept it in our hearts and know how to apply it to our lives. The apostle Paul informed the church at Corinth of this truth.

When I came to you, I did not come with eloquence or human wisdom as I proclaimed to you the testimony about God. For I resolved to know nothing while I was with you except Jesus Christ and him crucified. I came to you in weakness with great fear and trembling. My message and my preaching were not with wise and persuasive words, but with a demonstration of the Spirit's power, so that your faith might not rest on human wisdom, but on God's power.

We do, however, speak a message of wisdom among the mature, but not the wisdom of this age or of the rulers of this age, who are coming to nothing. No, we declare God's wisdom, a mystery that has been hidden and that God destined for our glory before time began. None of the rulers of this age understood it, for if they had, they would not have crucified the Lord of glory. However, as it is written:

> "What no eye has seen,
>   what no ear has heard,
> and what no human mind has conceived" —
>   the things God has prepared for those who love him —

these are the things God has revealed to us by his Spirit.

The Spirit searches all things, even the deep things of God. For who knows a person's thoughts except their own spirit within them? In the same way no one knows the thoughts of God except the Spirit of God. What we have received is not the spirit of the world, but the Spirit who is from God, so that we may understand what God has freely given us. This is what we speak, not in words taught us by human wisdom but in words taught by the Spirit, explaining spiritual realities with Spirit-taught words. The person without the Spirit does not accept the things that come from the Spirit of God but considers them foolishness, and cannot understand them because they are discerned only through the Spirit. The person with the Spirit makes judgments about all things, but such a person is not subject to merely human judgments, for,

> "Who has known the mind of the Lord
>   so as to instruct him?"

But we have the mind of Christ.   1 CORINTHIANS 2:1–16

What we believe matters. Anchoring our beliefs in the truth of God's Word is critical for the believer. Because of this, teachers of God's Word have a special calling to deliver the teachings of God's Word correctly, to call out false teachings and to model the message before the congregation and community.

The Spirit clearly says that in later times some will abandon the faith and follow deceiving spirits and things taught by demons. Such teachings come through hypocritical liars, whose consciences have been seared as with a hot iron. They forbid people to marry and order them to abstain from certain foods, which God created to be received with thanksgiving by those who believe and who know the truth. For everything God created is good, and nothing is to be rejected if it is received with thanksgiving, because it is consecrated by the word of God and prayer.

If you point these things out to the brothers and sisters, you will be a good minister of Christ Jesus, nourished on the truths of the faith and of the good teaching that you have followed. Have nothing to do with godless myths and old wives' tales; rather, train yourself to be godly. For physical training is of some value, but godliness has value for all things, holding promise for both the present life and the life to come. This is a trustworthy saying that deserves full acceptance. That is why we labor and strive, because we have put our hope in the living God, who is the Savior of all people, and especially of those who believe.

Command and teach these things. Don't let anyone look down on you because you are young, but set an example for the believers in speech, in conduct, in love, in faith and in purity. Until I come, devote yourself to the public reading of Scripture, to preaching and to teaching. Do not neglect your gift, which was given you through prophecy when the body of elders laid their hands on you.

Be diligent in these matters; give yourself wholly to them, so that everyone may see your progress. Watch your life and doctrine closely. Persevere in them, because if you do, you will save both yourself and your hearers. 1 TIMOTHY 4:1–16

Keep reminding God's people of these things. Warn them before God against quarreling about words; it is of no value, and only ruins those who listen. Do your best to present yourself to God as one approved, a worker who does not need to be ashamed and who correctly handles the word of truth. Avoid godless chatter, because those who indulge in it will become more and more ungodly.

2 TIMOTHY 2:14–16

A TRANSFORMED LIFE

The desired outcome of studying God's truth is transformation. It guides us along a path of maturity in Christ. We get into the Bible and the Bible turns around and gets into us and changes us for the good.

We have much to say about this, but it is hard to make it clear to you because you no longer try to understand. In fact, though by this time you ought to be teachers, you need someone to teach you the elementary truths of God's word all over again. You need milk, not solid food! Anyone who lives on milk, being still an infant, is not acquainted with the teaching about righteousness. But solid food is for the mature, who by constant use have trained themselves to distinguish good from evil.

Therefore let us move beyond the elementary teachings about Christ and be taken forward to maturity, not laying again the foundation of repentance from acts that lead to death, and of faith in God, instruction about cleansing rites, the laying on of hands, the resurrection of the dead, and eternal judgment. And God permitting, we will do so.   HEBREWS 5:11—6:3

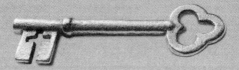

CHAPTER

14

Single-Mindedness

KEY IDEA

I focus on God and his priorities for my life.

KEY VERSE

But seek first his kingdom and his righteousness,
and all these things will be given to you as well.
Matthew 6:33

To be single-minded means to have one desire that trumps all others. One goal. One focus. From the beginning God made clear what his people's main focus should be — him.

PRINCIPLES OF SINGLE-MINDEDNESS

"I am the LORD your God, who brought you out of Egypt, out of the land of slavery. You shall have no other gods before me."

EXODUS 20:2–3

In the first of the Ten Commandments, God commanded the Israelites to serve him exclusively because he was worthy of their trust, as he had proved by delivering them from Egypt. Later, just before Moses died and the Israelites entered the promised land, God inspired Moses to remind the people of their single-minded calling.

These are the commands, decrees and laws the LORD your God directed me to teach you to observe in the land that you are crossing the Jordan to possess, so that you, your children and their children after them may fear the LORD your God as long as you live by keeping all his decrees and commands that I give you, and so that you may enjoy long life. Hear, Israel, and be careful to obey so that it may go well with you and that you may increase greatly in a land flowing with milk and honey, just as the LORD, the God of your ancestors, promised you.

Hear, O Israel: The LORD our God, the LORD is one. Love the LORD your God with all your heart and with all your soul and with all your strength. These commandments that I give you today are to be on your hearts. Impress them on your children. Talk about them when you sit at home and when you walk along the road, when you lie down and when you get up. Tie them as symbols on your hands and bind them on your foreheads. Write them on the doorframes of your houses and on your gates. DEUTERONOMY 6:1–9

God's people needed to submit fully to his authority and believe he could provide all they needed. It's this kind of trust that Jesus calls us to demonstrate as his disciples.

"Do not store up for yourselves treasures on earth, where moths and vermin destroy, and where thieves break in and steal. But store up for yourselves treasures in heaven, where moths and vermin do not destroy, and where thieves do not break in and steal. For where your treasure is, there your heart will be also.

"The eye is the lamp of the body. If your eyes are healthy, your whole body will be full of light. But if your eyes are unhealthy, your whole body will be full of darkness. If then the light within you is darkness, how great is that darkness!

"No one can serve two masters. Either you will hate the one and love the other, or you will be devoted to the one and despise the other. You cannot serve both God and money.

"Therefore I tell you, do not worry about your life, what you will eat or drink; or about your body, what you will wear. Is not life more than food, and the body more than clothes? Look at the birds of the air; they do not sow or reap or store away in barns, and yet your heavenly Father feeds them. Are you not much more valuable than they? Can any one of you by worrying add a single hour to your life?

"And why do you worry about clothes? See how the flowers of the field grow. They do not labor or spin. Yet I tell you that not even Solomon in all his splendor was dressed like one of these. If that is how God clothes the grass of the field, which is here today and tomorrow is thrown into the fire, will he not much more clothe you — you of little faith? So do not worry, saying, 'What shall we eat?' or 'What shall we drink?' or 'What shall we wear?' For the pagans run after all these things, and your heavenly Father knows that you need them. But seek first his kingdom and his righteousness, and all these things will be given to you as well."   MATTHEW 6:19–33

During the first century, the apostle Paul traveled from city to city teaching people about the gift of salvation through Jesus and how believers could single-mindedly follow Christ. In many cases, a combative group of religious leaders approached the new churches after Paul left and tried to undermine his authority and teaching. They boasted about their religious credentials and weighed down Paul's message with Jewish laws and traditions. This infuriated Paul, who then urged the believers to follow his example in keeping their focus steadfastly on Jesus.

Further, my brothers and sisters, rejoice in the Lord! It is no trouble for me to write the same things to you again, and it is a safeguard for you. Watch out for those dogs, those evildoers, those mutilators of the flesh. For it is we who are the circumcision, we who serve God by his Spirit, who boast in Christ Jesus, and who put no confidence in the flesh — though I myself have reasons for such confidence.

If someone else thinks they have reasons to put confidence in the flesh, I have more: circumcised on the eighth day, of the people of Israel, of the tribe of Benjamin, a Hebrew of Hebrews; in regard to the law, a Pharisee; as for zeal, persecuting the church; as for righteousness based on the law, faultless.

But whatever were gains to me I now consider loss for the sake of Christ. What is more, I consider everything a loss because of the surpassing worth of knowing Christ Jesus my Lord, for whose sake I have lost all things. I consider them garbage, that I may gain Christ and be found in him, not having a righteousness of my own that comes from the law, but that which is through faith in Christ — the righteousness that comes from God on the basis of faith. I want to know Christ — yes, to know the power of his resurrection and participation in his sufferings, becoming like him in his death, and so, somehow, attaining to the resurrection from the dead.

Not that I have already obtained all this, or have already arrived at my goal, but I press on to take hold of that for which Christ Jesus took hold of me. Brothers and sisters, I do not consider myself yet to have taken hold of it. But one thing I do: Forgetting what is behind and straining toward what is ahead, I press on toward the goal to win the prize for which God has called me heavenward in Christ Jesus.   PHILIPPIANS 3:1–14

PROFILES OF SINGLE-MINDEDNESS

King Jehoshaphat of the southern kingdom of Judah faced a tremendous challenge. His land was threatened by a hostile army. Rather than being overcome by fear, Jehoshaphat led the people to turn to the Lord in single-minded and wholehearted trust.

The Moabites and Ammonites with some of the Meunites came to wage war against Jehoshaphat.

Some people came and told Jehoshaphat, "A vast army is coming against you from Edom, from the other side of the Dead Sea. It is already in Hazezon Tamar" (that is, En Gedi). Alarmed, Jehoshaphat resolved to inquire of the LORD, and he proclaimed a fast for all Judah. The people of Judah came together to seek help from the LORD; indeed, they came from every town in Judah to seek him.

Then Jehoshaphat stood up in the assembly of Judah and Jerusalem at the temple of the LORD in the front of the new courtyard and said:

"LORD, the God of our ancestors, are you not the God who is in heaven? You rule over all the kingdoms of the nations. Power and might are in your hand, and no one can withstand you. Our God, did you not drive out the inhabitants of this land before your people Israel and give it forever to the descendants of Abraham your friend? They have lived in it and have built in it a sanctuary for your Name, saying, 'If calamity comes upon us, whether the sword of judgment, or plague or famine, we will stand in your presence before this temple that bears your Name and will cry out to you in our distress, and you will hear us and save us.'

"But now here are men from Ammon, Moab and Mount Seir, whose territory you would not allow Israel to invade when they came from Egypt; so they turned away from them and did not destroy them. See how they are repaying us by coming to drive us out of the possession you gave us as an inheritance. Our God, will you not judge them? For we have no power to face this vast army that is attacking us. We do not know what to do, but our eyes are on you."

All the men of Judah, with their wives and children and little ones, stood there before the LORD.

Then the Spirit of the LORD came on Jahaziel son of Zechariah, the son of Benaiah, the son of Jeiel, the son of Mattaniah, a Levite and descendant of Asaph, as he stood in the assembly.

He said: "Listen, King Jehoshaphat and all who live in Judah and Jerusalem! This is what the LORD says to you: 'Do not be afraid or discouraged because of this vast army. For the battle is not yours, but God's. Tomorrow march down against them. They will be climbing up by the Pass of Ziz, and you will find them at the end of the gorge in the Desert of Jeruel. You will not have to fight this battle. Take up your positions; stand firm and see the deliverance the LORD will give you, Judah and Jerusalem. Do not be afraid; do not be discouraged. Go out to face them tomorrow, and the LORD will be with you.'"

Jehoshaphat bowed down with his face to the ground, and all the people of Judah and Jerusalem fell down in worship before the LORD. Then some Levites from the Kohathites and Korahites stood up and praised the LORD, the God of Israel, with a very loud voice.

Early in the morning they left for the Desert of Tekoa. As they set out, Jehoshaphat stood and said, "Listen to me, Judah and people of Jerusalem! Have faith in the LORD your God and you will be upheld; have faith in his prophets and you will be successful." After consulting the people, Jehoshaphat appointed men to sing to the LORD and to praise him for the splendor of his holiness as they went out at the head of the army, saying:

> "Give thanks to the LORD,
>   for his love endures forever."

As they began to sing and praise, the LORD set ambushes against the men of Ammon and Moab and Mount Seir who were invading Judah, and they were defeated. The Ammonites and Moabites rose up against the men from Mount Seir to destroy and annihilate them. After they finished slaughtering the men from Seir, they helped to destroy one another.

When the men of Judah came to the place that overlooks the desert and looked toward the vast army, they saw only dead bodies lying on the ground; no one had escaped. So Jehoshaphat and his men went to carry off their plunder, and they found among them a great amount of equipment and clothing and also articles of value — more than they could take away. There was so much plunder that it took three days to collect it. On the fourth day they assembled in the Valley of Berakah, where they praised the LORD. This is why it is called the Valley of Berakah to this day.

Then, led by Jehoshaphat, all the men of Judah and Jerusalem returned joyfully to Jerusalem, for the LORD had given them cause to rejoice over their enemies. They entered Jerusalem and went to the temple of the LORD with harps and lyres and trumpets.

The fear of God came on all the surrounding kingdoms when they heard how the LORD had fought against the enemies of Israel.

And the kingdom of Jehoshaphat was at peace, for his God had given him rest on every side.   2 CHRONICLES 20:1–30

> While Jehoshaphat certainly proved that his focus was on God, Jesus serves as the exemplary model for the type of single-mindedness God had in mind when he announced in the first of his Ten Commandments: "You shall have no other gods before me." Living out those ancient rules, Jesus didn't make choices based on his desires or anyone else's expectations. His sole goal was to live according to his Father's will.

When Jesus spoke again to the people, he said, "I am the light of the world. Whoever follows me will never walk in darkness, but will have the light of life."

The Pharisees challenged him, "Here you are, appearing as your own witness; your testimony is not valid."

Jesus answered, "Even if I testify on my own behalf, my testimony is valid, for I know where I came from and where I am going. But you have no idea where I come from or where I am going. You judge by human standards; I pass judgment on no one. But if I do judge, my decisions are true, because I am not alone. I stand with the Father, who sent me. In your own Law it is written that the testimony of two witnesses is true. I am one who testifies for myself; my other witness is the Father, who sent me."

Then they asked him, "Where is your father?"

"You do not know me or my Father," Jesus replied. "If you knew me, you would know my Father also." He spoke these words while teaching in the temple courts near the place where the offerings were put. Yet no one seized him, because his hour had not yet come.

Once more Jesus said to them, "I am going away, and you will look for me, and you will die in your sin. Where I go, you cannot come."

This made the Jews ask, "Will he kill himself? Is that why he says, 'Where I go, you cannot come'?"

But he continued, "You are from below; I am from above. You are of this world; I am not of this world. I told you that you would die in your sins; if you do not believe that I am he, you will indeed die in your sins."

"Who are you?" they asked.

"Just what I have been telling you from the beginning," Jesus replied. "I have much to say in judgment of you. But he who sent me is trustworthy, and what I have heard from him I tell the world."

They did not understand that he was telling them about his Father. So Jesus said, "When you have lifted up the Son of Man, then you will know that I am he and that I do nothing on my own but speak just what the Father has taught me. The one who sent me is with me; he has not left me alone, for I always do what pleases him." Even as he spoke, many believed in him.   JOHN 8:12–30

Unfortunately, Jesus' disciple Peter had a bit more trouble retaining his single-minded focus when he was met with distraction. Peter's experience is a good reminder of how we are to think about Jesus, and keep our eyes on him, even when our thoughts get sidetracked or we feel frightened.

Jesus made the disciples get into the boat and go on ahead of him to the other side, while he dismissed the crowd. After he had dismissed them, he went up on a mountainside by himself to pray. Later that night, he was there alone, and the boat was already a considerable distance from land, buffeted by the waves because the wind was against it.

Shortly before dawn Jesus went out to them, walking on the lake. When the disciples saw him walking on the lake, they were terrified. "It's a ghost," they said, and cried out in fear.

But Jesus immediately said to them: "Take courage! It is I. Don't be afraid."

"Lord, if it's you," Peter replied, "tell me to come to you on the water."

"Come," he said.

Then Peter got down out of the boat, walked on the water and came toward Jesus. But when he saw the wind, he was afraid and, beginning to sink, cried out, "Lord, save me!"

Immediately Jesus reached out his hand and caught him. "You of little faith," he said, "why did you doubt?"

And when they climbed into the boat, the wind died down. Then those who were in the boat worshiped him, saying, "Truly you are the Son of God."

When they had crossed over, they landed at Gennesaret. And when the men of that place recognized Jesus, they sent word to all the surrounding country. People brought all their sick to him and begged him to let the sick just touch the edge of his cloak, and all who touched it were healed.   MATTHEW 14:22–36

Ultimately, the disciples adopted Jesus' bold and unwavering devotion to God and his purposes.

The apostles performed many signs and wonders among the people. And all the believers used to meet together in Solomon's Colonnade. No one else dared join them, even though they were highly regarded by the people. Nevertheless, more and more men and women believed in the Lord and were added to their number. As a result, people brought the sick into the streets and laid them on beds and mats so that at least Peter's shadow might fall on some of them as he passed by. Crowds gathered also from the towns around Jerusalem, bringing their sick and those tormented by impure spirits, and all of them were healed.

Then the high priest and all his associates, who were members of the party of the Sadducees, were filled with jealousy. They arrested the apostles and put them in the public jail. But during the night an angel of the Lord opened the doors of the jail and brought them out. "Go, stand in the temple courts," he said, "and tell the people all about this new life."

At daybreak they entered the temple courts, as they had been told, and began to teach the people.

When the high priest and his associates arrived, they called together the Sanhedrin — the full assembly of the elders of Israel — and sent to the jail for the apostles. But on arriving at the jail, the officers did not find them there. So they went back and reported, "We found the jail securely locked, with the guards standing at the doors; but when we opened them, we found no one inside." On hearing this report, the captain of the temple guard and the chief priests were at a loss, wondering what this might lead to.

Then someone came and said, "Look! The men you put in jail are standing in the temple courts teaching the people." At that, the captain went with his officers and brought the apostles. They did not use force, because they feared that the people would stone them.

The apostles were brought in and made to appear before the Sanhedrin to be questioned by the high priest. "We gave you strict orders not to teach in this name," he said. "Yet you have filled Jerusalem with your teaching and are determined to make us guilty of this man's blood."

Peter and the other apostles replied: "We must obey God rather than human beings! The God of our ancestors raised Jesus from the dead — whom you killed by hanging him on a cross. God exalted him to his own right hand as Prince and Savior that he might bring Israel to repentance and forgive their sins. We are witnesses of these things, and so is the Holy Spirit, whom God has given to those who obey him."

When they heard this, they were furious and wanted to put them to death. But a Pharisee named Gamaliel, a teacher of the law, who was honored by all the people, stood up in the Sanhedrin and ordered that the men be put outside for a little while. Then he addressed the Sanhedrin: "Men of Israel, consider carefully what you intend to do to these men. Some time ago Theudas appeared, claiming to be somebody, and about four hundred men rallied to him. He was killed, all his followers were dispersed, and it all came to nothing. After him, Judas the Galilean appeared in the days of the census and led a band of people in revolt. He too was killed, and all his followers were scattered. Therefore, in the present case I advise you: Leave these men alone! Let them go! For if their purpose or activity is of human origin, it will fail. But if it is from God, you will not be able to stop these men; you will only find yourselves fighting against God."

His speech persuaded them. They called the apostles in and had them flogged. Then they ordered them not to speak in the name of Jesus, and let them go.

The apostles left the Sanhedrin, rejoicing because they had been counted worthy of suffering disgrace for the Name. Day after day, in the temple courts and from house to house, they never stopped teaching and proclaiming the good news that Jesus is the Messiah.   ACTS 5:12–42

PRODUCT OF SINGLE-MINDEDNESS

*Near the end of the book of Deuteronomy—and Moses' life—
the Lord called the Israelites to make a choice: Trust and obey his
commands or go their own way. Speaking through Moses, God
gave this message to his people. And what was the result of the
people's decision? Because they chose obedience, the following
seven years were the most fruitful years in Israel's history—the
Glory Days!*

You yourselves know how we lived in Egypt and how we passed
through the countries on the way here. You saw among them
their detestable images and idols of wood and stone, of silver and
gold. Make sure there is no man or woman, clan or tribe among
you today whose heart turns away from the LORD our God to go
and worship the gods of those nations; make sure there is no root
among you that produces such bitter poison.

When such a person hears the words of this oath and they
invoke a blessing on themselves, thinking, "I will be safe, even
though I persist in going my own way," they will bring disaster on
the watered land as well as the dry. The LORD will never be willing to forgive them; his wrath and zeal will burn against them. All
the curses written in this book will fall on them, and the LORD
will blot out their names from under heaven. The LORD will single
them out from all the tribes of Israel for disaster, according to all
the curses of the covenant written in this Book of the Law.

Your children who follow you in later generations and foreigners who come from distant lands will see the calamities that have
fallen on the land and the diseases with which the LORD has afflicted it. The whole land will be a burning waste of salt and sulfur — nothing planted, nothing sprouting, no vegetation growing
on it. It will be like the destruction of Sodom and Gomorrah, Admah and Zeboyim, which the LORD overthrew in fierce anger. All
the nations will ask: "Why has the LORD done this to this land?
Why this fierce, burning anger?"

And the answer will be: "It is because this people abandoned
the covenant of the LORD, the God of their ancestors, the covenant
he made with them when he brought them out of Egypt. They
went off and worshiped other gods and bowed down to them, gods

they did not know, gods he had not given them. Therefore the LORD's anger burned against this land, so that he brought on it all the curses written in this book. In furious anger and in great wrath the LORD uprooted them from their land and thrust them into another land, as it is now."

The secret things belong to the LORD our God, but the things revealed belong to us and to our children forever, that we may follow all the words of this law.

When all these blessings and curses I have set before you come on you and you take them to heart wherever the LORD your God disperses you among the nations, and when you and your children return to the LORD your God and obey him with all your heart and with all your soul according to everything I command you today, then the LORD your God will restore your fortunes and have compassion on you and gather you again from all the nations where he scattered you. Even if you have been banished to the most distant land under the heavens, from there the LORD your God will gather you and bring you back. He will bring you to the land that belonged to your ancestors, and you will take possession of it. He will make you more prosperous and numerous than your ancestors. The LORD your God will circumcise your hearts and the hearts of your descendants, so that you may love him with all your heart and with all your soul, and live. The LORD your God will put all these curses on your enemies who hate and persecute you. You will again obey the LORD and follow all his commands I am giving you today. Then the LORD your God will make you most prosperous in all the work of your hands and in the fruit of your womb, the young of your livestock and the crops of your land. The LORD will again delight in you and make you prosperous, just as he delighted in your ancestors, if you obey the LORD your God and keep his commands and decrees that are written in this Book of the Law and turn to the LORD your God with all your heart and with all your soul.

Now what I am commanding you today is not too difficult for you or beyond your reach. It is not up in heaven, so that you have to ask, "Who will ascend into heaven to get it and proclaim it to us so we may obey it?" Nor is it beyond the sea, so that you have to ask, "Who will cross the sea to get it and proclaim it to us so we may obey it?" No, the word is very near you; it is in your mouth and in your heart so you may obey it.

See, I set before you today life and prosperity, death and destruction. For I command you today to love the LORD your God, to walk in obedience to him, and to keep his commands, decrees and laws; then you will live and increase, and the LORD your God will bless you in the land you are entering to possess.

But if your heart turns away and you are not obedient, and if you are drawn away to bow down to other gods and worship them, I declare to you this day that you will certainly be destroyed. You will not live long in the land you are crossing the Jordan to enter and possess.

This day I call the heavens and the earth as witnesses against you that I have set before you life and death, blessings and curses. Now choose life, so that you and your children may live and that you may love the LORD your God, listen to his voice, and hold fast to him. For the LORD is your life, and he will give you many years in the land he swore to give to your fathers, Abraham, Isaac and Jacob. DEUTERONOMY 29:16—30:20

In the New Testament, the apostle Paul also challenged believers to a single-minded commitment to God. And with his exhortations came encouraging promises about the fruitful results of such devotion. As with Israel, so with us today: If we single-mindedly focus on Christ and his priorities for our lives, we will experience our Glory Days!

Therefore, I urge you, brothers and sisters, in view of God's mercy, to offer your bodies as a living sacrifice, holy and pleasing to God — this is your true and proper worship. Do not conform to the pattern of this world, but be transformed by the renewing of your mind. Then you will be able to test and approve what God's will is — his good, pleasing and perfect will. ROMANS 12:1–2

Since, then, you have been raised with Christ, set your hearts on things above, where Christ is, seated at the right hand of God. Set your minds on things above, not on earthly things. For you died, and your life is now hidden with Christ in God. When

Christ, who is your life, appears, then you also will appear with him in glory. COLOSSIANS 3:1–4

Let the peace of Christ rule in your hearts, since as members of one body you were called to peace. And be thankful. Let the message of Christ dwell among you richly as you teach and admonish one another with all wisdom through psalms, hymns, and songs from the Spirit, singing to God with gratitude in your hearts. And whatever you do, whether in word or deed, do it all in the name of the Lord Jesus, giving thanks to God the Father through him.

COLOSSIANS 3:15–17

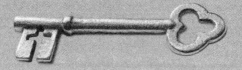

ACT

CHAPTER

15

Total Surrender

KEY IDEA

I dedicate my life to God's purposes.

KEY VERSE

I urge you, brothers and sisters, in view of God's mercy,
to offer your bodies as a living sacrifice,
holy and pleasing to God — this is
your true and proper worship.
Romans 12:1

A genuine decision to follow and obey God is a decision of total surrender. When God the Father offered up his Son for our redemption, he revealed how valuable we are to him. The gift of salvation was an act of total surrender by our Savior. Are you willing to change the way you live? Are you prepared to surrender your life for his purposes?

THE EXPECTATION

God is often referred to in the Old Testament as "jealous." This passionate description comes out of the language of love, similar to that of a marriage covenant. God is totally committed to us. He, in turn, asks us to be totally committed to him. He will not share our allegiance with anyone or anything else. He made this very clear to the Israelites when he etched the Ten Commandments on the stone tablets. The first three commandments clearly communicate the exclusivity of our relationship with God.

And God spoke all these words:

"I am the LORD your God, who brought you out of Egypt, out of the land of slavery.

"You shall have no other gods before me.

"You shall not make for yourself an image in the form of anything in heaven above or on the earth beneath or in the waters below. You shall not bow down to them or worship them; for I, the LORD your God, am a jealous God, punishing the children for the sin of the parents to the third and fourth generation of those who hate me, but showing love to a thousand generations of those who love me and keep my commandments.

"You shall not misuse the name of the LORD your God, for the LORD will not hold anyone guiltless who misuses his name."

EXODUS 20:1–7

PROFILES OF TOTAL SURRENDER

Despite having God's expectations written in stone, the Israelites failed to remain faithful. After many years of disobedience, the people suffered when God removed his protection. The northern kingdom of Israel was destroyed by the Assyrians and the southern kingdom of Judah was conquered by the Babylonians.

Before Judah was captured, some of the people were carried off in deportations. Along with Daniel, a small group of bright young men — Shadrach, Meshach and Abednego — were selected from the captives to be trained to serve the king. While in captivity, they were forced to make a crucial choice: worship the one true God or compromise and save their lives. They chose total surrender.

King Nebuchadnezzar made an image of gold, sixty cubits high and six cubits wide, and set it up on the plain of Dura in the province of Babylon. He then summoned the satraps, prefects, governors, advisers, treasurers, judges, magistrates and all the other provincial officials to come to the dedication of the image he had set up. So the satraps, prefects, governors, advisers, treasurers, judges, magistrates and all the other provincial officials assembled for the dedication of the image that King Nebuchadnezzar had set up, and they stood before it.

Then the herald loudly proclaimed, "Nations and peoples of every language, this is what you are commanded to do: As soon as you hear the sound of the horn, flute, zither, lyre, harp, pipe and all kinds of music, you must fall down and worship the image of gold that King Nebuchadnezzar has set up. Whoever does not fall down and worship will immediately be thrown into a blazing furnace."

Therefore, as soon as they heard the sound of the horn, flute, zither, lyre, harp and all kinds of music, all the nations and peoples of every language fell down and worshiped the image of gold that King Nebuchadnezzar had set up.

At this time some astrologers came forward and denounced the Jews. They said to King Nebuchadnezzar, "May the king live forever! Your Majesty has issued a decree that everyone who hears the sound of the horn, flute, zither, lyre, harp, pipe and all kinds of music must fall down and worship the image of gold, and that whoever does not fall down and worship will be thrown into a blazing furnace. But there are some Jews whom you have set over the affairs of the province of Babylon — Shadrach, Meshach and Abednego — who pay no attention to you, Your Majesty. They neither serve your gods nor worship the image of gold you have set up."

Furious with rage, Nebuchadnezzar summoned Shadrach, Meshach and Abednego. So these men were brought before the king, and Nebuchadnezzar said to them, "Is it true, Shadrach, Meshach and Abednego, that you do not serve my gods or worship the image of gold I have set up? Now when you hear the sound of the horn, flute, zither, lyre, harp, pipe and all kinds of music, if you are ready to fall down and worship the image I made, very good. But if you do not worship it, you will be thrown immediately into a blazing furnace. Then what god will be able to rescue you from my hand?"

Shadrach, Meshach and Abednego replied to him, "King Nebuchadnezzar, we do not need to defend ourselves before you in this matter. If we are thrown into the blazing furnace, the God we serve is able to deliver us from it, and he will deliver us from Your Majesty's hand. But even if he does not, we want you to know, Your Majesty, that we will not serve your gods or worship the image of gold you have set up."

Then Nebuchadnezzar was furious with Shadrach, Meshach and Abednego, and his attitude toward them changed. He ordered the furnace heated seven times hotter than usual and commanded some of the strongest soldiers in his army to tie up Shadrach, Meshach and Abednego and throw them into the blazing furnace. So these men, wearing their robes, trousers, turbans and other clothes, were bound and thrown into the blazing furnace. The king's command was so urgent and the furnace so hot that the flames of the fire killed the soldiers who took up Shadrach, Meshach and Abednego, and these three men, firmly tied, fell into the blazing furnace.

Then King Nebuchadnezzar leaped to his feet in amazement and asked his advisers, "Weren't there three men that we tied up and threw into the fire?"

They replied, "Certainly, Your Majesty."

He said, "Look! I see four men walking around in the fire, unbound and unharmed, and the fourth looks like a son of the gods."

Nebuchadnezzar then approached the opening of the blazing furnace and shouted, "Shadrach, Meshach and Abednego, servants of the Most High God, come out! Come here!"

So Shadrach, Meshach and Abednego came out of the fire, and

the satraps, prefects, governors and royal advisers crowded around them. They saw that the fire had not harmed their bodies, nor was a hair of their heads singed; their robes were not scorched, and there was no smell of fire on them.

Then Nebuchadnezzar said, "Praise be to the God of Shadrach, Meshach and Abednego, who has sent his angel and rescued his servants! They trusted in him and defied the king's command and were willing to give up their lives rather than serve or worship any god except their own God."   DANIEL 3:1–28

About 70 years after the first deportation of Jews to Babylon, the Babylonians were conquered by the Persians. Although King Cyrus of Persia decreed in 538 BC that the Jews could return to Judah, many of them chose not to go home. We know that Esther and her cousin Mordecai stayed in Susa under the rule of the Persian king Xerxes. When the reigning queen was removed from power, Esther (who kept her heritage a secret) was selected to replace her. Haman, the king's highest official, hated Mordecai because Mordecai refused to bow down and honor him. As revenge, Haman made plans to kill Mordecai and all the Jews in Xerxes' kingdom. Like Shadrach, Meshach and Abednego, Esther had a difficult decision to make: protect her people or protect her position as queen—and perhaps her own life. She chose total surrender.

King Xerxes honored Haman son of Hammedatha, the Agagite, elevating him and giving him a seat of honor higher than that of all the other nobles. All the royal officials at the king's gate knelt down and paid honor to Haman, for the king had commanded this concerning him. But Mordecai would not kneel down or pay him honor.

Then the royal officials at the king's gate asked Mordecai, "Why do you disobey the king's command?" Day after day they spoke to him but he refused to comply. Therefore they told Haman about it to see whether Mordecai's behavior would be tolerated, for he had told them he was a Jew.

When Haman saw that Mordecai would not kneel down or pay him honor, he was enraged. Yet having learned who Mordecai's people were, he scorned the idea of killing only Mordecai. Instead Haman looked for a way to destroy all Mordecai's people, the Jews, throughout the whole kingdom of Xerxes.

In the twelfth year of King Xerxes, in the first month, the month of Nisan, the *pur* (that is, the lot) was cast in the presence of Haman to select a day and month. And the lot fell on the twelfth month, the month of Adar.

Then Haman said to King Xerxes, "There is a certain people dispersed among the peoples in all the provinces of your kingdom who keep themselves separate. Their customs are different from those of all other people, and they do not obey the king's laws; it is not in the king's best interest to tolerate them. If it pleases the king, let a decree be issued to destroy them, and I will give ten thousand talents of silver to the king's administrators for the royal treasury."

So the king took his signet ring from his finger and gave it to Haman son of Hammedatha, the Agagite, the enemy of the Jews. "Keep the money," the king said to Haman, "and do with the people as you please."

Then on the thirteenth day of the first month the royal secretaries were summoned. They wrote out in the script of each province and in the language of each people all Haman's orders to the king's satraps, the governors of the various provinces and the nobles of the various peoples. These were written in the name of King Xerxes himself and sealed with his own ring. Dispatches were sent by couriers to all the king's provinces with the order to destroy, kill and annihilate all the Jews — young and old, women and children — on a single day, the thirteenth day of the twelfth month, the month of Adar, and to plunder their goods. A copy of the text of the edict was to be issued as law in every province and made known to the people of every nationality so they would be ready for that day.

The couriers went out, spurred on by the king's command, and the edict was issued in the citadel of Susa. The king and Haman sat down to drink, but the city of Susa was bewildered.

When Mordecai learned of all that had been done, he tore his clothes, put on sackcloth and ashes, and went out into the city, wailing loudly and bitterly. But he went only as far as the king's gate, because no one clothed in sackcloth was allowed to enter it. In every province to which the edict and order of the king came, there was great mourning among the Jews, with fasting, weeping and wailing. Many lay in sackcloth and ashes.

When Esther's eunuchs and female attendants came and told her about Mordecai, she was in great distress. She sent clothes for him to put on instead of his sackcloth, but he would not accept them. Then Esther summoned Hathak, one of the king's eunuchs assigned to attend her, and ordered him to find out what was troubling Mordecai and why.

So Hathak went out to Mordecai in the open square of the city in front of the king's gate. Mordecai told him everything that had happened to him, including the exact amount of money Haman had promised to pay into the royal treasury for the destruction of the Jews. He also gave him a copy of the text of the edict for their annihilation, which had been published in Susa, to show to Esther and explain it to her, and he told him to instruct her to go into the king's presence to beg for mercy and plead with him for her people.

Hathak went back and reported to Esther what Mordecai had said. Then she instructed him to say to Mordecai, "All the king's officials and the people of the royal provinces know that for any man or woman who approaches the king in the inner court without being summoned the king has but one law: that they be put to death unless the king extends the gold scepter to them and spares their lives. But thirty days have passed since I was called to go to the king."

When Esther's words were reported to Mordecai, he sent back this answer: "Do not think that because you are in the king's house you alone of all the Jews will escape. For if you remain silent at this time, relief and deliverance for the Jews will arise from another place, but you and your father's family will perish. And who knows but that you have come to your royal position for such a time as this?"

Then Esther sent this reply to Mordecai: "Go, gather together all the Jews who are in Susa, and fast for me. Do not eat or drink for three days, night or day. I and my attendants will fast as you do. When this is done, I will go to the king, even though it is against the law. And if I perish, I perish." ESTHER 3:1—4:16

THE COST OF TOTAL SURRENDER

A commitment to surrender completely to God's purposes is easy to say but hard to do. Jesus made this clear to his disciples and never masked the harsh reality they would encounter or the impact it would have on their lives. He also never shied away from difficult conversations, as is obvious from his interactions with Peter regarding the disciple's betrayal before Jesus' death. Through Peter, we learn that the cost of total surrender can sometimes feel like it's too much to bear.

Then [Jesus] said to them all: "Whoever wants to be my disciple must deny themselves and take up their cross daily and follow me. For whoever wants to save their life will lose it, but whoever loses their life for me will save it. What good is it for someone to gain the whole world, and yet lose or forfeit their very self? Whoever is ashamed of me and my words, the Son of Man will be ashamed of them when he comes in his glory and in the glory of the Father and of the holy angels."

LUKE 9:23–26

Then came the day of Unleavened Bread on which the Passover lamb had to be sacrificed. Jesus sent Peter and John, saying, "Go and make preparations for us to eat the Passover."

"Where do you want us to prepare for it?" they asked.

He replied, "As you enter the city, a man carrying a jar of water will meet you. Follow him to the house that he enters, and say to the owner of the house, 'The Teacher asks: Where is the guest room, where I may eat the Passover with my disciples?' He will show you a large room upstairs, all furnished. Make preparations there."

They left and found things just as Jesus had told them. So they prepared the Passover.

When the hour came, Jesus and his apostles reclined at the table. And he said to them, "I have eagerly desired to eat this Passover with you before I suffer. For I tell you, I will not eat it again until it finds fulfillment in the kingdom of God."

After taking the cup, he gave thanks and said, "Take this and divide it among you. For I tell you I will not drink again from the fruit of the vine until the kingdom of God comes."

And he took bread, gave thanks and broke it, and gave it to

them, saying, "This is my body given for you; do this in remembrance of me."

In the same way, after the supper he took the cup, saying, "This cup is the new covenant in my blood, which is poured out for you. But the hand of him who is going to betray me is with mine on the table. The Son of Man will go as it has been decreed. But woe to that man who betrays him!" They began to question among themselves which of them it might be who would do this.

A dispute also arose among them as to which of them was considered to be greatest. Jesus said to them, "The kings of the Gentiles lord it over them; and those who exercise authority over them call themselves Benefactors. But you are not to be like that. Instead, the greatest among you should be like the youngest, and the one who rules like the one who serves. For who is greater, the one who is at the table or the one who serves? Is it not the one who is at the table? But I am among you as one who serves. You are those who have stood by me in my trials. And I confer on you a kingdom, just as my Father conferred one on me, so that you may eat and drink at my table in my kingdom and sit on thrones, judging the twelve tribes of Israel.

"Simon, Simon, Satan has asked to sift all of you as wheat. But I have prayed for you, Simon, that your faith may not fail. And when you have turned back, strengthen your brothers."

But he replied, "Lord, I am ready to go with you to prison and to death."

Jesus answered, "I tell you, Peter, before the rooster crows today, you will deny three times that you know me."

Then Jesus asked them, "When I sent you without purse, bag or sandals, did you lack anything?"

"Nothing," they answered.

He said to them, "But now if you have a purse, take it, and also a bag; and if you don't have a sword, sell your cloak and buy one. It is written: 'And he was numbered with the transgressors'; and I tell you that this must be fulfilled in me. Yes, what is written about me is reaching its fulfillment."

The disciples said, "See, Lord, here are two swords."

"That's enough!" he replied.

Jesus went out as usual to the Mount of Olives, and his disciples followed him. On reaching the place, he said to them, "Pray that you will not fall into temptation." He withdrew about a stone's throw beyond them, knelt down and prayed, "Father, if you are willing, take this cup from me; yet not my will, but yours be done." An angel from heaven appeared to him and strengthened him. And being in anguish, he prayed more earnestly, and his sweat was like drops of blood falling to the ground.

When he rose from prayer and went back to the disciples, he found them asleep, exhausted from sorrow. "Why are you sleeping?" he asked them. "Get up and pray so that you will not fall into temptation."

While he was still speaking a crowd came up, and the man who was called Judas, one of the Twelve, was leading them. He approached Jesus to kiss him, but Jesus asked him, "Judas, are you betraying the Son of Man with a kiss?"

When Jesus' followers saw what was going to happen, they said, "Lord, should we strike with our swords?" And one of them struck the servant of the high priest, cutting off his right ear.

But Jesus answered, "No more of this!" And he touched the man's ear and healed him.

Then Jesus said to the chief priests, the officers of the temple guard, and the elders, who had come for him, "Am I leading a rebellion, that you have come with swords and clubs? Every day I was with you in the temple courts, and you did not lay a hand on me. But this is your hour — when darkness reigns."

Then seizing him, they led him away and took him into the house of the high priest. Peter followed at a distance. And when some there had kindled a fire in the middle of the courtyard and had sat down together, Peter sat down with them. A servant girl saw him seated there in the firelight. She looked closely at him and said, "This man was with him."

But he denied it. "Woman, I don't know him," he said.

A little later someone else saw him and said, "You also are one of them."

"Man, I am not!" Peter replied.

About an hour later another asserted, "Certainly this fellow was with him, for he is a Galilean."

Peter replied, "Man, I don't know what you're talking about!"

Just as he was speaking, the rooster crowed. The Lord turned and looked straight at Peter. Then Peter remembered the word the Lord had spoken to him: "Before the rooster crows today, you will disown me three times." And he went outside and wept bitterly.

LUKE 22:7–62

THE INSPIRATION OF MARTYRS

Despite his betrayal, Peter was graciously given a second chance to prove he was totally surrendered to God's purposes. After Jesus' resurrection, Jesus forgave and reinstated Peter to a leadership position. Peter boldly lived out his faith and, according to ancient tradition, was crucified upside down—perhaps because he didn't feel worthy of dying like Christ.

Stephen, however, was the first martyr of the Christian church. Although he was not an apostle, he played an important role in the early church by ministering to the widows in Jerusalem and by being a powerful witness for Jesus. His death triggered a tidal wave of persecution in the first century. Stephen was brought before the Sanhedrin where he put his total surrender to God courageously on display.

Now Stephen, a man full of God's grace and power, performed great wonders and signs among the people. Opposition arose, however, from members of the Synagogue of the Freedmen (as it was called) — Jews of Cyrene and Alexandria as well as the provinces of Cilicia and Asia — who began to argue with Stephen. But they could not stand up against the wisdom the Spirit gave him as he spoke.

Then they secretly persuaded some men to say, "We have heard Stephen speak blasphemous words against Moses and against God."

So they stirred up the people and the elders and the teachers of the law. They seized Stephen and brought him before the Sanhedrin. They produced false witnesses, who testified, "This fellow never stops speaking against this holy place and against the law. For we have heard him say that this Jesus of Nazareth will destroy this place and change the customs Moses handed down to us."

All who were sitting in the Sanhedrin looked intently at Stephen, and they saw that his face was like the face of an angel.

Then the high priest asked Stephen, "Are these charges true?"

To this he replied: "Brothers and fathers, listen to me! The God of glory appeared to our father Abraham while he was still in Mesopotamia, before he lived in Harran. 'Leave your country and your people,' God said, 'and go to the land I will show you.'

"So he left the land of the Chaldeans and settled in Harran. After the death of his father, God sent him to this land where you are now living. He gave him no inheritance here, not even enough ground to set his foot on. But God promised him that he and his descendants after him would possess the land, even though at that time Abraham had no child. God spoke to him in this way: 'For four hundred years your descendants will be strangers in a country not their own, and they will be enslaved and mistreated. But I will punish the nation they serve as slaves,' God said, 'and afterward they will come out of that country and worship me in this place.' Then he gave Abraham the covenant of circumcision. And Abraham became the father of Isaac and circumcised him eight days after his birth. Later Isaac became the father of Jacob, and Jacob became the father of the twelve patriarchs.

"Because the patriarchs were jealous of Joseph, they sold him as a slave into Egypt. But God was with him and rescued him from all his troubles. He gave Joseph wisdom and enabled him to gain the goodwill of Pharaoh king of Egypt. So Pharaoh made him ruler over Egypt and all his palace.

"Then a famine struck all Egypt and Canaan, bringing great suffering, and our ancestors could not find food. When Jacob heard that there was grain in Egypt, he sent our forefathers on their first visit. On their second visit, Joseph told his brothers who he was, and Pharaoh learned about Joseph's family. After this, Joseph sent for his father Jacob and his whole family, seventy-five in all. Then Jacob went down to Egypt, where he and our ancestors died. Their bodies were brought back to Shechem and placed in the tomb that Abraham had bought from the sons of Hamor at Shechem for a certain sum of money.

"As the time drew near for God to fulfill his promise to Abraham, the number of our people in Egypt had greatly increased. Then 'a new king, to whom Joseph meant nothing, came to power in Egypt.' He dealt treacherously with our people and oppressed our ancestors by forcing them to throw out their newborn babies so that they would die.

"At that time Moses was born, and he was no ordinary child. For three months he was cared for by his family. When he was placed outside, Pharaoh's daughter took him and brought him up as her own son. Moses was educated in all the wisdom of the Egyptians and was powerful in speech and action.

"When Moses was forty years old, he decided to visit his own people, the Israelites. He saw one of them being mistreated by an Egyptian, so he went to his defense and avenged him by killing the Egyptian. Moses thought that his own people would realize that God was using him to rescue them, but they did not. The next day Moses came upon two Israelites who were fighting. He tried to reconcile them by saying, 'Men, you are brothers; why do you want to hurt each other?'

"But the man who was mistreating the other pushed Moses aside and said, 'Who made you ruler and judge over us? Are you thinking of killing me as you killed the Egyptian yesterday?' When Moses heard this, he fled to Midian, where he settled as a foreigner and had two sons.

"After forty years had passed, an angel appeared to Moses in the flames of a burning bush in the desert near Mount Sinai. When he saw this, he was amazed at the sight. As he went over to get a closer look, he heard the Lord say: 'I am the God of your fathers, the God of Abraham, Isaac and Jacob.' Moses trembled with fear and did not dare to look.

"Then the Lord said to him, 'Take off your sandals, for the place where you are standing is holy ground. I have indeed seen the oppression of my people in Egypt. I have heard their groaning and have come down to set them free. Now come, I will send you back to Egypt.'

"This is the same Moses they had rejected with the words, 'Who made you ruler and judge?' He was sent to be their ruler and deliverer by God himself, through the angel who appeared to him in the bush. He led them out of Egypt and performed wonders and signs in Egypt, at the Red Sea and for forty years in the wilderness.

"This is the Moses who told the Israelites, 'God will raise up for you a prophet like me from your own people.' He was in the assembly in the wilderness, with the angel who spoke to him on Mount Sinai, and with our ancestors; and he received living words to pass on to us.

"But our ancestors refused to obey him. Instead, they rejected him and in their hearts turned back to Egypt. They told Aaron, 'Make us gods who will go before us. As for this fellow Moses who led us out of Egypt — we don't know what has happened to him!' That was the time they made an idol in the form of a calf. They brought sacrifices to it and reveled in what their own hands had made. But God turned away from them and gave them over to the worship of the sun, moon and stars. This agrees with what is written in the book of the prophets:

> "'Did you bring me sacrifices and offerings
>   forty years in the wilderness, people of Israel?
> You have taken up the tabernacle of Molek
>   and the star of your god Rephan,
>   the idols you made to worship.
> Therefore I will send you into exile' beyond Babylon.

"Our ancestors had the tabernacle of the covenant law with them in the wilderness. It had been made as God directed Moses, according to the pattern he had seen. After receiving the tabernacle, our ancestors under Joshua brought it with them when they took the land from the nations God drove out before them. It remained in the land until the time of David, who enjoyed God's favor and asked that he might provide a dwelling place for the God of Jacob. But it was Solomon who built a house for him.

"However, the Most High does not live in houses made by human hands. As the prophet says:

> "'Heaven is my throne,
>   and the earth is my footstool.
> What kind of house will you build for me?
>
>   says the Lord.
>   Or where will my resting place be?
> Has not my hand made all these things?'

"You stiff-necked people! Your hearts and ears are still uncircumcised. You are just like your ancestors: You always resist the

Holy Spirit! Was there ever a prophet your ancestors did not persecute? They even killed those who predicted the coming of the Righteous One. And now you have betrayed and murdered him — you who have received the law that was given through angels but have not obeyed it."

When the members of the Sanhedrin heard this, they were furious and gnashed their teeth at him. But Stephen, full of the Holy Spirit, looked up to heaven and saw the glory of God, and Jesus standing at the right hand of God. "Look," he said, "I see heaven open and the Son of Man standing at the right hand of God."

At this they covered their ears and, yelling at the top of their voices, they all rushed at him, dragged him out of the city and began to stone him. Meanwhile, the witnesses laid their coats at the feet of a young man named Saul.

While they were stoning him, Stephen prayed, "Lord Jesus, receive my spirit." Then he fell on his knees and cried out, "Lord, do not hold this sin against them." When he had said this, he fell asleep.   ACTS 6:8—7:60

Another martyr of the early church was the apostle Paul. While traveling throughout the Roman Empire on numerous missionary journeys, Paul formed countless close friendships and made some serious enemies. Knowing that severe hardship was in his future, he met with many believers for what he assumed would be one last time.

Through the Spirit they urged Paul not to go on to Jerusalem. When it was time to leave, we left and continued on our way. All of them, including wives and children, accompanied us out of the city, and there on the beach we knelt to pray. After saying goodbye to each other, we went aboard the ship, and they returned home.

We continued our voyage from Tyre and landed at Ptolemais, where we greeted the brothers and sisters and stayed with them for a day. Leaving the next day, we reached Caesarea and stayed at the house of Philip the evangelist, one of the Seven. He had four unmarried daughters who prophesied.

After we had been there a number of days, a prophet named Agabus came down from Judea. Coming over to us, he took Paul's belt, tied his own hands and feet with it and said, "The Holy Spirit says, 'In this way the Jewish leaders in Jerusalem will bind the owner of this belt and will hand him over to the Gentiles.'"

When we heard this, we and the people there pleaded with Paul not to go up to Jerusalem. Then Paul answered, "Why are you weeping and breaking my heart? I am ready not only to be bound, but also to die in Jerusalem for the name of the Lord Jesus." When he would not be dissuaded, we gave up and said, "The Lord's will be done." ACTS 21:4–14

The predictions made by Agabus were correct. Paul was arrested in Jerusalem and spent a couple of years imprisoned in Caesarea before finally being shipped to Rome, where he remained under house arrest for a couple more years. Jesus promised that when we lose our life we will truly find it. Surrendering his life for God's purposes was Paul's ultimate goal. Will you make it yours?

Now I want you to know, brothers and sisters, that what has happened to me has actually served to advance the gospel. As a result, it has become clear throughout the whole palace guard and to everyone else that I am in chains for Christ. And because of my chains, most of the brothers and sisters have become confident in the Lord and dare all the more to proclaim the gospel without fear.

It is true that some preach Christ out of envy and rivalry, but others out of goodwill. The latter do so out of love, knowing that I am put here for the defense of the gospel. The former preach Christ out of selfish ambition, not sincerely, supposing that they can stir up trouble for me while I am in chains. But what does it matter? The important thing is that in every way, whether from false motives or true, Christ is preached. And because of this I rejoice.

Yes, and I will continue to rejoice, for I know that through your prayers and God's provision of the Spirit of Jesus Christ what has happened to me will turn out for my deliverance. I eagerly expect and hope that I will in no way be ashamed, but will have sufficient courage so that now as always Christ will be exalted in my body, whether by life or by death. For to me, to live is Christ and to die is gain. PHILIPPIANS 1:12–21

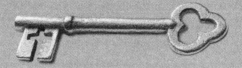

ACT

CHAPTER

16

Biblical Community

---------------------------------- KEY IDEA ----------------------------------

I fellowship with Christians to accomplish God's purposes
in my life, in the lives of others and in the world.

---------------------------------- KEY VERSE ----------------------------------

All the believers were together and had everything in
common. They sold property and possessions to give to anyone
who had need. Every day they continued to meet together
in the temple courts. They broke bread in their homes and ate
together with glad and sincere hearts, praising God and
enjoying the favor of all the people. And the Lord added to
their number daily those who were being saved.

Acts 2:44 – 47

250

CREATED FOR COMMUNITY
From the beginning, God designed and hardwired us for community.

This is the account of the heavens and the earth when they were created, when the LORD God made the earth and the heavens.

Now no shrub had yet appeared on the earth and no plant had yet sprung up, for the LORD God had not sent rain on the earth and there was no one to work the ground, but streams came up from the earth and watered the whole surface of the ground. Then the LORD God formed a man from the dust of the ground and breathed into his nostrils the breath of life, and the man became a living being.

Now the LORD God had planted a garden in the east, in Eden; and there he put the man he had formed. The LORD God made all kinds of trees grow out of the ground — trees that were pleasing to the eye and good for food. In the middle of the garden were the tree of life and the tree of the knowledge of good and evil.

A river watering the garden flowed from Eden; from there it was separated into four headwaters. The name of the first is the Pishon; it winds through the entire land of Havilah, where there is gold. (The gold of that land is good; aromatic resin and onyx are also there.) The name of the second river is the Gihon; it winds through the entire land of Cush. The name of the third river is the Tigris; it runs along the east side of Ashur. And the fourth river is the Euphrates.

The LORD God took the man and put him in the Garden of Eden to work it and take care of it. And the LORD God commanded the man, "You are free to eat from any tree in the garden; but you must not eat from the tree of the knowledge of good and evil, for when you eat from it you will certainly die."

The LORD God said, "It is not good for the man to be alone. I will make a helper suitable for him."

Now the LORD God had formed out of the ground all the wild animals and all the birds in the sky. He brought them to the man to see what he would name them; and whatever the man called each living creature, that was its name. So the man gave names to all the livestock, the birds in the sky and all the wild animals.

But for Adam no suitable helper was found. So the LORD God caused the man to fall into a deep sleep; and while he was sleeping, he took one of the man's ribs and then closed up the place with flesh. Then the LORD God made a woman from the rib he had taken out of the man, and he brought her to the man.

The man said,

> "This is now bone of my bones
>   and flesh of my flesh;
> she shall be called 'woman,'
>   for she was taken out of man."

That is why a man leaves his father and mother and is united to his wife, and they become one flesh.

Adam and his wife were both naked, and they felt no shame.

GENESIS 2:4–25

Community is not a "nice-to-have" addition, but an essential experience for living a godly and healthy life. God intended for humans to have rich, life-giving relationships with each other; relationships energized and motivated by the actual presence of God among them. Adam and Eve experienced this perfect ideal in the garden. But their rejection of God's vision for life together caused humankind to be escorted from the garden and out of community with God. This separation from God and the presence of sin in every human being's nature is a perpetual challenge to creating strong community. But it is clear from God's Word that people were not meant for separation and isolation.

> There was a man all alone;
>   he had neither son nor brother.
> There was no end to his toil,
>   yet his eyes were not content with his wealth.
> "For whom am I toiling," he asked,
>   "and why am I depriving myself of enjoyment?"
> This too is meaningless —
>   a miserable business!
>
> Two are better than one,
>   because they have a good return for their labor:

If either of them falls down,
    one can help the other up.
But pity anyone who falls
    and has no one to help them up.
Also, if two lie down together, they will keep warm.
    But how can one keep warm alone?
Though one may be overpowered,
    two can defend themselves.
A cord of three strands is not quickly broken.

ECCLESIASTES 4:8–12

THE PRESENCE OF GOD

In order to sustain life-giving community, God must be the center. After delivering the nation of Israel from bondage in Egypt, the Lord informed Moses of his intent to be with his people in a tent known as the tabernacle.

The LORD said to Moses, "Tell the Israelites to bring me an offering. You are to receive the offering for me from everyone whose heart prompts them to give. These are the offerings you are to receive from them: gold, silver and bronze; blue, purple and scarlet yarn and fine linen; goat hair; ram skins dyed red and another type of durable leather; acacia wood; olive oil for the light; spices for the anointing oil and for the fragrant incense; and onyx stones and other gems to be mounted on the ephod and breastpiece.

"Then have them make a sanctuary for me, and I will dwell among them. Make this tabernacle and all its furnishings exactly like the pattern I will show you. EXODUS 25:1–9

God's presence would be represented by the ark of the covenant—an elaborate box containing the Ten Commandments tablets, a gold jar filled with manna and Aaron's staff. The ark was placed in a special room in the tabernacle called the Most Holy Place, which was sectioned off by a thick curtain. While Moses and the Israelites were camped at the foot of Mount Sinai, they finished the building and preparation necessary to set up the tabernacle.

Then the LORD said to Moses: "Set up the tabernacle, the tent of meeting, on the first day of the first month. Place the ark of the covenant law in it and shield the ark with the curtain. Bring in the table and set out what belongs on it. Then bring in the lampstand and set up its lamps. Place the gold altar of incense in front of the ark of the covenant law and put the curtain at the entrance to the tabernacle.

"Place the altar of burnt offering in front of the entrance to the tabernacle, the tent of meeting; place the basin between the tent of meeting and the altar and put water in it. Set up the courtyard around it and put the curtain at the entrance to the courtyard.

"Take the anointing oil and anoint the tabernacle and everything in it; consecrate it and all its furnishings, and it will be holy. Then anoint the altar of burnt offering and all its utensils; consecrate the altar, and it will be most holy. Anoint the basin and its stand and consecrate them.

"Bring Aaron and his sons to the entrance to the tent of meeting and wash them with water. Then dress Aaron in the sacred garments, anoint him and consecrate him so he may serve me as priest. Bring his sons and dress them in tunics. Anoint them just as you anointed their father, so they may serve me as priests. Their anointing will be to a priesthood that will continue throughout their generations." Moses did everything just as the LORD commanded him.

So the tabernacle was set up on the first day of the first month in the second year. When Moses set up the tabernacle, he put the bases in place, erected the frames, inserted the crossbars and set up the posts. Then he spread the tent over the tabernacle and put the covering over the tent, as the LORD commanded him.

He took the tablets of the covenant law and placed them in the ark, attached the poles to the ark and put the atonement cover over it. Then he brought the ark into the tabernacle and hung the shielding curtain and shielded the ark of the covenant law, as the LORD commanded him.

Moses placed the table in the tent of meeting on the north side of the tabernacle outside the curtain and set out the bread on it before the LORD, as the LORD commanded him.

He placed the lampstand in the tent of meeting opposite the table on the south side of the tabernacle and set up the lamps before the LORD, as the LORD commanded him.

Moses placed the gold altar in the tent of meeting in front of the curtain and burned fragrant incense on it, as the LORD commanded him.

Then he put up the curtain at the entrance to the tabernacle. He set the altar of burnt offering near the entrance to the tabernacle, the tent of meeting, and offered on it burnt offerings and grain offerings, as the LORD commanded him.

He placed the basin between the tent of meeting and the altar and put water in it for washing, and Moses and Aaron and his sons used it to wash their hands and feet. They washed whenever they entered the tent of meeting or approached the altar, as the LORD commanded Moses.

Then Moses set up the courtyard around the tabernacle and altar and put up the curtain at the entrance to the courtyard. And so Moses finished the work.

Then the cloud covered the tent of meeting, and the glory of the LORD filled the tabernacle. Moses could not enter the tent of meeting because the cloud had settled on it, and the glory of the LORD filled the tabernacle. EXODUS 40:1–35

The cloud, symbolic of God's glory, that had led the Israelites after their escape from Egypt covered and filled the newly established tabernacle. About 500 years later, the Israelites built a temple in Jerusalem to replace the tabernacle with a permanent place where they could meet with God. And something similar happened after King Solomon's prayer at the dedication of that temple.

When Solomon finished praying, fire came down from heaven and consumed the burnt offering and the sacrifices, and the glory of the LORD filled the temple. The priests could not enter the temple of the LORD because the glory of the LORD filled it. When all the Israelites saw the fire coming down and the glory of the LORD above the temple, they knelt on the pavement with their faces to the ground, and they worshiped and gave thanks to the LORD, saying,

> "He is good;
> his love endures forever." 2 CHRONICLES 7:1–3

In the New Testament, God's presence among his people changed. Simultaneous with the death of Jesus on the cross, the heavy curtain hanging in front of the Holy Place that quarantined God's people from God's presence was torn from top to bottom. The presence of God was no longer isolated to this small room in the temple. Forgiveness of sins was now available to all. Paul instructs us on the new "temple" for God's presence.

Remember that formerly you who are Gentiles by birth and called "uncircumcised" by those who call themselves "the circumcision" (which is done in the body by human hands) — remember that at that time you were separate from Christ, excluded from citizenship in Israel and foreigners to the covenants of the promise, without hope and without God in the world. But now in Christ Jesus you who once were far away have been brought near by the blood of Christ.

For he himself is our peace, who has made the two groups one and has destroyed the barrier, the dividing wall of hostility, by setting aside in his flesh the law with its commands and regulations. His purpose was to create in himself one new humanity out of the two, thus making peace, and in one body to reconcile both of them to God through the cross, by which he put to death their hostility. He came and preached peace to you who were far away and peace to those who were near. For through him we both have access to the Father by one Spirit.

Consequently, you are no longer foreigners and strangers, but fellow citizens with God's people and also members of his household, built on the foundation of the apostles and prophets, with Christ Jesus himself as the chief cornerstone. In him the whole building is joined together and rises to become a holy temple in the Lord. And in him you too are being built together to become a dwelling in which God lives by his Spirit. EPHESIANS 2:11–22

THE NEW COMMUNITY

After the resurrection of Jesus and before his ascension back to the Father, Jesus told the disciples to wait in Jerusalem for the indwelling of the Holy Spirit. As promised, the actual presence of God descended on the believers in Jesus Christ—the new "temple." With God's presence dwelling in the hearts of believers, their potential for vibrant community with each other escalated.

When the day of Pentecost came, they were all together in one place. Suddenly a sound like the blowing of a violent wind came from heaven and filled the whole house where they were sitting. They saw what seemed to be tongues of fire that separated and came to rest on each of them. All of them were filled with the Holy Spirit and began to speak in other tongues as the Spirit enabled them.   ACTS 2:1–4

They devoted themselves to the apostles' teaching and to fellowship, to the breaking of bread and to prayer. Everyone was filled with awe at the many wonders and signs performed by the apostles. All the believers were together and had everything in common. They sold property and possessions to give to anyone who had need. Every day they continued to meet together in the temple courts. They broke bread in their homes and ate together with glad and sincere hearts, praising God and enjoying the favor of all the people. And the Lord added to their number daily those who were being saved.   ACTS 2:42–47

All the believers were one in heart and mind. No one claimed that any of their possessions was their own, but they shared everything they had. With great power the apostles continued to testify to the resurrection of the Lord Jesus. And God's grace was so powerfully at work in them all that there were no needy persons among them. For from time to time those who owned land or houses sold them, brought the money from the sales and put it at the apostles' feet, and it was distributed to anyone who had need.

Joseph, a Levite from Cyprus, whom the apostles called Barnabas (which means "son of encouragement"), sold a field he owned and brought the money and put it at the apostles' feet.   ACTS 4:32–37

During the first century, it proved difficult for many Jewish converts to overcome the pressure and persecution they received from other family members who remained in Judaism. The author of Hebrews wrote that letter to these believers to convince them of the superiority of Christ over the law and to encourage them to lean heavily into their new community of faith to persevere.

Therefore, brothers and sisters, since we have confidence to enter the Most Holy Place by the blood of Jesus, by a new and living way opened for us through the curtain, that is, his body, and since we have a great priest over the house of God, let us draw near to God with a sincere heart and with the full assurance that faith brings, having our hearts sprinkled to cleanse us from a guilty conscience and having our bodies washed with pure water. Let us hold unswervingly to the hope we profess, for he who promised is faithful. And let us consider how we may spur one another on toward love and good deeds, not giving up meeting together, as some are in the habit of doing, but encouraging one another — and all the more as you see the Day approaching.   HEBREWS 10:19–25

MARKS OF BIBLICAL COMMUNITY

Biblical community engages everyone in the community to use their gifts, resources and time in unison to accomplish a task important to the plan of God. The Israelites returned from 70 years of captivity and were rebuilding their lives under the reign of God. Nehemiah returned to spearhead the rebuilding of the wall around the city to protect them from bullying from the surrounding nations. Everyone in the community, including children, was called to help with this massive and important project.

I [Nehemiah] went to Jerusalem, and after staying there three days I set out during the night with a few others. I had not told anyone what my God had put in my heart to do for Jerusalem. There were no mounts with me except the one I was riding on.

By night I went out through the Valley Gate toward the Jackal Well and the Dung Gate, examining the walls of Jerusalem, which had been broken down, and its gates, which had been destroyed by fire. Then I moved on toward the Fountain Gate and the King's Pool, but there was not enough room for my mount to get through; so I went up the valley by night, examining the wall. Finally, I turned back and reentered through the Valley Gate. The officials did not know where I had gone or what I was doing, because as yet

I had said nothing to the Jews or the priests or nobles or officials or any others who would be doing the work.

Then I said to them, "You see the trouble we are in: Jerusalem lies in ruins, and its gates have been burned with fire. Come, let us rebuild the wall of Jerusalem, and we will no longer be in disgrace." I also told them about the gracious hand of my God on me and what the king had said to me.

They replied, "Let us start rebuilding." So they began this good work.

But when Sanballat the Horonite, Tobiah the Ammonite official and Geshem the Arab heard about it, they mocked and ridiculed us. "What is this you are doing?" they asked. "Are you rebelling against the king?"

I answered them by saying, "The God of heaven will give us success. We his servants will start rebuilding, but as for you, you have no share in Jerusalem or any claim or historic right to it."

Eliashib the high priest and his fellow priests went to work and rebuilt the Sheep Gate. They dedicated it and set its doors in place, building as far as the Tower of the Hundred, which they dedicated, and as far as the Tower of Hananel. The men of Jericho built the adjoining section, and Zakkur son of Imri built next to them.

The Fish Gate was rebuilt by the sons of Hassenaah. They laid its beams and put its doors and bolts and bars in place. Meremoth son of Uriah, the son of Hakkoz, repaired the next section. Next to him Meshullam son of Berekiah, the son of Meshezabel, made repairs, and next to him Zadok son of Baana also made repairs. The next section was repaired by the men of Tekoa, but their nobles would not put their shoulders to the work under their supervisors.

The Jeshanah Gate was repaired by Joiada son of Paseah and Meshullam son of Besodeiah. They laid its beams and put its doors with their bolts and bars in place. Next to them, repairs were made by men from Gibeon and Mizpah — Melatiah of Gibeon and Jadon of Meronoth — places under the authority of the governor of Trans-Euphrates. Uzziel son of Harhaiah, one of the goldsmiths, repaired the next section; and Hananiah, one of the perfume-makers, made repairs next to that. They restored Jerusalem as far as the Broad Wall. Rephaiah son of Hur, ruler of a half-district of

Jerusalem, repaired the next section. Adjoining this, Jedaiah son of Harumaph made repairs opposite his house, and Hattush son of Hashabneiah made repairs next to him. Malkijah son of Harim and Hasshub son of Pahath-Moab repaired another section and the Tower of the Ovens. Shallum son of Hallohesh, ruler of a half-district of Jerusalem, repaired the next section with the help of his daughters.

The Valley Gate was repaired by Hanun and the residents of Zanoah. They rebuilt it and put its doors with their bolts and bars in place. They also repaired a thousand cubits of the wall as far as the Dung Gate.

The Dung Gate was repaired by Malkijah son of Rekab, ruler of the district of Beth Hakkerem. He rebuilt it and put its doors with their bolts and bars in place.

The Fountain Gate was repaired by Shallun son of Kol-Hozeh, ruler of the district of Mizpah. He rebuilt it, roofing it over and putting its doors and bolts and bars in place. He also repaired the wall of the Pool of Siloam, by the King's Garden, as far as the steps going down from the City of David. Beyond him, Nehemiah son of Azbuk, ruler of a half-district of Beth Zur, made repairs up to a point opposite the tombs of David, as far as the artificial pool and the House of the Heroes.

Next to him, the repairs were made by the Levites under Rehum son of Bani. Beside him, Hashabiah, ruler of half the district of Keilah, carried out repairs for his district. Next to him, the repairs were made by their fellow Levites under Binnui son of Henadad, ruler of the other half-district of Keilah. Next to him, Ezer son of Jeshua, ruler of Mizpah, repaired another section, from a point facing the ascent to the armory as far as the angle of the wall. Next to him, Baruch son of Zabbai zealously repaired another section, from the angle to the entrance of the house of Eliashib the high priest. Next to him, Meremoth son of Uriah, the son of Hakkoz, repaired another section, from the entrance of Eliashib's house to the end of it.

The repairs next to him were made by the priests from the surrounding region. Beyond them, Benjamin and Hasshub made repairs in front of their house; and next to them, Azariah son of Maaseiah, the son of Ananiah, made repairs beside his house. Next to him, Binnui son of Henadad repaired another section, from Azariah's house to the angle and the corner, and Palal son of Uzai worked opposite the angle and the tower projecting from the upper palace near the court of the guard. Next to him, Pedaiah son of Parosh and the temple servants living on the hill of Ophel made repairs up to a point opposite the Water Gate toward the east and the projecting tower. Next to them, the men of Tekoa repaired another section, from the great projecting tower to the wall of Ophel.

Above the Horse Gate, the priests made repairs, each in front of his own house. Next to them, Zadok son of Immer made repairs opposite his house. Next to him, Shemaiah son of Shekaniah, the guard at the East Gate, made repairs. Next to him, Hananiah son of Shelemiah, and Hanun, the sixth son of Zalaph, repaired another section. Next to them, Meshullam son of Berekiah made repairs opposite his living quarters. Next to him, Malkijah, one of the goldsmiths, made repairs as far as the house of the temple servants and the merchants, opposite the Inspection Gate, and as far as the room above the corner; and between the room above the corner and the Sheep Gate the goldsmiths and merchants made repairs.

NEHEMIAH 2:11—3:32

So the wall was completed on the twenty-fifth of Elul, in fifty-two days. NEHEMIAH 6:15

The wall in Jerusalem was built so quickly because the Biblical community pitched in and made it happen. In the New Testament, Jesus modeled the attitude and life of the new community he was forming through the first disciples. Those in Biblical community seek to serve, not to be served.

It was just before the Passover Festival. Jesus knew that the hour had come for him to leave this world and go to the Father. Having loved his own who were in the world, he loved them to the end.

The evening meal was in progress, and the devil had already prompted Judas, the son of Simon Iscariot, to betray Jesus. Jesus knew that the Father had put all things under his power, and that he had come from God and was returning to God; so he got up from the meal, took off his outer clothing, and wrapped a towel around his waist. After that, he poured water into a basin and began to wash his disciples' feet, drying them with the towel that was wrapped around him.

He came to Simon Peter, who said to him, "Lord, are you going to wash my feet?"

Jesus replied, "You do not realize now what I am doing, but later you will understand."

"No," said Peter, "you shall never wash my feet."

Jesus answered, "Unless I wash you, you have no part with me."

"Then, Lord," Simon Peter replied, "not just my feet but my hands and my head as well!"

Jesus answered, "Those who have had a bath need only to wash their feet; their whole body is clean. And you are clean, though not every one of you." For he knew who was going to betray him, and that was why he said not every one was clean.

When he had finished washing their feet, he put on his clothes and returned to his place. "Do you understand what I have done for you?" he asked them. "You call me 'Teacher' and 'Lord,' and rightly so, for that is what I am. Now that I, your Lord and Teacher, have washed your feet, you also should wash one another's feet. I have set you an example that you should do as I have done for you. Very truly I tell you, no servant is greater than his master, nor is a messenger greater than the one who sent him. Now that you know these things, you will be blessed if you do them." JOHN 13:1–17

One of the marked differences between the church and the rest of society is the call to live for others. Throughout the New Testament, followers of Jesus were urged to look out for "one another." When the early Christians did this in faith, it created an irresistible attraction for outsiders to belong to the family of God.

For just as each of us has one body with many members, and these members do not all have the same function, so in Christ we, though many, form one body, and each member belongs to all the others. ROMANS 12:4–5

Be devoted to one another in love. Honor one another above
yourselves.   ROMANS 12:10

Let no debt remain outstanding, except the continuing debt to
love one another, for whoever loves others has fulfilled the law.
                                                               ROMANS 13:8

May the God who gives endurance and encouragement give
you the same attitude of mind toward each other that Christ Jesus
had, so that with one mind and one voice you may glorify the God
and Father of our Lord Jesus Christ.
Accept one another, then, just as Christ accepted you, in order
to bring praise to God.   ROMANS 15:5–7

I myself am convinced, my brothers and sisters, that you yourselves are full of goodness, filled with knowledge and competent to
instruct one another.   ROMANS 15:14

You, my brothers and sisters, were called to be free. But do not
use your freedom to indulge the flesh; rather, serve one another
humbly in love.   GALATIANS 5:13

Carry each other's burdens, and in this way you will fulfill the
law of Christ.   GALATIANS 6:2

Be completely humble and gentle; be patient, bearing with one
another in love.   EPHESIANS 4:2

Submit to one another out of reverence for Christ. EPHESIANS 5:21

For God did not appoint us to suffer wrath but to receive salvation through our Lord Jesus Christ. He died for us so that, whether
we are awake or asleep, we may live together with him. Therefore
encourage one another and build each other up, just as in fact you
are doing.   1 THESSALONIANS 5:9–11

*The calling among the early church to care for one another was
also demonstrated through simple hospitality. This mandate
to show love and demonstrate an open-door policy greatly*

enhanced the quality of community and always left room for new people to belong, regardless of their station in life.

Keep on loving one another as brothers and sisters. Do not forget to show hospitality to strangers, for by so doing some people have shown hospitality to angels without knowing it. Continue to remember those in prison as if you were together with them in prison, and those who are mistreated as if you yourselves were suffering.   HEBREWS 13:1–3

Through Jesus, therefore, let us continually offer to God a sacrifice of praise — the fruit of lips that openly profess his name. And do not forget to do good and to share with others, for with such sacrifices God is pleased.   HEBREWS 13:15–16

A couple named Priscilla and Aquila serve as a beautiful example of how to be hospitable. In the first century, inns were not commonplace, and the early church didn't own buildings. For Biblical community to be experienced, people who owned homes had to open them up for the church to meet. Paul was on his second missionary journey when he first encountered this warm-hearted couple, who invited him to stay with them.

Paul left Athens and went to Corinth. There he met a Jew named Aquila, a native of Pontus, who had recently come from Italy with his wife Priscilla, because Claudius had ordered all Jews to leave Rome. Paul went to see them, and because he was a tentmaker as they were, he stayed and worked with them.   ACTS 18:1–3

Paul stayed on in Corinth for some time. Then he left the brothers and sisters and sailed for Syria, accompanied by Priscilla and Aquila. Before he sailed, he had his hair cut off at Cenchreae because of a vow he had taken. They arrived at Ephesus, where Paul left Priscilla and Aquila.   ACTS 18:18–19

Meanwhile a Jew named Apollos, a native of Alexandria, came to Ephesus. He was a learned man, with a thorough knowledge of the Scriptures. He had been instructed in the way of the Lord, and he spoke with great fervor and taught about Jesus accurately, though he knew only the baptism of John. He began to speak boldly in the synagogue. When Priscilla and Aquila heard him, they invited him to their home and explained to him the way of God more adequately. Acts 18:24–26

Paul's admiration for Priscilla and Aquila can be found throughout his letters. Paul wrote 1 Corinthians when he was in Ephesus. He sent greetings on behalf of Aquila and Priscilla, who were hosting the church in their home.

The churches in the province of Asia send you greetings. Aquila and Priscilla greet you warmly in the Lord, and so does the church that meets at their house. 1 Corinthians 16:19

Also, a couple years later when Paul penned the letter to the Romans, he expressed his gratitude to Priscilla and Aquila, who were now in Rome.

Greet Priscilla and Aquila, my co-workers in Christ Jesus. They risked their lives for me. Not only I but all the churches of the Gentiles are grateful to them. Romans 16:3–4

In order for the church to accomplish its full mission, all believers, looking to the example of Priscilla and Aquila, need to use the gifts God has given them to serve others. In 1 John, the apostle John emphasized the value of Christian fellowship. If we practice this quality and depth of fellowship with other Christians, we will accomplish God's purposes in our lives, in others' lives and in the world.

That which was from the beginning, which we have heard, which we have seen with our eyes, which we have looked at and our hands have touched — this we proclaim concerning the Word of life. The life appeared; we have seen it and testify to it, and we proclaim to you the eternal life, which was with the Father and has appeared to us. We proclaim to you what we have seen and heard, so that you also may have fellowship with us. And our fellowship is with the Father and with his Son, Jesus Christ. We write this to make our joy complete.

This is the message we have heard from him and declare to you: God is light; in him there is no darkness at all. If we claim to have fellowship with him and yet walk in the darkness, we lie and do not live out the truth. But if we walk in the light, as he is in the light, we have fellowship with one another, and the blood of Jesus, his Son, purifies us from all sin.   1 JOHN 1:1–7

Dear friends, I am not writing you a new command but an old one, which you have had since the beginning. This old command is the message you have heard. Yet I am writing you a new command; its truth is seen in him and in you, because the darkness is passing and the true light is already shining.

Anyone who claims to be in the light but hates a brother or sister is still in the darkness. Anyone who loves their brother and sister lives in the light, and there is nothing in them to make them stumble. But anyone who hates a brother or sister is in the darkness and walks around in the darkness. They do not know where they are going, because the darkness has blinded them.   1 JOHN 2:7–11

This is how we know what love is: Jesus Christ laid down his life for us. And we ought to lay down our lives for our brothers and sisters. If anyone has material possessions and sees a brother or sister in need but has no pity on them, how can the love of God be in that person? Dear children, let us not love with words or speech but with actions and in truth.   1 JOHN 3:16–18

Dear friends, let us love one another, for love comes from God. Everyone who loves has been born of God and knows God. Whoever does not love does not know God, because God is love. This is how God showed his love among us: He sent his one and only Son into the world that we might live through him. This is love: not that we loved God, but that he loved us and sent his Son as an atoning sacrifice for our sins. Dear friends, since God so loved us, we also ought to love one another. No one has ever seen God; but if we love one another, God lives in us and his love is made complete in us.

This is how we know that we live in him and he in us: He has given us of his Spirit. And we have seen and testify that the Father has sent his Son to be the Savior of the world. If anyone acknowledges that Jesus is the Son of God, God lives in them and they in God. And so we know and rely on the love God has for us.

God is love. Whoever lives in love lives in God, and God in them. This is how love is made complete among us so that we will have confidence on the day of judgment: In this world we are like Jesus. There is no fear in love. But perfect love drives out fear, because fear has to do with punishment. The one who fears is not made perfect in love.

We love because he first loved us. Whoever claims to love God yet hates a brother or sister is a liar. For whoever does not love their brother and sister, whom they have seen, cannot love God, whom they have not seen. And he has given us this command: Anyone who loves God must also love their brother and sister.

1 JOHN 4:7–21

CHAPTER

17

Spiritual Gifts

KEY IDEA

I know my spiritual gifts and
use them to fulfill God's purposes.

KEY VERSE

For just as each of us has one body with many members,
and these members do not all have the same function,
so in Christ we, though many, form one body, and each
member belongs to all the others. We have different gifts,
according to the grace given to each of us.

Romans 12:4–6

The term "spiritual gifts" originates from the Greek words pneu-matika (spiritual or of the Spirit) and charisma (gift). Spiritual gifts are special abilities or functions given by the Holy Spirit that are meant to be used by God's people to complete God's work.

SPIRITUAL GIFTS IN THE OLD TESTAMENT

Although the term "spiritual gift" isn't found in the Old Testament, we see clear evidence of the Holy Spirit working through people during this time. In the Old Testament the unique empowering of the Spirit was given to individuals (often only temporarily) primarily to enable them to carry out the special responsibilities God had given them. The Spirit of the Lord came upon Saul, the first king of Israel, to empower him to accomplish his task given to him by God. Saul repeatedly disobeyed the instruction of the Lord until God finally intervened and commissioned Samuel to anoint a new king for Israel.

The LORD said to Samuel, "How long will you mourn for Saul, since I have rejected him as king over Israel? Fill your horn with oil and be on your way; I am sending you to Jesse of Bethlehem. I have chosen one of his sons to be king."

But Samuel said, "How can I go? If Saul hears about it, he will kill me."

The LORD said, "Take a heifer with you and say, 'I have come to sacrifice to the LORD.' Invite Jesse to the sacrifice, and I will show you what to do. You are to anoint for me the one I indicate."

Samuel did what the LORD said. When he arrived at Bethlehem, the elders of the town trembled when they met him. They asked, "Do you come in peace?"

Samuel replied, "Yes, in peace; I have come to sacrifice to the LORD. Consecrate yourselves and come to the sacrifice with me." Then he consecrated Jesse and his sons and invited them to the sacrifice.

When they arrived, Samuel saw Eliab and thought, "Surely the LORD's anointed stands here before the LORD."

But the LORD said to Samuel, "Do not consider his appearance or his height, for I have rejected him. The LORD does not look at the things people look at. People look at the outward appearance, but the LORD looks at the heart."

Then Jesse called Abinadab and had him pass in front of Samuel. But Samuel said, "The LORD has not chosen this one either." Jesse then had Shammah pass by, but Samuel said, "Nor has the LORD chosen this one." Jesse had seven of his sons pass before Samuel, but Samuel said to him, "The LORD has not chosen these." So he asked Jesse, "Are these all the sons you have?"

"There is still the youngest," Jesse answered. "He is tending the sheep."

Samuel said, "Send for him; we will not sit down until he arrives."

So he sent for him and had him brought in. He was glowing with health and had a fine appearance and handsome features.

Then the LORD said, "Rise and anoint him; this is the one."

So Samuel took the horn of oil and anointed him in the presence of his brothers, and from that day on the Spirit of the LORD came powerfully upon David. Samuel then went to Ramah.

Now the Spirit of the LORD had departed from Saul, and an evil spirit from the LORD tormented him.

Saul's attendants said to him, "See, an evil spirit from God is tormenting you. Let our lord command his servants here to search for someone who can play the lyre. He will play when the evil spirit from God comes on you, and you will feel better."

So Saul said to his attendants, "Find someone who plays well and bring him to me."

One of the servants answered, "I have seen a son of Jesse of Bethlehem who knows how to play the lyre. He is a brave man and a warrior. He speaks well and is a fine-looking man. And the LORD is with him."

Then Saul sent messengers to Jesse and said, "Send me your son David, who is with the sheep." So Jesse took a donkey loaded with bread, a skin of wine and a young goat and sent them with his son David to Saul.

David came to Saul and entered his service. Saul liked him very much, and David became one of his armor-bearers. Then Saul sent word to Jesse, saying, "Allow David to remain in my service, for I am pleased with him."

Whenever the spirit from God came on Saul, David would take up his lyre and play. Then relief would come to Saul; he would feel better, and the evil spirit would leave him. 1 SAMUEL 16:1–23

Occasionally in the Old Testament, spiritual gifts were used for the sake of outsiders. In these situations, God used miraculous signs to reveal himself as the one true God. For instance, while the Israelites were living in exile under the rule of King Nebuchadnezzar, God empowered Daniel with the ability to interpret complex dreams.

In the second year of his reign, Nebuchadnezzar had dreams; his mind was troubled and he could not sleep. So the king summoned the magicians, enchanters, sorcerers and astrologers to tell him what he had dreamed. When they came in and stood before the king, he said to them, "I have had a dream that troubles me and I want to know what it means."

Then the astrologers answered the king, "May the king live forever! Tell your servants the dream, and we will interpret it."

The king replied to the astrologers, "This is what I have firmly decided: If you do not tell me what my dream was and interpret it, I will have you cut into pieces and your houses turned into piles of rubble. But if you tell me the dream and explain it, you will receive from me gifts and rewards and great honor. So tell me the dream and interpret it for me."

Once more they replied, "Let the king tell his servants the dream, and we will interpret it."

Then the king answered, "I am certain that you are trying to gain time, because you realize that this is what I have firmly decided: If you do not tell me the dream, there is only one penalty for you. You have conspired to tell me misleading and wicked things, hoping the situation will change. So then, tell me the dream, and I will know that you can interpret it for me."

The astrologers answered the king, "There is no one on earth who can do what the king asks! No king, however great and mighty, has ever asked such a thing of any magician or enchanter or astrologer. What the king asks is too difficult. No one can reveal it to the king except the gods, and they do not live among humans."

This made the king so angry and furious that he ordered the execution of all the wise men of Babylon. So the decree was issued to put the wise men to death, and men were sent to look for Daniel and his friends to put them to death.

When Arioch, the commander of the king's guard, had gone out to put to death the wise men of Babylon, Daniel spoke to him with wisdom and tact. He asked the king's officer, "Why did the king issue such a harsh decree?" Arioch then explained the matter to Daniel. At this, Daniel went in to the king and asked for time, so that he might interpret the dream for him.

Then Daniel returned to his house and explained the matter to his friends Hananiah, Mishael and Azariah. He urged them to plead for mercy from the God of heaven concerning this mystery, so that he and his friends might not be executed with the rest of the wise men of Babylon. During the night the mystery was revealed to Daniel in a vision. Then Daniel praised the God of heaven and said:

> "Praise be to the name of God for ever and ever;
>> wisdom and power are his.
> He changes times and seasons;
>> he deposes kings and raises up others.
> He gives wisdom to the wise
>> and knowledge to the discerning.
> He reveals deep and hidden things;
>> he knows what lies in darkness,
>> and light dwells with him.
> I thank and praise you, God of my ancestors:
>> You have given me wisdom and power,
> you have made known to me what we asked of you,
>> you have made known to us the dream of the king."

Then Daniel went to Arioch, whom the king had appointed to execute the wise men of Babylon, and said to him, "Do not execute the wise men of Babylon. Take me to the king, and I will interpret his dream for him."

Arioch took Daniel to the king at once and said, "I have found a man among the exiles from Judah who can tell the king what his dream means."

The king asked Daniel (also called Belteshazzar), "Are you able to tell me what I saw in my dream and interpret it?"

Daniel replied, "No wise man, enchanter, magician or diviner can explain to the king the mystery he has asked about, but there is a God in heaven who reveals mysteries. He has shown King Nebuchadnezzar what will happen in days to come. Your dream and the visions that passed through your mind as you were lying in bed are these:

"As Your Majesty was lying there, your mind turned to things to come, and the revealer of mysteries showed you what is going to happen. As for me, this mystery has been revealed to me, not because I have greater wisdom than anyone else alive, but so that Your Majesty may know the interpretation and that you may understand what went through your mind.

"Your Majesty looked, and there before you stood a large statue — an enormous, dazzling statue, awesome in appearance. The head of the statue was made of pure gold, its chest and arms of silver, its belly and thighs of bronze, its legs of iron, its feet partly of iron and partly of baked clay. While you were watching, a rock was cut out, but not by human hands. It struck the statue on its feet of iron and clay and smashed them. Then the iron, the clay, the bronze, the silver and the gold were all broken to pieces and became like chaff on a threshing floor in the summer. The wind swept them away without leaving a trace. But the rock that struck the statue became a huge mountain and filled the whole earth.

"This was the dream, and now we will interpret it to the king. Your Majesty, you are the king of kings. The God of heaven has given you dominion and power and might and glory; in your hands he has placed all mankind and the beasts of the field and the birds in the sky. Wherever they live, he has made you ruler over them all. You are that head of gold.

"After you, another kingdom will arise, inferior to yours. Next, a third kingdom, one of bronze, will rule over the whole earth. Finally, there will be a fourth kingdom, strong as iron — for iron breaks and smashes everything — and as iron breaks things to pieces, so it will crush and break all the others. Just as you saw that the feet and toes were partly of baked clay and partly of iron, so this will be a divided kingdom; yet it will have some of the strength of iron in it, even as you saw iron mixed with clay. As the toes were partly iron and partly clay, so this kingdom will be partly strong and partly brittle. And just as you saw the iron mixed with baked clay, so the people will be a mixture and will not remain united, any more than iron mixes with clay.

"In the time of those kings, the God of heaven will set up a kingdom that will never be destroyed, nor will it be left to another people. It will crush all those kingdoms and bring them to an end, but it will itself endure forever. This is the meaning of the vision of the rock cut out of a mountain, but not by human hands — a rock that broke the iron, the bronze, the clay, the silver and the gold to pieces.

"The great God has shown the king what will take place in the future. The dream is true and its interpretation is trustworthy."

Then King Nebuchadnezzar fell prostrate before Daniel and paid him honor and ordered that an offering and incense be presented to him. The king said to Daniel, "Surely your God is the God of gods and the Lord of kings and a revealer of mysteries, for you were able to reveal this mystery."   DANIEL 2:1–47

THE PROMISED GIFT OF THE HOLY SPIRIT

In the New Testament, when Jesus ate the Last Supper with his disciples, he knew he would soon be put to death. Wanting them to be encouraged and prepared for life without him walking by their side, Jesus promised to send the Holy Spirit — who would empower them with hope and guidance and the ability to get through the difficult days ahead.

"If you love me, keep my commands. And I will ask the Father, and he will give you another advocate to help you and be with you forever — the Spirit of truth. The world cannot accept him, because it neither sees him nor knows him. But you know him, for he lives with you and will be in you. I will not leave you as orphans; I will come to you. Before long, the world will not see me anymore, but you will see me. Because I live, you also will live. On that day you will realize that I am in my Father, and you are in me, and I am in you. Whoever has my commands and keeps them is the one who loves me. The one who loves me will be loved by my Father, and I too will love them and show myself to them."

Then Judas (not Judas Iscariot) said, "But, Lord, why do you intend to show yourself to us and not to the world?"

Jesus replied, "Anyone who loves me will obey my teaching. My Father will love them, and we will come to them and make our home with them. Anyone who does not love me will not obey my teaching. These words you hear are not my own; they belong to the Father who sent me.

"All this I have spoken while still with you. But the Advocate, the Holy Spirit, whom the Father will send in my name, will teach you all things and will remind you of everything I have said to you. Peace I leave with you; my peace I give you. I do not give to you as the world gives. Do not let your hearts be troubled and do not be afraid.

"You heard me say, 'I am going away and I am coming back to you.' If you loved me, you would be glad that I am going to the Father, for the Father is greater than I. I have told you now before it happens, so that when it does happen you will believe. I will not say much more to you, for the prince of this world is coming. He has no hold over me, but he comes so that the world may learn that I love the Father and do exactly what my Father has commanded me."

JOHN 14:15–31

Later, Jesus' last words to his disciples before he ascended to heaven instructed them to wait in Jerusalem for the promised gift of the Holy Spirit. Ten days later the Holy Spirit arrived on the Jewish celebration of Pentecost (i.e., 50 days after Passover), the disciples were filled with incredible boldness and the church was born. Jews use this celebration to commemorate the giving of the law. Christians use this day to commemorate the giving of the Spirit.

When the day of Pentecost came, they were all together in one place. Suddenly a sound like the blowing of a violent wind came from heaven and filled the whole house where they were sitting. They saw what seemed to be tongues of fire that separated and came to rest on each of them. All of them were filled with the Holy Spirit and began to speak in other tongues as the Spirit enabled them.

Now there were staying in Jerusalem God-fearing Jews from every nation under heaven. When they heard this sound, a crowd came together in bewilderment, because each one heard their own language being spoken. Utterly amazed, they asked: "Aren't all these who are speaking Galileans? Then how is it that each of us hears them in our native language? Parthians, Medes and Elamites; residents of Mesopotamia, Judea and Cappadocia, Pontus and Asia, Phrygia and Pamphylia, Egypt and the parts of Libya near Cyrene; visitors from Rome (both Jews and converts to Judaism); Cretans and Arabs — we hear them declaring the wonders of God in our own tongues!" Amazed and perplexed, they asked one another, "What does this mean?"

Some, however, made fun of them and said, "They have had too much wine."

Then Peter stood up with the Eleven, raised his voice and addressed the crowd: "Fellow Jews and all of you who live in Jerusalem, let me explain this to you; listen carefully to what I say. These people are not drunk, as you suppose. It's only nine in the morning! No, this is what was spoken by the prophet Joel:

> " 'In the last days, God says,
>   I will pour out my Spirit on all people.
> Your sons and daughters will prophesy,
>   your young men will see visions,
>   your old men will dream dreams.
> Even on my servants, both men and women,
>   I will pour out my Spirit in those days,
>   and they will prophesy.
> I will show wonders in the heavens above
>   and signs on the earth below,
>   blood and fire and billows of smoke.
> The sun will be turned to darkness
>   and the moon to blood
>   before the coming of the great and glorious
>   day of the Lord.
> And everyone who calls
>   on the name of the Lord will be saved.' "   ACTS 2:1–21

PURPOSE AND FUNCTION OF SPIRITUAL GIFTS

Spiritual gifts are given with a purpose. God wants to redeem this broken world, and he has chosen to use us, the church, to do it.

Whereas in the Old Testament the Holy Spirit temporarily came upon followers of God to enable them to fulfill specific tasks, the New Testament clearly indicates that the Holy Spirit indwells all believers and that all believers have spiritual gifts. And since the New Testament refers to specific gifts, it seems safe to assume that God wants us to identify our gifts in order to best use them.

For just as each of us has one body with many members, and these members do not all have the same function, so in Christ we, though many, form one body, and each member belongs to all the others. We have different gifts, according to the grace given to each of us. If your gift is prophesying, then prophesy in accordance with your faith; if it is serving, then serve; if it is teaching, then teach; if it is to encourage, then give encouragement; if it is giving, then give generously; if it is to lead, do it diligently; if it is to show mercy, do it cheerfully. ROMANS 12:4–8

There are different kinds of gifts, but the same Spirit distributes them. There are different kinds of service, but the same Lord. There are different kinds of working, but in all of them and in everyone it is the same God at work.

Now to each one the manifestation of the Spirit is given for the common good. To one there is given through the Spirit a message of wisdom, to another a message of knowledge by means of the same Spirit, to another faith by the same Spirit, to another gifts of healing by that one Spirit, to another miraculous powers, to another prophecy, to another distinguishing between spirits, to another speaking in different kinds of tongues, and to still another the interpretation of tongues. All these are the work of one and the same Spirit, and he distributes them to each one, just as he determines.

Just as a body, though one, has many parts, but all its many parts form one body, so it is with Christ. For we were all baptized by one Spirit so as to form one body — whether Jews or Gentiles, slave or free — and we were all given the one Spirit to drink. Even so the body is not made up of one part but of many.

Now if the foot should say, "Because I am not a hand, I do not belong to the body," it would not for that reason stop being part of the body. And if the ear should say, "Because I am not an eye, I do not belong to the body," it would not for that reason stop being part of the body. If the whole body were an eye, where would the sense of hearing be? If the whole body were an ear, where would the sense of smell be? But in fact God has placed the parts in the body, every one of them, just as he wanted them to be. If they were all one part, where would the body be? As it is, there are many parts, but one body.

The eye cannot say to the hand, "I don't need you!" And the head cannot say to the feet, "I don't need you!" On the contrary, those parts of the body that seem to be weaker are indispensable, and the parts that we think are less honorable we treat with special honor. And the parts that are unpresentable are treated with special modesty, while our presentable parts need no special treatment. But God has put the body together, giving greater honor to the parts that lacked it, so that there should be no division in the body, but that its parts should have equal concern for each other. If one part suffers, every part suffers with it; if one part is honored, every part rejoices with it.

Now you are the body of Christ, and each one of you is a part of it. And God has placed in the church first of all apostles, second prophets, third teachers, then miracles, then gifts of healing, of helping, of guidance, and of different kinds of tongues. Are all apostles? Are all prophets? Are all teachers? Do all work miracles? Do all have gifts of healing? Do all speak in tongues? Do all interpret? Now eagerly desire the greater gifts.

And yet I will show you the most excellent way.

If I speak in the tongues of men or of angels, but do not have love, I am only a resounding gong or a clanging cymbal. If I have the gift of prophecy and can fathom all mysteries and all knowledge, and if I have a faith that can move mountains, but do not have love, I am nothing. If I give all I possess to the poor and give over my body to hardship that I may boast, but do not have love, I gain nothing.

Love is patient, love is kind. It does not envy, it does not boast, it is not proud. It does not dishonor others, it is not self-seeking, it is not easily angered, it keeps no record of wrongs. Love does not delight in evil but rejoices with the truth. It always protects, always trusts, always hopes, always perseveres.

Love never fails. But where there are prophecies, they will cease; where there are tongues, they will be stilled; where there is knowledge, it will pass away. For we know in part and we prophesy in part, but when completeness comes, what is in part disappears. When I was a child, I talked like a child, I thought like a child, I reasoned like a child. When I became a man, I put the ways of childhood behind me. For now we see only a reflection as in a mirror; then we shall see face to face. Now I know in part; then I shall know fully, even as I am fully known.

And now these three remain: faith, hope and love. But the greatest of these is love.   1 CORINTHIANS 12:4—13:13

STEWARDSHIP OF OUR GIFTS

Spiritual gifts are tools that are meant to be used. The divine task of restoring broken people to God has been imparted to us, and we must put these tools to work. In this parable about the bags of gold, Jesus illustrated this principle for his disciples.

"Again, it will be like a man going on a journey, who called his servants and entrusted his wealth to them. To one he gave five bags of gold, to another two bags, and to another one bag, each according to his ability. Then he went on his journey. The man who had received five bags of gold went at once and put his money to work and gained five bags more. So also, the one with two bags of gold gained two more. But the man who had received one bag went off, dug a hole in the ground and hid his master's money.

"After a long time the master of those servants returned and settled accounts with them. The man who had received five bags of gold brought the other five. 'Master,' he said, 'you entrusted me with five bags of gold. See, I have gained five more.'

"His master replied, 'Well done, good and faithful servant! You have been faithful with a few things; I will put you in charge of many things. Come and share your master's happiness!'

"The man with two bags of gold also came. 'Master,' he said, 'you entrusted me with two bags of gold; see, I have gained two more.'

"His master replied, 'Well done, good and faithful servant! You have been faithful with a few things; I will put you in charge of many things. Come and share your master's happiness!'

"Then the man who had received one bag of gold came. 'Master,' he said, 'I knew that you are a hard man, harvesting where you have not sown and gathering where you have not scattered seed. So I was afraid and went out and hid your gold in the ground. See, here is what belongs to you.'

"His master replied, 'You wicked, lazy servant! So you knew that I harvest where I have not sown and gather where I have not scattered seed? Well then, you should have put my money on deposit with the bankers, so that when I returned I would have received it back with interest.

"'So take the bag of gold from him and give it to the one who has ten bags. For whoever has will be given more, and they will have an abundance. Whoever does not have, even what they have will be taken from them. And throw that worthless servant outside, into the darkness, where there will be weeping and gnashing of teeth.'"   MATTHEW 25:14–30

> *Just as a piston engine requires pure gasoline to run smoothly, our gifts must be fueled with loving intentions. Spiritual gifts that are driven by selfish ambition and pride will sputter and fail. Church leaders are a gift to the church, and as they use their spiritual gifts, other believers will be equipped to steward theirs— resulting in the body of Christ being built up and individual believers becoming mature.*

The end of all things is near. Therefore be alert and of sober mind so that you may pray. Above all, love each other deeply, because love covers over a multitude of sins. Offer hospitality to one another without grumbling. Each of you should use whatever gift you have received to serve others, as faithful stewards of God's grace in its various forms. If anyone speaks, they should do so as one who speaks the very words of God. If anyone serves, they should do so with the strength God provides, so that in all things God may be praised through Jesus Christ.   1 PETER 4:7–11

As a prisoner for the Lord, then, I urge you to live a life worthy of the calling you have received. Be completely humble and gentle; be patient, bearing with one another in love. Make every effort to keep the unity of the Spirit through the bond of peace. There is one body and one Spirit, just as you were called to one hope when you were called; one Lord, one faith, one baptism; one God and Father of all, who is over all and through all and in all.

But to each one of us grace has been given as Christ apportioned it. This is why it says:

> "When he ascended on high,
> he took many captives
> and gave gifts to his people."

(What does "he ascended" mean except that he also descended to the lower, earthly regions? He who descended is the very one who ascended higher than all the heavens, in order to fill the whole universe.) So Christ himself gave the apostles, the prophets, the evangelists, the pastors and teachers, to equip his people for works of service, so that the body of Christ may be built up until we all reach unity in the faith and in the knowledge of the Son of God and become mature, attaining to the whole measure of the fullness of Christ.

Then we will no longer be infants, tossed back and forth by the waves, and blown here and there by every wind of teaching and by the cunning and craftiness of people in their deceitful scheming. Instead, speaking the truth in love, we will grow to become in every respect the mature body of him who is the head, that is, Christ. From him the whole body, joined and held together by every supporting ligament, grows and builds itself up in love, as each part does its work. EPHESIANS 4:1–16

CHAPTER

18

Offering My Time

---- KEY IDEA ----

I offer my time to fulfill God's purposes.

---- KEY VERSE ----

Whatever you do, whether in word or deed,
do it all in the name of the Lord Jesus, giving
thanks to God the Father through him.
Colossians 3:17

GIVING GOD OUR TIME

In essence, we cannot talk about "our" time since all time belongs to God. Every moment we have is a gift from him. It is because of this fact that we are called to use that time to honor our Father. The prophet Jonah learned this the hard way. God called Jonah to redirect his time from the popular job of serving Israel to the unpopular assignment of traveling to Nineveh to give their enemy a chance to repent and be saved by God.

The word of the LORD came to Jonah son of Amittai: "Go to the great city of Nineveh and preach against it, because its wickedness has come up before me."

But Jonah ran away from the LORD and headed for Tarshish. He went down to Joppa, where he found a ship bound for that port. After paying the fare, he went aboard and sailed for Tarshish to flee from the LORD.

Then the LORD sent a great wind on the sea, and such a violent storm arose that the ship threatened to break up. All the sailors were afraid and each cried out to his own god. And they threw the cargo into the sea to lighten the ship.

But Jonah had gone below deck, where he lay down and fell into a deep sleep. The captain went to him and said, "How can you sleep? Get up and call on your god! Maybe he will take notice of us so that we will not perish."

Then the sailors said to each other, "Come, let us cast lots to find out who is responsible for this calamity." They cast lots and the lot fell on Jonah. So they asked him, "Tell us, who is responsible for making all this trouble for us? What kind of work do you do? Where do you come from? What is your country? From what people are you?"

He answered, "I am a Hebrew and I worship the LORD, the God of heaven, who made the sea and the dry land."

This terrified them and they asked, "What have you done?" (They knew he was running away from the LORD, because he had already told them so.)

The sea was getting rougher and rougher. So they asked him, "What should we do to you to make the sea calm down for us?"

"Pick me up and throw me into the sea," he replied, "and it will become calm. I know that it is my fault that this great storm has come upon you."

Instead, the men did their best to row back to land. But they could not, for the sea grew even wilder than before. Then they cried out to the LORD, "Please, LORD, do not let us die for taking this man's life. Do not hold us accountable for killing an innocent man, for you, LORD, have done as you pleased." Then they took Jonah and threw him overboard, and the raging sea grew calm. At this the men greatly feared the LORD, and they offered a sacrifice to the LORD and made vows to him.

Now the LORD provided a huge fish to swallow Jonah, and Jonah was in the belly of the fish three days and three nights.

From inside the fish Jonah prayed to the LORD his God. He said:

> "In my distress I called to the LORD,
>   and he answered me.
> From deep in the realm of the dead I called for help,
>   and you listened to my cry.
> You hurled me into the depths,
>   into the very heart of the seas,
>   and the currents swirled about me;
> all your waves and breakers
>   swept over me.
> I said, 'I have been banished
>   from your sight;
> yet I will look again
>   toward your holy temple.'
> The engulfing waters threatened me,
>   the deep surrounded me;
>   seaweed was wrapped around my head.
> To the roots of the mountains I sank down;
>   the earth beneath barred me in forever.
> But you, LORD my God,
>   brought my life up from the pit.
>
> "When my life was ebbing away,
>   I remembered you, LORD,
> and my prayer rose to you,
>   to your holy temple.

"Those who cling to worthless idols
   turn away from God's love for them.
But I, with shouts of grateful praise,
   will sacrifice to you.
What I have vowed I will make good.
   I will say, 'Salvation comes from the LORD.'"

And the LORD commanded the fish, and it vomited Jonah onto dry land. JONAH 1:1—2:10

SERVING GOD'S PURPOSES

Not only are we to give our time to God, but we are also to use that time to serve his purposes, which can mean many different things. Like Jonah, God's people often needed reminders about this. When the first exiles returned to Judah from captivity in Babylon, one of their first priorities was to rebuild the temple and restore worship to the one true God. In 536 BC, under the leadership of Zerubbabel, the building project began. When opposition from the Samaritans and other neighbors intensified, the people got discouraged and the building came to a complete halt. For ten years the project lay dormant. The prophet Haggai delivered a chilling and effective message from God encouraging the people of God to reconsider how they prioritized their time.

In the second year of King Darius, on the first day of the sixth month, the word of the LORD came through the prophet Haggai to Zerubbabel son of Shealtiel, governor of Judah, and to Joshua son of Jozadak, the high priest:

This is what the LORD Almighty says: "These people say, 'The time has not yet come to rebuild the LORD's house.'"

Then the word of the LORD came through the prophet Haggai: "Is it a time for you yourselves to be living in your paneled houses, while this house remains a ruin?"

Now this is what the LORD Almighty says: "Give careful thought to your ways. You have planted much, but harvested little. You eat, but never have enough. You drink, but never have your fill. You put on clothes, but are not warm. You earn wages, only to put them in a purse with holes in it."

This is what the LORD Almighty says: "Give careful thought to your ways. Go up into the mountains and bring down timber and build my house, so that I may take pleasure in it and be honored," says the LORD. "You expected much, but see, it turned out to be little. What you brought home, I blew away. Why?" declares the LORD Almighty. "Because of my house, which remains a ruin, while each of you is busy with your own house. Therefore, because of you the heavens have withheld their dew and the earth its crops. I called for a drought on the fields and the mountains, on the grain, the new wine, the olive oil and everything else the ground produces, on people and livestock, and on all the labor of your hands."

Then Zerubbabel son of Shealtiel, Joshua son of Jozadak, the high priest, and the whole remnant of the people obeyed the voice of the LORD their God and the message of the prophet Haggai, because the LORD their God had sent him. And the people feared the LORD.

Then Haggai, the LORD's messenger, gave this message of the LORD to the people: "I am with you," declares the LORD. So the LORD stirred up the spirit of Zerubbabel son of Shealtiel, governor of Judah, and the spirit of Joshua son of Jozadak, the high priest, and the spirit of the whole remnant of the people. They came and began to work on the house of the LORD Almighty, their God, on the twenty-fourth day of the sixth month.   HAGGAI 1:1–15

One person who never needed reminding of the fact that his time was to be dedicated to God was God's Son, Jesus. After attending the Festival of Passover with his earthly parents, Jesus made the decision to stay a little longer and spend some time in the house of his heavenly Father. Even at the young age of twelve, Jesus understood how best to use his time.

Every year Jesus' parents went to Jerusalem for the Festival of the Passover. When he was twelve years old, they went up to the festival, according to the custom. After the festival was over, while his parents were returning home, the boy Jesus stayed behind in Jerusalem, but they were unaware of it. Thinking he was in their company, they traveled on for a day. Then they began looking for him among their relatives and friends. When they did not find him, they went back to Jerusalem to look for him. After three days they found him in the temple courts, sitting among the teachers, listening to them and asking them questions. Everyone who heard him was amazed at his understanding and his answers. When his parents saw him, they were astonished. His mother said to him, "Son, why have you treated us like this? Your father and I have been anxiously searching for you."

"Why were you searching for me?" he asked. "Didn't you know I had to be in my Father's house?" But they did not understand what he was saying to them.

Then he went down to Nazareth with them and was obedient to them. But his mother treasured all these things in her heart. And Jesus grew in wisdom and stature, and in favor with God and man.   LUKE 2:41–52

MANAGING OUR TIME

Managing our time involves discovering God's rhythms and balance. He desires for us to be replenished and renewed to face the assignments that lie ahead. One of the Ten Commandments instructs God's people to set aside the Sabbath as a day of rest. Christians today have sincere disagreements concerning whether or not Sabbath-keeping is obligatory. But before God gave the Israelites the Ten Commandments at Mount Sinai, he gave them a command and a lesson regarding the Sabbath and collecting manna. God clearly designed people with the need for regular and deliberate rest.

The whole Israelite community set out from Elim and came to the Desert of Sin, which is between Elim and Sinai, on the fifteenth day of the second month after they had come out of Egypt. In the desert the whole community grumbled against Moses and Aaron. The Israelites said to them, "If only we had died by the LORD's hand in Egypt! There we sat around pots of meat and ate all the food we wanted, but you have brought us out into this desert to starve this entire assembly to death."

Then the LORD said to Moses, "I will rain down bread from heaven for you. The people are to go out each day and gather enough for that day. In this way I will test them and see whether they will follow my instructions. On the sixth day they are to prepare what they bring in, and that is to be twice as much as they gather on the other days."

So Moses and Aaron said to all the Israelites, "In the evening you will know that it was the LORD who brought you out of Egypt, and in the morning you will see the glory of the LORD, because he has heard your grumbling against him. Who are we, that you should grumble against us?" Moses also said, "You will know that it was the LORD when he gives you meat to eat in the evening and all the bread you want in the morning, because he has heard your grumbling against him. Who are we? You are not grumbling against us, but against the LORD."

Then Moses told Aaron, "Say to the entire Israelite community, 'Come before the LORD, for he has heard your grumbling.'"

While Aaron was speaking to the whole Israelite community, they looked toward the desert, and there was the glory of the LORD appearing in the cloud.

The LORD said to Moses, "I have heard the grumbling of the Israelites. Tell them, 'At twilight you will eat meat, and in the morning you will be filled with bread. Then you will know that I am the LORD your God.'"

That evening quail came and covered the camp, and in the morning there was a layer of dew around the camp. When the dew was gone, thin flakes like frost on the ground appeared on the desert floor. When the Israelites saw it, they said to each other, "What is it?" For they did not know what it was.

Moses said to them, "It is the bread the LORD has given you to eat. This is what the LORD has commanded: 'Everyone is to gather as much as they need. Take an omer for each person you have in your tent.'"

The Israelites did as they were told; some gathered much, some little. And when they measured it by the omer, the one who gathered much did not have too much, and the one who gathered little did not have too little. Everyone had gathered just as much as they needed.

Then Moses said to them, "No one is to keep any of it until morning."

However, some of them paid no attention to Moses; they kept

part of it until morning, but it was full of maggots and began to smell. So Moses was angry with them.

Each morning everyone gathered as much as they needed, and when the sun grew hot, it melted away. On the sixth day, they gathered twice as much — two omers for each person — and the leaders of the community came and reported this to Moses. He said to them, "This is what the LORD commanded: 'Tomorrow is to be a day of sabbath rest, a holy sabbath to the LORD. So bake what you want to bake and boil what you want to boil. Save whatever is left and keep it until morning.'"

So they saved it until morning, as Moses commanded, and it did not stink or get maggots in it. "Eat it today," Moses said, "because today is a sabbath to the LORD. You will not find any of it on the ground today. Six days you are to gather it, but on the seventh day, the Sabbath, there will not be any."

Nevertheless, some of the people went out on the seventh day to gather it, but they found none. Then the LORD said to Moses, "How long will you refuse to keep my commands and my instructions? Bear in mind that the LORD has given you the Sabbath; that is why on the sixth day he gives you bread for two days. Everyone is to stay where they are on the seventh day; no one is to go out." So the people rested on the seventh day.   EXODUS 16:1–30

Clearly, God's Word, the Bible, contains stories and flat-out advice that illustrate healthy and godly time management. For example, the Israelites' needs were daunting after they escaped from Egypt. Living together in the harsh wilderness created an overwhelming docket of conflicts that needed refereeing. As the leader of the community, Moses tried his best to deal with each and every case on his own. Apparently Moses sent his wife, Zipporah, to her father with the news that the Lord had blessed his mission and that he was in the vicinity of Mount Sinai. When his father-in-law came to visit, he was deeply concerned with what he saw and gave Moses a lesson in time management.

Jethro, Moses' father-in-law, together with Moses' sons and wife, came to him in the wilderness, where he was camped near the mountain of God. Jethro had sent word to him, "I, your father-in-law Jethro, am coming to you with your wife and her two sons."

So Moses went out to meet his father-in-law and bowed down and kissed him. They greeted each other and then went into the tent. Moses told his father-in-law about everything the LORD had done to Pharaoh and the Egyptians for Israel's sake and about all the hardships they had met along the way and how the LORD had saved them.

Jethro was delighted to hear about all the good things the LORD had done for Israel in rescuing them from the hand of the Egyptians. He said, "Praise be to the LORD, who rescued you from the hand of the Egyptians and of Pharaoh, and who rescued the people from the hand of the Egyptians. Now I know that the LORD is greater than all other gods, for he did this to those who had treated Israel arrogantly." Then Jethro, Moses' father-in-law, brought a burnt offering and other sacrifices to God, and Aaron came with all the elders of Israel to eat a meal with Moses' father-in-law in the presence of God.

The next day Moses took his seat to serve as judge for the people, and they stood around him from morning till evening. When his father-in-law saw all that Moses was doing for the people, he said, "What is this you are doing for the people? Why do you alone sit as judge, while all these people stand around you from morning till evening?"

Moses answered him, "Because the people come to me to seek God's will. Whenever they have a dispute, it is brought to me, and I decide between the parties and inform them of God's decrees and instructions."

Moses' father-in-law replied, "What you are doing is not good. You and these people who come to you will only wear yourselves out. The work is too heavy for you; you cannot handle it alone. Listen now to me and I will give you some advice, and may God be with you. You must be the people's representative before God and bring their disputes to him. Teach them his decrees and instructions, and show them the way they are to live and how they are to behave. But select capable men from all the people — men who fear God, trustworthy men who hate dishonest gain — and appoint them as officials over thousands, hundreds, fifties and tens. Have them serve as judges for the people at all times, but have them bring every difficult case to you; the simple cases they can decide themselves. That will make your load lighter, because they will share it with you. If you do this and God so commands, you will be able to stand the strain, and all these people will go home satisfied."

Moses listened to his father-in-law and did everything he said. He chose capable men from all Israel and made them leaders of the people, officials over thousands, hundreds, fifties and tens. They served as judges for the people at all times. The difficult cases they brought to Moses, but the simple ones they decided themselves.

Then Moses sent his father-in-law on his way, and Jethro returned to his own country.   EXODUS 18:5–27

The book of Proverbs in the Old Testament is a collection of brief words of wisdom loosely bound together to teach the reader skills for living, including time management. The last chapter in the book is unique. In detail, it describes the day-to-day workings of the "wife of noble character," who is essentially a personification of wisdom. The way she juggled her responsibilities while keeping God's purposes at the center of it all is an inspiration to every follower of God.

A wife of noble character who can find?
    She is worth far more than rubies.
Her husband has full confidence in her
    and lacks nothing of value.
She brings him good, not harm,
    all the days of her life.
She selects wool and flax
    and works with eager hands.
She is like the merchant ships,
    bringing her food from afar.
She gets up while it is still night;
    she provides food for her family
    and portions for her female servants.
She considers a field and buys it;
    out of her earnings she plants a vineyard.
She sets about her work vigorously;
    her arms are strong for her tasks.

She sees that her trading is profitable,
    and her lamp does not go out at night.
In her hand she holds the distaff
    and grasps the spindle with her fingers.
She opens her arms to the poor
    and extends her hands to the needy.
When it snows, she has no fear for her household;
    for all of them are clothed in scarlet.
She makes coverings for her bed;
    she is clothed in fine linen and purple.
Her husband is respected at the city gate,
    where he takes his seat among the elders of the land.
She makes linen garments and sells them,
    and supplies the merchants with sashes.
She is clothed with strength and dignity;
    she can laugh at the days to come.
She speaks with wisdom,
    and faithful instruction is on her tongue.
She watches over the affairs of her household
    and does not eat the bread of idleness.
Her children arise and call her blessed;
    her husband also, and he praises her:
"Many women do noble things,
    but you surpass them all."
Charm is deceptive, and beauty is fleeting;
    but a woman who fears the LORD is to be praised.
Honor her for all that her hands have done,
    and let her works bring her praise at the city gate.

PROVERBS 31:10–31

Like the wife of noble character, Jesus also kept God as his focus in everything he did, including how he managed his time. When Jesus' ministry was in full swing, the demands on his schedule were intense. At this time in his journey, his brothers did not embrace his position as Messiah. With tongue in cheek they suggested Jesus make his way to Judea in time for a major Jewish festival to expedite his "campaign." Jesus informed them of an important principle of his life—he managed his priorities according to the timing of God the Father.

After this, Jesus went around in Galilee. He did not want to go about in Judea because the Jewish leaders there were looking for a way to kill him. But when the Jewish Festival of Tabernacles was near, Jesus' brothers said to him, "Leave Galilee and go to Judea, so that your disciples there may see the works you do. No one who wants to become a public figure acts in secret. Since you are doing these things, show yourself to the world." For even his own brothers did not believe in him.

Therefore Jesus told them, "My time is not yet here; for you any time will do. The world cannot hate you, but it hates me because I testify that its works are evil. You go to the festival. I am not going up to this festival, because my time has not yet fully come." After he had said this, he stayed in Galilee.

However, after his brothers had left for the festival, he went also, not publicly, but in secret. Now at the festival the Jewish leaders were watching for Jesus and asking, "Where is he?"

Among the crowds there was widespread whispering about him. Some said, "He is a good man."

Others replied, "No, he deceives the people." But no one would say anything publicly about him for fear of the leaders.

Not until halfway through the festival did Jesus go up to the temple courts and begin to teach. The Jews there were amazed and asked, "How did this man get such learning without having been taught?"

Jesus answered, "My teaching is not my own. It comes from the one who sent me." JOHN 7:1–16

THE REWARDS OF GIVING AWAY OUR TIME

When we give our time to serve the purposes of God, particularly to those who cannot reciprocate, God not only takes notice but may also reward us greatly.

"When the Son of Man comes in his glory, and all the angels with him, he will sit on his glorious throne. All the nations will be gathered before him, and he will separate the people one from another as a shepherd separates the sheep from the goats. He will put the sheep on his right and the goats on his left.

"Then the King will say to those on his right, 'Come, you who are blessed by my Father; take your inheritance, the kingdom prepared for you since the creation of the world. For I was hungry and you gave me something to eat, I was thirsty and you gave me something to drink, I was a stranger and you invited me in, I needed clothes and you clothed me, I was sick and you looked after me, I was in prison and you came to visit me.'

"Then the righteous will answer him, 'Lord, when did we see you hungry and feed you, or thirsty and give you something to drink? When did we see you a stranger and invite you in, or needing clothes and clothe you? When did we see you sick or in prison and go to visit you?'

"The King will reply, 'Truly I tell you, whatever you did for one of the least of these brothers and sisters of mine, you did for me.'

"Then he will say to those on his left, 'Depart from me, you who are cursed, into the eternal fire prepared for the devil and his angels. For I was hungry and you gave me nothing to eat, I was thirsty and you gave me nothing to drink, I was a stranger and you did not invite me in, I needed clothes and you did not clothe me, I was sick and in prison and you did not look after me.'

"They also will answer, 'Lord, when did we see you hungry or thirsty or a stranger or needing clothes or sick or in prison, and did not help you?'

"He will reply, 'Truly I tell you, whatever you did not do for one of the least of these, you did not do for me.'

"Then they will go away to eternal punishment, but the righteous to eternal life." MATTHEW 25:31–46

Be very careful, then, how you live — not as unwise but as wise, making the most of every opportunity, because the days are evil. Therefore do not be foolish, but understand what the Lord's will is. EPHESIANS 5:15–17

Do not be deceived: God cannot be mocked. A man reaps what he sows. Whoever sows to please their flesh, from the flesh will reap destruction; whoever sows to please the Spirit, from the Spirit will reap eternal life. Let us not become weary in doing good, for at the proper time we will reap a harvest if we do not give up. Therefore, as we have opportunity, let us do good to all people, especially to those who belong to the family of believers. GALATIANS 6:7–10

CHAPTER

19

Giving My Resources

---- KEY IDEA ----

I give my resources to fulfill God's purposes.

---- KEY VERSE ----

Since you excel in everything — in faith,
in speech, in knowledge, in complete earnestness
and in the love we have kindled in you — see that
you also excel in this grace of giving.
2 Corinthians 8:7

GIVING TITHES AND OFFERINGS

*Throughout the Old Testament, God's people set aside a tenth
of their proceeds of land, herds and flocks for God's purposes.
This principle is called tithing. Giving a tithe started as a nonreli-
gious, political tradition in the ancient world where giving a tribute or tax of a tenth (tithe) to the king was customary. This offering
demonstrated allegiance to the monarch's kingdom. When we
give a tenth of our income to God's purposes, we declare our
allegiance to God and his kingdom.*

*Jacob was one of the first followers of God who made a dec-
laration to honor the Lord with a tithe. He was the grandson of
Abraham, the son of Isaac and Rebekah, and the twin brother of
Esau. Jacob and Esau had a deeply strained relationship. Esau
was the firstborn, yet Jacob manipulated him to acquire his birth-
right and then—with the help of his mother—deceived his father
in order to receive the firstborn's special blessing. Although
Jacob's decisions weren't always upright, he did choose to honor
God with his wealth.*

Esau held a grudge against Jacob because of the blessing his father had given him. He said to himself, "The days of mourning for
my father are near; then I will kill my brother Jacob."

When Rebekah was told what her older son Esau had said, she
sent for her younger son Jacob and said to him, "Your brother Esau
is planning to avenge himself by killing you. Now then, my son,
do what I say: Flee at once to my brother Laban in Harran. Stay
with him for a while until your brother's fury subsides. When your
brother is no longer angry with you and forgets what you did to
him, I'll send word for you to come back from there. Why should I
lose both of you in one day?"

Then Rebekah said to Isaac, "I'm disgusted with living because
of these Hittite women. If Jacob takes a wife from among the wom-
en of this land, from Hittite women like these, my life will not be
worth living."

So Isaac called for Jacob and blessed him. Then he commanded him: "Do not marry a Canaanite woman. Go at once to Paddan
Aram, to the house of your mother's father Bethuel. Take a wife for
yourself there, from among the daughters of Laban, your mother's

brother. May God Almighty bless you and make you fruitful and increase your numbers until you become a community of peoples. May he give you and your descendants the blessing given to Abraham, so that you may take possession of the land where you now reside as a foreigner, the land God gave to Abraham." Then Isaac sent Jacob on his way, and he went to Paddan Aram, to Laban son of Bethuel the Aramean, the brother of Rebekah, who was the mother of Jacob and Esau.

Now Esau learned that Isaac had blessed Jacob and had sent him to Paddan Aram to take a wife from there, and that when he blessed him he commanded him, "Do not marry a Canaanite woman," and that Jacob had obeyed his father and mother and had gone to Paddan Aram. Esau then realized how displeasing the Canaanite women were to his father Isaac; so he went to Ishmael and married Mahalath, the sister of Nebaioth and daughter of Ishmael son of Abraham, in addition to the wives he already had.

Jacob left Beersheba and set out for Harran. When he reached a certain place, he stopped for the night because the sun had set. Taking one of the stones there, he put it under his head and lay down to sleep. He had a dream in which he saw a stairway resting on the earth, with its top reaching to heaven, and the angels of God were ascending and descending on it. There above it stood the LORD, and he said: "I am the LORD, the God of your father Abraham and the God of Isaac. I will give you and your descendants the land on which you are lying. Your descendants will be like the dust of the earth, and you will spread out to the west and to the east, to the north and to the south. All peoples on earth will be blessed through you and your offspring. I am with you and will watch over you wherever you go, and I will bring you back to this land. I will not leave you until I have done what I have promised you."

When Jacob awoke from his sleep, he thought, "Surely the LORD is in this place, and I was not aware of it." He was afraid and said, "How awesome is this place! This is none other than the house of God; this is the gate of heaven."

Early the next morning Jacob took the stone he had placed under his head and set it up as a pillar and poured oil on top of it. He called that place Bethel, though the city used to be called Luz.

Then Jacob made a vow, saying, "If God will be with me and will watch over me on this journey I am taking and will give me food to eat and clothes to wear so that I return safely to my father's household, then the LORD will be my God and this stone that I have set up as a pillar will be God's house, and of all that you give me I will give you a tenth."   GENESIS 27:41—28:22

It is evident from many examples in the Bible that our offerings to God need not be confined to our money, but can extend to our possessions, skills, labor, creativity and time. Remarkably, at a point in Israel's history when the Israelites were at their most vulnerable, wandering in the wilderness as nomads, they demonstrated their greatest generosity. God asked Moses to build a place called the tabernacle for him to dwell with his people. In order for this to happen, God's people needed to contribute their treasures and talents. Their generous response was so overwhelming that Moses had to tell them to stop bringing their gifts for the tabernacle.

Moses said to the whole Israelite community, "This is what the LORD has commanded: From what you have, take an offering for the LORD. Everyone who is willing is to bring to the LORD an offering of gold, silver and bronze; blue, purple and scarlet yarn and fine linen; goat hair; ram skins dyed red and another type of durable leather; acacia wood; olive oil for the light; spices for the anointing oil and for the fragrant incense; and onyx stones and other gems to be mounted on the ephod and breastpiece.

"All who are skilled among you are to come and make everything the LORD has commanded: the tabernacle with its tent and its covering, clasps, frames, crossbars, posts and bases; the ark with its poles and the atonement cover and the curtain that shields it; the table with its poles and all its articles and the bread of the Presence; the lampstand that is for light with its accessories, lamps and oil for the light; the altar of incense with its poles, the anointing oil and the fragrant incense; the curtain for the doorway at the entrance to the tabernacle; the altar of burnt offering with its bronze grating, its poles and all its utensils; the bronze basin with its stand; the curtains of the courtyard with its posts and bases, and the curtain for the entrance to the courtyard; the tent pegs for the tabernacle and for the courtyard, and their ropes; the woven garments worn for ministering in the sanctuary — both the sacred garments for Aaron the priest and the garments for his sons when they serve as priests."

Then the whole Israelite community withdrew from Moses' presence, and everyone who was willing and whose heart moved them came and brought an offering to the LORD for the work on the tent of meeting, for all its service, and for the sacred garments. All who were willing, men and women alike, came and brought gold jewelry of all kinds: brooches, earrings, rings and ornaments. They all presented their gold as a wave offering to the LORD. Everyone who had blue, purple or scarlet yarn or fine linen, or goat hair, ram skins dyed red or the other durable leather brought them. Those presenting an offering of silver or bronze brought it as an offering to the LORD, and everyone who had acacia wood for any part of the work brought it. Every skilled woman spun with her hands and brought what she had spun — blue, purple or scarlet yarn or fine linen. And all the women who were willing and had the skill spun the goat hair. The leaders brought onyx stones and other gems to be mounted on the ephod and breastpiece. They also brought spices and olive oil for the light and for the anointing oil and for the fragrant incense. All the Israelite men and women who were willing brought to the LORD freewill offerings for all the work the LORD through Moses had commanded them to do.   EXODUS 35:4–29

The people continued to bring freewill offerings morning after morning. So all the skilled workers who were doing all the work on the sanctuary left what they were doing and said to Moses, "The people are bringing more than enough for doing the work the LORD commanded to be done."

Then Moses gave an order and they sent this word throughout the camp: "No man or woman is to make anything else as an offering for the sanctuary." And so the people were restrained from bringing more, because what they already had was more than enough to do all the work.   EXODUS 36:3–7

While the Israelites moved from place to place in the wilderness during the time of Moses, they took the tabernacle with them wherever they relocated. Hundreds of years later after Israel had occupied the promised land and become a stable nation, the people once again generously and wholeheartedly gave from their resources, which they acknowledged God had given them in the first place, to build a house worthy of God's presence.

Then King David said to the whole assembly: "My son Solomon, the one whom God has chosen, is young and inexperienced. The task is great, because this palatial structure is not for man but for the LORD God. With all my resources I have provided for the temple of my God — gold for the gold work, silver for the silver, bronze for the bronze, iron for the iron and wood for the wood, as well as onyx for the settings, turquoise, stones of various colors, and all kinds of fine stone and marble — all of these in large quantities. Besides, in my devotion to the temple of my God I now give my personal treasures of gold and silver for the temple of my God, over and above everything I have provided for this holy temple: three thousand talents of gold (gold of Ophir) and seven thousand talents of refined silver, for the overlaying of the walls of the buildings, for the gold work and the silver work, and for all the work to be done by the craftsmen. Now, who is willing to consecrate themselves to the LORD today?"

Then the leaders of families, the officers of the tribes of Israel, the commanders of thousands and commanders of hundreds, and the officials in charge of the king's work gave willingly. They gave toward the work on the temple of God five thousand talents and ten thousand darics of gold, ten thousand talents of silver, eighteen thousand talents of bronze and a hundred thousand talents of iron. Anyone who had precious stones gave them to the treasury of the temple of the LORD in the custody of Jehiel the Gershonite. The people rejoiced at the willing response of their leaders, for they had given freely and wholeheartedly to the LORD. David the king also rejoiced greatly.

David praised the LORD in the presence of the whole assembly, saying,

> "Praise be to you, LORD,
> 　　the God of our father Israel,
> 　　from everlasting to everlasting.

Yours, LORD, is the greatness and the power
　　and the glory and the majesty and the splendor,
　　for everything in heaven and earth is yours.
Yours, LORD, is the kingdom;
　　you are exalted as head over all.
Wealth and honor come from you;
　　you are the ruler of all things.
In your hands are strength and power
　　to exalt and give strength to all.
Now, our God, we give you thanks,
　　and praise your glorious name.

"But who am I, and who are my people, that we should be able to give as generously as this? Everything comes from you, and we have given you only what comes from your hand. We are foreigners and strangers in your sight, as were all our ancestors. Our days on earth are like a shadow, without hope. LORD our God, all this abundance that we have provided for building you a temple for your Holy Name comes from your hand, and all of it belongs to you. I know, my God, that you test the heart and are pleased with integrity. All these things I have given willingly and with honest intent. And now I have seen with joy how willingly your people who are here have given to you. LORD, the God of our fathers Abraham, Isaac and Israel, keep these desires and thoughts in the hearts of your people forever, and keep their hearts loyal to you. 　　1 CHRONICLES 29:1–18

WHY WE GIVE

Giving away our money and resources is beneficial not only for the recipients but also for us. When we make giving to God's purposes part of our regular spending habits, we honor God and keep our greed at bay. The writers of the Proverbs offered the following words of wisdom.

Honor the LORD with your wealth,
　　with the firstfruits of all your crops;
then your barns will be filled to overflowing,
　　and your vats will brim over with new wine.

　　　　　　　　　　　　　　　　　PROVERBS 3:9–10

One person gives freely, yet gains even more;
    another withholds unduly, but comes to poverty.

A generous person will prosper;
    whoever refreshes others will be refreshed.

PROVERBS 11:24–25

Those who trust in their riches will fall,
    but the righteous will thrive like a green leaf.   PROVERBS 11:28

Solomon, one of the writers of Proverbs and the son of King David, experienced immense wealth during his lifetime. In the book of Ecclesiastes, traditionally considered to be written by Solomon, he reflects on his life and shares his words of wisdom with us regarding the dangers of wealth. Money itself is not evil, but the love of money can lead to sin. More wealth does not mean more satisfaction in life. To avoid falling victim to money's seductive lure, we are to use what we have for the Lord.

Whoever loves money never has enough;
    whoever loves wealth is never satisfied with their income.
    This too is meaningless.

As goods increase,
    so do those who consume them.
And what benefit are they to the owners
    except to feast their eyes on them?

The sleep of a laborer is sweet,
    whether they eat little or much,
but as for the rich, their abundance
    permits them no sleep.

I have seen a grievous evil under the sun:

wealth hoarded to the harm of its owners,
    or wealth lost through some misfortune,
so that when they have children
    there is nothing left for them to inherit.
Everyone comes naked from their mother's womb,
    and as everyone comes, so they depart.

> They take nothing from their toil
>> that they can carry in their hands.

This too is a grievous evil:

> As everyone comes, so they depart,
>> and what do they gain,
>> since they toil for the wind?
> All their days they eat in darkness,
>> with great frustration, affliction and anger.

This is what I have observed to be good: that it is appropriate for a person to eat, to drink and to find satisfaction in their toilsome labor under the sun during the few days of life God has given them — for this is their lot. Moreover, when God gives someone wealth and possessions, and the ability to enjoy them, to accept their lot and be happy in their toil — this is a gift of God. They seldom reflect on the days of their life, because God keeps them occupied with gladness of heart.   ECCLESIASTES 5:10–20

CONTENTMENT IS FOUND IN GOD, NOT MONEY

Jesus said more about money than the topics of heaven and hell combined. Our attitude toward money and personal resources says so much about our lives. Giving should flow from a pure heart desiring to meet a need. It should not be a way to draw attention to ourselves. We should also strive to think beyond our earthly life and share what we've been given in order to build God's kingdom.

"Be careful not to practice your righteousness in front of others to be seen by them. If you do, you will have no reward from your Father in heaven.

"So when you give to the needy, do not announce it with trumpets, as the hypocrites do in the synagogues and on the streets, to be honored by others. Truly I tell you, they have received their reward in full. But when you give to the needy, do not let your left hand know what your right hand is doing, so that your giving may be in secret. Then your Father, who sees what is done in secret, will reward you.   MATTHEW 6:1–4

"Do not store up for yourselves treasures on earth, where moths and vermin destroy, and where thieves break in and steal. But store up for yourselves treasures in heaven, where moths and vermin do not destroy, and where thieves do not break in and steal. For where your treasure is, there your heart will be also.

"The eye is the lamp of the body. If your eyes are healthy, your whole body will be full of light. But if your eyes are unhealthy, your whole body will be full of darkness. If then the light within you is darkness, how great is that darkness!

"No one can serve two masters. Either you will hate the one and love the other, or you will be devoted to the one and despise the other. You cannot serve both God and money." MATTHEW 6:19–24

Someone in the crowd said to him, "Teacher, tell my brother to divide the inheritance with me."

Jesus replied, "Man, who appointed me a judge or an arbiter between you?" Then he said to them, "Watch out! Be on your guard against all kinds of greed; life does not consist in an abundance of possessions."

And he told them this parable: "The ground of a certain rich man yielded an abundant harvest. He thought to himself, 'What shall I do? I have no place to store my crops.'

"Then he said, 'This is what I'll do. I will tear down my barns and build bigger ones, and there I will store my surplus grain. And I'll say to myself, "You have plenty of grain laid up for many years. Take life easy; eat, drink and be merry."'

"But God said to him, 'You fool! This very night your life will be demanded from you. Then who will get what you have prepared for yourself?'

"This is how it will be with whoever stores up things for themselves but is not rich toward God." LUKE 12:13–21

As is evident from the above parable of the rich fool, Jesus had a knack for noticing teachable moments. Everyday encounters with fig trees, water wells and simple dinner parties provided illustrations for Jesus to explain what matters the most to God. In this situation, Jesus was observing the daily activities at the temple when an opportunity arose for Jesus to teach his disciples what type of giving touches God's heart.

Jesus sat down opposite the place where the offerings were put and watched the crowd putting their money into the temple treasury. Many rich people threw in large amounts. But a poor widow came and put in two very small copper coins, worth only a few cents.

Calling his disciples to him, Jesus said, "Truly I tell you, this poor widow has put more into the treasury than all the others. They all gave out of their wealth; but she, out of her poverty, put in everything — all she had to live on."   MARK 12:41–44

It's easy to give when we know we will receive something in return. Jesus challenges us to remember that true giving has no strings attached.

"If you love those who love you, what credit is that to you? Even sinners love those who love them. And if you do good to those who are good to you, what credit is that to you? Even sinners do that. And if you lend to those from whom you expect repayment, what credit is that to you? Even sinners lend to sinners, expecting to be repaid in full. But love your enemies, do good to them, and lend to them without expecting to get anything back. Then your reward will be great, and you will be children of the Most High, because he is kind to the ungrateful and wicked. Be merciful, just as your Father is merciful."   LUKE 6:32–36

After Jesus' death, resurrection and ascension to heaven, his followers committed to give their money generously to help the needy among them and fulfill God's purposes.

All the believers were one in heart and mind. No one claimed that any of their possessions was their own, but they shared everything they had. With great power the apostles continued to testify to the resurrection of the Lord Jesus. And God's grace was so powerfully at work in them all that there were no needy persons among them. For from time to time those who owned land or houses sold them, brought the money from the sales and put it at the apostles' feet, and it was distributed to anyone who had need.

Joseph, a Levite from Cyprus, whom the apostles called Barnabas (which means "son of encouragement"), sold a field he owned and brought the money and put it at the apostles' feet.   ACTS 4:32–37

Evidence of the generosity of the early church can be seen in many circumstances. For instance, Paul encouraged the believers at Corinth to send an offering to their needy fellow believers in Jerusalem, something the Corinthians had intended to do but had not finished.

And now, brothers and sisters, we want you to know about the grace that God has given the Macedonian churches. In the midst of a very severe trial, their overflowing joy and their extreme poverty welled up in rich generosity. For I testify that they gave as much as they were able, and even beyond their ability. Entirely on their own, they urgently pleaded with us for the privilege of sharing in this service to the Lord's people. And they exceeded our expectations: They gave themselves first of all to the Lord, and then by the will of God also to us. So we urged Titus, just as he had earlier made a beginning, to bring also to completion this act of grace on your part. But since you excel in everything — in faith, in speech, in knowledge, in complete earnestness and in the love we have kindled in you — see that you also excel in this grace of giving.

I am not commanding you, but I want to test the sincerity of your love by comparing it with the earnestness of others. For you know the grace of our Lord Jesus Christ, that though he was rich, yet for your sake he became poor, so that you through his poverty might become rich.

And here is my judgment about what is best for you in this matter. Last year you were the first not only to give but also to have the desire to do so. Now finish the work, so that your eager willingness to do it may be matched by your completion of it, according to your means. For if the willingness is there, the gift is acceptable according to what one has, not according to what one does not have.

Our desire is not that others might be relieved while you are hard pressed, but that there might be equality. At the present time your plenty will supply what they need, so that in turn their plenty will supply what you need. The goal is equality, as it is written: "The one who gathered much did not have too much, and the one who gathered little did not have too little."

Thanks be to God, who put into the heart of Titus the same concern I have for you. For Titus not only welcomed our appeal, but he is coming to you with much enthusiasm and on his own initiative. And we are sending along with him the brother who is praised by all the churches for his service to the gospel. What is more, he was chosen by the churches to accompany us as we carry the offering, which we administer in order to honor the Lord himself and to show our eagerness to help. We want to avoid any criticism of the way we administer this liberal gift. For we are taking pains to do what is right, not only in the eyes of the Lord but also in the eyes of man.

In addition, we are sending with them our brother who has often proved to us in many ways that he is zealous, and now even more so because of his great confidence in you. As for Titus, he is my partner and co-worker among you; as for our brothers, they are representatives of the churches and an honor to Christ. Therefore show these men the proof of your love and the reason for our pride in you, so that the churches can see it.

There is no need for me to write to you about this service to the Lord's people. For I know your eagerness to help, and I have been boasting about it to the Macedonians, telling them that since last year you in Achaia were ready to give; and your enthusiasm has stirred most of them to action. But I am sending the brothers in order that our boasting about you in this matter should not prove hollow, but that you may be ready, as I said you would be. For if any Macedonians come with me and find you unprepared, we — not to say anything about you — would be ashamed of having been so confident. So I thought it necessary to urge the brothers to visit you in advance and finish the arrangements for the generous gift you had promised. Then it will be ready as a generous gift, not as one grudgingly given.

Remember this: Whoever sows sparingly will also reap sparingly, and whoever sows generously will also reap generously. Each of you should give what you have decided in your heart to give, not reluctantly or under compulsion, for God loves a cheerful giver.

And God is able to bless you abundantly, so that in all things at all times, having all that you need, you will abound in every good work. As it is written:

> "They have freely scattered their gifts to the poor;
>   their righteousness endures forever."

Now he who supplies seed to the sower and bread for food will also supply and increase your store of seed and will enlarge the harvest of your righteousness. You will be enriched in every way so that you can be generous on every occasion, and through us your generosity will result in thanksgiving to God.

This service that you perform is not only supplying the needs of the Lord's people but is also overflowing in many expressions of thanks to God. Because of the service by which you have proved yourselves, others will praise God for the obedience that accompanies your confession of the gospel of Christ, and for your generosity in sharing with them and with everyone else. And in their prayers for you their hearts will go out to you, because of the surpassing grace God has given you. Thanks be to God for his indescribable gift!   2 CORINTHIANS 8:1—9:15

Paul earned his living as a tentmaker during his missionary journeys, though he was grateful for the financial support he received from some churches, such as the church at Philippi. He preached the gospel sincerely and free of charge, taking care not to be a financial burden to believers. Regardless of his circumstances, Paul learned a vital lesson: Having enough doesn't bring contentment; contentment makes what you have enough.

I rejoiced greatly in the Lord that at last you renewed your concern for me. Indeed, you were concerned, but you had no opportunity to show it. I am not saying this because I am in need, for I have learned to be content whatever the circumstances. I know what it is to be in need, and I know what it is to have plenty. I have learned the secret of being content in any and every situation, whether well fed or hungry, whether living in plenty or in want. I can do all this through him who gives me strength.

Yet it was good of you to share in my troubles. Moreover, as you Philippians know, in the early days of your acquaintance with the gospel, when I set out from Macedonia, not one church shared with me in the matter of giving and receiving, except you only; for even when I was in Thessalonica, you sent me aid more than once when I was in need. Not that I desire your gifts; what I desire is that more be credited to your account. I have received full payment and have more than enough. I am amply supplied, now that I have received from Epaphroditus the gifts you sent. They are a fragrant offering, an acceptable sacrifice, pleasing to God. And my God will meet all your needs according to the riches of his glory in Christ Jesus.   PHILIPPIANS 4:10–19

Command those who are rich in this present world not to be arrogant nor to put their hope in wealth, which is so uncertain, but to put their hope in God, who richly provides us with everything for our enjoyment. Command them to do good, to be rich in good deeds, and to be generous and willing to share. In this way they will lay up treasure for themselves as a firm foundation for the coming age, so that they may take hold of the life that is truly life.

1 TIMOTHY 6:17–19

CHAPTER

20

Sharing My Faith

--------- KEY IDEA ---------

I share my faith with others
to fulfill God's purposes.

--------- KEY VERSE ---------

Pray also for me, that whenever I speak,
words may be given me so that I will fearlessly
make known the mystery of the gospel,
for which I am an ambassador in chains.
Pray that I may declare it fearlessly, as I should.
Ephesians 6:19 – 20

THE CALL TO SHARE OUR FAITH

Catastrophically, the fall of humankind in the Garden of Eden shattered humanity's connection with God—the connection he originally intended when he created people. So God unfolded a plan to provide the way for all people to come back into a relationship with him. His grand plan included the founding of a brand-new nation. Two thousand years before the arrival of Jesus, God called Abram (later renamed Abraham) to start this new nation, eventually known as Israel. People from all nations would come to know God through Abraham's offspring.

The LORD had said to Abram, "Go from your country, your people and your father's household to the land I will show you.

"I will make you into a great nation,
    and I will bless you;
I will make your name great,
    and you will be a blessing.
I will bless those who bless you,
    and whoever curses you I will curse;
and all peoples on earth
    will be blessed through you."

So Abram went, as the LORD had told him.   GENESIS 12:1–4

In the two thousand years that followed, Israel was a living demonstration to the world of the lengths to which God would go to reestablish his relationship with his people. Then, with the ultimate sacrifice of his Son, the reconciliation with God that was formerly confined to Israel now became available to all humankind. What's remarkable is that we can play a pivotal role in God's restoration plan. By responding to the call to share our faith, we partner with God in his divine pursuit of broken souls.

For Christ's love compels us, because we are convinced that one died for all, and therefore all died. And he died for all, that those who live should no longer live for themselves but for him who died for them and was raised again.

So from now on we regard no one from a worldly point of view.

Though we once regarded Christ in this way, we do so no longer. Therefore, if anyone is in Christ, the new creation has come: The old has gone, the new is here! All this is from God, who reconciled us to himself through Christ and gave us the ministry of reconciliation: that God was reconciling the world to himself in Christ, not counting people's sins against them. And he has committed to us the message of reconciliation. We are therefore Christ's ambassadors, as though God were making his appeal through us. We implore you on Christ's behalf: Be reconciled to God. God made him who had no sin to be sin for us, so that in him we might become the righteousness of God.   2 CORINTHIANS 5:14–21

SHARING OUR FAITH THROUGH OUR LIFE

The most powerful way to share our faith in God is through our life—being a positive example to all in how we live every day. When others see the faith, hope and love in our life, they are drawn to live the same way. After paying attention over time, they will notice our confidence in and relationship with the one true God. In 2 Kings we find a story in which a young girl from Israel who had been taken captive speaks up because of her faith and her noble concern for her master, the commander of the army of Aram—Israel's enemy. The girl's words eventually led to the healing of this foreign soldier and inspired his belief in the one true God.

Now Naaman was commander of the army of the king of Aram. He was a great man in the sight of his master and highly regarded, because through him the LORD had given victory to Aram. He was a valiant soldier, but he had leprosy.

Now bands of raiders from Aram had gone out and had taken captive a young girl from Israel, and she served Naaman's wife. She said to her mistress, "If only my master would see the prophet who is in Samaria! He would cure him of his leprosy."

Naaman went to his master and told him what the girl from Israel had said. "By all means, go," the king of Aram replied. "I will send a letter to the king of Israel." So Naaman left, taking with him ten talents of silver, six thousand shekels of gold and ten sets of clothing. The letter that he took to the king of Israel read: "With this letter I am sending my servant Naaman to you so that you may cure him of his leprosy."

As soon as the king of Israel read the letter, he tore his robes and said, "Am I God? Can I kill and bring back to life? Why does this fellow send someone to me to be cured of his leprosy? See how he is trying to pick a quarrel with me!"

When Elisha the man of God heard that the king of Israel had torn his robes, he sent him this message: "Why have you torn your robes? Have the man come to me and he will know that there is a prophet in Israel." So Naaman went with his horses and chariots and stopped at the door of Elisha's house. Elisha sent a messenger to say to him, "Go, wash yourself seven times in the Jordan, and your flesh will be restored and you will be cleansed."

But Naaman went away angry and said, "I thought that he would surely come out to me and stand and call on the name of the LORD his God, wave his hand over the spot and cure me of my leprosy. Are not Abana and Pharpar, the rivers of Damascus, better than all the waters of Israel? Couldn't I wash in them and be cleansed?" So he turned and went off in a rage.

Naaman's servants went to him and said, "My father, if the prophet had told you to do some great thing, would you not have done it? How much more, then, when he tells you, 'Wash and be cleansed'!" So he went down and dipped himself in the Jordan seven times, as the man of God had told him, and his flesh was restored and became clean like that of a young boy.

Then Naaman and all his attendants went back to the man of God. He stood before him and said, "Now I know that there is no God in all the world except in Israel." 2 KINGS 5:1–15

The God of all the world wants us to reflect his will in our life. In his famous Sermon on the Mount, Jesus used the metaphor of "salt and light" to express the power of a life lived in faith and obedience to God.

"You are the salt of the earth. But if the salt loses its saltiness, how can it be made salty again? It is no longer good for anything, except to be thrown out and trampled underfoot.

"You are the light of the world. A town built on a hill cannot be hidden. Neither do people light a lamp and put it under a bowl. Instead they put it on its stand, and it gives light to everyone in the house. In the same way, let your light shine before others, that they may see your good deeds and glorify your Father in heaven."

MATTHEW 5:13–16

Being the light of the world requires a humble servant attitude, a willingness to adapt our approach to meet the needs of the people we are trying to reach. Others were drawn to the Christian faith by the way the people of the church lived and served those around them.

They devoted themselves to the apostles' teaching and to fellowship, to the breaking of bread and to prayer. Everyone was filled with awe at the many wonders and signs performed by the apostles. All the believers were together and had everything in common. They sold property and possessions to give to anyone who had need. Every day they continued to meet together in the temple courts. They broke bread in their homes and ate together with glad and sincere hearts, praising God and enjoying the favor of all the people. And the Lord added to their number daily those who were being saved.

ACTS 2:42–47

Paul too illustrated well a humble servant attitude, which is captured in 1 Corinthians.

Though I am free and belong to no one, I have made myself a slave to everyone, to win as many as possible. To the Jews I became like a Jew, to win the Jews. To those under the law I became like one under the law (though I myself am not under the law), so as to win those under the law. To those not having the law I became like one not having the law (though I am not free from God's law but am under Christ's law), so as to win those not having the law. To the weak I became weak, to win the weak. I have become all things to all people so that by all possible means I might save some. I do all this for the sake of the gospel, that I may share in its blessings.

1 CORINTHIANS 9:19–23

SHARING OUR FAITH THROUGH OUR WORDS

In addition to sharing our faith by the way we live our life, we are also called to share who God is and what great things he has done for us through our words. David, overwhelmed with God's involvement in his life, was a strong witness through his words to God's character and acts.

I waited patiently for the LORD;
  he turned to me and heard my cry.
He lifted me out of the slimy pit,
  out of the mud and mire;
he set my feet on a rock
  and gave me a firm place to stand.
He put a new song in my mouth,
  a hymn of praise to our God.
Many will see and fear the LORD
  and put their trust in him.

Blessed is the one
  who trusts in the LORD,
who does not look to the proud,
  to those who turn aside to false gods.
Many, LORD my God,
  are the wonders you have done,
  the things you planned for us.
None can compare with you;
  were I to speak and tell of your deeds,
  they would be too many to declare.

Sacrifice and offering you did not desire —
  but my ears you have opened —
  burnt offerings and sin offerings you did not require.
Then I said, "Here I am, I have come —
  it is written about me in the scroll.
I desire to do your will, my God;
  your law is within my heart."

I proclaim your saving acts in the great assembly;
  I do not seal my lips, LORD,
  as you know.

I do not hide your righteousness in my heart;
    I speak of your faithfulness and your saving help.
I do not conceal your love and your faithfulness
    from the great assembly. PSALM 40:1–10

The entire early church had a mission to share the truth about God's love and faithfulness, which they accomplished by testifying with their mouths about the resurrected Christ. Although we may feel we are not as eloquent as David or as knowledgeable as Paul, like the early church members, we all have a mission to share our faith with others. It is through God that we have been given the power to carry out that assignment.

In my former book, Theophilus, I [Luke] wrote about all that Jesus began to do and to teach until the day he was taken up to heaven, after giving instructions through the Holy Spirit to the apostles he had chosen. After his suffering, he presented himself to them and gave many convincing proofs that he was alive. He appeared to them over a period of forty days and spoke about the kingdom of God. On one occasion, while he was eating with them, he gave them this command: "Do not leave Jerusalem, but wait for the gift my Father promised, which you have heard me speak about. For John baptized with water, but in a few days you will be baptized with the Holy Spirit."

Then they gathered around him and asked him, "Lord, are you at this time going to restore the kingdom to Israel?"

He said to them: "It is not for you to know the times or dates the Father has set by his own authority. But you will receive power when the Holy Spirit comes on you; and you will be my witnesses in Jerusalem, and in all Judea and Samaria, and to the ends of the earth." ACTS 1:1–8

Jesus had told his disciples of God's plan for them to be witnesses in Jerusalem, and in all Judea and Samaria, and to the ends of the earth, but none of them ventured outside of Jerusalem with the good news ... until they were forced to do so because of persecution. In the moment, the horrible harassment the believers experienced must have seemed to be a setback.

They may have left their belongings in Jerusalem, but they took their faith with them.

A great persecution broke out against the church in Jerusalem, and all except the apostles were scattered throughout Judea and Samaria ... But Saul began to destroy the church. Going from house to house, he dragged off both men and women and put them in prison.

Those who had been scattered preached the word wherever they went. Philip went down to a city in Samaria and proclaimed the Messiah there. When the crowds heard Philip and saw the signs he performed, they all paid close attention to what he said. For with shrieks, impure spirits came out of many, and many who were paralyzed or lame were healed. So there was great joy in that city.

ACTS 8:1–8

Now an angel of the Lord said to Philip, "Go south to the road — the desert road — that goes down from Jerusalem to Gaza." So he started out, and on his way he met an Ethiopian eunuch, an important official in charge of all the treasury of the Kandake (which means "queen of the Ethiopians"). This man had gone to Jerusalem to worship, and on his way home was sitting in his chariot reading the Book of Isaiah the prophet. The Spirit told Philip, "Go to that chariot and stay near it."

Then Philip ran up to the chariot and heard the man reading Isaiah the prophet. "Do you understand what you are reading?" Philip asked.

"How can I," he said, "unless someone explains it to me?" So he invited Philip to come up and sit with him.

This is the passage of Scripture the eunuch was reading:

> "He was led like a sheep to the slaughter,
>   and as a lamb before its shearer is silent,
>   so he did not open his mouth.
> In his humiliation he was deprived of justice.
>   Who can speak of his descendants?
>   For his life was taken from the earth."

The eunuch asked Philip, "Tell me, please, who is the prophet talking about, himself or someone else?" Then Philip began with that very passage of Scripture and told him the good news about Jesus.

As they traveled along the road, they came to some water and the eunuch said, "Look, here is water. What can stand in the way of my being baptized?" And he gave orders to stop the chariot. Then both Philip and the eunuch went down into the water and Philip baptized him. When they came up out of the water, the Spirit of the Lord suddenly took Philip away, and the eunuch did not see him again, but went on his way rejoicing. Philip, however, appeared at Azotus and traveled about, preaching the gospel in all the towns until he reached Caesarea.   ACTS 8:26–40

> Like Philip illustrated in his own life, when we choose to partner with God in his plan to piece together this broken world, we become his ambassadors, his representatives on earth. Being an ambassador of Christ is not easy. The apostle Paul, who suffered greatly for sharing his faith, understood this well. Despite the persecution, he was passionate about spreading the good news. While headed to Jerusalem during his third missionary journey, he requested a meeting with his good friends from Ephesus, since he knew there was a chance he'd never see them again.

From Miletus, Paul sent to Ephesus for the elders of the church. When they arrived, he said to them: "You know how I lived the whole time I was with you, from the first day I came into the province of Asia. I served the Lord with great humility and with tears and in the midst of severe testing by the plots of my Jewish opponents. You know that I have not hesitated to preach anything that would be helpful to you but have taught you publicly and from house to house. I have declared to both Jews and Greeks that they must turn to God in repentance and have faith in our Lord Jesus.

"And now, compelled by the Spirit, I am going to Jerusalem, not knowing what will happen to me there. I only know that in every city the Holy Spirit warns me that prison and hardships are facing me. However, I consider my life worth nothing to me; my only aim is to finish the race and complete the task the Lord Jesus has given me — the task of testifying to the good news of God's grace."

ACTS 20:17–24

In his letters, Paul asked fellow believers to pray for him as he shared his faith. And he called them to make the most of every opportunity to share the message of the good news. Paul's words are precious to us as well as we work to share our faith with those in our life.

Pray also for me, that whenever I speak, words may be given me so that I will fearlessly make known the mystery of the gospel, for which I am an ambassador in chains. Pray that I may declare it fearlessly, as I should. Ephesians 6:19–20

Devote yourselves to prayer, being watchful and thankful. And pray for us, too, that God may open a door for our message, so that we may proclaim the mystery of Christ, for which I am in chains. Pray that I may proclaim it clearly, as I should. Be wise in the way you act toward outsiders; make the most of every opportunity. Let your conversation be always full of grace, seasoned with salt, so that you may know how to answer everyone. Colossians 4:2–6

Sharing Our Faith with All

It was God's plan from the very beginning for all nations and all people to be a part of God's plan of redemption and restoration. The Israelites resisted God's calling to be the channel of his redemptive purposes for the peoples of the world. This sentiment was demonstrated in the story of Jonah. He was called by God to take God's message to the Assyrian people in the great city of Nineveh. When this assignment came to Jonah from God, he ran away in the opposite direction. God gave Jonah an opportunity to rethink his decision by placing him in the belly of a giant fish for three days. After God had the fish vomit Jonah onto dry land, he offered him an opportunity to change his mind.

Then the word of the Lord came to Jonah a second time: "Go to the great city of Nineveh and proclaim to it the message I give you."

Jonah obeyed the word of the Lord and went to Nineveh. Now Nineveh was a very large city; it took three days to go through it. Jonah began by going a day's journey into the city, proclaiming, "Forty more days and Nineveh will be overthrown." The Ninevites believed God. A fast was proclaimed, and all of them, from the greatest to the least, put on sackcloth.

When Jonah's warning reached the king of Nineveh, he rose from his throne, took off his royal robes, covered himself with sackcloth and sat down in the dust. This is the proclamation he issued in Nineveh:

"By the decree of the king and his nobles:

Do not let people or animals, herds or flocks, taste anything; do not let them eat or drink. But let people and animals be covered with sackcloth. Let everyone call urgently on God. Let them give up their evil ways and their violence. Who knows? God may yet relent and with compassion turn from his fierce anger so that we will not perish."

When God saw what they did and how they turned from their evil ways, he relented and did not bring on them the destruction he had threatened.

But to Jonah this seemed very wrong, and he became angry. He prayed to the LORD, "Isn't this what I said, LORD, when I was still at home? That is what I tried to forestall by fleeing to Tarshish. I knew that you are a gracious and compassionate God, slow to anger and abounding in love, a God who relents from sending calamity. Now, LORD, take away my life, for it is better for me to die than to live."

But the LORD replied, "Is it right for you to be angry?"

Jonah had gone out and sat down at a place east of the city. There he made himself a shelter, sat in its shade and waited to see what would happen to the city. Then the LORD God provided a leafy plant and made it grow up over Jonah to give shade for his head to ease his discomfort, and Jonah was very happy about the plant. But at dawn the next day God provided a worm, which chewed the plant so that it withered. When the sun rose, God provided a scorching east wind, and the sun blazed on Jonah's head so that he grew faint. He wanted to die, and said, "It would be better for me to die than to live."

But God said to Jonah, "Is it right for you to be angry about the plant?"

"It is," he said. "And I'm so angry I wish I were dead."

But the LORD said, "You have been concerned about this plant, though you did not tend it or make it grow. It sprang up overnight and died overnight. And should I not have concern for the great city of Nineveh, in which there are more than a hundred and twenty thousand people who cannot tell their right hand from their left — and also many animals?"   JONAH 3:1—4:11

The resistance of the Jews to share their faith with outsiders carried over into the time of Jesus. The Samaritans were a mixed-blood race resulting from the intermarriage of Israelites left behind when the people of the northern kingdom were exiled and Gentiles were brought into the land by the Assyrians. Resentful hostility existed between Jews and Samaritans in Jesus' day. To avoid these people who lived in the large region between Judea and Galilee, Jews would often go out of their way and cross over the Jordan River and travel on the east side. Modeling the value of inclusivity to his disciples, Jesus traveled directly through Samaria and went out of his way to talk to a Samaritan woman.

[Jesus] left Judea and went back once more to Galilee.

Now he had to go through Samaria. So he came to a town in Samaria called Sychar, near the plot of ground Jacob had given to his son Joseph. Jacob's well was there, and Jesus, tired as he was from the journey, sat down by the well. It was about noon.

When a Samaritan woman came to draw water, Jesus said to her, "Will you give me a drink?" (His disciples had gone into the town to buy food.)

The Samaritan woman said to him, "You are a Jew and I am a Samaritan woman. How can you ask me for a drink?" (For Jews do not associate with Samaritans.)

Jesus answered her, "If you knew the gift of God and who it is that asks you for a drink, you would have asked him and he would have given you living water."

"Sir," the woman said, "you have nothing to draw with and the well is deep. Where can you get this living water? Are you greater than our father Jacob, who gave us the well and drank from it himself, as did also his sons and his livestock?"

Jesus answered, "Everyone who drinks this water will be thirsty again, but whoever drinks the water I give them will never thirst. Indeed, the water I give them will become in them a spring of water welling up to eternal life."

The woman said to him, "Sir, give me this water so that I won't get thirsty and have to keep coming here to draw water."

He told her, "Go, call your husband and come back."

"I have no husband," she replied.

Jesus said to her, "You are right when you say you have no husband. The fact is, you have had five husbands, and the man you now have is not your husband. What you have just said is quite true."

"Sir," the woman said, "I can see that you are a prophet. Our ancestors worshiped on this mountain, but you Jews claim that the place where we must worship is in Jerusalem."

"Woman," Jesus replied, "believe me, a time is coming when you will worship the Father neither on this mountain nor in Jerusalem. You Samaritans worship what you do not know; we worship what we do know, for salvation is from the Jews. Yet a time is coming and has now come when the true worshipers will worship the Father in the Spirit and in truth, for they are the kind of worshipers the Father seeks. God is spirit, and his worshipers must worship in the Spirit and in truth."

The woman said, "I know that Messiah" (called Christ) "is coming. When he comes, he will explain everything to us."

Then Jesus declared, "I, the one speaking to you — I am he."

Just then his disciples returned and were surprised to find him talking with a woman. But no one asked, "What do you want?" or "Why are you talking with her?"

Then, leaving her water jar, the woman went back to the town and said to the people, "Come, see a man who told me everything I ever did. Could this be the Messiah?" They came out of the town and made their way toward him.

Meanwhile his disciples urged him, "Rabbi, eat something."

But he said to them, "I have food to eat that you know nothing about."

Then his disciples said to each other, "Could someone have brought him food?"

"My food," said Jesus, "is to do the will of him who sent me and to finish his work. Don't you have a saying, 'It's still four months until harvest'? I tell you, open your eyes and look at the fields! They are ripe for harvest. Even now the one who reaps draws a wage and harvests a crop for eternal life, so that the sower and the reaper may be glad together. Thus the saying 'One sows and another reaps' is true. I sent you to reap what you have not worked for. Others have done the hard work, and you have reaped the benefits of their labor."

Many of the Samaritans from that town believed in him because of the woman's testimony, "He told me everything I ever did." So when the Samaritans came to him, they urged him to stay with them, and he stayed two days. And because of his words many more became believers.

They said to the woman, "We no longer believe just because of what you said; now we have heard for ourselves, and we know that this man really is the Savior of the world."   JOHN 4:3–42

Although Paul was known as the apostle to the Gentiles, his heart longed for his fellow Jews to respond to the message about Jesus. In his letter to the Romans, Paul declares God's plan and desire for both Jew and Gentile—all people—to hear the gospel and know Jesus as Lord. Paul also communicates that we must share God's critical message of salvation with others so they can act.

Brothers and sisters, my heart's desire and prayer to God for the Israelites is that they may be saved. For I can testify about them that they are zealous for God, but their zeal is not based on knowledge. Since they did not know the righteousness of God and sought to establish their own, they did not submit to God's righteousness. Christ is the culmination of the law so that there may be righteousness for everyone who believes.

Moses writes this about the righteousness that is by the law: "The person who does these things will live by them." But the righteousness that is by faith says: "Do not say in your heart, 'Who will ascend into heaven?'" (that is, to bring Christ down) "or 'Who will descend into the deep?'" (that is, to bring Christ up from the dead).

But what does it say? "The word is near you; it is in your mouth and in your heart," that is, the message concerning faith that we proclaim: If you declare with your mouth, "Jesus is Lord," and believe in your heart that God raised him from the dead, you will be saved. For it is with your heart that you believe and are justified, and it is with your mouth that you profess your faith and are saved. As Scripture says, "Anyone who believes in him will never be put to shame." For there is no difference between Jew and Gentile — the same Lord is Lord of all and richly blesses all who call on him, for, "Everyone who calls on the name of the Lord will be saved."

How, then, can they call on the one they have not believed in? And how can they believe in the one of whom they have not heard? And how can they hear without someone preaching to them? And how can anyone preach unless they are sent? As it is written: "How beautiful are the feet of those who bring good news!" ROMANS 10:1–15

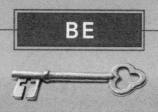

Who Am I Becoming?

I am the vine; you are the branches.
If you remain in me and I in you, you will bear
much fruit; apart from me you can do nothing.
John 15:5

In the passage above Jesus compares the Christian life to a vine. He is the vine; we are the branches. If we remain in the vine of Christ, over time it will produce amazing and scrumptious fruit at the end of our branches for all to see and taste.

People love ripe, delicious-tasting fruit, but grimace at green, rotten or artificial fruit. Jesus wants to produce in us fruit that brings great joy to us and to others. For this to happen, we must remain in Christ. To remain simply means to "stay put." Becoming like Jesus is a journey. Spiritual growth is compounding. The longer we remain consistent with Christ, the better it gets.

Nurturing the passion and discipline to *think* and *act* like Jesus is our proactive part in remaining in the vine of Christ, but we are not alone. The Father is the gardener. He waters, tills the soil, makes sure we have the proper exposure to the sun and prunes us.

As we remain in Christ and the Gardener does his work, eventually the bud of fruit appears on the end of our branches. With more time the fruit grows and ripens. Mature fruit on the outside gives evidence to the health of the branch on the inside. Mature fruit on the outside ministers to the people God has put in our life. It draws them to us; it nurtures them and gives them refreshment. This pleases God when we "pay forward" the love he first deposited in us.

The final ten chapters lay out the ten key virtues God desires to see developed in your life. As you read, silently whisper, "This is who I want to become!" And with God's help you will.

I can do all this through him who gives me strength.
Philippians 4:13

CHAPTER

21

Love

--- KEY IDEA ---

I am committed to loving God and loving others.

--- KEY VERSE ---

This is love: not that we loved God, but that he loved us and
sent his Son as an atoning sacrifice for our sins. Dear friends,
since God so loved us, we also ought to love one another.
No one has ever seen God; but if we love one another,
God lives in us and his love is made complete in us.
1 John 4:10 – 12

The Bible is a complex narrative. But what is the big—yet simple—idea behind all the stories and teachings contained in this ancient book? Love—love dominates God's story. First Corinthians 13 provides us with an earnest description of love that resonates throughout Scripture.

If I speak in the tongues of men or of angels, but do not have love, I am only a resounding gong or a clanging cymbal. If I have the gift of prophecy and can fathom all mysteries and all knowledge, and if I have a faith that can move mountains, but do not have love, I am nothing. If I give all I possess to the poor and give over my body to hardship that I may boast, but do not have love, I gain nothing.

Love is patient, love is kind. It does not envy, it does not boast, it is not proud. It does not dishonor others, it is not self-seeking, it is not easily angered, it keeps no record of wrongs. Love does not delight in evil but rejoices with the truth. It always protects, always trusts, always hopes, always perseveres.

Love never fails. But where there are prophecies, they will cease; where there are tongues, they will be stilled; where there is knowledge, it will pass away. For we know in part and we prophesy in part, but when completeness comes, what is in part disappears. When I was a child, I talked like a child, I thought like a child, I reasoned like a child. When I became a man, I put the ways of childhood behind me. For now we see only a reflection as in a mirror; then we shall see face to face. Now I know in part; then I shall know fully, even as I am fully known.

And now these three remain: faith, hope and love. But the greatest of these is love. 1 CORINTHIANS 13:1–13

THE GREATEST COMMANDMENT

Love as the greatest commandment can be found early in God's story with his people. For example, near the end of his life Moses gathered the Israelites together to remind them of what truly mattered as they readied themselves to enter the promised land. His words, recorded in the book of Deuteronomy, include a passage known as the Shema (Hebrew for "hear"), which later became the Jewish confession of faith, recited twice daily at the morning and evening prayer services. As the Shema articulates, the love between God and his people has always been the driver behind a life of faith.

Hear, O Israel: The LORD our God, the LORD is one. Love the LORD your God with all your heart and with all your soul and with all your strength. These commandments that I give you today are to be on your hearts. Impress them on your children. Talk about them when you sit at home and when you walk along the road, when you lie down and when you get up. Tie them as symbols on your hands and bind them on your foreheads. Write them on the doorframes of your houses and on your gates.   DEUTERONOMY 6:4–9

Flowing from the priority to love God with our whole heart, soul and strength was the command to love our neighbor as ourselves.

" 'Do not hate a fellow Israelite in your heart. Rebuke your neighbor frankly so you will not share in their guilt.
" 'Do not seek revenge or bear a grudge against anyone among your people, but love your neighbor as yourself. I am the LORD.' "
                                                                LEVITICUS 19:17–18

Jesus confirmed these two commands from the Old Testament—love God and love others—as the greatest of all the commandments during an encounter recorded in the New Testament between Jesus and the religious leaders.

One of the teachers of the law came and heard them debating. Noticing that Jesus had given them a good answer, he asked him, "Of all the commandments, which is the most important?"
"The most important one," answered Jesus, "is this: 'Hear, O Israel: The Lord our God, the Lord is one. Love the Lord your God with all your heart and with all your soul and with all your mind and with all your strength.' The second is this: 'Love your neighbor as yourself.' There is no commandment greater than these."
"Well said, teacher," the man replied. "You are right in saying that God is one and there is no other but him. To love him with all your heart, with all your understanding and with all your strength,

and to love your neighbor as yourself is more important than all burnt offerings and sacrifices."

When Jesus saw that he had answered wisely, he said to him, "You are not far from the kingdom of God." And from then on no one dared ask him any more questions. MARK 12:28–34

Followers of God are to live lives distinctly different from those around them. They are to be forgiving and self-giving, showing love to all. The command to love God and other people did not fade into the sunset with the rise of the church. The same principles that guided Israel remained essential for the church in New Testament times, as it does for the church today. Love is the ultimate fulfillment of all the laws of the Old Testament. The law of love is the only one that should rule the hearts and lives of Christians.

"You have heard that it was said, 'Love your neighbor and hate your enemy.' But I tell you, love your enemies and pray for those who persecute you, that you may be children of your Father in heaven. He causes his sun to rise on the evil and the good, and sends rain on the righteous and the unrighteous. If you love those who love you, what reward will you get? Are not even the tax collectors doing that? And if you greet only your own people, what are you doing more than others? Do not even pagans do that? Be perfect, therefore, as your heavenly Father is perfect."

MATTHEW 5:43–48

Let no debt remain outstanding, except the continuing debt to love one another, for whoever loves others has fulfilled the law. The commandments, "You shall not commit adultery," "You shall not murder," "You shall not steal," "You shall not covet," and whatever other command there may be, are summed up in this one command: "Love your neighbor as yourself." Love does no harm to a neighbor. Therefore love is the fulfillment of the law. ROMANS 13:8–10

THE CAPACITY OF LOVE
Left to our own sinful nature, or flesh, we move away from unconditional and sacrificial love and instead crave to satisfy our own wants over the needs and interests of others. Living a life of love

requires the presence of God's love and power within us. When we yield to this presence in our lives, it produces within us love for others. The law provides some instruction regarding how to live a life of love; the Spirit empowers us to actually do it.

You, my brothers and sisters, were called to be free. But do not use your freedom to indulge the flesh; rather, serve one another humbly in love. For the entire law is fulfilled in keeping this one command: "Love your neighbor as yourself." If you bite and devour each other, watch out or you will be destroyed by each other.

So I say, walk by the Spirit, and you will not gratify the desires of the flesh. For the flesh desires what is contrary to the Spirit, and the Spirit what is contrary to the flesh. They are in conflict with each other, so that you are not to do whatever you want. But if you are led by the Spirit, you are not under the law.

The acts of the flesh are obvious: sexual immorality, impurity and debauchery; idolatry and witchcraft; hatred, discord, jealousy, fits of rage, selfish ambition, dissensions, factions and envy; drunkenness, orgies, and the like. I warn you, as I did before, that those who live like this will not inherit the kingdom of God.

But the fruit of the Spirit is love, joy, peace, forbearance, kindness, goodness, faithfulness, gentleness and self-control. Against such things there is no law. Those who belong to Christ Jesus have crucified the flesh with its passions and desires. Since we live by the Spirit, let us keep in step with the Spirit. GALATIANS 5:13–25

Furthermore, our capacity to love begins with receiving God's love for us. From this reservoir we pour out love toward each other. The presence of God's Spirit in us, working through us to overcome our passion for self in favor of loving others, is confirmation that we are in fact children of God.

Dear friends, let us love one another, for love comes from God. Everyone who loves has been born of God and knows God. Whoever does not love does not know God, because God is love. This is how God showed his love among us: He sent his one and only Son into the world that we might live through him. This is love: not that we loved God, but that he loved us and sent his Son as an atoning sacrifice for our sins. Dear friends, since God so loved us, we also ought to love one another. No one has ever seen God; but if we love one another, God lives in us and his love is made complete in us.

This is how we know that we live in him and he in us: He has given us of his Spirit. And we have seen and testify that the Father has sent his Son to be the Savior of the world. If anyone acknowledges that Jesus is the Son of God, God lives in them and they in God. And so we know and rely on the love God has for us.

God is love. Whoever lives in love lives in God, and God in them. This is how love is made complete among us so that we will have confidence on the day of judgment: In this world we are like Jesus. There is no fear in love. But perfect love drives out fear, because fear has to do with punishment. The one who fears is not made perfect in love.

We love because he first loved us. Whoever claims to love God yet hates a brother or sister is a liar. For whoever does not love their brother and sister, whom they have seen, cannot love God, whom they have not seen. And he has given us this command: Anyone who loves God must also love their brother and sister.

1 JOHN 4:7–21

Although we may love our brother or sister, all relationships have their issues. Unfortunately, dissonance can replace the love when we leave those hurts and offenses unresolved. When Peter approached Jesus with a question about forgiveness, Jesus answered the question and followed it up with a poignant parable to illustrate his point. It is forgiveness that keeps relationships connected and prevents a root of bitterness from dividing people.

Then Peter came to Jesus and asked, "Lord, how many times shall I forgive my brother or sister who sins against me? Up to seven times?"

Jesus answered, "I tell you, not seven times, but seventy-seven times.

"Therefore, the kingdom of heaven is like a king who wanted to settle accounts with his servants. As he began the settlement, a man who owed him ten thousand bags of gold was brought to him.

Since he was not able to pay, the master ordered that he and his wife and his children and all that he had be sold to repay the debt.

"At this the servant fell on his knees before him. 'Be patient with me,' he begged, 'and I will pay back everything.' The servant's master took pity on him, canceled the debt and let him go.

"But when that servant went out, he found one of his fellow servants who owed him a hundred silver coins. He grabbed him and began to choke him. 'Pay back what you owe me!' he demanded.

"His fellow servant fell to his knees and begged him, 'Be patient with me, and I will pay it back.'

"But he refused. Instead, he went off and had the man thrown into prison until he could pay the debt. When the other servants saw what had happened, they were outraged and went and told their master everything that had happened.

"Then the master called the servant in. 'You wicked servant,' he said, 'I canceled all that debt of yours because you begged me to. Shouldn't you have had mercy on your fellow servant just as I had on you?' In anger his master handed him over to the jailers to be tortured, until he should pay back all he owed.

"This is how my heavenly Father will treat each of you unless you forgive your brother or sister from your heart." MATTHEW 18:21–35

A LOVING EXAMPLE: DAVID AND JONATHAN

Now that we have a clear understanding of love as God has intended it to be, it's powerful to look at how that love has been exemplified by God's people in the Bible. One of the most beautiful and inspiring stories of someone loving another as they would themselves is Jonathan and David. Jonathan, the son of King Saul, the first monarch of Israel, was next in line to reign. But when young David emerged into the limelight after killing the Philistine giant Goliath with a mere slingshot, it was clear that God had other plans. Jonathan recognized God's hand on David and graciously stepped aside and even protected David. King Saul saw the same thing, but instead became driven by jealousy and insecurity.

Jonathan became one in spirit with David, and he loved him as himself. From that day Saul kept David with him and did not let him return home to his family. And Jonathan made a covenant with David because he loved him as himself. Jonathan took off the robe he was wearing and gave it to David, along with his tunic, and even his sword, his bow and his belt.   1 SAMUEL 18:1–4

Saul told his son Jonathan and all the attendants to kill David. But Jonathan had taken a great liking to David and warned him, "My father Saul is looking for a chance to kill you. Be on your guard tomorrow morning; go into hiding and stay there. I will go out and stand with my father in the field where you are. I'll speak to him about you and will tell you what I find out."

Jonathan spoke well of David to Saul his father and said to him, "Let not the king do wrong to his servant David; he has not wronged you, and what he has done has benefited you greatly. He took his life in his hands when he killed the Philistine. The LORD won a great victory for all Israel, and you saw it and were glad. Why then would you do wrong to an innocent man like David by killing him for no reason?"

Saul listened to Jonathan and took this oath: "As surely as the LORD lives, David will not be put to death."

So Jonathan called David and told him the whole conversation. He brought him to Saul, and David was with Saul as before.

                                                              1 SAMUEL 19:1–7

Before long, Saul jealously turned against David again and threw a spear at David with the intent of killing him. David escaped and found himself on the run. It appears the purpose of this hardship in David's life was to give him the opportunity to see God's hand in his life and to learn to trust God unreservedly. David eventually found his way safely to Jonathan. David apparently wanted to make one more attempt to come alongside Saul and serve him if Saul would accept him. David and Jonathan agreed on a plan to expose the intent of Saul's heart.

Then David fled from Naioth at Ramah and went to Jonathan and asked, "What have I done? What is my crime? How have I wronged your father, that he is trying to kill me?"

"Never!" Jonathan replied. "You are not going to die! Look, my father doesn't do anything, great or small, without letting me know. Why would he hide this from me? It isn't so!"

But David took an oath and said, "Your father knows very well that I have found favor in your eyes, and he has said to himself, 'Jonathan must not know this or he will be grieved.' Yet as surely as the LORD lives and as you live, there is only a step between me and death."

Jonathan said to David, "Whatever you want me to do, I'll do for you."

So David said, "Look, tomorrow is the New Moon feast, and I am supposed to dine with the king; but let me go and hide in the field until the evening of the day after tomorrow. If your father misses me at all, tell him, 'David earnestly asked my permission to hurry to Bethlehem, his hometown, because an annual sacrifice is being made there for his whole clan.' If he says, 'Very well,' then your servant is safe. But if he loses his temper, you can be sure that he is determined to harm me. As for you, show kindness to your servant, for you have brought him into a covenant with you before the LORD. If I am guilty, then kill me yourself! Why hand me over to your father?"

"Never!" Jonathan said. "If I had the least inkling that my father was determined to harm you, wouldn't I tell you?"

David asked, "Who will tell me if your father answers you harshly?"

"Come," Jonathan said, "let's go out into the field." So they went there together.

Then Jonathan said to David, "I swear by the LORD, the God of Israel, that I will surely sound out my father by this time the day after tomorrow! If he is favorably disposed toward you, will I not send you word and let you know? But if my father intends to harm you, may the LORD deal with Jonathan, be it ever so severely, if I do not let you know and send you away in peace. May the LORD be with you as he has been with my father. But show me unfailing kindness like the LORD's kindness as long as I live, so that I may not be killed, and do not ever cut off your kindness from my family — not even when the LORD has cut off every one of David's enemies from the face of the earth."

So Jonathan made a covenant with the house of David, saying, "May the LORD call David's enemies to account." And Jonathan had David reaffirm his oath out of love for him, because he loved him as he loved himself.

Then Jonathan said to David, "Tomorrow is the New Moon feast. You will be missed, because your seat will be empty. The day after tomorrow, toward evening, go to the place where you hid when this trouble began, and wait by the stone Ezel. I will shoot three arrows to the side of it, as though I were shooting at a target. Then I will send a boy and say, 'Go, find the arrows.' If I say to him, 'Look, the arrows are on this side of you; bring them here,' then come, because, as surely as the LORD lives, you are safe; there is no danger. But if I say to the boy, 'Look, the arrows are beyond you,' then you must go, because the LORD has sent you away. And about the matter you and I discussed — remember, the LORD is witness between you and me forever."

So David hid in the field, and when the New Moon feast came, the king sat down to eat. He sat in his customary place by the wall, opposite Jonathan, and Abner sat next to Saul, but David's place was empty. Saul said nothing that day, for he thought, "Something must have happened to David to make him ceremonially unclean — surely he is unclean." But the next day, the second day of the month, David's place was empty again. Then Saul said to his son Jonathan, "Why hasn't the son of Jesse come to the meal, either yesterday or today?"

Jonathan answered, "David earnestly asked me for permission to go to Bethlehem. He said, 'Let me go, because our family is observing a sacrifice in the town and my brother has ordered me to be there. If I have found favor in your eyes, let me get away to see my brothers.' That is why he has not come to the king's table."

Saul's anger flared up at Jonathan and he said to him, "You son of a perverse and rebellious woman! Don't I know that you have sided with the son of Jesse to your own shame and to the shame of the mother who bore you? As long as the son of Jesse lives on this earth, neither you nor your kingdom will be established. Now send someone to bring him to me, for he must die!"

"Why should he be put to death? What has he done?" Jonathan asked his father. But Saul hurled his spear at him to kill him. Then Jonathan knew that his father intended to kill David.

Jonathan got up from the table in fierce anger; on that second day of the feast he did not eat, because he was grieved at his father's shameful treatment of David.

In the morning Jonathan went out to the field for his meeting with David. He had a small boy with him, and he said to the boy, "Run and find the arrows I shoot." As the boy ran, he shot an arrow beyond him. When the boy came to the place where Jonathan's arrow had fallen, Jonathan called out after him, "Isn't the arrow beyond you?" Then he shouted, "Hurry! Go quickly! Don't stop!" The boy picked up the arrow and returned to his master. (The boy knew nothing about all this; only Jonathan and David knew.) Then Jonathan gave his weapons to the boy and said, "Go, carry them back to town."

After the boy had gone, David got up from the south side of the stone and bowed down before Jonathan three times, with his face to the ground. Then they kissed each other and wept together — but David wept the most.

Jonathan said to David, "Go in peace, for we have sworn friendship with each other in the name of the LORD, saying, 'The LORD is witness between you and me, and between your descendants and my descendants forever.'" Then David left, and Jonathan went back to the town.   1 SAMUEL 20:1–42

David was a fugitive, on the run from King Saul for several years. While David was hiding from Saul, the Philistines — the same enemy David defeated as a young man — attacked and defeated Israel. Jonathan was killed in battle and Saul took his own life as the enemy closed in on him. A short time later David was inaugurated as the king of Israel. When David's kingdom was well established, he demonstrated that he hadn't forgotten his promise to show kindness to Jonathan's family by taking care of Jonathan's son Mephibosheth. In his relationship with both Jonathan and Mephibosheth and throughout his reign as king, David demonstrated his commitment to love God and others.

CHAPTER

22

Joy

--- KEY IDEA ---

Despite my circumstances,
I feel inner contentment and understand
my purpose in life.

--- KEY VERSE ---

I have told you this so that my joy may be in you
and that your joy may be complete.
John 15:11

SOURCE OF JOY

God may shower us with blessings and circumstances that bring joy to our lives, but true joy is found not in those things themselves but in their source. Joy can also be fueled and found in living out God's Word and trusting in the promises God gives us in his Word. The psalmist declared this truth with great confidence in this song.

Keep me safe, my God,
 for in you I take refuge.

I say to the LORD, "You are my Lord;
 apart from you I have no good thing."
I say of the holy people who are in the land,
 "They are the noble ones in whom is all my delight."
Those who run after other gods will suffer more and
   more.
 I will not pour out libations of blood to such gods
 or take up their names on my lips.

LORD, you alone are my portion and my cup;
 you make my lot secure.
The boundary lines have fallen for me in pleasant places;
 surely I have a delightful inheritance.
I will praise the LORD, who counsels me;
 even at night my heart instructs me.
I keep my eyes always on the LORD.
 With him at my right hand, I will not be shaken.

Therefore my heart is glad and my tongue rejoices;
 my body also will rest secure,
because you will not abandon me to the realm of the dead,
 nor will you let your faithful one see decay.
You make known to me the path of life;
 you will fill me with joy in your presence,
 with eternal pleasures at your right hand. PSALM 16:1–11

The precepts of the LORD are right,
 giving joy to the heart.

The commands of the LORD are radiant,
   giving light to the eyes.   PSALM 19:8

I rejoice in following your statutes
   as one rejoices in great riches.   PSALM 119:14

I rejoice in your promise
   like one who finds great spoil.   PSALM 119:162

God's promises find their ultimate fulfillment in his Son Jesus.
So when we abide in the vine of Christ through obedience to
his commands, his nutrients of joy run through our spiritual veins
from the inside out and produce the ripe, juicy fruit of joy in and
through our lives.

"I am the true vine, and my Father is the gardener. He cuts off
every branch in me that bears no fruit, while every branch that
does bear fruit he prunes so that it will be even more fruitful. You
are already clean because of the word I have spoken to you. Remain in me, as I also remain in you. No branch can bear fruit by
itself; it must remain in the vine. Neither can you bear fruit unless
you remain in me.

"I am the vine; you are the branches. If you remain in me and I
in you, you will bear much fruit; apart from me you can do nothing. If you do not remain in me, you are like a branch that is thrown
away and withers; such branches are picked up, thrown into the
fire and burned. If you remain in me and my words remain in you,
ask whatever you wish, and it will be done for you. This is to my
Father's glory, that you bear much fruit, showing yourselves to be
my disciples.

"As the Father has loved me, so have I loved you. Now remain
in my love. If you keep my commands, you will remain in my love,
just as I have kept my Father's commands and remain in his love.
I have told you this so that my joy may be in you and that your joy
may be complete."   JOHN 15:1–11

James wrote one of the first letters in the New Testament that
instructed believers regarding this new life in Christ. Followers of

Jesus can not only experience joy in spite of trials, but the trials themselves can be beneficial because they force us back to the true source of joy—God.

Consider it pure joy, my brothers and sisters, whenever you face trials of many kinds, because you know that the testing of your faith produces perseverance. Let perseverance finish its work so that you may be mature and complete, not lacking anything. If any of you lacks wisdom, you should ask God, who gives generously to all without finding fault, and it will be given to you. But when you ask, you must believe and not doubt, because the one who doubts is like a wave of the sea, blown and tossed by the wind. That person should not expect to receive anything from the Lord. Such a person is double-minded and unstable in all they do.

Believers in humble circumstances ought to take pride in their high position. But the rich should take pride in their humiliation — since they will pass away like a wild flower. For the sun rises with scorching heat and withers the plant; its blossom falls and its beauty is destroyed. In the same way, the rich will fade away even while they go about their business.

Blessed is the one who perseveres under trial because, having stood the test, that person will receive the crown of life that the Lord has promised to those who love him.

When tempted, no one should say, "God is tempting me." For God cannot be tempted by evil, nor does he tempt anyone; but each person is tempted when they are dragged away by their own evil desire and enticed. Then, after desire has conceived, it gives birth to sin; and sin, when it is full-grown, gives birth to death.

Don't be deceived, my dear brothers and sisters. Every good and perfect gift is from above, coming down from the Father of the heavenly lights, who does not change like shifting shadows.

JAMES 1:2–17

JOYFUL CELEBRATIONS

In the Old Testament people often responded to God's blessings with joyful celebrations. Coming together intentionally to remember God stimulated joy in the hearts of the people. The annual Festival of Tabernacles especially provided an opportunity

*for the Israelites to celebrate God's goodness, since the focus
was the blessing of God on their harvest and the work of their
hands. Moses instructed the Israelites to make this festival an
occasion to express their joy.*

Celebrate the Festival of Tabernacles for seven days after you
have gathered the produce of your threshing floor and your winepress. Be joyful at your festival — you, your sons and daughters,
your male and female servants, and the Levites, the foreigners,
the fatherless and the widows who live in your towns. For seven
days celebrate the festival to the LORD your God at the place the
LORD will choose. For the LORD your God will bless you in all your
harvest and in all the work of your hands, and your joy will be
complete.

Three times a year all your men must appear before the LORD
your God at the place he will choose: at the Festival of Unleavened
Bread, the Festival of Weeks and the Festival of Tabernacles. No
one should appear before the LORD empty-handed: Each of you
must bring a gift in proportion to the way the LORD your God has
blessed you.   DEUTERONOMY 16:13–17

*Another joyful celebration recorded in the Old Testament
occurred when David retrieved the ark of the covenant from the
Philistines. David understood the power of God's presence in
the center of Israelite life and community. After he built a tent to
store the ark he wrote a grand song to celebrate God for who he
is and what he had consistently done for Israel.*

David first appointed Asaph and his associates to give praise to
the LORD in this manner:

> Give praise to the LORD, proclaim his name;
>   make known among the nations what he has done.
> Sing to him, sing praise to him;
>   tell of all his wonderful acts.
> Glory in his holy name;
>   let the hearts of those who seek the LORD rejoice.
> Look to the LORD and his strength;
>   seek his face always.

Remember the wonders he has done,
    his miracles, and the judgments he pronounced,
you his servants, the descendants of Israel,
    his chosen ones, the children of Jacob.
He is the LORD our God;
    his judgments are in all the earth.

He remembers his covenant forever,
    the promise he made, for a thousand generations,
the covenant he made with Abraham,
    the oath he swore to Isaac.
He confirmed it to Jacob as a decree,
    to Israel as an everlasting covenant:
"To you I will give the land of Canaan
    as the portion you will inherit."

When they were but few in number,
    few indeed, and strangers in it,
they wandered from nation to nation,
    from one kingdom to another.
He allowed no one to oppress them;
    for their sake he rebuked kings:
"Do not touch my anointed ones;
    do my prophets no harm."

Sing to the LORD, all the earth;
    proclaim his salvation day after day.
Declare his glory among the nations,
    his marvelous deeds among all peoples.

For great is the LORD and most worthy of praise;
    he is to be feared above all gods.
For all the gods of the nations are idols,
    but the LORD made the heavens.
Splendor and majesty are before him;
    strength and joy are in his dwelling place.

Ascribe to the LORD, all you families of nations,
    ascribe to the LORD glory and strength.
Ascribe to the LORD the glory due his name;
    bring an offering and come before him.

Worship the LORD in the splendor of his holiness.
    Tremble before him, all the earth!
    The world is firmly established; it cannot be moved.

Let the heavens rejoice, let the earth be glad;
    let them say among the nations, "The LORD reigns!"
Let the sea resound, and all that is in it;
    let the fields be jubilant, and everything in them!
Let the trees of the forest sing,
    let them sing for joy before the LORD,
    for he comes to judge the earth.

Give thanks to the LORD, for he is good;
    his love endures forever.
Cry out, "Save us, God our Savior;
    gather us and deliver us from the nations,
that we may give thanks to your holy name,
    and glory in your praise."
Praise be to the LORD, the God of Israel,
    from everlasting to everlasting.

Then all the people said "Amen" and "Praise the LORD."

1 CHRONICLES 16:7–36

A little over 350 years after the death of David, the Babylonians exiled the people of Israel from the southern kingdom of Judah. The magnificent temple built by David's son Solomon was destroyed. Roughly 70 years later, according to God's plan, the people began to return home and immediately started rebuilding the temple. Opposition from the neighboring people, however, brought the project to a halt. God wielded the heart of a foreign ruler with immense power, King Darius of Persia (also known as the king of Assyria), to demand the opposition stand down and allow the temple to be completed. Finally, 20 years after the work began, the second temple was completed. With joy the returned exiles dedicated the temple and then about a month later celebrated the Passover (a yearly festival commemorating the night in Egypt when God "passed over" all the Israelites who had the blood of a lamb on the doorpost of their homes, thus sparing the lives

*of their firstborn sons) and the Festival of Unleavened Bread
(a seven-day festival beginning the day after Passover where the
Israelites ate only unleavened bread and presented their first
fruits of the harvest to the priests).*

Because of the decree King Darius had sent, Tattenai, governor of Trans-Euphrates, and Shethar-Bozenai and their associates carried it out with diligence. So the elders of the Jews continued to build and prosper under the preaching of Haggai the prophet and Zechariah, a descendant of Iddo. They finished building the temple according to the command of the God of Israel and the decrees of Cyrus, Darius and Artaxerxes, kings of Persia. The temple was completed on the third day of the month Adar, in the sixth year of the reign of King Darius.

Then the people of Israel — the priests, the Levites and the rest of the exiles — celebrated the dedication of the house of God with joy. For the dedication of this house of God they offered a hundred bulls, two hundred rams, four hundred male lambs and, as a sin offering for all Israel, twelve male goats, one for each of the tribes of Israel. And they installed the priests in their divisions and the Levites in their groups for the service of God at Jerusalem, according to what is written in the Book of Moses.

On the fourteenth day of the first month, the exiles celebrated the Passover. The priests and Levites had purified themselves and were all ceremonially clean. The Levites slaughtered the Passover lamb for all the exiles, for their relatives the priests and for themselves. So the Israelites who had returned from the exile ate it, together with all who had separated themselves from the unclean practices of their Gentile neighbors in order to seek the LORD, the God of Israel. For seven days they celebrated with joy the Festival of Unleavened Bread, because the LORD had filled them with joy by changing the attitude of the king of Assyria so that he assisted them in the work on the house of God, the God of Israel.   EZRA 6:13–22

JOY DESPITE OUR CIRCUMSTANCES

*Prior to the exile and return of the southern kingdom of Judah
was a dark season. The people were led, almost without interruption, by a succession of evil kings. Habakkuk was a prophet trying*

desperately to get the people back on track. He asked God how long he was going to let injustice and wickedness go on before he disciplined the nation. God informed the prophet that he was going to use the Babylonians to deal with Judah's persistent disobedience. Habakkuk struggled with this idea at first but in the end found resolve. Even though God's people were going to go through a difficult season, Habakkuk knew they could retain their joy based on what God had done for them in the past and his promises for the future.

LORD, I have heard of your fame;
    I stand in awe of your deeds, LORD.
Repeat them in our day,
    in our time make them known;
    in wrath remember mercy.

God came from Teman,
    the Holy One from Mount Paran.
His glory covered the heavens
    and his praise filled the earth.
His splendor was like the sunrise;
    rays flashed from his hand,
    where his power was hidden.
Plague went before him;
    pestilence followed his steps.
He stood, and shook the earth;
    he looked, and made the nations tremble.
The ancient mountains crumbled
    and the age-old hills collapsed —
    but he marches on forever.
I saw the tents of Cushan in distress,
    the dwellings of Midian in anguish.

Were you angry with the rivers, LORD?
    Was your wrath against the streams?
Did you rage against the sea
    when you rode your horses
    and your chariots to victory?
You uncovered your bow,
    you called for many arrows.

You split the earth with rivers;
    the mountains saw you and writhed.
Torrents of water swept by;
    the deep roared
    and lifted its waves on high.

Sun and moon stood still in the heavens
    at the glint of your flying arrows,
    at the lightning of your flashing spear.
In wrath you strode through the earth
    and in anger you threshed the nations.
You came out to deliver your people,
    to save your anointed one.
You crushed the leader of the land of wickedness,
    you stripped him from head to foot.
With his own spear you pierced his head
    when his warriors stormed out to scatter us,
gloating as though about to devour
    the wretched who were in hiding.
You trampled the sea with your horses,
    churning the great waters.

I heard and my heart pounded,
    my lips quivered at the sound;
decay crept into my bones,
    and my legs trembled.
Yet I will wait patiently for the day of calamity
    to come on the nation invading us.
Though the fig tree does not bud
    and there are no grapes on the vines,
though the olive crop fails
    and the fields produce no food,
though there are no sheep in the pen
    and no cattle in the stalls,
yet I will rejoice in the LORD,
    I will be joyful in God my Savior.

The Sovereign LORD is my strength;
    he makes my feet like the feet of a deer,
    he enables me to tread on the heights.   HABAKKUK 3:2–19

Just as God's people found joy and strength in God's promises amid dark times during Habakkuk's day, Jesus' disciples drew comfort and strength from Jesus' promises as they prepared for his death. A few hours before he was crucified Jesus sat with them and reassured them that their grief would be short-lived—three days to be exact. After that time something was going to happen to secure their joy in any and all circumstances.

It was just before the Passover Festival. Jesus knew that the hour had come for him to leave this world and go to the Father. Having loved his own who were in the world, he loved them to the end.

JOHN 13:1

Jesus went on to say, "In a little while you will see me no more, and then after a little while you will see me."

At this, some of his disciples said to one another, "What does he mean by saying, 'In a little while you will see me no more, and then after a little while you will see me,' and 'Because I am going to the Father'?" They kept asking, "What does he mean by 'a little while'? We don't understand what he is saying."

Jesus saw that they wanted to ask him about this, so he said to them, "Are you asking one another what I meant when I said, 'In a little while you will see me no more, and then after a little while you will see me'? Very truly I tell you, you will weep and mourn while the world rejoices. You will grieve, but your grief will turn to joy. A woman giving birth to a child has pain because her time has come; but when her baby is born she forgets the anguish because of her joy that a child is born into the world. So with you: Now is your time of grief, but I will see you again and you will rejoice, and no one will take away your joy. In that day you will no longer ask me anything. Very truly I tell you, my Father will give you whatever you ask in my name. Until now you have not asked for anything in my name. Ask and you will receive, and your joy will be complete."

JOHN 16:16–24

One of those disciples, the apostle Paul, later wrote a joyful treatise of sorts while under house arrest and chained to a Roman guard. In a passionate letter to the church at Philippi,

Paul fervently expressed his joy in Christ. Half of the lessons on increasing our joy are "taught" explicitly by Paul. Half of the lessons are "caught" implicitly by observing how Paul found joy despite his circumstances. At the letter's opening, notice how he found joy in the people God had placed in his life. Then we learn that Paul even saw his imprisonment as a blessing, for it helped bring attention to the gospel message.

Paul and Timothy, servants of Christ Jesus,

To all God's holy people in Christ Jesus at Philippi, together with the overseers and deacons:

Grace and peace to you from God our Father and the Lord Jesus Christ.

I thank my God every time I remember you. In all my prayers for all of you, I always pray with joy because of your partnership in the gospel from the first day until now, being confident of this, that he who began a good work in you will carry it on to completion until the day of Christ Jesus.

It is right for me to feel this way about all of you, since I have you in my heart and, whether I am in chains or defending and confirming the gospel, all of you share in God's grace with me. God can testify how I long for all of you with the affection of Christ Jesus.

And this is my prayer: that your love may abound more and more in knowledge and depth of insight, so that you may be able to discern what is best and may be pure and blameless for the day of Christ, filled with the fruit of righteousness that comes through Jesus Christ — to the glory and praise of God.

Now I want you to know, brothers and sisters, that what has happened to me has actually served to advance the gospel. As a result, it has become clear throughout the whole palace guard and to everyone else that I am in chains for Christ. And because of my chains, most of the brothers and sisters have become confident in the Lord and dare all the more to proclaim the gospel without fear.

It is true that some preach Christ out of envy and rivalry, but others out of goodwill. The latter do so out of love, knowing that I am put here for the defense of the gospel. The former preach Christ out of selfish ambition, not sincerely, supposing that they can stir up trouble for me while I am in chains. But what does it matter? The important thing is that in every way, whether from false motives or true, Christ is preached. And because of this I rejoice.

Yes, and I will continue to rejoice, for I know that through your prayers and God's provision of the Spirit of Jesus Christ what has happened to me will turn out for my deliverance.   PHILIPPIANS 1:1–19

> *Paul also instructed the Philippian believers on how to rise above the fear spurred by those who opposed them. He invited them to remove grumbling and arguing from their vocabulary as a means to increase their joy. The ultimate source of joy is in knowing Christ better, so Paul encouraged his readers to put the past behind them and stay focused on the future, giving all their troubles to God and rehearsing his blessings continuously.*

Whatever happens, conduct yourselves in a manner worthy of the gospel of Christ. Then, whether I come and see you or only hear about you in my absence, I will know that you stand firm in the one Spirit, striving together as one for the faith of the gospel without being frightened in any way by those who oppose you. This is a sign to them that they will be destroyed, but that you will be saved — and that by God. For it has been granted to you on behalf of Christ not only to believe in him, but also to suffer for him, since you are going through the same struggle you saw I had, and now hear that I still have.   PHILIPPIANS 1:27–30

Therefore, my dear friends, as you have always obeyed — not only in my presence, but now much more in my absence — continue to work out your salvation with fear and trembling, for it is God who works in you to will and to act in order to fulfill his good purpose.

Do everything without grumbling or arguing, so that you may become blameless and pure, "children of God without fault in a warped and crooked generation." Then you will shine among them like stars in the sky as you hold firmly to the word of life. And then I will be able to boast on the day of Christ that I did not run or labor in vain. But even if I am being poured out like a drink offering on the sacrifice and service coming from your faith, I am glad and rejoice with all of you. So you too should be glad and rejoice with me.　　　　　　　　　　　　　　　PHILIPPIANS 2:12–18

Further, my brothers and sisters, rejoice in the Lord! It is no trouble for me to write the same things to you again, and it is a safeguard for you. Watch out for those dogs, those evildoers, those mutilators of the flesh. For it is we who are the circumcision, we who serve God by his Spirit, who boast in Christ Jesus, and who put no confidence in the flesh — though I myself have reasons for such confidence.

If someone else thinks they have reasons to put confidence in the flesh, I have more: circumcised on the eighth day, of the people of Israel, of the tribe of Benjamin, a Hebrew of Hebrews; in regard to the law, a Pharisee; as for zeal, persecuting the church; as for righteousness based on the law, faultless.

But whatever were gains to me I now consider loss for the sake of Christ. What is more, I consider everything a loss because of the surpassing worth of knowing Christ Jesus my Lord, for whose sake I have lost all things. I consider them garbage, that I may gain Christ and be found in him, not having a righteousness of my own that comes from the law, but that which is through faith in Christ — the righteousness that comes from God on the basis of faith. I want to know Christ — yes, to know the power of his resurrection and participation in his sufferings, becoming like him in his death, and so, somehow, attaining to the resurrection from the dead.

Not that I have already obtained all this, or have already arrived at my goal, but I press on to take hold of that for which Christ Jesus took hold of me. Brothers and sisters, I do not consider myself yet to have taken hold of it. But one thing I do: Forgetting what is behind and straining toward what is ahead, I press on toward the goal to win the prize for which God has called me heavenward in Christ Jesus.

All of us, then, who are mature should take such a view of things. And if on some point you think differently, that too God will make clear to you. Only let us live up to what we have already attained.

Join together in following my example, brothers and sisters, and just as you have us as a model, keep your eyes on those who live as we do. For, as I have often told you before and now tell you again even with tears, many live as enemies of the cross of Christ. Their destiny is destruction, their god is their stomach, and their glory is in their shame. Their mind is set on earthly things. But our citizenship is in heaven. And we eagerly await a Savior from there, the Lord Jesus Christ, who, by the power that enables him to bring everything under his control, will transform our lowly bodies so that they will be like his glorious body.   PHILIPPIANS 3:1–21

Therefore, my brothers and sisters, you whom I love and long for, my joy and crown, stand firm in the Lord in this way, dear friends!

I plead with Euodia and I plead with Syntyche to be of the same mind in the Lord. Yes, and I ask you, my true companion, help these women since they have contended at my side in the cause of the gospel, along with Clement and the rest of my co-workers, whose names are in the book of life.

Rejoice in the Lord always. I will say it again: Rejoice! Let your gentleness be evident to all. The Lord is near. Do not be anxious about anything, but in every situation, by prayer and petition, with thanksgiving, present your requests to God. And the peace of God, which transcends all understanding, will guard your hearts and your minds in Christ Jesus.

Finally, brothers and sisters, whatever is true, whatever is noble, whatever is right, whatever is pure, whatever is lovely, whatever is admirable — if anything is excellent or praiseworthy — think about such things. Whatever you have learned or received or heard from me, or seen in me — put it into practice. And the God of peace will be with you.   PHILIPPIANS 4:1–9

Paul wrapped up his thoughts by disclosing the secret to contentment despite life's varying circumstances.

I rejoiced greatly in the Lord that at last you renewed your concern for me. Indeed, you were concerned, but you had no opportunity to show it. I am not saying this because I am in need, for I have learned to be content whatever the circumstances. I know what it is to be in need, and I know what it is to have plenty. I have learned the secret of being content in any and every situation, whether well fed or hungry, whether living in plenty or in want. I can do all this through him who gives me strength.   PHILIPPIANS 4:10–13

> *Like Paul, the apostle Peter also taught through his letters to the Christians scattered throughout Asia Minor that believers are in a position to experience joy in spite of, and because of, their difficult circumstances. The same is true for followers of Jesus today.*

Praise be to the God and Father of our Lord Jesus Christ! In his great mercy he has given us new birth into a living hope through the resurrection of Jesus Christ from the dead, and into an inheritance that can never perish, spoil or fade. This inheritance is kept in heaven for you, who through faith are shielded by God's power until the coming of the salvation that is ready to be revealed in the last time. In all this you greatly rejoice, though now for a little while you may have had to suffer grief in all kinds of trials. These have come so that the proven genuineness of your faith — of greater worth than gold, which perishes even though refined by fire — may result in praise, glory and honor when Jesus Christ is revealed. Though you have not seen him, you love him; and even though you do not see him now, you believe in him and are filled with an inexpressible and glorious joy, for you are receiving the end result of your faith, the salvation of your souls.   1 PETER 1:3–9

Dear friends, do not be surprised at the fiery ordeal that has come on you to test you, as though something strange were happening to you. But rejoice inasmuch as you participate in the sufferings of Christ, so that you may be overjoyed when his glory is revealed. If you are insulted because of the name of Christ, you are blessed, for the Spirit of glory and of God rests on you. If you suffer, it should not be as a murderer or thief or any other kind of criminal, or even as a meddler. However, if you suffer as a Christian, do not be ashamed, but praise God that you bear that name.

1 PETER 4:12–16

Humble yourselves, therefore, under God's mighty hand, that he may lift you up in due time. Cast all your anxiety on him because he cares for you.

Be alert and of sober mind. Your enemy the devil prowls around like a roaring lion looking for someone to devour. Resist him, standing firm in the faith, because you know that the family of believers throughout the world is undergoing the same kind of sufferings.

And the God of all grace, who called you to his eternal glory in Christ, after you have suffered a little while, will himself restore you and make you strong, firm and steadfast. To him be the power for ever and ever. Amen.   1 PETER 5:6–11

CHAPTER

23

Peace

KEY IDEA

I am free from anxiety because I have found peace with God,
peace with others and peace with myself.

KEY VERSE

Do not be anxious about anything, but in every situation,
by prayer and petition, with thanksgiving, present
your requests to God. And the peace of God,
which transcends all understanding, will guard
your hearts and your minds in Christ Jesus.
Philippians 4:6 – 7

PEACE WITH GOD

Most of us think of peace as a feeling. We want to trade our anxiety, depression and fear for calming tranquility. There are many harmful and ineffective ways people attempt to achieve this feeling, most notably by using alcohol or drugs. Biblical peace, however, starts not with the feeling of peace but with the root cause of it, meaning a strong and healthy relationship with God and with others. Of course, peace with God is made possible only through the Prince of Peace. When Christ establishes his eternal kingdom, societal peace will be the norm. Around seven hundred years before Jesus was born, Isaiah foretold of Jesus' arrival to earth and the far-reaching impact of his reign.

> For to us a child is born,
>> to us a son is given,
>> and the government will be on his shoulders.
> And he will be called
>> Wonderful Counselor, Mighty God,
>> Everlasting Father, Prince of Peace.
> Of the greatness of his government and peace
>> there will be no end.
> He will reign on David's throne
>> and over his kingdom,
> establishing and upholding it
>> with justice and righteousness
>> from that time on and forever.
> The zeal of the LORD Almighty
>> will accomplish this.   ISAIAH 9:6–7

> Who has believed our message
>> and to whom has the arm of the LORD been revealed?
> He grew up before him like a tender shoot,
>> and like a root out of dry ground.
> He had no beauty or majesty to attract us to him,
>> nothing in his appearance that we should desire him.
> He was despised and rejected by mankind,
>> a man of suffering, and familiar with pain.
> Like one from whom people hide their faces
>> he was despised, and we held him in low esteem.

Surely he took up our pain
   and bore our suffering,
yet we considered him punished by God,
   stricken by him, and afflicted.
But he was pierced for our transgressions,
   he was crushed for our iniquities;
the punishment that brought us peace was on him,
   and by his wounds we are healed.
We all, like sheep, have gone astray,
   each of us has turned to our own way;
and the Lord has laid on him
   the iniquity of us all.

He was oppressed and afflicted,
   yet he did not open his mouth;
he was led like a lamb to the slaughter,
   and as a sheep before its shearers is silent,
   so he did not open his mouth.
By oppression and judgment he was taken away.
   Yet who of his generation protested?
For he was cut off from the land of the living;
   for the transgression of my people he was punished.
He was assigned a grave with the wicked,
   and with the rich in his death,
though he had done no violence,
   nor was any deceit in his mouth.

Yet it was the Lord's will to crush him and cause him
      to suffer,
   and though the Lord makes his life an offering
      for sin,
he will see his offspring and prolong his days,
   and the will of the Lord will prosper in his hand.
After he has suffered,
   he will see the light of life and be satisfied;
by his knowledge my righteous servant will justify many,
   and he will bear their iniquities.
Therefore I will give him a portion among the great,
   and he will divide the spoils with the strong,

because he poured out his life unto death,
   and was numbered with the transgressors.
For he bore the sin of many,
   and made intercession for the transgressors. ISAIAH 53:1–12

While Christ's life on this earth was often troublesome and tumul-
tuous, it was his pouring out of his life unto death that produced
the possibility of a life of peace. For instance, in Paul's day, there
were enormous barriers of cultural prejudice and religious isola-
tion between Jews and Gentiles. The Jews arrogantly despised
the pagan Gentiles as dogs and viewed them contemptuously
as the "uncircumcised." Those attitudes went both ways; for
instance, the Greeks divided all people into two classes — Greeks
and barbarians. But these barriers came crashing down because
of Christ. Through the sacrifice of Jesus' death and resurrection,
all believers share mutual citizenship in God's kingdom of peace.

Therefore, since we have been justified through faith, we have
peace with God through our Lord Jesus Christ, through whom we
have gained access by faith into this grace in which we now stand.
And we boast in the hope of the glory of God. Not only so, but we
also glory in our sufferings, because we know that suffering produces perseverance; perseverance, character; and character, hope.
And hope does not put us to shame, because God's love has been
poured out into our hearts through the Holy Spirit, who has been
given to us.

You see, at just the right time, when we were still powerless,
Christ died for the ungodly. Very rarely will anyone die for a righteous person, though for a good person someone might possibly
dare to die. But God demonstrates his own love for us in this:
While we were still sinners, Christ died for us.

Since we have now been justified by his blood, how much more
shall we be saved from God's wrath through him! For if, while we
were God's enemies, we were reconciled to him through the death
of his Son, how much more, having been reconciled, shall we be
saved through his life! Not only is this so, but we also boast in God
through our Lord Jesus Christ, through whom we have now received reconciliation. ROMANS 5:1–11

Since, then, we know what it is to fear the Lord, we try to persuade others. What we are is plain to God, and I hope it is also plain to your conscience. We are not trying to commend ourselves to you again, but are giving you an opportunity to take pride in us, so that you can answer those who take pride in what is seen rather than in what is in the heart. If we are "out of our mind," as some say, it is for God; if we are in our right mind, it is for you. For Christ's love compels us, because we are convinced that one died for all, and therefore all died. And he died for all, that those who live should no longer live for themselves but for him who died for them and was raised again.

So from now on we regard no one from a worldly point of view. Though we once regarded Christ in this way, we do so no longer. Therefore, if anyone is in Christ, the new creation has come: The old has gone, the new is here! All this is from God, who reconciled us to himself through Christ and gave us the ministry of reconciliation: that God was reconciling the world to himself in Christ, not counting people's sins against them. And he has committed to us the message of reconciliation. We are therefore Christ's ambassadors, as though God were making his appeal through us. We implore you on Christ's behalf: Be reconciled to God. God made him who had no sin to be sin for us, so that in him we might become the righteousness of God.

As God's co-workers we urge you not to receive God's grace in vain. For he says,

> "In the time of my favor I heard you,
> and in the day of salvation I helped you."

I tell you, now is the time of God's favor, now is the day of salvation.   2 CORINTHIANS 5:11—6:2

As for you, you were dead in your transgressions and sins, in which you used to live when you followed the ways of this world and of the ruler of the kingdom of the air, the spirit who is now at work in those who are disobedient. All of us also lived among them at one time, gratifying the cravings of our flesh and following its desires and thoughts. Like the rest, we were by nature deserving of wrath. But because of his great love for us, God, who is rich in mercy, made us alive with Christ even when we were dead in transgressions — it is by grace you have been saved. And God raised us up with Christ and seated us with him in the heavenly realms in Christ Jesus, in order that in the coming ages he might show the incomparable riches of his grace, expressed in his kindness to us in Christ Jesus. For it is by grace you have been saved, through faith — and this is not from yourselves, it is the gift of God — not by works, so that no one can boast. For we are God's handiwork, created in Christ Jesus to do good works, which God prepared in advance for us to do.

Therefore, remember that formerly you who are Gentiles by birth and called "uncircumcised" by those who call themselves "the circumcision" (which is done in the body by human hands) — remember that at that time you were separate from Christ, excluded from citizenship in Israel and foreigners to the covenants of the promise, without hope and without God in the world. But now in Christ Jesus you who once were far away have been brought near by the blood of Christ.

For he himself is our peace, who has made the two groups one and has destroyed the barrier, the dividing wall of hostility, by setting aside in his flesh the law with its commands and regulations. His purpose was to create in himself one new humanity out of the two, thus making peace, and in one body to reconcile both of them to God through the cross, by which he put to death their hostility. He came and preached peace to you who were far away and peace to those who were near. For through him we both have access to the Father by one Spirit.

Consequently, you are no longer foreigners and strangers, but fellow citizens with God's people and also members of his household, built on the foundation of the apostles and prophets, with Christ Jesus himself as the chief cornerstone. In him the whole building is joined together and rises to become a holy temple in the Lord. And in him you too are being built together to become a dwelling in which God lives by his Spirit.   EPHESIANS 2:1–22

PEACE WITH OTHERS

While the Bible is brimming with examples of hostility and fighting, it also contains notable examples of people striving for peace. For instance, in the Old Testament Abram (later named Abraham) and his wife, Sarai (later named Sarah), and nephew Lot moved to Canaan and lived as nomadic shepherds. When conflict arose between the two men regarding space and land, Abram took the initiative to calm their dispute. Although Abram, as the elder, would normally have first pick of the land, he put the peace of the family above his own wishes.

So Abram went up from Egypt to the Negev, with his wife and everything he had, and Lot went with him. Abram had become very wealthy in livestock and in silver and gold.

From the Negev he went from place to place until he came to Bethel, to the place between Bethel and Ai where his tent had been earlier and where he had first built an altar. There Abram called on the name of the LORD.

Now Lot, who was moving about with Abram, also had flocks and herds and tents. But the land could not support them while they stayed together, for their possessions were so great that they were not able to stay together. And quarreling arose between Abram's herders and Lot's. The Canaanites and Perizzites were also living in the land at that time.

So Abram said to Lot, "Let's not have any quarreling between you and me, or between your herders and mine, for we are close relatives. Is not the whole land before you? Let's part company. If you go to the left, I'll go to the right; if you go to the right, I'll go to the left."

Lot looked around and saw that the whole plain of the Jordan toward Zoar was well watered, like the garden of the LORD, like the land of Egypt. (This was before the LORD destroyed Sodom and Gomorrah.) So Lot chose for himself the whole plain of the Jordan and set out toward the east. The two men parted company: Abram lived in the land of Canaan, while Lot lived among the cities of the plain and pitched his tents near Sodom. Now the people of Sodom were wicked and were sinning greatly against the LORD.

The LORD said to Abram after Lot had parted from him, "Look around from where you are, to the north and south, to the east and west. All the land that you see I will give to you and your offspring forever. I will make your offspring like the dust of the earth, so that if anyone could count the dust, then your offspring could be counted. Go, walk through the length and breadth of the land, for I am giving it to you."

So Abram went to live near the great trees of Mamre at Hebron, where he pitched his tents. There he built an altar to the LORD. GENESIS 13:1–18

Another example of people striving for peace in the Bible is found in the life of Jesus. In the Sermon on the Mount, Jesus encourages us to make living at peace with each other one of our top priorities, even above acts of worship. God makes it clear throughout Scripture that he values obedience over sacrifice. So if we are not at peace in our relationships, Jesus urges us not to keep performing acts of worship, but to pursue reconciliation first.

"You have heard that it was said to the people long ago, 'You shall not murder, and anyone who murders will be subject to judgment.' But I tell you that anyone who is angry with a brother or sister will be subject to judgment. Again, anyone who says to a brother or sister, 'Raca,' is answerable to the court. And anyone who says, 'You fool!' will be in danger of the fire of hell.

"Therefore, if you are offering your gift at the altar and there remember that your brother or sister has something against you, leave your gift there in front of the altar. First go and be reconciled to them; then come and offer your gift.

"Settle matters quickly with your adversary who is taking you to court. Do it while you are still together on the way, or your adversary may hand you over to the judge, and the judge may hand you over to the officer, and you may be thrown into prison. Truly I tell you, you will not get out until you have paid the last penny."

MATTHEW 5:21–26

Living at peace, even with fellow followers of Jesus, can be a challenge. We each think and feel differently. Naturally there are bound to be conflicts. The church in New Testament times was made up of both Jews and Gentiles. Many Jewish converts held on to the rituals of the Old Testament Law regarding diets and festivals. Some Jewish followers gladly left these rules behind in favor of their new freedom in Christ. Because the Gentiles had little regard for these traditions, it created tension in their community. Paul instructed the church in Rome how to experience peace even amid intense disagreements.

Accept the one whose faith is weak, without quarreling over disputable matters. One person's faith allows them to eat anything, but another, whose faith is weak, eats only vegetables. The one who eats everything must not treat with contempt the one who does not, and the one who does not eat everything must not judge the one who does, for God has accepted them. Who are you to judge someone else's servant? To their own master, servants stand or fall. And they will stand, for the Lord is able to make them stand.

One person considers one day more sacred than another; another considers every day alike. Each of them should be fully convinced in their own mind. Whoever regards one day as special does so to the Lord. Whoever eats meat does so to the Lord, for they give thanks to God; and whoever abstains does so to the Lord and gives thanks to God. For none of us lives for ourselves alone, and none of us dies for ourselves alone. If we live, we live for the Lord; and if we die, we die for the Lord. So, whether we live or die, we belong to the Lord. For this very reason, Christ died and returned to life so that he might be the Lord of both the dead and the living.

You, then, why do you judge your brother or sister? Or why do you treat them with contempt? For we will all stand before God's judgment seat. It is written:

> "'As surely as I live,' says the Lord,
> 'every knee will bow before me;
>   every tongue will acknowledge God.'"

So then, each of us will give an account of ourselves to God.

Therefore let us stop passing judgment on one another. Instead, make up your mind not to put any stumbling block or obstacle in the way of a brother or sister. I am convinced, being fully persuaded in the Lord Jesus, that nothing is unclean in itself. But if anyone regards something as unclean, then for that person it is unclean. If your brother or sister is distressed because of what you eat, you are no longer acting in love. Do not by your eating destroy someone for whom Christ died. Therefore do not let what you know is good be spoken of as evil. For the kingdom of God is not a matter of eating and drinking, but of righteousness, peace and joy in the Holy Spirit, because anyone who serves Christ in this way is pleasing to God and receives human approval.

Let us therefore make every effort to do what leads to peace and to mutual edification. Do not destroy the work of God for the sake of food. All food is clean, but it is wrong for a person to eat anything that causes someone else to stumble. It is better not to eat meat or drink wine or to do anything else that will cause your brother or sister to fall.

So whatever you believe about these things keep between yourself and God. Blessed is the one who does not condemn himself by what he approves. But whoever has doubts is condemned if they eat, because their eating is not from faith; and everything that does not come from faith is sin.

We who are strong ought to bear with the failings of the weak and not to please ourselves. Each of us should please our neighbors for their good, to build them up. For even Christ did not please himself but, as it is written: "The insults of those who insult you have fallen on me." For everything that was written in the past was written to teach us, so that through the endurance taught in the Scriptures and the encouragement they provide we might have hope.

May the God who gives endurance and encouragement give you the same attitude of mind toward each other that Christ Jesus had, so that with one mind and one voice you may glorify the God and Father of our Lord Jesus Christ.

Accept one another, then, just as Christ accepted you, in order to bring praise to God. For I tell you that Christ has become a servant of the Jews on behalf of God's truth, so that the promises made to the patriarchs might be confirmed and, moreover, that the Gentiles might glorify God for his mercy. As it is written:

"Therefore I will praise you among the Gentiles;
    I will sing the praises of your name."

Again, it says,

> "Rejoice, you Gentiles, with his people."

And again,

> "Praise the Lord, all you Gentiles;
> let all the peoples extol him."

And again, Isaiah says,

> "The Root of Jesse will spring up,
> one who will arise to rule over the nations;
> in him the Gentiles will hope."

May the God of hope fill you with all joy and peace as you trust in him, so that you may overflow with hope by the power of the Holy Spirit.   ROMANS 14:1—15:13

Many of the New Testament letters helped to resocialize the church to live in God's kingdom—a kingdom of righteousness, peace and joy. Paul offered specific instruction to believers in the various churches regarding how to achieve this divine vision through Christ. Believers were to set their sights on living at peace with everyone to the best of their ability.

Since, then, you have been raised with Christ, set your hearts on things above, where Christ is, seated at the right hand of God. Set your minds on things above, not on earthly things. For you died, and your life is now hidden with Christ in God. When Christ, who is your life, appears, then you also will appear with him in glory.

Put to death, therefore, whatever belongs to your earthly nature: sexual immorality, impurity, lust, evil desires and greed, which is idolatry. Because of these, the wrath of God is coming. You used to walk in these ways, in the life you once lived. But now you must also rid yourselves of all such things as these: anger, rage, malice, slander, and filthy language from your lips. Do not lie to each other, since you have taken off your old self with its practices and have put on the new self, which is being renewed in knowledge in the image of its Creator. Here there is no Gentile or Jew, circumcised or uncircumcised, barbarian, Scythian, slave or free, but Christ is all, and is in all.

Therefore, as God's chosen people, holy and dearly loved, clothe yourselves with compassion, kindness, humility, gentleness and patience. Bear with each other and forgive one another if any of you has a grievance against someone. Forgive as the Lord forgave you. And over all these virtues put on love, which binds them all together in perfect unity.

Let the peace of Christ rule in your hearts, since as members of one body you were called to peace. And be thankful. Let the message of Christ dwell among you richly as you teach and admonish one another with all wisdom through psalms, hymns, and songs from the Spirit, singing to God with gratitude in your hearts. And whatever you do, whether in word or deed, do it all in the name of the Lord Jesus, giving thanks to God the Father through him.

COLOSSIANS 3:1–17

Do not repay anyone evil for evil. Be careful to do what is right in the eyes of everyone. If it is possible, as far as it depends on you, live at peace with everyone. Do not take revenge, my dear friends, but leave room for God's wrath, for it is written: "It is mine to avenge; I will repay," says the Lord. On the contrary:

"If your enemy is hungry, feed him;
    if he is thirsty, give him something to drink.
In doing this, you will heap burning coals on his head."

Do not be overcome by evil, but overcome evil with good.

ROMANS 12:17–21

Paul offered a similar discourse to the church in Ephesus.

I urge, then, first of all, that petitions, prayers, intercession and thanksgiving be made for all people — for kings and all those in authority, that we may live peaceful and quiet lives in all godliness and holiness. This is good, and pleases God our Savior, who wants all people to be saved and to come to a knowledge of the truth. For there is one God and one mediator between God and mankind, the man Christ Jesus, who gave himself as a ransom for all people. This has now been witnessed to at the proper time. And for this purpose I was appointed a herald and an apostle — I am telling the truth, I am not lying — and a true and faithful teacher of the Gentiles.

Therefore I want the men everywhere to pray, lifting up holy hands without anger or disputing.   1 Timothy 2:1–8

Paul penned a letter to his faithful ministry partner Titus while Titus was leading the new believers on the Mediterranean Sea island of Crete. At this time Crete was known as an immoral, dishonest place filled with selfish people—all the ingredients for conflict and strife. Paul gave Titus tangible and practical advice to guide the believers there regarding how to live a life of peace.

Remind the people to be subject to rulers and authorities, to be obedient, to be ready to do whatever is good, to slander no one, to be peaceable and considerate, and always to be gentle toward everyone.

At one time we too were foolish, disobedient, deceived and enslaved by all kinds of passions and pleasures. We lived in malice and envy, being hated and hating one another. But when the kindness and love of God our Savior appeared, he saved us, not because of righteous things we had done, but because of his mercy. He saved us through the washing of rebirth and renewal by the Holy Spirit, whom he poured out on us generously through Jesus Christ our Savior, so that, having been justified by his grace, we might become heirs having the hope of eternal life. This is a trustworthy saying. And I want you to stress these things, so that those who have trusted in God may be careful to devote themselves to doing what is good. These things are excellent and profitable for everyone.

But avoid foolish controversies and genealogies and arguments and quarrels about the law, because these are unprofitable and useless. Warn a divisive person once, and then warn them a second time. After that, have nothing to do with them. You may be sure that such people are warped and sinful; they are self-condemned.

Titus 3:1–11

Peace With Yourself (Inner Peace)

Two-thirds of the use of the word "peace" (shalom) in the Old Testament involves the fulfillment that comes to humans when they experience God's presence. Such peace can be experienced from God's presence in our lives even in difficult circumstances. King David went through many difficult seasons during his life,

*but one of his most painful was when his own son Absalom con-
spired against him. When there is a deep schism with a loved
one, inner peace is at its most elusive.*

In the course of time, Absalom provided himself with a chariot and horses and with fifty men to run ahead of him. He would
get up early and stand by the side of the road leading to the city
gate. Whenever anyone came with a complaint to be placed before the king for a decision, Absalom would call out to him, "What
town are you from?" He would answer, "Your servant is from one
of the tribes of Israel." Then Absalom would say to him, "Look,
your claims are valid and proper, but there is no representative of
the king to hear you." And Absalom would add, "If only I were appointed judge in the land! Then everyone who has a complaint or
case could come to me and I would see that they receive justice."

Also, whenever anyone approached him to bow down before
him, Absalom would reach out his hand, take hold of him and kiss
him. Absalom behaved in this way toward all the Israelites who
came to the king asking for justice, and so he stole the hearts of the
people of Israel.

At the end of four years, Absalom said to the king, "Let me go
to Hebron and fulfill a vow I made to the LORD. While your servant was living at Geshur in Aram, I made this vow: 'If the LORD
takes me back to Jerusalem, I will worship the LORD in Hebron.'"

The king said to him, "Go in peace." So he went to Hebron.

Then Absalom sent secret messengers throughout the tribes of
Israel to say, "As soon as you hear the sound of the trumpets, then
say, 'Absalom is king in Hebron.'" Two hundred men from Jerusalem had accompanied Absalom. They had been invited as guests
and went quite innocently, knowing nothing about the matter.
While Absalom was offering sacrifices, he also sent for Ahithophel
the Gilonite, David's counselor, to come from Giloh, his hometown. And so the conspiracy gained strength, and Absalom's following kept on increasing.

A messenger came and told David, "The hearts of the people of
Israel are with Absalom."

Then David said to all his officials who were with him in Jerusalem, "Come! We must flee, or none of us will escape from

Absalom. We must leave immediately, or he will move quickly to overtake us and bring ruin on us and put the city to the sword."

The king's officials answered him, "Your servants are ready to do whatever our lord the king chooses."

The king set out, with his entire household following him; but he left ten concubines to take care of the palace.   2 Samuel 15:1–16

The whole countryside wept aloud as all the people passed by. The king also crossed the Kidron Valley, and all the people moved on toward the wilderness.   2 Samuel 15:23

David continued up the Mount of Olives, weeping as he went; his head was covered and he was barefoot. All the people with him covered their heads too and were weeping as they went up.

2 Samuel 15:30

David wrote many of his psalms from a place of anguish and despair, yet they all seem to take a turn and end in trust and even rejoicing. The editors of the book of Psalms connected Psalm 3 with this specific situation between Absalom and David. Although inner peace would seem impossible for one who is fleeing in anguish from his own son, in the end David found inner peace because he fixed his thoughts on God's presence in his life.

A psalm of David. When he fled from his son Absalom.

Lord, how many are my foes!
   How many rise up against me!
Many are saying of me,
   "God will not deliver him."

But you, Lord, are a shield around me,
   my glory, the One who lifts my head high.
I call out to the Lord,
   and he answers me from his holy mountain.

I lie down and sleep;
   I wake again, because the Lord sustains me.
I will not fear though tens of thousands
   assail me on every side.

> Arise, LORD!
>> Deliver me, my God!
> Strike all my enemies on the jaw;
>> break the teeth of the wicked.
>
> From the LORD comes deliverance.
>> May your blessing be on your people.   PSALM 3:1–8

Worry is the chief robber of peace in our lives. It prevents us from lying down and sleeping in peace at night. It keeps us on edge during the day. Our Prince of Peace, Jesus, emphasized the immense capacity of God the Father to love and care for his people individually before they let the worries of this life overtake them. He also stressed the important role of the Holy Spirit, the gift of the Father, in supporting God's people.

"Therefore I tell you, do not worry about your life, what you will eat or drink; or about your body, what you will wear. Is not life more than food, and the body more than clothes? Look at the birds of the air; they do not sow or reap or store away in barns, and yet your heavenly Father feeds them. Are you not much more valuable than they? Can any one of you by worrying add a single hour to your life?

"And why do you worry about clothes? See how the flowers of the field grow. They do not labor or spin. Yet I tell you that not even Solomon in all his splendor was dressed like one of these. If that is how God clothes the grass of the field, which is here today and tomorrow is thrown into the fire, will he not much more clothe you — you of little faith? So do not worry, saying, 'What shall we eat?' or 'What shall we drink?' or 'What shall we wear?' For the pagans run after all these things, and your heavenly Father knows that you need them. But seek first his kingdom and his righteousness, and all these things will be given to you as well. Therefore do not worry about tomorrow, for tomorrow will worry about itself. Each day has enough trouble of its own."   MATTHEW 6:25–34

It's true that each day has enough trouble of its own and, as followers of Christ, we must be prepared to deal with these troubles. It might be tempting to give in to the stress but, as Jesus vividly illustrated to his disciples, through our faith we can find peace and remain in control.

That day when evening came, he said to his disciples, "Let us go over to the other side." Leaving the crowd behind, they took him along, just as he was, in the boat. There were also other boats with him. A furious squall came up, and the waves broke over the boat, so that it was nearly swamped. Jesus was in the stern, sleeping on a cushion. The disciples woke him and said to him, "Teacher, don't you care if we drown?"

He got up, rebuked the wind and said to the waves, "Quiet! Be still!" Then the wind died down and it was completely calm.

He said to his disciples, "Why are you so afraid? Do you still have no faith?"

They were terrified and asked each other, "Who is this? Even the wind and the waves obey him!" MARK 4:35–41

Jesus was constantly working to educate and reassure his followers. On the day before his crucifixion, Jesus talked to his disciples about a unique offer of peace. This peace comes only from God and is wholly different from the peace offered by the world.

"If you love me, keep my commands. And I will ask the Father, and he will give you another advocate to help you and be with you forever — the Spirit of truth. The world cannot accept him, because it neither sees him nor knows him. But you know him, for he lives with you and will be in you. I will not leave you as orphans; I will come to you. Before long, the world will not see me anymore, but you will see me. Because I live, you also will live. On that day you will realize that I am in my Father, and you are in me, and I am in you. Whoever has my commands and keeps them is the one who loves me. The one who loves me will be loved by my Father, and I too will love them and show myself to them."

Then Judas (not Judas Iscariot) said, "But, Lord, why do you intend to show yourself to us and not to the world?"

Jesus replied, "Anyone who loves me will obey my teaching. My Father will love them, and we will come to them and make our home with them. Anyone who does not love me will not obey my teaching. These words you hear are not my own; they belong to the Father who sent me.

"All this I have spoken while still with you. But the Advocate, the Holy Spirit, whom the Father will send in my name, will teach you all things and will remind you of everything I have said to you. Peace I leave with you; my peace I give you. I do not give to you as the world gives. Do not let your hearts be troubled and do not be afraid." JOHN 14:15–27

As Paul wrapped up his personal letter to the believers at Philippi, he spoke to them directly on how to obtain a peace that transcends all understanding.

Rejoice in the Lord always. I will say it again: Rejoice! Let your gentleness be evident to all. The Lord is near. Do not be anxious about anything, but in every situation, by prayer and petition, with thanksgiving, present your requests to God. And the peace of God, which transcends all understanding, will guard your hearts and your minds in Christ Jesus.

Finally, brothers and sisters, whatever is true, whatever is noble, whatever is right, whatever is pure, whatever is lovely, whatever is admirable — if anything is excellent or praiseworthy — think about such things. Whatever you have learned or received or heard from me, or seen in me — put it into practice. And the God of peace will be with you. PHILIPPIANS 4:4–9

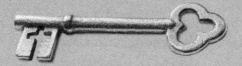

CHAPTER

24

Self-Control

KEY IDEA

I have the power through Christ to control myself.

KEY VERSE

For the grace of God has appeared that offers salvation
to all people. It teaches us to say "No" to ungodliness
and worldly passions, and to live self-controlled,
upright and godly lives in this present age, while we wait
for the blessed hope — the appearing of the glory
of our great God and Savior, Jesus Christ.

Titus 2:11 – 13

THE CALL AND THE CHALLENGE

God desires all of us to have self-control over things that can destroy us and others. The writer of Proverbs places options before us, clearly showing the virtue and benefit of self-control.

Better a patient person than a warrior,
   one with self-control than one who takes a city.

PROVERBS 16:32

The one who has knowledge uses words with restraint,
   and whoever has understanding is even-tempered.

PROVERBS 17:27

Like a city whose walls are broken through
   is a person who lacks self-control.

PROVERBS 25:28

Fools give full vent to their rage,
   but the wise bring calm in the end.

PROVERBS 29:11

In essence, self-control means having power over one's own impulses, reactions and desires. Paul wrote a personal letter to his ministry partner Titus instructing him to appoint elders in the church gathered on the island of Crete. Self-control was a prominent characteristic Titus was to look for in these spiritual leaders. Paul also instructed Titus to call all believers of all ages to this virtue, which obviously was much needed in Crete.

To Titus, my true son in our common faith:

Grace and peace from God the Father and Christ Jesus our Savior.

The reason I left you in Crete was that you might put in order what was left unfinished and appoint elders in every town, as I directed you. An elder must be blameless, faithful to his wife, a man whose children believe and are not open to the charge of being wild and disobedient. Since an overseer manages God's household, he must be blameless — not overbearing, not quick-tempered, not given to drunkenness, not violent, not pursuing dishonest gain.

Rather, he must be hospitable, one who loves what is good, who is self-controlled, upright, holy and disciplined. He must hold firmly to the trustworthy message as it has been taught, so that he can encourage others by sound doctrine and refute those who oppose it.

TITUS 1:4–9

You, however, must teach what is appropriate to sound doctrine. Teach the older men to be temperate, worthy of respect, self-controlled, and sound in faith, in love and in endurance.

Likewise, teach the older women to be reverent in the way they live, not to be slanderers or addicted to much wine, but to teach what is good. Then they can urge the younger women to love their husbands and children, to be self-controlled and pure, to be busy at home, to be kind, and to be subject to their husbands, so that no one will malign the word of God.

Similarly, encourage the young men to be self-controlled. In everything set them an example by doing what is good. In your teaching show integrity, seriousness and soundness of speech that cannot be condemned, so that those who oppose you may be ashamed because they have nothing bad to say about us.

Teach slaves to be subject to their masters in everything, to try to please them, not to talk back to them, and not to steal from them, but to show that they can be fully trusted, so that in every way they will make the teaching about God our Savior attractive.

For the grace of God has appeared that offers salvation to all people. It teaches us to say "No" to ungodliness and worldly passions, and to live self-controlled, upright and godly lives in this present age, while we wait for the blessed hope — the appearing of the glory of our great God and Savior, Jesus Christ, who gave himself for us to redeem us from all wickedness and to purify for himself a people that are his very own, eager to do what is good.

These, then, are the things you should teach. Encourage and rebuke with all authority. Do not let anyone despise you.   TITUS 2:1–15

MODELS OF SELF-CONTROL — BAD AND GOOD

During the days of the judges, the Philistines bullied Israel for 40 years. But time after time God raised up a special person, a judge, to deliver Israel from this oppression. God intervened in

*the life of a childless Israelite couple and enabled the wife to con-
ceive and give birth to Samson, who would be used by God to
set Israel free from this bondage. From conception Samson was
a Nazirite—which comes from the Hebrew word meaning "separated"—and God blessed him with supernatural strength. As a
spiritual and physical sign of this vow, Samson was to never cut his
hair. Interestingly, this special man, one of the last judges of Israel,
struggled mightily with self-control over his sexual passions; and
ironically he was particularly attracted to Philistine women. Eventually Samson let his lack of self-control get the best of him.*

One day Samson went to Gaza, where he saw a prostitute. He
went in to spend the night with her. The people of Gaza were told,
"Samson is here!" So they surrounded the place and lay in wait
for him all night at the city gate. They made no move during the
night, saying, "At dawn we'll kill him."

But Samson lay there only until the middle of the night. Then
he got up and took hold of the doors of the city gate, together with
the two posts, and tore them loose, bar and all. He lifted them to
his shoulders and carried them to the top of the hill that faces Hebron.

Some time later, he fell in love with a woman in the Valley of
Sorek whose name was Delilah. The rulers of the Philistines went
to her and said, "See if you can lure him into showing you the secret of his great strength and how we can overpower him so we
may tie him up and subdue him. Each one of us will give you elev-
en hundred shekels of silver."

So Delilah said to Samson, "Tell me the secret of your great
strength and how you can be tied up and subdued."

Samson answered her, "If anyone ties me with seven fresh bowstrings that have not been dried, I'll become as weak as any other
man."

Then the rulers of the Philistines brought her seven fresh bowstrings that had not been dried, and she tied him with them. With
men hidden in the room, she called to him, "Samson, the Philistines are upon you!" But he snapped the bowstrings as easily as a
piece of string snaps when it comes close to a flame. So the secret
of his strength was not discovered.

Then Delilah said to Samson, "You have made a fool of me; you lied to me. Come now, tell me how you can be tied."

He said, "If anyone ties me securely with new ropes that have never been used, I'll become as weak as any other man."

So Delilah took new ropes and tied him with them. Then, with men hidden in the room, she called to him, "Samson, the Philistines are upon you!" But he snapped the ropes off his arms as if they were threads.

Delilah then said to Samson, "All this time you have been making a fool of me and lying to me. Tell me how you can be tied."

He replied, "If you weave the seven braids of my head into the fabric on the loom and tighten it with the pin, I'll become as weak as any other man." So while he was sleeping, Delilah took the seven braids of his head, wove them into the fabric and tightened it with the pin.

Again she called to him, "Samson, the Philistines are upon you!" He awoke from his sleep and pulled up the pin and the loom, with the fabric.

Then she said to him, "How can you say, 'I love you,' when you won't confide in me? This is the third time you have made a fool of me and haven't told me the secret of your great strength." With such nagging she prodded him day after day until he was sick to death of it.

So he told her everything. "No razor has ever been used on my head," he said, "because I have been a Nazirite dedicated to God from my mother's womb. If my head were shaved, my strength would leave me, and I would become as weak as any other man."

When Delilah saw that he had told her everything, she sent word to the rulers of the Philistines, "Come back once more; he has told me everything." So the rulers of the Philistines returned with the silver in their hands. After putting him to sleep on her lap, she called for someone to shave off the seven braids of his hair, and so began to subdue him. And his strength left him.

Then she called, "Samson, the Philistines are upon you!"

He awoke from his sleep and thought, "I'll go out as before and shake myself free." But he did not know that the LORD had left him.

Then the Philistines seized him, gouged out his eyes and took him down to Gaza. Binding him with bronze shackles, they set him to grinding grain in the prison. JUDGES 16:1–21

Unlike Samson, Joseph offers one of the best examples in the Bible of a man who exercised excellent self-control. Joseph was sold into slavery at the hands of his jealous brothers. The band of traveling merchants who purchased him took him from his home in Canaan to Egypt to be resold to an important official in Pharaoh's court. Although Joseph was punished by his captors for his self-control, God rewarded his faithfulness.

Now Joseph had been taken down to Egypt. Potiphar, an Egyptian who was one of Pharaoh's officials, the captain of the guard, bought him from the Ishmaelites who had taken him there.

The LORD was with Joseph so that he prospered, and he lived in the house of his Egyptian master. When his master saw that the LORD was with him and that the LORD gave him success in everything he did, Joseph found favor in his eyes and became his attendant. Potiphar put him in charge of his household, and he entrusted to his care everything he owned. From the time he put him in charge of his household and of all that he owned, the LORD blessed the household of the Egyptian because of Joseph. The blessing of the LORD was on everything Potiphar had, both in the house and in the field. So Potiphar left everything he had in Joseph's care; with Joseph in charge, he did not concern himself with anything except the food he ate.

Now Joseph was well-built and handsome, and after a while his master's wife took notice of Joseph and said, "Come to bed with me!"

But he refused. "With me in charge," he told her, "my master does not concern himself with anything in the house; everything he owns he has entrusted to my care. No one is greater in this house than I am. My master has withheld nothing from me except you, because you are his wife. How then could I do such a wicked thing and sin against God?" And though she spoke to Joseph day after day, he refused to go to bed with her or even be with her.

One day he went into the house to attend to his duties, and

none of the household servants was inside. She caught him by his cloak and said, "Come to bed with me!" But he left his cloak in her hand and ran out of the house.

When she saw that he had left his cloak in her hand and had run out of the house, she called her household servants. "Look," she said to them, "this Hebrew has been brought to us to make sport of us! He came in here to sleep with me, but I screamed. When he heard me scream for help, he left his cloak beside me and ran out of the house."

She kept his cloak beside her until his master came home. Then she told him this story: "That Hebrew slave you brought us came to me to make sport of me. But as soon as I screamed for help, he left his cloak beside me and ran out of the house."

When his master heard the story his wife told him, saying, "This is how your slave treated me," he burned with anger. Joseph's master took him and put him in prison, the place where the king's prisoners were confined.

But while Joseph was there in the prison, the LORD was with him; he showed him kindness and granted him favor in the eyes of the prison warden. So the warden put Joseph in charge of all those held in the prison, and he was made responsible for all that was done there. The warden paid no attention to anything under Joseph's care, because the LORD was with Joseph and gave him success in whatever he did.   GENESIS 39:1–23

Titus 2:11 – 12 tells us that "the grace of God ... teaches us to say 'No' to ungodliness and worldly passions, and to live self-controlled, upright and godly lives in this present age." One would think the law would do a better job of teaching us self-control by labeling our behavior as sin and describing a punishment. While laws and rules are helpful and even necessary in a sin-filled world, people are not motivated by them. People are motivated by grace and love. The law restrains our darkness from the outside. Grace reaches our heart and transforms us from the inside. Jesus told a beautiful story of the grace and love of a father who restores a son who has lost control. Of course, Jesus ultimately points to the grace and love offered by our Heavenly Father.

Jesus continued: "There was a man who had two sons. The younger one said to his father, 'Father, give me my share of the estate.' So he divided his property between them.

"Not long after that, the younger son got together all he had, set off for a distant country and there squandered his wealth in wild living. After he had spent everything, there was a severe famine in that whole country, and he began to be in need. So he went and hired himself out to a citizen of that country, who sent him to his fields to feed pigs. He longed to fill his stomach with the pods that the pigs were eating, but no one gave him anything.

"When he came to his senses, he said, 'How many of my father's hired servants have food to spare, and here I am starving to death! I will set out and go back to my father and say to him: Father, I have sinned against heaven and against you. I am no longer worthy to be called your son; make me like one of your hired servants.' So he got up and went to his father.

"But while he was still a long way off, his father saw him and was filled with compassion for him; he ran to his son, threw his arms around him and kissed him.

"The son said to him, 'Father, I have sinned against heaven and against you. I am no longer worthy to be called your son.'

"But the father said to his servants, 'Quick! Bring the best robe and put it on him. Put a ring on his finger and sandals on his feet. Bring the fattened calf and kill it. Let's have a feast and celebrate. For this son of mine was dead and is alive again; he was lost and is found.' So they began to celebrate.

"Meanwhile, the older son was in the field. When he came near the house, he heard music and dancing. So he called one of the servants and asked him what was going on. 'Your brother has come,' he replied, 'and your father has killed the fattened calf because he has him back safe and sound.'

"The older brother became angry and refused to go in. So his father went out and pleaded with him. But he answered his father, 'Look! All these years I've been slaving for you and never disobeyed your orders. Yet you never gave me even a young goat so I could celebrate with my friends. But when this son of yours who has squandered your property with prostitutes comes home, you kill the fattened calf for him!'

"'My son,' the father said, 'you are always with me, and everything I have is yours. But we had to celebrate and be glad, because this brother of yours was dead and is alive again; he was lost and is found.'"

LUKE 15:11–32

THE HOW-TOS

The Bible offers practical instruction on how to grow in the virtue of self-control. One of the primary applications is to "flee" — flee from the person, environment or situation that tempts us to lose control. Corinth was a place given to boundaryless living. In Paul's letter known to us as 1 Corinthians, he instructed the believers in Corinth to keep themselves out of harm's way lest they fall.

"I have the right to do anything," you say — but not everything is beneficial. "I have the right to do anything" — but I will not be mastered by anything. You say, "Food for the stomach and the stomach for food, and God will destroy them both." The body, however, is not meant for sexual immorality but for the Lord, and the Lord for the body. By his power God raised the Lord from the dead, and he will raise us also. Do you not know that your bodies are members of Christ himself? Shall I then take the members of Christ and unite them with a prostitute? Never! Do you not know that he who unites himself with a prostitute is one with her in body? For it is said, "The two will become one flesh." But whoever is united with the Lord is one with him in spirit.

Flee from sexual immorality. All other sins a person commits are outside the body, but whoever sins sexually, sins against their own body. Do you not know that your bodies are temples of the Holy Spirit, who is in you, whom you have received from God? You are not your own; you were bought at a price. Therefore honor God with your bodies.

1 CORINTHIANS 6:12–20

My dear friends, flee from idolatry. I speak to sensible people; judge for yourselves what I say. Is not the cup of thanksgiving for which we give thanks a participation in the blood of Christ? And is not the bread that we break a participation in the body of Christ? Because there is one loaf, we, who are many, are one body, for we all share the one loaf.

Consider the people of Israel: Do not those who eat the sacrifices participate in the altar? Do I mean then that food sacrificed to an idol is anything, or that an idol is anything? No, but the sacrifices of pagans are offered to demons, not to God, and I do not want you to be participants with demons. You cannot drink the cup of the Lord and the cup of demons too; you cannot have a part in both the Lord's table and the table of demons. Are we trying to arouse the Lord's jealousy? Are we stronger than he?

1 CORINTHIANS 10:14–22

Paul reiterated the charge to flee in his letters to Timothy, which he penned to give the young leader instructions regarding how to spiritually guide the church at Ephesus. He wrote about how to avoid false teachers and the lure of the love of money. He also urged Timothy and the church members not to keep company with people who will draw them into ungodly behaviors.

These are the things you are to teach and insist on. If anyone teaches otherwise and does not agree to the sound instruction of our Lord Jesus Christ and to godly teaching, they are conceited and understand nothing. They have an unhealthy interest in controversies and quarrels about words that result in envy, strife, malicious talk, evil suspicions and constant friction between people of corrupt mind, who have been robbed of the truth and who think that godliness is a means to financial gain.

But godliness with contentment is great gain. For we brought nothing into the world, and we can take nothing out of it. But if we have food and clothing, we will be content with that. Those who want to get rich fall into temptation and a trap and into many foolish and harmful desires that plunge people into ruin and destruction. For the love of money is a root of all kinds of evil. Some people, eager for money, have wandered from the faith and pierced themselves with many griefs.

But you, man of God, flee from all this, and pursue righteousness, godliness, faith, love, endurance and gentleness. Fight the good fight of the faith. Take hold of the eternal life to which you were called when you made your good confession in the presence of many witnesses. In the sight of God, who gives life to everything, and of Christ Jesus, who while testifying before Pontius Pilate made the good confession, I charge you to keep this command without spot or blame until the appearing of our Lord Jesus Christ, which God will bring about in his own time — God, the blessed and only Ruler, the King of kings and Lord of lords, who alone is immortal and who lives in unapproachable light, whom no one has seen or can see.   1 TIMOTHY 6:2–16

Flee the evil desires of youth and pursue righteousness, faith, love and peace, along with those who call on the Lord out of a pure heart. Don't have anything to do with foolish and stupid arguments, because you know they produce quarrels. And the Lord's servant must not be quarrelsome but must be kind to everyone, able to teach, not resentful. Opponents must be gently instructed, in the hope that God will grant them repentance leading them to a knowledge of the truth, and that they will come to their senses and escape from the trap of the devil, who has taken them captive to do his will.

But mark this: There will be terrible times in the last days. People will be lovers of themselves, lovers of money, boastful, proud, abusive, disobedient to their parents, ungrateful, unholy, without love, unforgiving, slanderous, without self-control, brutal, not lovers of the good, treacherous, rash, conceited, lovers of pleasure rather than lovers of God — having a form of godliness but denying its power. Have nothing to do with such people.

They are the kind who worm their way into homes and gain control over gullible women, who are loaded down with sins and are swayed by all kinds of evil desires, always learning but never able to come to a knowledge of the truth.   2 TIMOTHY 2:22—3:7

A second strategy, also defensive in nature, in the fight to preserve self-control is to resist. We can tame our tongues, reduce fights and quarrels amongst us, control our selfish desires and mitigate against the negative influences of the world and the devil. But ultimately complete self-control is unattainable. Our sin nature, or flesh, eventually wears us down and gets the best of us. The ultimate solution to gain self-control is "God-control." The believer has the presence and power of God within them to live a life not undermined by our inner desires and the corruption of the world. As believers, we are to draw on this power to live productive and effective lives.

Not many of you should become teachers, my fellow believers, because you know that we who teach will be judged more strictly. We all stumble in many ways. Anyone who is never at fault in what they say is perfect, able to keep their whole body in check.

When we put bits into the mouths of horses to make them obey us, we can turn the whole animal. Or take ships as an example. Although they are so large and are driven by strong winds, they are steered by a very small rudder wherever the pilot wants to go. Likewise, the tongue is a small part of the body, but it makes great boasts. Consider what a great forest is set on fire by a small spark. The tongue also is a fire, a world of evil among the parts of the body. It corrupts the whole body, sets the whole course of one's life on fire, and is itself set on fire by hell.

All kinds of animals, birds, reptiles and sea creatures are being tamed and have been tamed by mankind, but no human being can tame the tongue. It is a restless evil, full of deadly poison.

With the tongue we praise our Lord and Father, and with it we curse human beings, who have been made in God's likeness. Out of the same mouth come praise and cursing. My brothers and sisters, this should not be. Can both fresh water and salt water flow from the same spring? My brothers and sisters, can a fig tree bear olives, or a grapevine bear figs? Neither can a salt spring produce fresh water.

Who is wise and understanding among you? Let them show it by their good life, by deeds done in the humility that comes from wisdom. But if you harbor bitter envy and selfish ambition in your hearts, do not boast about it or deny the truth. Such "wisdom" does not come down from heaven but is earthly, unspiritual, demonic. For where you have envy and selfish ambition, there you find disorder and every evil practice.

But the wisdom that comes from heaven is first of all pure; then peace-loving, considerate, submissive, full of mercy and good fruit, impartial and sincere. Peacemakers who sow in peace reap a harvest of righteousness.

What causes fights and quarrels among you? Don't they come from your desires that battle within you? You desire but do not have, so you kill. You covet but you cannot get what you want, so you quarrel and fight. You do not have because you do not ask God. When you ask, you do not receive, because you ask with wrong motives, that you may spend what you get on your pleasures.

You adulterous people, don't you know that friendship with the world means enmity against God? Therefore, anyone who chooses to be a friend of the world becomes an enemy of God. Or do you think Scripture says without reason that he jealously longs for the spirit he has caused to dwell in us? But he gives us more grace. That is why Scripture says:

> "God opposes the proud
>   but shows favor to the humble."

Submit yourselves, then, to God. Resist the devil, and he will flee from you. Come near to God and he will come near to you. Wash your hands, you sinners, and purify your hearts, you double-minded. Grieve, mourn and wail. Change your laughter to mourning and your joy to gloom. Humble yourselves before the Lord, and he will lift you up.   JAMES 3:1—4:10

Peter offered similar advice in his first letter to the Christians scattered throughout the regions of Asia Minor (modern-day Turkey).

Be alert and of sober mind. Your enemy the devil prowls around like a roaring lion looking for someone to devour. Resist him, standing firm in the faith, because you know that the family of believers throughout the world is undergoing the same kind of sufferings.

And the God of all grace, who called you to his eternal glory in Christ, after you have suffered a little while, will himself restore you and make you strong, firm and steadfast. To him be the power for ever and ever. Amen.   1 PETER 5:8–11

The apostle Paul presented a different strategy to practice self-control in our lives—particularly in the area of sexual passions. Engage these natural desires within the boundaries of God's design.

Now for the matters you wrote about: "It is good for a man not to have sexual relations with a woman." But since sexual immorality is occurring, each man should have sexual relations with his own wife, and each woman with her own husband. The husband should fulfill his marital duty to his wife, and likewise the wife to her husband. The wife does not have authority over her own body but yields it to her husband. In the same way, the husband does not have authority over his own body but yields it to his wife. Do not deprive each other except perhaps by mutual consent and for a time, so that you may devote yourselves to prayer. Then come together again so that Satan will not tempt you because of your lack of self-control. I say this as a concession, not as a command. I wish that all of you were as I am. But each of you has your own gift from God; one has this gift, another has that.

Now to the unmarried and the widows I say: It is good for them to stay unmarried, as I do. But if they cannot control themselves, they should marry, for it is better to marry than to burn with passion.   1 CORINTHIANS 7:1–9

Self-control is truly impossible. Our sin nature eventually wears us down and gets the best of us. Thankfully we, as believers, have the presence and power of God within to live a life not undermined by our inner desires and the corruption of the world. In Peter's second letter he challenged believers to draw on this power to live productive and effective lives.

His divine power has given us everything we need for a godly life through our knowledge of him who called us by his own glory and goodness. Through these he has given us his very great and precious promises, so that through them you may participate in the divine nature, having escaped the corruption in the world caused by evil desires.

For this very reason, make every effort to add to your faith goodness; and to goodness, knowledge; and to knowledge, self-control; and to self-control, perseverance; and to perseverance, godliness; and to godliness, mutual affection; and to mutual affection, love. For if you possess these qualities in increasing measure, they will keep you from being ineffective and unproductive in your knowledge of our Lord Jesus Christ. But whoever does not have them is nearsighted and blind, forgetting that they have been cleansed from their past sins.

Therefore, my brothers and sisters, make every effort to confirm your calling and election. For if you do these things, you will never stumble, and you will receive a rich welcome into the eternal kingdom of our Lord and Savior Jesus Christ. 2 PETER 1:3–11

Paul also stresses the importance of relying on the power of God, walking with the Holy Spirit, to remain in control. The ultimate solution to gain self-control is "God-control."

So I say, walk by the Spirit, and you will not gratify the desires of the flesh. For the flesh desires what is contrary to the Spirit, and the Spirit what is contrary to the flesh. They are in conflict with each other, so that you are not to do whatever you want. But if you are led by the Spirit, you are not under the law.

The acts of the flesh are obvious: sexual immorality, impurity and debauchery; idolatry and witchcraft; hatred, discord, jealousy, fits of rage, selfish ambition, dissensions, factions and envy; drunkenness, orgies, and the like. I warn you, as I did before, that those who live like this will not inherit the kingdom of God.

But the fruit of the Spirit is love, joy, peace, forbearance, kindness, goodness, faithfulness, gentleness and self-control. Against such things there is no law. Those who belong to Christ Jesus have crucified the flesh with its passions and desires. Since we live by the Spirit, let us keep in step with the Spirit. GALATIANS 5:16–25

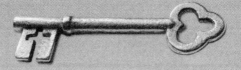

CHAPTER

25

Hope

KEY IDEA

I can cope with the hardships of life
because of the hope I have in Jesus Christ.

KEY VERSE

We have this hope as an anchor for the soul,
firm and secure. It enters the inner sanctuary
behind the curtain, where our forerunner,
Jesus, has entered on our behalf.
Hebrews 6:19–20

THE NEED FOR HOPE

It is impossible to cope without hope. Job had lost everything and was running out of strength. He wanted to die. His "friends" came to comfort him. His response to his unhelpful friends is the expression of a man without hope.

Job replied:

> "If only my anguish could be weighed
>   and all my misery be placed on the scales!
> It would surely outweigh the sand of the seas —
>   no wonder my words have been impetuous.
> The arrows of the Almighty are in me,
>   my spirit drinks in their poison;
>   God's terrors are marshaled against me.
> Does a wild donkey bray when it has grass,
>   or an ox bellow when it has fodder?
> Is tasteless food eaten without salt,
>   or is there flavor in the sap of the mallow?
> I refuse to touch it;
>   such food makes me ill.
>
> "Oh, that I might have my request,
>   that God would grant what I hope for,
> that God would be willing to crush me,
>   to let loose his hand and cut off my life!
> Then I would still have this consolation —
>   my joy in unrelenting pain —
>   that I had not denied the words of the Holy One.
>
> "What strength do I have, that I should still hope?
>   What prospects, that I should be patient?
> Do I have the strength of stone?
>   Is my flesh bronze?
> Do I have any power to help myself,
>   now that success has been driven from me?"   JOB 6:1–13

> "Do not mortals have hard service on earth?
>   Are not their days like those of hired laborers?
> Like a slave longing for the evening shadows,
>   or a hired laborer waiting to be paid,

so I have been allotted months of futility,
    and nights of misery have been assigned to me.
When I lie down I think, 'How long before I get up?'
    The night drags on, and I toss and turn until dawn.
My body is clothed with worms and scabs,
    my skin is broken and festering.

"My days are swifter than a weaver's shuttle,
    and they come to an end without hope."   JOB 7:1–6

SOURCES OF FALSE HOPE

False hope causes people to plan, build and risk for something that is not likely to happen. The Bible identifies several things humans unfortunately place their hope in only to be disappointed in the end.

False hope ... in riches.

Because of his fearless confidence in God, David is able to hurl condemnation at his enemy who trusts in wealth.

Why do you boast of evil, you mighty hero?
    Why do you boast all day long,
        you who are a disgrace in the eyes of God?
You who practice deceit,
    your tongue plots destruction;
        it is like a sharpened razor.
You love evil rather than good,
    falsehood rather than speaking the truth.
You love every harmful word,
    you deceitful tongue!

Surely God will bring you down to everlasting ruin:
    He will snatch you up and pluck you from your tent;
    he will uproot you from the land of the living.
The righteous will see and fear;
    they will laugh at you, saying,
"Here now is the man
    who did not make God his stronghold
but trusted in his great wealth
    and grew strong by destroying others!"

> But I am like an olive tree
>> flourishing in the house of God;
> I trust in God's unfailing love
>> for ever and ever.
> For what you have done I will always praise you
>> in the presence of your faithful people.
> And I will hope in your name,
>> for your name is good. Psalm 52:1–9

Paul tells Timothy to instruct the believers in Ephesus about the false hope of trusting in riches.

Command those who are rich in this present world not to be arrogant nor to put their hope in wealth, which is so uncertain, but to put their hope in God, who richly provides us with everything for our enjoyment. 1 Timothy 6:17

False hope . . . in people.
    The psalmists tell us that we will be disappointed if we place our hope in people rather than God.

> It is better to take refuge in the Lord
>> than to trust in humans.
> It is better to take refuge in the Lord
>> than to trust in princes. Psalm 118:8–9

> Do not put your trust in princes,
>> in human beings, who cannot save.
> When their spirit departs, they return to the ground;
>> on that very day their plans come to nothing. Psalm 146:3–4

The prophet Jeremiah declares the same sentiment.

This is what the Lord says:

> "Cursed is the one who trusts in man,
>> who draws strength from mere flesh
>> and whose heart turns away from the Lord.

That person will be like a bush in the wastelands;
   they will not see prosperity when it comes.
They will dwell in the parched places of the desert,
   in a salt land where no one lives.   JEREMIAH 17:5–6

False hope ... in idols
   An idol is any object we place above God. The prophet Habakkuk declares how foolish it is to place our hope in such man-made inventions.

"Of what value is an idol carved by a craftsman?
   Or an image that teaches lies?
For the one who makes it trusts in his own creation;
   he makes idols that cannot speak.
Woe to him who says to wood, 'Come to life!'
   Or to lifeless stone, 'Wake up!'
Can it give guidance?
   It is covered with gold and silver;
   there is no breath in it."   HABAKKUK 2:18–19

False hope ... in human government
   It is easy and often more tangible for people to place their trust and hope in nations. Isaiah warns the people of Judah to avoid such a mistake, even with the mighty nation of Egypt.

Woe to those who go down to Egypt for help,
   who rely on horses,
who trust in the multitude of their chariots
   and in the great strength of their horsemen,
but do not look to the Holy One of Israel,
   or seek help from the LORD.   ISAIAH 31:1

But the Egyptians are mere mortals and not God;
   their horses are flesh and not spirit.
When the LORD stretches out his hand,
   those who help will stumble,
   those who are helped will fall;
   all will perish together.   ISAIAH 31:3

THE SOURCE OF TRUE HOPE

True hope is found only in God.

Hope is only as good as the power and character of the one who offers it. The psalmist expresses with deep passion his trust in God for his source of hope when present times are tough.

As the deer pants for streams of water,
    so my soul pants for you, my God.
My soul thirsts for God, for the living God.
    When can I go and meet with God?
My tears have been my food
    day and night,
while people say to me all day long,
    "Where is your God?"
These things I remember
    as I pour out my soul:
how I used to go to the house of God
    under the protection of the Mighty One
with shouts of joy and praise
    among the festive throng.

Why, my soul, are you downcast?
    Why so disturbed within me?
Put your hope in God,
    for I will yet praise him,
    my Savior and my God.

My soul is downcast within me;
    therefore I will remember you
from the land of the Jordan,
    the heights of Hermon — from Mount Mizar.
Deep calls to deep
    in the roar of your waterfalls;
all your waves and breakers
    have swept over me.

By day the LORD directs his love,
    at night his song is with me —
    a prayer to the God of my life.

I say to God my Rock,
   "Why have you forgotten me?
Why must I go about mourning,
   oppressed by the enemy?"
My bones suffer mortal agony
   as my foes taunt me,
saying to me all day long,
   "Where is your God?"

Why, my soul, are you downcast?
   Why so disturbed within me?
Put your hope in God,
   for I will yet praise him,
   my Savior and my God.   PSALM 42:1–11

True hope is found in God's promises.

All the authors of the New Testament wrote on the topic of hope. It is clearly one of the unique and powerful benefits of following God. The writer of Hebrews drew on the character of God to confirm God's promises.

When God made his promise to Abraham, since there was no one greater for him to swear by, he swore by himself, saying, "I will surely bless you and give you many descendants." And so after waiting patiently, Abraham received what was promised.

People swear by someone greater than themselves, and the oath confirms what is said and puts an end to all argument. Because God wanted to make the unchanging nature of his purpose very clear to the heirs of what was promised, he confirmed it with an oath. God did this so that, by two unchangeable things in which it is impossible for God to lie, we who have fled to take hold of the hope set before us may be greatly encouraged. We have this hope as an anchor for the soul, firm and secure. It enters the inner sanctuary behind the curtain, where our forerunner, Jesus, has entered on our behalf. He has become a high priest forever, in the order of Melchizedek.

HEBREWS 6:13–20

Since God's character is rock solid, trustworthy and true, we anchor our hope in his promises to us. Paul wrote a letter to the church at

Colossae while he was under house arrest in Rome. God had been unfolding his grand promise of redemption since the fall of Adam and Eve. The true and full content of this promise was a mystery to the people of the Old Testament era. Now, God has fulfilled his promise and revealed it to us — the source of our hope has come.

Now I rejoice in what I am suffering for you, and I fill up in my flesh what is still lacking in regard to Christ's afflictions, for the sake of his body, which is the church. I have become its servant by the commission God gave me to present to you the word of God in its fullness — the mystery that has been kept hidden for ages and generations, but is now disclosed to the Lord's people. To them God has chosen to make known among the Gentiles the glorious riches of this mystery, which is Christ in you, the hope of glory.

He is the one we proclaim, admonishing and teaching everyone with all wisdom, so that we may present everyone fully mature in Christ. To this end I strenuously contend with all the energy Christ so powerfully works in me.   COLOSSIANS 1:24–29

What God has promised to all believers in Jesus enables us to endure the hardships of life. Peter opened his first letter proclaiming this truth. The ultimate promise of God is our future resurrection. The hope of this promise trumps all momentary trials.

Peter, an apostle of Jesus Christ,

To God's elect, exiles scattered throughout the provinces of Pontus, Galatia, Cappadocia, Asia and Bithynia, who have been chosen according to the foreknowledge of God the Father, through the sanctifying work of the Spirit, to be obedient to Jesus Christ and sprinkled with his blood:

Grace and peace be yours in abundance.

Praise be to the God and Father of our Lord Jesus Christ! In his great mercy he has given us new birth into a living hope through the resurrection of Jesus Christ from the dead, and into an inheritance that can never perish, spoil or fade. This inheritance is kept in heaven for you, who through faith are shielded by God's power until the coming of the salvation that is ready to be revealed in the last time. In all this you greatly rejoice, though now for a little while you may have had to suffer grief in all kinds of trials. These have come so that the proven genuineness of your faith — of greater worth than gold, which perishes even though refined by fire — may result in praise, glory and honor when Jesus Christ is revealed. Though you have not seen him, you love him; and even though you do not see him now, you believe in him and are filled with an inexpressible and glorious joy, for you are receiving the end result of your faith, the salvation of your souls.

Concerning this salvation, the prophets, who spoke of the grace that was to come to you, searched intently and with the greatest care, trying to find out the time and circumstances to which the Spirit of Christ in them was pointing when he predicted the sufferings of the Messiah and the glories that would follow. It was revealed to them that they were not serving themselves but you, when they spoke of the things that have now been told you by those who have preached the gospel to you by the Holy Spirit sent from heaven. Even angels long to look into these things.

Therefore, with minds that are alert and fully sober, set your hope on the grace to be brought to you when Jesus Christ is revealed at his coming. As obedient children, do not conform to the evil desires you had when you lived in ignorance. But just as he who called you is holy, so be holy in all you do; for it is written: "Be holy, because I am holy."

Since you call on a Father who judges each person's work impartially, live out your time as foreigners here in reverent fear. For you know that it was not with perishable things such as silver or gold that you were redeemed from the empty way of life handed down to you from your ancestors, but with the precious blood of Christ, a lamb without blemish or defect. He was chosen before the creation of the world, but was revealed in these last times for your sake. Through him you believe in God, who raised him from the dead and glorified him, and so your faith and hope are in God.

Now that you have purified yourselves by obeying the truth so that you have sincere love for each other, love one another deeply, from the heart. For you have been born again, not of perishable seed, but of imperishable, through the living and enduring word of God. For,

"All people are like grass,
    and all their glory is like the flowers of the field;
the grass withers and the flowers fall,
    but the word of the Lord endures forever."

And this is the word that was preached to you.   1 PETER 1:1–25

The Christians in Thessalonica had misunderstood Paul and thought that all believers would live until Christ returns. That caused them distress when some in the church died. Paul wrote his first letter to them to clear up this matter. The promise to all believers, past and present, of being with the Lord forever is the foundation of our hope.

Brothers and sisters, we do not want you to be uninformed about those who sleep in death, so that you do not grieve like the rest of mankind, who have no hope. For we believe that Jesus died and rose again, and so we believe that God will bring with Jesus those who have fallen asleep in him. According to the Lord's word, we tell you that we who are still alive, who are left until the coming of the Lord, will certainly not precede those who have fallen asleep. For the Lord himself will come down from heaven, with a loud command, with the voice of the archangel and with the trumpet call of God, and the dead in Christ will rise first. After that, we who are still alive and are left will be caught up together with them in the clouds to meet the Lord in the air. And so we will be with the Lord forever. Therefore encourage one another with these words.   1 THESSALONIANS 4:13–18

John echoed the writings of Paul and Peter regarding the hope we have through the promised resurrection. He challenged his readers to live pure lives in anticipation of this guaranteed event.

See what great love the Father has lavished on us, that we should be called children of God! And that is what we are! The reason the world does not know us is that it did not know him. Dear friends, now we are children of God, and what we will be has not yet been made known. But we know that when Christ appears, we shall be like him, for we shall see him as he is. All who have this hope in him purify themselves, just as he is pure.   1 JOHN 3:1–3

THE EFFECT OF HOPE

God and his promises are the reason for our hope. When we embrace this hope, it has a dramatic effect on our daily lives. Hope gives us the ability to get through our days, to persevere. Simeon waited many long years without seeing the fulfillment of his hope, but he carried on, letting hope give him strength for each new day.

Now there was a man in Jerusalem called Simeon, who was righteous and devout. He was waiting for the consolation of Israel, and the Holy Spirit was on him. It had been revealed to him by the Holy Spirit that he would not die before he had seen the Lord's Messiah. Moved by the Spirit, he went into the temple courts. When the parents brought in the child Jesus to do for him what the custom of the Law required, Simeon took him in his arms and praised God, saying:

> "Sovereign Lord, as you have promised,
>   you may now dismiss your servant in peace.
> For my eyes have seen your salvation,
>   which you have prepared in the sight of all nations:
> a light for revelation to the Gentiles,
>   and the glory of your people Israel."

The child's father and mother marveled at what was said about him. Then Simeon blessed them and said to Mary, his mother: "This child is destined to cause the falling and rising of many in Israel, and to be a sign that will be spoken against, so that the thoughts of many hearts will be revealed. And a sword will pierce your own soul too."   LUKE 2:25–35

Isaiah prophesied about the coming captivity of the people of Judah by the Babylonians. This portion of the book of Isaiah looks beyond that and assumes the 70 years of exile are almost over. Isaiah was able to encourage the people with confidence because he based his hope in God and his promise to bring the people home. The exiles could live full, happy lives because they knew God would keep his promise.

> Comfort, comfort my people,
>> says your God.
> Speak tenderly to Jerusalem,
>> and proclaim to her
> that her hard service has been completed,
>> that her sin has been paid for,
> that she has received from the LORD's hand
>> double for all her sins.
>
> A voice of one calling:
> "In the wilderness prepare
>> the way for the LORD;
> make straight in the desert
>> a highway for our God.
> Every valley shall be raised up,
>> every mountain and hill made low;
> the rough ground shall become level,
>> the rugged places a plain.
> And the glory of the LORD will be revealed,
>> and all people will see it together.
>>>> For the mouth of the LORD has spoken."
>
> A voice says, "Cry out."
>> And I said, "What shall I cry?"
>
> "All people are like grass,
>> and all their faithfulness is like the flowers of the field.
> The grass withers and the flowers fall,
>> because the breath of the LORD blows on them.
>> Surely the people are grass.
> The grass withers and the flowers fall,
>> but the word of our God endures forever."
>
> You who bring good news to Zion,
>> go up on a high mountain.
> You who bring good news to Jerusalem,
>> lift up your voice with a shout,

lift it up, do not be afraid;
    say to the towns of Judah,
    "Here is your God!"
See, the Sovereign LORD comes with power,
    and he rules with a mighty arm.
See, his reward is with him,
    and his recompense accompanies him.
He tends his flock like a shepherd:
    He gathers the lambs in his arms
and carries them close to his heart;
    he gently leads those that have young.

Who has measured the waters in the hollow of his hand,
    or with the breadth of his hand marked off the
        heavens?
Who has held the dust of the earth in a basket,
    or weighed the mountains on the scales
    and the hills in a balance?
Who can fathom the Spirit of the LORD,
    or instruct the LORD as his counselor?
Whom did the LORD consult to enlighten him,
    and who taught him the right way?
Who was it that taught him knowledge,
    or showed him the path of understanding?

Surely the nations are like a drop in a bucket;
    they are regarded as dust on the scales;
    he weighs the islands as though they were fine dust.
Lebanon is not sufficient for altar fires,
    nor its animals enough for burnt offerings.
Before him all the nations are as nothing;
    they are regarded by him as worthless
    and less than nothing.

With whom, then, will you compare God?
    To what image will you liken him?
As for an idol, a metalworker casts it,
    and a goldsmith overlays it with gold
    and fashions silver chains for it.

A person too poor to present such an offering
   selects wood that will not rot;
they look for a skilled worker
   to set up an idol that will not topple.

Do you not know?
   Have you not heard?
Has it not been told you from the beginning?
   Have you not understood since the earth was
     founded?
He sits enthroned above the circle of the earth,
   and its people are like grasshoppers.
He stretches out the heavens like a canopy,
   and spreads them out like a tent to live in.
He brings princes to naught
   and reduces the rulers of this world to nothing.
No sooner are they planted,
   no sooner are they sown,
   no sooner do they take root in the ground,
than he blows on them and they wither,
   and a whirlwind sweeps them away like chaff.

"To whom will you compare me?
   Or who is my equal?" says the Holy One.
Lift up your eyes and look to the heavens:
   Who created all these?
He who brings out the starry host one by one
   and calls forth each of them by name.
Because of his great power and mighty strength,
   not one of them is missing.

Why do you complain, Jacob?
   Why do you say, Israel,
"My way is hidden from the LORD;
   my cause is disregarded by my God"?
Do you not know?
   Have you not heard?
The LORD is the everlasting God,
   the Creator of the ends of the earth.

He will not grow tired or weary,
and his understanding no one can fathom.
He gives strength to the weary
and increases the power of the weak.
Even youths grow tired and weary,
and young men stumble and fall;
but those who hope in the LORD
will renew their strength.
They will soar on wings like eagles;
they will run and not grow weary,
they will walk and not be faint.   ISAIAH 40:1–31

About a century after Isaiah died, his prediction of the Babylonian captivity was fulfilled during the lifetime of the prophet Jeremiah. Jeremiah's message to God's people was similar to Isaiah's: Although the people were captive, God's promises could give them hope for their daily living. And he offers that same hope to Christians today.

This is the text of the letter that the prophet Jeremiah sent from Jerusalem to the surviving elders among the exiles and to the priests, the prophets and all the other people Nebuchadnezzar had carried into exile from Jerusalem to Babylon. (This was after King Jehoiachin and the queen mother, the court officials and the leaders of Judah and Jerusalem, the skilled workers and the artisans had gone into exile from Jerusalem.) He entrusted the letter to Elasah son of Shaphan and to Gemariah son of Hilkiah, whom Zedekiah king of Judah sent to King Nebuchadnezzar in Babylon. It said:

This is what the LORD Almighty, the God of Israel, says to all those I carried into exile from Jerusalem to Babylon: "Build houses and settle down; plant gardens and eat what they produce. Marry and have sons and daughters; find wives for your sons and give your daughters in marriage, so that they too may have sons and daughters. Increase in number there; do not decrease. Also, seek the peace and prosperity of the city to which I have carried you into exile. Pray to the LORD for it, because if it prospers, you too will prosper." Yes, this is what the LORD Almighty, the God of Israel, says: "Do not let the prophets and diviners among you deceive you. Do not listen to the dreams you encourage them to have. They are prophesying lies to you in my name. I have not sent them," declares the LORD.

This is what the LORD says: "When seventy years are completed for Babylon, I will come to you and fulfill my good promise to bring you back to this place. For I know the plans I have for you," declares the LORD, "plans to prosper you and not to harm you, plans to give you hope and a future." JEREMIAH 29:1–11

HOPE ACTIVATES FAITH, FAITH DEEPENS HOPE

Hope is available to all followers of God, but not everyone takes hold of it. It can be hard for us to trust in a God we cannot see and hold fast to fantastic promises yet to come. To activate the power of hope in our lives, we need to have faith in God and his promises. The writer of Hebrews preached this message to his readers. He then listed people from the past who placed their faith in God and experienced amazing results in their lives. God offers this same opportunity to us today. In fact, God has "something better" planned for those who know Jesus.

Now faith is confidence in what we hope for and assurance about what we do not see. This is what the ancients were commended for.

By faith we understand that the universe was formed at God's command, so that what is seen was not made out of what was visible.

By faith Abel brought God a better offering than Cain did. By faith he was commended as righteous, when God spoke well of his offerings. And by faith Abel still speaks, even though he is dead.

By faith Enoch was taken from this life, so that he did not experience death: "He could not be found, because God had taken him away." For before he was taken, he was commended as one who pleased God. And without faith it is impossible to please God, because anyone who comes to him must believe that he exists and that he rewards those who earnestly seek him.

By faith Noah, when warned about things not yet seen, in holy fear built an ark to save his family. By his faith he condemned the world and became heir of the righteousness that is in keeping with faith.

By faith Abraham, when called to go to a place he would later receive as his inheritance, obeyed and went, even though he did not know where he was going. By faith he made his home in the promised land like a stranger in a foreign country; he lived in tents, as did Isaac and Jacob, who were heirs with him of the same promise. For he was looking forward to the city with foundations, whose architect and builder is God. And by faith even Sarah, who was past childbearing age, was enabled to bear children because she considered him faithful who had made the promise. And so from this one man, and he as good as dead, came descendants as numerous as the stars in the sky and as countless as the sand on the seashore.

All these people were still living by faith when they died. They did not receive the things promised; they only saw them and welcomed them from a distance, admitting that they were foreigners and strangers on earth. People who say such things show that they are looking for a country of their own. If they had been thinking of the country they had left, they would have had opportunity to return. Instead, they were longing for a better country — a heavenly one. Therefore God is not ashamed to be called their God, for he has prepared a city for them.

By faith Abraham, when God tested him, offered Isaac as a sacrifice. He who had embraced the promises was about to sacrifice his one and only son, even though God had said to him, "It is through Isaac that your offspring will be reckoned." Abraham reasoned that God could even raise the dead, and so in a manner of speaking he did receive Isaac back from death.

By faith Isaac blessed Jacob and Esau in regard to their future.

By faith Jacob, when he was dying, blessed each of Joseph's sons, and worshiped as he leaned on the top of his staff.

By faith Joseph, when his end was near, spoke about the exodus of the Israelites from Egypt and gave instructions concerning the burial of his bones.

By faith Moses' parents hid him for three months after he was born, because they saw he was no ordinary child, and they were not afraid of the king's edict.

By faith Moses, when he had grown up, refused to be known as the son of Pharaoh's daughter. He chose to be mistreated along with the people of God rather than to enjoy the fleeting pleasures of sin. He regarded disgrace for the sake of Christ as of greater value than the treasures of Egypt, because he was looking ahead to his reward. By faith he left Egypt, not fearing the king's anger; he persevered because he saw him who is invisible. By faith he kept the Passover and the application of blood, so that the destroyer of the firstborn would not touch the firstborn of Israel.

By faith the people passed through the Red Sea as on dry land; but when the Egyptians tried to do so, they were drowned.

By faith the walls of Jericho fell, after the army had marched around them for seven days.

By faith the prostitute Rahab, because she welcomed the spies, was not killed with those who were disobedient.

And what more shall I say? I do not have time to tell about Gideon, Barak, Samson and Jephthah, about David and Samuel and the prophets, who through faith conquered kingdoms, administered justice, and gained what was promised; who shut the mouths of lions, quenched the fury of the flames, and escaped the edge of the sword; whose weakness was turned to strength; and who became powerful in battle and routed foreign armies. Women received back their dead, raised to life again. There were others who were tortured, refusing to be released so that they might gain an even better resurrection. Some faced jeers and flogging, and even chains and imprisonment. They were put to death by stoning; they were sawed in two; they were killed by the sword. They went about in sheepskins and goatskins, destitute, persecuted and mistreated — the world was not worthy of them. They wandered in deserts and mountains, living in caves and in holes in the ground.

These were all commended for their faith, yet none of them received what had been promised, since God had planned something better for us so that only together with us would they be made perfect.

Therefore, since we are surrounded by such a great cloud of witnesses, let us throw off everything that hinders and the sin that so easily entangles. And let us run with perseverance the race marked out for us, fixing our eyes on Jesus, the pioneer and perfecter of faith. For the joy set before him he endured the cross, scorning its shame, and sat down at the right hand of the throne of God. Consider him who endured such opposition from sinners, so that you will not grow weary and lose heart.   Hebrews 11:1—12:3

BE

CHAPTER

26

Patience

KEY IDEA

I am slow to anger and endure patiently
under the unavoidable pressures of life.

KEY VERSE

Whoever is patient has great understanding,
but one who is quick-tempered displays folly.
Proverbs 14:29

GOD IS PATIENT WITH US

But you, Lord, are a compassionate and gracious God,
slow to anger, abounding in love and faithfulness.

PSALM 86:15

God loved the people of Israel and had a wonderful plan for them. The Israelites, on the other hand, struggled to trust God even after he proved himself to them over and over in mighty ways.

The Israelites had spent four hundred long years in Egypt, but now the land God had promised to Abraham for his descendants was ready. But the people had to step forward in faith. God would accomplish the rest. In the book of Exodus, we read how God, through Moses, led the people out of Egypt, and how God even parted the Red Sea.

In the book of Numbers, the people are poised to enter the promised land. They send twelve spies into the land to scope out the situation. Upon their return, the spies report: The size and strength of the enemy is great. Except for Joshua and Caleb, all the spies give in to their fear and say, "We can't attack those people; they are stronger than we are." After the report is given to the people they make their decision. They would rather go back to Egypt and subject themselves to slavery than trust God to lay hold of a life of freedom.

That night all the members of the community raised their voices and wept aloud. All the Israelites grumbled against Moses and Aaron, and the whole assembly said to them, "If only we had died in Egypt! Or in this wilderness! Why is the LORD bringing us to this land only to let us fall by the sword? Our wives and children will be taken as plunder. Wouldn't it be better for us to go back to Egypt?" And they said to each other, "We should choose a leader and go back to Egypt."

Then Moses and Aaron fell facedown in front of the whole Israelite assembly gathered there. Joshua son of Nun and Caleb son of Jephunneh, who were among those who had explored the land, tore their clothes and said to the entire Israelite assembly, "The land we passed through and explored is exceedingly good. If the LORD is pleased with us, he will lead us into that land, a land flowing with milk and honey, and will give it to us. Only do not rebel against the Lord. And do not be afraid of the people of the land, because we will devour them. Their protection is gone, but the Lord is with us. Do not be afraid of them."

But the whole assembly talked about stoning them. Then the glory of the Lord appeared at the tent of meeting to all the Israelites. The Lord said to Moses, "How long will these people treat me with contempt? How long will they refuse to believe in me, in spite of all the signs I have performed among them? I will strike them down with a plague and destroy them, but I will make you into a nation greater and stronger than they."

Moses said to the Lord, "Then the Egyptians will hear about it! By your power you brought these people up from among them. And they will tell the inhabitants of this land about it. They have already heard that you, Lord, are with these people and that you, Lord, have been seen face to face, that your cloud stays over them, and that you go before them in a pillar of cloud by day and a pillar of fire by night. If you put all these people to death, leaving none alive, the nations who have heard this report about you will say, 'The Lord was not able to bring these people into the land he promised them on oath, so he slaughtered them in the wilderness.'

"Now may the Lord's strength be displayed, just as you have declared: 'The Lord is slow to anger, abounding in love and forgiving sin and rebellion. Yet he does not leave the guilty unpunished; he punishes the children for the sin of the parents to the third and fourth generation.' In accordance with your great love, forgive the sin of these people, just as you have pardoned them from the time they left Egypt until now."

The Lord replied, "I have forgiven them, as you asked. Nevertheless, as surely as I live and as surely as the glory of the Lord fills the whole earth, not one of those who saw my glory and the signs I performed in Egypt and in the wilderness but who disobeyed me and tested me ten times — not one of them will ever see the land I promised on oath to their ancestors." Numbers 14:1–23

"Not one of you will enter the land I swore with uplifted hand to make your home, except Caleb son of Jephunneh and Joshua son of Nun. As for your children that you said would be taken as plunder, I will bring them in to enjoy the land you have rejected.

But as for you, your bodies will fall in this wilderness. Your children will be shepherds here for forty years, suffering for your unfaithfulness, until the last of your bodies lies in the wilderness."

NUMBERS 14:30–33

Although God didn't wipe out the rebellious Israelites as they deserved, he made them wander in the wilderness for forty years—one year for each of the forty days the spies explored the land. Nevertheless, God patiently demonstrated his commitment to his covenant with Israel and established the next generation in the promised land.

God's patience extends beyond the Israelites to all people. God is just. In Peter's second letter he tells his readers about "the day of the Lord" when Christ will return and bring to consummation all things. This will be the day of judgment for unbelievers, but the day of redemption for believers. God demonstrates his patience toward all humanity by delaying this ultimate and final judgment to give more people an opportunity to reach out and take hold of his forgiveness.

Dear friends, this is now my second letter to you. I have written both of them as reminders to stimulate you to wholesome thinking. I want you to recall the words spoken in the past by the holy prophets and the command given by our Lord and Savior through your apostles.

Above all, you must understand that in the last days scoffers will come, scoffing and following their own evil desires. They will say, "Where is this 'coming' he promised? Ever since our ancestors died, everything goes on as it has since the beginning of creation." But they deliberately forget that long ago by God's word the heavens came into being and the earth was formed out of water and by water. By these waters also the world of that time was deluged and destroyed. By the same word the present heavens and earth are reserved for fire, being kept for the day of judgment and destruction of the ungodly.

But do not forget this one thing, dear friends: With the Lord a day is like a thousand years, and a thousand years are like a day. The Lord is not slow in keeping his promise, as some understand slowness. Instead he is patient with you, not wanting anyone to perish, but everyone to come to repentance.

But the day of the Lord will come like a thief. The heavens will disappear with a roar; the elements will be destroyed by fire, and the earth and everything done in it will be laid bare.

Since everything will be destroyed in this way, what kind of people ought you to be? You ought to live holy and godly lives as you look forward to the day of God and speed its coming. That day will bring about the destruction of the heavens by fire, and the elements will melt in the heat. But in keeping with his promise we are looking forward to a new heaven and a new earth, where righteousness dwells.

So then, dear friends, since you are looking forward to this, make every effort to be found spotless, blameless and at peace with him. Bear in mind that our Lord's patience means salvation, just as our dear brother Paul also wrote you with the wisdom that God gave him. He writes the same way in all his letters, speaking in them of these matters. His letters contain some things that are hard to understand, which ignorant and unstable people distort, as they do the other Scriptures, to their own destruction.

Therefore, dear friends, since you have been forewarned, be on your guard so that you may not be carried away by the error of the lawless and fall from your secure position. But grow in the grace and knowledge of our Lord and Savior Jesus Christ. To him be glory both now and forever! Amen.   2 PETER 3:1–18

BEING SLOW TO BECOME ANGRY

One of the primary ideas behind the virtue of patience is taking a long time to overheat. The Greek word carries the idea of a thermometer. If a spiritual thermometer were placed in our mouths as we faced a difficult situation, how long would it take for our temperature to rise? As we mature, we learn to control our anger and practice patience in all circumstances.

Young David was a threat to King Saul. While it was not David's goal, he was popular with the people of Israel. King Saul burned with anger and jealousy toward David. For the next several years, he pursued David, hoping to capture and kill him. David, forced to become a fugitive, proves he is a "man after God's own heart" when he waits on God's timing instead of taking matters into his own hands.

After Saul returned from pursuing the Philistines, he was told, "David is in the Desert of En Gedi." So Saul took three thousand able young men from all Israel and set out to look for David and his men near the Crags of the Wild Goats.

He came to the sheep pens along the way; a cave was there, and Saul went in to relieve himself. David and his men were far back in the cave. The men said, "This is the day the LORD spoke of when he said to you, 'I will give your enemy into your hands for you to deal with as you wish.'" Then David crept up unnoticed and cut off a corner of Saul's robe.

Afterward, David was conscience-stricken for having cut off a corner of his robe. He said to his men, "The LORD forbid that I should do such a thing to my master, the LORD's anointed, or lay my hand on him; for he is the anointed of the LORD." With these words David sharply rebuked his men and did not allow them to attack Saul. And Saul left the cave and went his way.

Then David went out of the cave and called out to Saul, "My lord the king!" When Saul looked behind him, David bowed down and prostrated himself with his face to the ground. He said to Saul, "Why do you listen when men say, 'David is bent on harming you'? This day you have seen with your own eyes how the LORD delivered you into my hands in the cave. Some urged me to kill you, but I spared you; I said, 'I will not lay my hand on my lord, because he is the LORD's anointed.' See, my father, look at this piece of your robe in my hand! I cut off the corner of your robe but did not kill you. See that there is nothing in my hand to indicate that I am guilty of wrongdoing or rebellion. I have not wronged you, but you are hunting me down to take my life. May the LORD judge between you and me. And may the LORD avenge the wrongs you have done to me, but my hand will not touch you. As the old saying goes, 'From evildoers come evil deeds,' so my hand will not touch you.

"Against whom has the king of Israel come out? Who are you pursuing? A dead dog? A flea? May the LORD be our judge and decide between us. May he consider my cause and uphold it; may he vindicate me by delivering me from your hand."

When David finished saying this, Saul asked, "Is that your voice, David my son?" And he wept aloud. "You are more righteous than I," he said. "You have treated me well, but I have treated you badly. You have just now told me about the good you did to me; the LORD delivered me into your hands, but you did not kill me. When a man finds his enemy, does he let him get away unharmed? May the LORD reward you well for the way you treated me today. I know that you will surely be king and that the kingdom of Israel will be established in your hands. Now swear to me by the LORD that you will not kill off my descendants or wipe out my name from my father's family."

So David gave his oath to Saul. Then Saul returned home, but David and his men went up to the stronghold.   1 SAMUEL 24:1–22

Saul returned home, but his jealousy remained. As the days passed, Saul allowed his anger against David to fester and grow. Once again Saul led three thousand troops on a mission to capture and kill David.

The Ziphites went to Saul at Gibeah and said, "Is not David hiding on the hill of Hakilah, which faces Jeshimon?"

So Saul went down to the Desert of Ziph, with his three thousand select Israelite troops, to search there for David. Saul made his camp beside the road on the hill of Hakilah facing Jeshimon, but David stayed in the wilderness. When he saw that Saul had followed him there, he sent out scouts and learned that Saul had definitely arrived.

Then David set out and went to the place where Saul had camped. He saw where Saul and Abner son of Ner, the commander of the army, had lain down. Saul was lying inside the camp, with the army encamped around him.

David then asked Ahimelek the Hittite and Abishai son of Zeruiah, Joab's brother, "Who will go down into the camp with me to Saul?"

"I'll go with you," said Abishai.

So David and Abishai went to the army by night, and there was Saul, lying asleep inside the camp with his spear stuck in the ground near his head. Abner and the soldiers were lying around him.

Abishai said to David, "Today God has delivered your enemy into your hands. Now let me pin him to the ground with one thrust of the spear; I won't strike him twice."

But David said to Abishai, "Don't destroy him! Who can lay a hand on the LORD's anointed and be guiltless? As surely as the LORD lives," he said, "the LORD himself will strike him, or his time will come and he will die, or he will go into battle and perish. But the LORD forbid that I should lay a hand on the LORD's anointed. Now get the spear and water jug that are near his head, and let's go."

So David took the spear and water jug near Saul's head, and they left. No one saw or knew about it, nor did anyone wake up. They were all sleeping, because the LORD had put them into a deep sleep.

Then David crossed over to the other side and stood on top of the hill some distance away; there was a wide space between them. He called out to the army and to Abner son of Ner, "Aren't you going to answer me, Abner?"

Abner replied, "Who are you who calls to the king?"

David said, "You're a man, aren't you? And who is like you in Israel? Why didn't you guard your lord the king? Someone came to destroy your lord the king. What you have done is not good. As surely as the LORD lives, you and your men must die, because you did not guard your master, the LORD's anointed. Look around you. Where are the king's spear and water jug that were near his head?"

Saul recognized David's voice and said, "Is that your voice, David my son?"

David replied, "Yes it is, my lord the king." And he added, "Why is my lord pursuing his servant? What have I done, and what wrong am I guilty of? Now let my lord the king listen to his servant's words. If the LORD has incited you against me, then may he accept an offering. If, however, people have done it, may they be cursed before the LORD! They have driven me today from my share in the LORD's inheritance and have said, 'Go, serve other gods.' Now do not let my blood fall to the ground far from the presence of the LORD. The king of Israel has come out to look for a flea — as one hunts a partridge in the mountains."

Then Saul said, "I have sinned. Come back, David my son. Because you considered my life precious today, I will not try to harm you again. Surely I have acted like a fool and have been terribly wrong."

"Here is the king's spear," David answered. "Let one of your young men come over and get it. The LORD rewards everyone for their righteousness and faithfulness. The LORD delivered you into my hands today, but I would not lay a hand on the LORD's anointed. As surely as I valued your life today, so may the LORD value my life and deliver me from all trouble."

Then Saul said to David, "May you be blessed, David my son; you will do great things and surely triumph."

So David went on his way, and Saul returned home.

1 SAMUEL 26:1–25

Saul was critically wounded in a battle against the Philistines and eventually died after falling on his own sword. When David got word of Saul and his son Jonathan's death, he refused to celebrate victory for himself but grieved the loss of Israel's king. David waited for God to work out his plan. In the course of time, David became king of his own tribe, Judah; seven years later he was crowned king of all Israel. David's son Solomon took the throne of Israel after David's death. In Proverbs, Solomon shares from his amazing reservoir of God-instilled wisdom. Listen to and learn from what he wrote about the virtue of patience.

Whoever is patient has great understanding,
but one who is quick-tempered displays folly. PROVERBS 14:29

A hot-tempered person stirs up conflict,
but the one who is patient calms a quarrel. PROVERBS 15:18

Better a patient person than a warrior,
one with self-control than one who takes a city.

PROVERBS 16:32

A person's wisdom yields patience;
it is to one's glory to overlook an offense. PROVERBS 19:11

Through patience a ruler can be persuaded,
and a gentle tongue can break a bone. PROVERBS 25:15

What does it take to learn to control anger and practice patience? The apostle Paul learned patience through a difficult relationship. In Acts, we read that Paul was disappointed in John Mark, who had deserted him on a previous missionary journey. Paul's anger ran deep, and he refused to work with John Mark, even choosing to travel without his good friend Barnabas if John Mark was a part of the package.

Some time later Paul said to Barnabas, "Let us go back and visit the believers in all the towns where we preached the word of the Lord and see how they are doing." Barnabas wanted to take John, also called Mark, with them, but Paul did not think it wise to take him, because he had deserted them in Pamphylia and had not continued with them in the work. They had such a sharp disagreement that they parted company. Barnabas took Mark and sailed for Cyprus, but Paul chose Silas and left, commended by the believers to the grace of the Lord. He went through Syria and Cilicia, strengthening the churches. ACTS 15:36–41

The next short verse carries behind it an amazing story. Paul, in prison, near the end of his life, asked his close friend and associate Timothy to bring John Mark with him to Rome. What a journey of forgiveness and reconciliation he must have undergone. He had forgiven Mark, who eventually had proven himself to Paul, and had come to view him with patience and respect.

Only Luke is with me. Get Mark and bring him with you, because he is helpful to me in my ministry. 2 TIMOTHY 4:11

James offered the following advice to Paul. We too can use it in our relationships with others—particularly those who "push our buttons."

My dear brothers and sisters, take note of this: Everyone should be quick to listen, slow to speak and slow to become angry, because human anger does not produce the righteousness that God desires. JAMES 1:19–20

PERSEVERING UNDER PRESSURE

Another aspect of patience is holding up under the pressures of life, waiting on the Lord for resolution. In the book of Job we read of a most unusual conversation taking place in heaven between

God and Satan. The outcome of this conversation will gravely affect the life of a righteous man named Job. What unfolds is the ultimate test of patience. Will Job curse God or will he offer up his praise to God?

In the land of Uz there lived a man whose name was Job. This man was blameless and upright; he feared God and shunned evil. He had seven sons and three daughters, and he owned seven thousand sheep, three thousand camels, five hundred yoke of oxen and five hundred donkeys, and had a large number of servants. He was the greatest man among all the people of the East.

His sons used to hold feasts in their homes on their birthdays, and they would invite their three sisters to eat and drink with them. When a period of feasting had run its course, Job would make arrangements for them to be purified. Early in the morning he would sacrifice a burnt offering for each of them, thinking, "Perhaps my children have sinned and cursed God in their hearts." This was Job's regular custom.

One day the angels came to present themselves before the LORD, and Satan also came with them. The LORD said to Satan, "Where have you come from?"

Satan answered the LORD, "From roaming throughout the earth, going back and forth on it."

Then the LORD said to Satan, "Have you considered my servant Job? There is no one on earth like him; he is blameless and upright, a man who fears God and shuns evil."

"Does Job fear God for nothing?" Satan replied. "Have you not put a hedge around him and his household and everything he has? You have blessed the work of his hands, so that his flocks and herds are spread throughout the land. But now stretch out your hand and strike everything he has, and he will surely curse you to your face."

The LORD said to Satan, "Very well, then, everything he has is in your power, but on the man himself do not lay a finger."

Then Satan went out from the presence of the LORD.

One day when Job's sons and daughters were feasting and drinking wine at the oldest brother's house, a messenger came to Job and said, "The oxen were plowing and the donkeys were grazing nearby, and the Sabeans attacked and made off with them.

They put the servants to the sword, and I am the only one who has escaped to tell you!"

While he was still speaking, another messenger came and said, "The fire of God fell from the heavens and burned up the sheep and the servants, and I am the only one who has escaped to tell you!"

While he was still speaking, another messenger came and said, "The Chaldeans formed three raiding parties and swept down on your camels and made off with them. They put the servants to the sword, and I am the only one who has escaped to tell you!"

While he was still speaking, yet another messenger came and said, "Your sons and daughters were feasting and drinking wine at the oldest brother's house, when suddenly a mighty wind swept in from the desert and struck the four corners of the house. It collapsed on them and they are dead, and I am the only one who has escaped to tell you!"

At this, Job got up and tore his robe and shaved his head. Then he fell to the ground in worship and said:

> "Naked I came from my mother's womb,
>   and naked I will depart.
> The LORD gave and the LORD has taken away;
>   may the name of the LORD be praised."

In all this, Job did not sin by charging God with wrongdoing.

On another day the angels came to present themselves before the LORD, and Satan also came with them to present himself before him. And the LORD said to Satan, "Where have you come from?"

Satan answered the LORD, "From roaming throughout the earth, going back and forth on it."

Then the LORD said to Satan, "Have you considered my servant Job? There is no one on earth like him; he is blameless and upright, a man who fears God and shuns evil. And he still maintains his integrity, though you incited me against him to ruin him without any reason."

"Skin for skin!" Satan replied. "A man will give all he has for his own life. But now stretch out your hand and strike his flesh and bones, and he will surely curse you to your face."

The LORD said to Satan, "Very well, then, he is in your hands; but you must spare his life."

So Satan went out from the presence of the LORD and afflicted Job with painful sores from the soles of his feet to the crown of his head. Then Job took a piece of broken pottery and scraped himself with it as he sat among the ashes.

His wife said to him, "Are you still maintaining your integrity? Curse God and die!"

He replied, "You are talking like a foolish woman. Shall we accept good from God, and not trouble?"

In all this, Job did not sin in what he said.

When Job's three friends, Eliphaz the Temanite, Bildad the Shuhite and Zophar the Naamathite, heard about all the troubles that had come upon him, they set out from their homes and met together by agreement to go and sympathize with him and comfort him. When they saw him from a distance, they could hardly recognize him; they began to weep aloud, and they tore their robes and sprinkled dust on their heads. Then they sat on the ground with him for seven days and seven nights. No one said a word to him, because they saw how great his suffering was.   JOB 1:1—2:13

Job's three friends did their best work when they merely sat silently with Job in the ashes. But they didn't stay silent. They felt an obligation to open their mouths and interpret the tragedy that befell Job. They suggested it could only be Job's sin that would cause such a catastrophe. Of course, this wasn't true. Understandably, Job contemplated giving up; he also had straight-forward questions for God and defended himself. But Job never cursed God as Satan claimed he would. Job's patience in the face of trials is a model for us. In the end, God restored Job.

After the LORD had said these things to Job, he said to Eliphaz the Temanite, "I am angry with you and your two friends, because you have not spoken the truth about me, as my servant Job has. So now take seven bulls and seven rams and go to my servant Job and sacrifice a burnt offering for yourselves. My servant Job will pray for you, and I will accept his prayer and not deal with you according to your folly. You have not spoken the truth about me, as my servant Job has." So Eliphaz the Temanite, Bildad the Shuhite and Zophar the Naamathite did what the LORD told them; and the LORD accepted Job's prayer.

After Job had prayed for his friends, the LORD restored his fortunes and gave him twice as much as he had before. All his brothers and sisters and everyone who had known him before came and ate with him in his house. They comforted and consoled him over all the trouble the LORD had brought on him, and each one gave him a piece of silver and a gold ring.

The LORD blessed the latter part of Job's life more than the former part. He had fourteen thousand sheep, six thousand camels, a thousand yoke of oxen and a thousand donkeys. And he also had seven sons and three daughters. The first daughter he named Jemimah, the second Keziah and the third Keren-Happuch. Nowhere in all the land were there found women as beautiful as Job's daughters, and their father granted them an inheritance along with their brothers.

After this, Job lived a hundred and forty years; he saw his children and their children to the fourth generation. And so Job died, an old man and full of years.   JOB 42:7–17

What can we learn from David, Paul, James and Job? Patience is a virtue that we develop through control of our anger, and we develop this virtue in the face of adversity. Our cultivation of patience pleases God, who is patient with us. Patience affects our relationships in a positive way and brings great joy to our lives and community. The writer of Hebrews tells us how God fosters this virtue in us over time.

Therefore, since we are surrounded by such a great cloud of witnesses, let us throw off everything that hinders and the sin that so easily entangles. And let us run with perseverance the race marked out for us, fixing our eyes on Jesus, the pioneer and perfecter of faith. For the joy set before him he endured the cross, scorning its shame, and sat down at the right hand of the throne of God. Consider him who endured such opposition from sinners, so that you will not grow weary and lose heart.

In your struggle against sin, you have not yet resisted to the point of shedding your blood. And have you completely forgotten this word of encouragement that addresses you as a father addresses his son? It says,

> "My son, do not make light of the Lord's discipline,
>   and do not lose heart when he rebukes you,
> because the Lord disciplines the one he loves,
>   and he chastens everyone he accepts as his son."

Endure hardship as discipline; God is treating you as his children. For what children are not disciplined by their father? If you are not disciplined — and everyone undergoes discipline — then you are not legitimate, not true sons and daughters at all. Moreover, we have all had human fathers who disciplined us and we respected them for it. How much more should we submit to the Father of spirits and live! They disciplined us for a little while as they thought best; but God disciplines us for our good, in order that we may share in his holiness. No discipline seems pleasant at the time, but painful. Later on, however, it produces a harvest of righteousness and peace for those who have been trained by it.

Therefore, strengthen your feeble arms and weak knees.

HEBREWS 12:1–12

BE

CHAPTER

27

Kindness/Goodness

KEY IDEA

I choose to be kind and good
in my relationships with others.

KEY VERSE

Make sure that nobody pays back wrong for wrong,
but always strive to do what is good
for each other and for everyone else.
1 Thessalonians 5:15

Our Kind and Good God

As with all the virtues, our God is the perfect example. This psalm was likely written after the Israelites returned from captivity in Babylon and was recited each year at one of the annual religious festivals. Throughout their history the Israelites cried out to God for mercy and help. Each time God responded from a tender and kind heart. As we look back on our own life we will see the same pattern of response from God.

Give thanks to the Lord, for he is good;
   his love endures forever.

Let the redeemed of the Lord tell their story—
   those he redeemed from the hand of the foe,
those he gathered from the lands,
   from east and west, from north and south.

Some wandered in desert wastelands,
   finding no way to a city where they could settle.
They were hungry and thirsty,
   and their lives ebbed away.
Then they cried out to the Lord in their trouble,
   and he delivered them from their distress.
He led them by a straight way
   to a city where they could settle.
Let them give thanks to the Lord for his unfailing love
   and his wonderful deeds for mankind,
for he satisfies the thirsty
   and fills the hungry with good things.

Some sat in darkness, in utter darkness,
   prisoners suffering in iron chains,
because they rebelled against God's commands
   and despised the plans of the Most High.
So he subjected them to bitter labor;
   they stumbled, and there was no one to help.
Then they cried to the Lord in their trouble,
   and he saved them from their distress.
He brought them out of darkness, the utter darkness,
   and broke away their chains.

Let them give thanks to the LORD for his unfailing love
  and his wonderful deeds for mankind,
for he breaks down gates of bronze
  and cuts through bars of iron.

Some became fools through their rebellious ways
  and suffered affliction because of their iniquities.
They loathed all food
  and drew near the gates of death.
Then they cried to the LORD in their trouble,
  and he saved them from their distress.
He sent out his word and healed them;
  he rescued them from the grave.
Let them give thanks to the LORD for his unfailing love
  and his wonderful deeds for mankind.
Let them sacrifice thank offerings
  and tell of his works with songs of joy.

Some went out on the sea in ships;
  they were merchants on the mighty waters.
They saw the works of the LORD,
  his wonderful deeds in the deep.
For he spoke and stirred up a tempest
  that lifted high the waves.
They mounted up to the heavens and went down to the
    depths;
  in their peril their courage melted away.
They reeled and staggered like drunkards;
  they were at their wits' end.
Then they cried out to the LORD in their trouble,
  and he brought them out of their distress.
He stilled the storm to a whisper;
  the waves of the sea were hushed.
They were glad when it grew calm,
  and he guided them to their desired haven.
Let them give thanks to the LORD for his unfailing love
  and his wonderful deeds for mankind.
Let them exalt him in the assembly of the people
  and praise him in the council of the elders.

He turned rivers into a desert,
    flowing springs into thirsty ground,
and fruitful land into a salt waste,
    because of the wickedness of those who lived there.
He turned the desert into pools of water
    and the parched ground into flowing springs;
there he brought the hungry to live,
    and they founded a city where they could settle.
They sowed fields and planted vineyards
    that yielded a fruitful harvest;
he blessed them, and their numbers greatly increased,
    and he did not let their herds diminish.

Then their numbers decreased, and they were humbled
    by oppression, calamity and sorrow;
he who pours contempt on nobles
    made them wander in a trackless waste.
But he lifted the needy out of their affliction
    and increased their families like flocks.
The upright see and rejoice,
    but all the wicked shut their mouths.

Let the one who is wise heed these things
    and ponder the loving deeds of the LORD.   PSALM 107:1–43

STORIES OF KINDNESS: RAHAB

The Bible contains many stories of kindness throughout its pages. In the Old Testament, Joshua, Israel's great and courageous leader, sent two spies to scope out the land of Canaan in preparation for the conquest. While they were deep in enemy territory, God used a most unusual character to show them kindness.

Then Joshua son of Nun secretly sent two spies from Shittim. "Go, look over the land," he said, "especially Jericho." So they went and entered the house of a prostitute named Rahab and stayed there.

The king of Jericho was told, "Look, some of the Israelites have come here tonight to spy out the land." So the king of Jericho sent this message to Rahab: "Bring out the men who came to you and entered your house, because they have come to spy out the whole land."

But the woman had taken the two men and hidden them. She said, "Yes, the men came to me, but I did not know where they had come from. At dusk, when it was time to close the city gate, they left. I don't know which way they went. Go after them quickly. You may catch up with them." (But she had taken them up to the roof and hidden them under the stalks of flax she had laid out on the roof.) So the men set out in pursuit of the spies on the road that leads to the fords of the Jordan, and as soon as the pursuers had gone out, the gate was shut.

Before the spies lay down for the night, she went up on the roof and said to them, "I know that the LORD has given you this land and that a great fear of you has fallen on us, so that all who live in this country are melting in fear because of you. We have heard how the LORD dried up the water of the Red Sea for you when you came out of Egypt, and what you did to Sihon and Og, the two kings of the Amorites east of the Jordan, whom you completely destroyed. When we heard of it, our hearts melted in fear and everyone's courage failed because of you, for the LORD your God is God in heaven above and on the earth below.

"Now then, please swear to me by the LORD that you will show kindness to my family, because I have shown kindness to you. Give me a sure sign that you will spare the lives of my father and mother, my brothers and sisters, and all who belong to them — and that you will save us from death."

"Our lives for your lives!" the men assured her. "If you don't tell what we are doing, we will treat you kindly and faithfully when the LORD gives us the land."

So she let them down by a rope through the window, for the house she lived in was part of the city wall. She said to them, "Go to the hills so the pursuers will not find you. Hide yourselves there three days until they return, and then go on your way."

Now the men had said to her, "This oath you made us swear will not be binding on us unless, when we enter the land, you have tied this scarlet cord in the window through which you let us down, and unless you have brought your father and mother, your brothers and all your family into your house. If any of them go outside your house into the street, their blood will be on their own heads; we will not be responsible. As for those who are in the house with you, their blood will be on our head if a hand is laid on them. But if you tell what we are doing, we will be released from the oath you made us swear."

"Agreed," she replied. "Let it be as you say."

So she sent them away, and they departed. And she tied the scarlet cord in the window.

When they left, they went into the hills and stayed there three days, until the pursuers had searched all along the road and returned without finding them. Then the two men started back. They went down out of the hills, forded the river and came to Joshua son of Nun and told him everything that had happened to them. They said to Joshua, "The LORD has surely given the whole land into our hands; all the people are melting in fear because of us."

JOSHUA 2:1–24

With the hand of God obviously on their side, the Israelites conquered the city of Jericho, and Rahab was rewarded for her act of kindness.

Joshua got up early the next morning and the priests took up the ark of the LORD. The seven priests carrying the seven trumpets went forward, marching before the ark of the LORD and blowing the trumpets. The armed men went ahead of them and the rear guard followed the ark of the LORD, while the trumpets kept sounding. So on the second day they marched around the city once and returned to the camp. They did this for six days.

On the seventh day, they got up at daybreak and marched around the city seven times in the same manner, except that on that day they circled the city seven times. The seventh time around, when the priests sounded the trumpet blast, Joshua commanded the army, "Shout! For the LORD has given you the city! The city and all that is in it are to be devoted to the LORD. Only Rahab the prostitute and all who are with her in her house shall be spared, because she hid the spies we sent. But keep away from the devoted things, so that you will not bring about your own destruction by taking any of them. Otherwise you will make the camp of Israel liable to destruction and bring trouble on it. All the silver and gold and the articles of bronze and iron are sacred to the LORD and must go into his treasury."

When the trumpets sounded, the army shouted, and at the sound of the trumpet, when the men gave a loud shout, the wall collapsed; so everyone charged straight in, and they took the city. They devoted the city to the LORD and destroyed with the sword every living thing in it — men and women, young and old, cattle, sheep and donkeys.

Joshua said to the two men who had spied out the land, "Go into the prostitute's house and bring her out and all who belong to her, in accordance with your oath to her." So the young men who had done the spying went in and brought out Rahab, her father and mother, her brothers and sisters and all who belonged to her. They brought out her entire family and put them in a place outside the camp of Israel.

Then they burned the whole city and everything in it, but they put the silver and gold and the articles of bronze and iron into the treasury of the LORD's house. But Joshua spared Rahab the prostitute, with her family and all who belonged to her, because she hid the men Joshua had sent as spies to Jericho — and she lives among the Israelites to this day. JOSHUA 6:12–25

STORIES OF KINDNESS: DAVID

The prophet Samuel anointed David, when he was just a teenager, to be the next king of Israel. His coronation, however, was a number of years away. Over the next several years God would use the rebellious heart of King Saul to grow David's trust in God. Before David took off running from King Saul, Jonathan, Saul's son and successor to the throne, had a sobering conversation with David. Jonathan acknowledged and accepted God's plan for David, not him, to be the next king. However, he made one request of the future king of Israel.

"If my father intends to harm you, may the LORD deal with Jonathan, be it ever so severely, if I do not let you know and send you away in peace. May the LORD be with you as he has been with my father. But show me unfailing kindness like the LORD's kindness as long as I live, so that I may not be killed, and do not ever cut off your kindness from my family—not even when the LORD has cut off every one of David's enemies from the face of the earth."

So Jonathan made a covenant with the house of David, saying, "May the LORD call David's enemies to account."   1 SAMUEL 20:13–16

Fast-forward many years. Saul and Jonathan were both dead, and David was now king. All potential threats from the old royal house of Saul had been neutralized, and David remembered his promise to Jonathan.

David asked, "Is there anyone still left of the house of Saul to whom I can show kindness for Jonathan's sake?"

Now there was a servant of Saul's household named Ziba. They summoned him to appear before David, and the king said to him, "Are you Ziba?"

"At your service," he replied.

The king asked, "Is there no one still alive from the house of Saul to whom I can show God's kindness?"

Ziba answered the king, "There is still a son of Jonathan; he is lame in both feet."

"Where is he?" the king asked.

Ziba answered, "He is at the house of Makir son of Ammiel in Lo Debar."

So King David had him brought from Lo Debar, from the house of Makir son of Ammiel.

When Mephibosheth son of Jonathan, the son of Saul, came to David, he bowed down to pay him honor.

David said, "Mephibosheth!"

"At your service," he replied.

"Don't be afraid," David said to him, "for I will surely show you kindness for the sake of your father Jonathan. I will restore to you all the land that belonged to your grandfather Saul, and you will always eat at my table."

Mephibosheth bowed down and said, "What is your servant, that you should notice a dead dog like me?"

Then the king summoned Ziba, Saul's steward, and said to him, "I have given your master's grandson everything that belonged to Saul and his family. You and your sons and your servants are to farm the land for him and bring in the crops, so that your master's grandson may be provided for. And Mephibosheth, grandson of your master, will always eat at my table." (Now Ziba had fifteen sons and twenty servants.)

Then Ziba said to the king, "Your servant will do whatever my lord the king commands his servant to do." So Mephibosheth ate at David's table like one of the king's sons.

Mephibosheth had a young son named Mika, and all the members of Ziba's household were servants of Mephibosheth. And Mephibosheth lived in Jerusalem, because he always ate at the king's table; he was lame in both feet. 2 SAMUEL 9:1–13

STORIES OF KINDNESS: THE DINNER GUEST

The Jewish religious leaders in Jesus' day held exclusive dinner parties. Only invited guests of significant public standing were allowed to attend. Upon arrival, the host would seat guests in order of importance. On one occasion when Jesus was invited to eat at the table of a well-known Pharisee, he took advantage of the opportunity to teach a lesson first about humility and then about the kind of people who should be on the guest list of such occasions.

One Sabbath, when Jesus went to eat in the house of a prominent Pharisee, he was being carefully watched. LUKE 14:1

When he noticed how the guests picked the places of honor at the table, he told them this parable: "When someone invites you to a wedding feast, do not take the place of honor, for a person more distinguished than you may have been invited. If so, the host who invited both of you will come and say to you, 'Give this person your seat.' Then, humiliated, you will have to take the least important place. But when you are invited, take the lowest place, so that when your host comes, he will say to you, 'Friend, move up to a better place.' Then you will be honored in the presence of all the other guests. For all those who exalt themselves will be humbled, and those who humble themselves will be exalted."

Then Jesus said to his host, "When you give a luncheon or dinner, do not invite your friends, your brothers or sisters, your relatives, or your rich neighbors; if you do, they may invite you back and so you will be repaid. But when you give a banquet, invite the poor, the crippled, the lame, the blind, and you will be blessed. Although they cannot repay you, you will be repaid at the resurrection of the righteous."

LUKE 14:7–14

STORIES OF KINDNESS: PAUL, ONESIMUS AND PHILEMON

While Paul was in prison, likely in Rome, he met a slave named Onesimus, who may have stolen from his master before running away. Through Paul's ministry, Onesimus became a Christian and eventually returned to his master. As it turned out, the master, a man name Philemon, was a Christian and Paul's close friend. Paul sent Onesimus home with a personal letter he had written to give to Philemon. The letter encouraged Philemon to exercise kindness toward his slave and accept Onesimus not as a slave but as a Christian brother.

Paul, a prisoner of Christ Jesus, and Timothy our brother,

To Philemon our dear friend and fellow worker — also to Apphia our sister and Archippus our fellow soldier — and to the church that meets in your home:

Grace and peace to you from God our Father and the Lord Jesus Christ.

I always thank my God as I remember you in my prayers, because I hear about your love for all his holy people and your faith in the Lord Jesus. I pray that your partnership with us in the faith may be effective in deepening your understanding of every good thing we share for the sake of Christ. Your love has given me great joy and encouragement, because you, brother, have refreshed the hearts of the Lord's people.

Therefore, although in Christ I could be bold and order you to do what you ought to do, yet I prefer to appeal to you on the basis of love. It is as none other than Paul — an old man and now also a prisoner of Christ Jesus — that I appeal to you for my son Onesimus, who became my son while I was in chains. Formerly he was useless to you, but now he has become useful both to you and to me.

I am sending him — who is my very heart — back to you. I would have liked to keep him with me so that he could take your place in helping me while I am in chains for the gospel. But I did not want to do anything without your consent, so that any favor you do would not seem forced but would be voluntary. Perhaps the reason he was separated from you for a little while was that you might have him back forever — no longer as a slave, but better than a slave, as a dear brother. He is very dear to me but even dearer to you, both as a fellow man and as a brother in the Lord.

So if you consider me a partner, welcome him as you would welcome me. If he has done you any wrong or owes you anything, charge it to me. I, Paul, am writing this with my own hand. I will pay it back — not to mention that you owe me your very self. I do wish, brother, that I may have some benefit from you in the Lord; refresh my heart in Christ. Confident of your obedience, I write to you, knowing that you will do even more than I ask.

And one thing more: Prepare a guest room for me, because I hope to be restored to you in answer to your prayers.

Epaphras, my fellow prisoner in Christ Jesus, sends you greetings. And so do Mark, Aristarchus, Demas and Luke, my fellow workers.

The grace of the Lord Jesus Christ be with your spirit.

PHILEMON 1–25

STORIES OF KINDNESS: ONESIPHORUS

While Paul spent his years in ministry encouraging others to show kindness, from time to time, he found himself on the receiving end and was grateful. At the end of his ministry and life, from a cold dungeon Paul penned his last letter to his prodigy Timothy, who was pastoring the church at Ephesus. Life in this season had been extremely hard for Paul. In the letter he shared with Timothy his gratitude for one particular believer.

You know that everyone in the province of Asia has deserted me, including Phygelus and Hermogenes.

May the Lord show mercy to the household of Onesiphorus, because he often refreshed me and was not ashamed of my chains.

On the contrary, when he was in Rome, he searched hard for me until he found me. May the Lord grant that he will find mercy from the Lord on that day! You know very well in how many ways he helped me in Ephesus.

2 TIMOTHY 1:15–18

TEACHINGS ON GOODNESS

Jesus not only showed his followers how to be good and kind to others, but he also left us instructions that are both practical and radical.

"But to you who are listening I say: Love your enemies, do good to those who hate you, bless those who curse you, pray for those who mistreat you. If someone slaps you on one cheek, turn to them the other also. If someone takes your coat, do not withhold your shirt from them. Give to everyone who asks you, and if anyone takes what belongs to you, do not demand it back. Do to others as you would have them do to you.

"If you love those who love you, what credit is that to you? Even sinners love those who love them. And if you do good to those who are good to you, what credit is that to you? Even sinners do that. And if you lend to those from whom you expect repayment, what credit is that to you? Even sinners lend to sinners, expecting to be repaid in full. But love your enemies, do good to them, and lend to them without expecting to get anything back. Then your reward will be great, and you will be children of the Most High, because he is kind to the ungrateful and wicked. Be merciful, just as your Father is merciful.

"Do not judge, and you will not be judged. Do not condemn, and you will not be condemned. Forgive, and you will be forgiven. Give, and it will be given to you. A good measure, pressed down, shaken together and running over, will be poured into your lap. For with the measure you use, it will be measured to you."

He also told them this parable: "Can the blind lead the blind? Will they not both fall into a pit? The student is not above the teacher, but everyone who is fully trained will be like their teacher.

"Why do you look at the speck of sawdust in your brother's eye and pay no attention to the plank in your own eye? How can you say to your brother, 'Brother, let me take the speck out of your eye,' when you yourself fail to see the plank in your own eye? You hypocrite, first take the plank out of your eye, and then you will see clearly to remove the speck from your brother's eye.

"No good tree bears bad fruit, nor does a bad tree bear good fruit. Each tree is recognized by its own fruit. People do not pick figs from thornbushes, or grapes from briers. A good man brings good things out of the good stored up in his heart, and an evil man brings evil things out of the evil stored up in his heart. For the mouth speaks what the heart is full of." LUKE 6:27–45

> Two good men who were followers of Jesus—the apostles Peter and Paul—offered instruction to the early believers on living a life of kindness and goodness. From these timeless principles we can find practical guidance for how our relationships with others can reflect the heart and desires of our kind God.

Finally, all of you, be like-minded, be sympathetic, love one another, be compassionate and humble. Do not repay evil with evil or insult with insult. On the contrary, repay evil with blessing, because to this you were called so that you may inherit a blessing. For,

"Whoever would love life
and see good days
must keep their tongue from evil
and their lips from deceitful speech.
They must turn from evil and do good;
they must seek peace and pursue it.
For the eyes of the Lord are on the righteous
and his ears are attentive to their prayer,
but the face of the Lord is against those who do evil."

Who is going to harm you if you are eager to do good? But even if you should suffer for what is right, you are blessed. "Do not fear their threats; do not be frightened." But in your hearts revere Christ as Lord. Always be prepared to give an answer to everyone who asks you to give the reason for the hope that you have. But do this with gentleness and respect, keeping a clear conscience, so that those who speak maliciously against your good behavior in Christ may be ashamed of their slander. For it is better, if it is God's will, to suffer for doing good than for doing evil. 1 Peter 3:8–17

We who are strong ought to bear with the failings of the weak and not to please ourselves. Each of us should please our neighbors for their good, to build them up. Romans 15:1–2

"I have the right to do anything," you say—but not everything is beneficial. "I have the right to do anything"—but not everything is constructive. No one should seek their own good, but the good of others. 1 Corinthians 10:23–24

Let us not become weary in doing good, for at the proper time we will reap a harvest if we do not give up. Therefore, as we have opportunity, let us do good to all people, especially to those who belong to the family of believers. Galatians 6:9–10

Get rid of all bitterness, rage and anger, brawling and slander, along with every form of malice. Be kind and compassionate to one another, forgiving each other, just as in Christ God forgave you. Follow God's example, therefore, as dearly loved children and walk in the way of love, just as Christ loved us and gave himself up for us as a fragrant offering and sacrifice to God. Ephesians 4:31—5:2

Make sure that nobody pays back wrong for wrong, but always strive to do what is good for each other and for everyone else. 1 Thessalonians 5:15

In everything set them an example by doing what is good. Titus 2:7

Remind the people to be subject to rulers and authorities, to be obedient, to be ready to do whatever is good, to slander no one, to be peaceable and considerate, and always to be gentle toward everyone.

At one time we too were foolish, disobedient, deceived and enslaved by all kinds of passions and pleasures. We lived in malice and envy, being hated and hating one another. But when the kindness and love of God our Savior appeared, he saved us, not because of righteous things we had done, but because of his mercy. He saved us through the washing of rebirth and renewal by the Holy Spirit, whom he poured out on us generously through Jesus Christ our Savior, so that, having been justified by his grace, we might become heirs having the hope of eternal life. This is a trustworthy saying. And I want you to stress these things, so that those who have trusted in God may be careful to devote themselves to doing what is good. These things are excellent and profitable for everyone.   TITUS 3:1–8

Our people must learn to devote themselves to doing what is good, in order to provide for urgent needs and not live unproductive lives.   TITUS 3:14

CHAPTER

28

Faithfulness

KEY IDEA

I have established a good name with God
and others based on my loyalty to those relationships.

KEY VERSE

Let love and faithfulness never leave you;
bind them around your neck,
write them on the tablet of your heart.
Then you will win favor and a good name
in the sight of God and man.

Proverbs 3:3–4

As with all the other virtues, faithfulness benefits the people in our lives. When we are faithful to them, they are blessed. And, over time, our faithfulness to others also has a reciprocal benefit. First, we win favor. As needs emerge in our life, people will be inclined to help us. Second, we establish a name. When our name is brought up, even when we are not present, it is spoken with high regard. A good name established through a life of faithfulness is a boundless gift to pass on to our children.

GOD'S FAITHFULNESS

Many of the authors of the Bible recorded their reflections about God's faithfulness. In the song of Moses recorded in Deuteronomy 32, Moses exalts the faithfulness of the covenant-keeping God.

> Listen, you heavens, and I will speak;
>   hear, you earth, the words of my mouth.
> Let my teaching fall like rain
>   and my words descend like dew,
> like showers on new grass,
>   like abundant rain on tender plants.
>
> I will proclaim the name of the LORD.
>   Oh, praise the greatness of our God!
> He is the Rock, his works are perfect,
>   and all his ways are just.
> A faithful God who does no wrong,
>   upright and just is he.   DEUTERONOMY 32:1–4

Likewise, while living in a world with so much uncertainty, the author of Psalm 36 took great comfort in the extent of God's devotion.

> Your love, LORD, reaches to the heavens,
>   your faithfulness to the skies.
> Your righteousness is like the highest mountains,
>   your justice like the great deep.
> You, LORD, preserve both people and animals.

How priceless is your unfailing love, O God!
    People take refuge in the shadow of your wings.
They feast on the abundance of your house;
    you give them drink from your river of delights.
For with you is the fountain of life;
    in your light we see light.   PSALM 36:5–9

While God always remained faithful, the Israelites did not, and he disciplined them for it. In 586 BC Jerusalem and the temple were destroyed and the people were exiled to Babylon. God called the prophet Jeremiah to witness these events and warn the southern kingdom of Judah of God's just punishment. The author (ancient tradition credits Jeremiah with writing Lamentations) of this series of alphabetic acrostic poems lamented about what he saw and felt but also reminded the people of God's consistent faithfulness.

I remember my affliction and my wandering,
    the bitterness and the gall.
I well remember them,
    and my soul is downcast within me.
Yet this I call to mind
    and therefore I have hope:

Because of the LORD's great love we are not consumed,
    for his compassions never fail.
They are new every morning;
    great is your faithfulness.
I say to myself, "The LORD is my portion;
    therefore I will wait for him."   LAMENTATIONS 3:19–24

CALLED TO FAITHFULNESS

The writers of the wisdom books call the reader to a life of faithfulness and also highlight its rich rewards in our lives.

My son, do not forget my teaching,
    but keep my commands in your heart,
for they will prolong your life many years
    and bring you peace and prosperity.

Let love and faithfulness never leave you;
 bind them around your neck,
 write them on the tablet of your heart.
Then you will win favor and a good name
 in the sight of God and man.

Trust in the LORD with all your heart
 and lean not on your own understanding;
in all your ways submit to him,
 and he will make your paths straight. PROVERBS 3:1–6

Many claim to have unfailing love,
 but a faithful person who can find? PROVERBS 20:6

A faithful person will be richly blessed,
 but one eager to get rich will not go unpunished.
         PROVERBS 28:20

The calling Paul shared with the Corinthians concerning his own life applies to all followers of Christ.

This, then, is how you ought to regard us: as servants of Christ and as those entrusted with the mysteries God has revealed. Now it is required that those who have been given a trust must prove faithful. 1 CORINTHIANS 4:1–2

STORIES OF FAITHFULNESS: JOSEPH

God built the nation of Israel from scratch, starting with Abraham, to reveal his name, his power and his plan to provide a way for everyone to come back into a relationship with him. Israel's faithfulness to God over the next 2,000 years was sketchy at best. They were essentially a dysfunctional family, generation after generation. However, there were a few bright spots of tenacious faithfulness both to God and to others. One such example is Joseph, one of the twelve sons of Jacob. He provides a human model of faithfulness for all believers.

Jacob lived in the land where his father had stayed, the land of Canaan.

This is the account of Jacob's family line.

Joseph, a young man of seventeen, was tending the flocks with his brothers, the sons of Bilhah and the sons of Zilpah, his father's wives, and he brought their father a bad report about them.

Now Israel loved Joseph more than any of his other sons, because he had been born to him in his old age; and he made an ornate robe for him. When his brothers saw that their father loved him more than any of them, they hated him and could not speak a kind word to him.

Joseph had a dream, and when he told it to his brothers, they hated him all the more. He said to them, "Listen to this dream I had: We were binding sheaves of grain out in the field when suddenly my sheaf rose and stood upright, while your sheaves gathered around mine and bowed down to it."

His brothers said to him, "Do you intend to reign over us? Will you actually rule us?" And they hated him all the more because of his dream and what he had said.

Then he had another dream, and he told it to his brothers. "Listen," he said, "I had another dream, and this time the sun and moon and eleven stars were bowing down to me."

When he told his father as well as his brothers, his father rebuked him and said, "What is this dream you had? Will your mother and I and your brothers actually come and bow down to the ground before you?" His brothers were jealous of him, but his father kept the matter in mind.

Now his brothers had gone to graze their father's flocks near Shechem, and Israel said to Joseph, "As you know, your brothers are grazing the flocks near Shechem. Come, I am going to send you to them."

"Very well," he replied.

So he said to him, "Go and see if all is well with your brothers and with the flocks, and bring word back to me." Then he sent him off from the Valley of Hebron.

When Joseph arrived at Shechem, a man found him wandering around in the fields and asked him, "What are you looking for?"

He replied, "I'm looking for my brothers. Can you tell me where they are grazing their flocks?"

"They have moved on from here," the man answered. "I heard them say, 'Let's go to Dothan.'"

So Joseph went after his brothers and found them near Dothan. But they saw him in the distance, and before he reached them, they plotted to kill him.

"Here comes that dreamer!" they said to each other. "Come now, let's kill him and throw him into one of these cisterns and say that a ferocious animal devoured him. Then we'll see what comes of his dreams."

When Reuben heard this, he tried to rescue him from their hands. "Let's not take his life," he said. "Don't shed any blood. Throw him into this cistern here in the wilderness, but don't lay a hand on him." Reuben said this to rescue him from them and take him back to his father.

So when Joseph came to his brothers, they stripped him of his robe — the ornate robe he was wearing — and they took him and threw him into the cistern. The cistern was empty; there was no water in it.

As they sat down to eat their meal, they looked up and saw a caravan of Ishmaelites coming from Gilead. Their camels were loaded with spices, balm and myrrh, and they were on their way to take them down to Egypt.

Judah said to his brothers, "What will we gain if we kill our brother and cover up his blood? Come, let's sell him to the Ishmaelites and not lay our hands on him; after all, he is our brother, our own flesh and blood." His brothers agreed.

So when the Midianite merchants came by, his brothers pulled Joseph up out of the cistern and sold him for twenty shekels of silver to the Ishmaelites, who took him to Egypt.

When Reuben returned to the cistern and saw that Joseph was not there, he tore his clothes. He went back to his brothers and said, "The boy isn't there! Where can I turn now?"

Then they got Joseph's robe, slaughtered a goat and dipped the robe in the blood. They took the ornate robe back to their father and said, "We found this. Examine it to see whether it is your son's robe."

He recognized it and said, "It is my son's robe! Some ferocious animal has devoured him. Joseph has surely been torn to pieces."

Then Jacob tore his clothes, put on sackcloth and mourned for his son many days. All his sons and daughters came to comfort him, but he refused to be comforted. "No," he said, "I will continue to mourn until I join my son in the grave." So his father wept for him.

Meanwhile, the Midianites sold Joseph in Egypt to Potiphar, one of Pharaoh's officials, the captain of the guard.   GENESIS 37:1–36

As a teenager Joseph was given dreams of greatness but was cast into a pit by his jealous brothers. From this first pit God lifted him up.

Now Joseph had been taken down to Egypt. Potiphar, an Egyptian who was one of Pharaoh's officials, the captain of the guard, bought him from the Ishmaelites who had taken him there.

The LORD was with Joseph so that he prospered, and he lived in the house of his Egyptian master. When his master saw that the LORD was with him and that the LORD gave him success in everything he did, Joseph found favor in his eyes and became his attendant. Potiphar put him in charge of his household, and he entrusted to his care everything he owned. From the time he put him in charge of his household and of all that he owned, the LORD blessed the household of the Egyptian because of Joseph. The blessing of the LORD was on everything Potiphar had, both in the house and in the field. So Potiphar left everything he had in Joseph's care; with Joseph in charge, he did not concern himself with anything except the food he ate.   GENESIS 39:1–6

As part of God's master plan, Joseph rose again only to be cast into another pit. Potiphar's wife tried to seduce Joseph, but Joseph maintained his integrity and faithfulness to both Potiphar and God by resisting the temptation. Because he rejected her, Potiphar's wife made false accusations against Joseph, and he was thrown into prison. But God was with him there too and lifted him up yet again.

Some time later, the cupbearer and the baker of the king of Egypt offended their master, the king of Egypt. Pharaoh was angry with his two officials, the chief cupbearer and the chief baker, and put them in custody in the house of the captain of the guard, in the same prison where Joseph was confined. The captain of the guard assigned them to Joseph, and he attended them.

After they had been in custody for some time, each of the two men — the cupbearer and the baker of the king of Egypt, who were being held in prison — had a dream the same night, and each dream had a meaning of its own.

When Joseph came to them the next morning, he saw that they were dejected. So he asked Pharaoh's officials who were in custody with him in his master's house, "Why do you look so sad today?"

"We both had dreams," they answered, "but there is no one to interpret them."

Then Joseph said to them, "Do not interpretations belong to God? Tell me your dreams."

So the chief cupbearer told Joseph his dream. He said to him, "In my dream I saw a vine in front of me, and on the vine were three branches. As soon as it budded, it blossomed, and its clusters ripened into grapes. Pharaoh's cup was in my hand, and I took the grapes, squeezed them into Pharaoh's cup and put the cup in his hand."

"This is what it means," Joseph said to him. "The three branches are three days. Within three days Pharaoh will lift up your head and restore you to your position, and you will put Pharaoh's cup in his hand, just as you used to do when you were his cupbearer. But when all goes well with you, remember me and show me kindness; mention me to Pharaoh and get me out of this prison. I was forcibly carried off from the land of the Hebrews, and even here I have done nothing to deserve being put in a dungeon."

When the chief baker saw that Joseph had given a favorable interpretation, he said to Joseph, "I too had a dream: On my head were three baskets of bread. In the top basket were all kinds of baked goods for Pharaoh, but the birds were eating them out of the basket on my head."

"This is what it means," Joseph said. "The three baskets are three days. Within three days Pharaoh will lift off your head and impale your body on a pole. And the birds will eat away your flesh."

Now the third day was Pharaoh's birthday, and he gave a feast for all his officials. He lifted up the heads of the chief cupbearer and the chief baker in the presence of his officials: He restored the chief cupbearer to his position, so that he once again put the cup into Pharaoh's hand — but he impaled the chief baker, just as Joseph had said to them in his interpretation.

The chief cupbearer, however, did not remember Joseph; he forgot him.   GENESIS 40:1–23

Joseph sat in prison two more years. It wasn't until Pharaoh had a dream that none of his magicians or wise men could interpret that the restored cupbearer finally remembered Joseph, and he was brought from the dungeon to explain the dream's meaning. As he stood before the king, Joseph maintained his faithfulness to God.

So Pharaoh sent for Joseph, and he was quickly brought from the dungeon. When he had shaved and changed his clothes, he came before Pharaoh.

Pharaoh said to Joseph, "I had a dream, and no one can interpret it. But I have heard it said of you that when you hear a dream you can interpret it."

"I cannot do it," Joseph replied to Pharaoh, "but God will give Pharaoh the answer he desires."

Then Pharaoh said to Joseph, "In my dream I was standing on the bank of the Nile, when out of the river there came up seven cows, fat and sleek, and they grazed among the reeds. After them, seven other cows came up — scrawny and very ugly and lean. I had never seen such ugly cows in all the land of Egypt. The lean, ugly cows ate up the seven fat cows that came up first. But even after they ate them, no one could tell that they had done so; they looked just as ugly as before. Then I woke up.

"In my dream I saw seven heads of grain, full and good, growing on a single stalk. After them, seven other heads sprouted — withered and thin and scorched by the east wind. The thin heads of grain swallowed up the seven good heads. I told this to the magicians, but none of them could explain it to me."

Then Joseph said to Pharaoh, "The dreams of Pharaoh are one and the same. God has revealed to Pharaoh what he is about to do.

The seven good cows are seven years, and the seven good heads of grain are seven years; it is one and the same dream. The seven lean, ugly cows that came up afterward are seven years, and so are the seven worthless heads of grain scorched by the east wind: They are seven years of famine.

"It is just as I said to Pharaoh: God has shown Pharaoh what he is about to do. Seven years of great abundance are coming throughout the land of Egypt, but seven years of famine will follow them. Then all the abundance in Egypt will be forgotten, and the famine will ravage the land. The abundance in the land will not be remembered, because the famine that follows it will be so severe. The reason the dream was given to Pharaoh in two forms is that the matter has been firmly decided by God, and God will do it soon.

"And now let Pharaoh look for a discerning and wise man and put him in charge of the land of Egypt. Let Pharaoh appoint commissioners over the land to take a fifth of the harvest of Egypt during the seven years of abundance. They should collect all the food of these good years that are coming and store up the grain under the authority of Pharaoh, to be kept in the cities for food. This food should be held in reserve for the country, to be used during the seven years of famine that will come upon Egypt, so that the country may not be ruined by the famine."

The plan seemed good to Pharaoh and to all his officials. So Pharaoh asked them, "Can we find anyone like this man, one in whom is the spirit of God?"

Then Pharaoh said to Joseph, "Since God has made all this known to you, there is no one so discerning and wise as you. You shall be in charge of my palace, and all my people are to submit to your orders. Only with respect to the throne will I be greater than you."

So Pharaoh said to Joseph, "I hereby put you in charge of the whole land of Egypt." Then Pharaoh took his signet ring from his finger and put it on Joseph's finger. He dressed him in robes of fine linen and put a gold chain around his neck. He had him ride in a chariot as his second-in-command, and people shouted before him, "Make way!" Thus he put him in charge of the whole land of Egypt.

Then Pharaoh said to Joseph, "I am Pharaoh, but without your word no one will lift hand or foot in all Egypt." Pharaoh gave Joseph the name Zaphenath-Paneah and gave him Asenath daughter of Potiphera, priest of On, to be his wife. And Joseph went throughout the land of Egypt.

Joseph was thirty years old when he entered the service of Pharaoh king of Egypt.   GENESIS 41:14–46

As Joseph had predicted, there were seven years of back-to-back bumper crops. Egypt was the only nation that adequately set aside food for the lean years to come. Sure enough, in the eighth year a severe famine broke out that would last a solid seven years. Meanwhile, back in the land of Canaan a conversation broke out in Jacob's household.

When Jacob learned that there was grain in Egypt, he said to his sons, "Why do you just keep looking at each other?" He continued, "I have heard that there is grain in Egypt. Go down there and buy some for us, so that we may live and not die."

Then ten of Joseph's brothers went down to buy grain from Egypt. But Jacob did not send Benjamin, Joseph's brother, with the others, because he was afraid that harm might come to him. So Israel's sons were among those who went to buy grain, for there was famine in the land of Canaan also.

Now Joseph was the governor of the land, the person who sold grain to all its people. So when Joseph's brothers arrived, they bowed down to him with their faces to the ground.   GENESIS 42:1–6

From pit to pinnacle. It took twenty-one years for Joseph's dreams to come to pass, but through it all God was faithful. Joseph also stayed faithful to God and the people he served. Through the faithfulness of God and Joseph, the emerging nation of Israel survived the famine. As a result, Joseph was reunited with his father and enjoyed a position of prosperity and blessing for more than 70 years until his death.

STORIES OF FAITHFULNESS: RUTH

Fast-forward to the period in Israel's history when the Israelites occupied the land of Canaan. One of the most heart-touching stories of faithfulness and loyalty does not involve an Israelite but a young Moabite woman.

In the days when the judges ruled, there was a famine in the land. So a man from Bethlehem in Judah, together with his wife and two sons, went to live for a while in the country of Moab. The man's name was Elimelek, his wife's name was Naomi, and the names of his two sons were Mahlon and Kilion. They were Ephrathites from Bethlehem, Judah. And they went to Moab and lived there.

Now Elimelek, Naomi's husband, died, and she was left with her two sons. They married Moabite women, one named Orpah and the other Ruth. After they had lived there about ten years, both Mahlon and Kilion also died, and Naomi was left without her two sons and her husband.

When Naomi heard in Moab that the LORD had come to the aid of his people by providing food for them, she and her daughters-in-law prepared to return home from there. With her two daughters-in-law she left the place where she had been living and set out on the road that would take them back to the land of Judah.

Then Naomi said to her two daughters-in-law, "Go back, each of you, to your mother's home. May the LORD show you kindness, as you have shown kindness to your dead husbands and to me. May the LORD grant that each of you will find rest in the home of another husband."

Then she kissed them goodbye and they wept aloud and said to her, "We will go back with you to your people."

But Naomi said, "Return home, my daughters. Why would you come with me? Am I going to have any more sons, who could become your husbands? Return home, my daughters; I am too old to have another husband. Even if I thought there was still hope for me — even if I had a husband tonight and then gave birth to sons — would you wait until they grew up? Would you remain unmarried for them? No, my daughters. It is more bitter for me than for you, because the LORD's hand has turned against me!"

At this they wept aloud again. Then Orpah kissed her mother-in-law goodbye, but Ruth clung to her.

"Look," said Naomi, "your sister-in-law is going back to her people and her gods. Go back with her."

But Ruth replied, "Don't urge me to leave you or to turn back from you. Where you go I will go, and where you stay I will stay.

Your people will be my people and your God my God. Where you die I will die, and there I will be buried. May the LORD deal with me, be it ever so severely, if even death separates you and me." When Naomi realized that Ruth was determined to go with her, she stopped urging her.

So the two women went on until they came to Bethlehem. When they arrived in Bethlehem, the whole town was stirred because of them, and the women exclaimed, "Can this be Naomi?"

"Don't call me Naomi," she told them. "Call me Mara, because the Almighty has made my life very bitter. I went away full, but the LORD has brought me back empty. Why call me Naomi? The LORD has afflicted me; the Almighty has brought misfortune upon me."

So Naomi returned from Moab accompanied by Ruth the Moabite, her daughter-in-law, arriving in Bethlehem as the barley harvest was beginning.   RUTH 1:1–22

STORIES OF FAITHFULNESS: MARY

God demonstrated his faithfulness to Naomi and Ruth through Boaz, their "guardian-redeemer," who provided for their needs and married Ruth. Boaz and Ruth had a son named Obed, who had a son named Jesse, who had a son named David—who became the great king of Israel. And later the prophet Micah prophesied that the Messiah would come from David's town of Bethlehem. A thousand years after David lived, the time had come for the Messiah to be born from the tribe of Judah, the family of David, in the city of Bethlehem. God would pull this off through a very young and faithful descendant of Ruth.

In the sixth month of Elizabeth's pregnancy, God sent the angel Gabriel to Nazareth, a town in Galilee, to a virgin pledged to be married to a man named Joseph, a descendant of David. The virgin's name was Mary. The angel went to her and said, "Greetings, you who are highly favored! The Lord is with you."

Mary was greatly troubled at his words and wondered what kind of greeting this might be. But the angel said to her, "Do not be afraid, Mary; you have found favor with God. You will conceive and give birth to a son, and you are to call him Jesus. He will be great and will be called the Son of the Most High. The Lord God will give him the throne of his father David, and he will reign over Jacob's descendants forever; his kingdom will never end."

"How will this be," Mary asked the angel, "since I am a virgin?"

The angel answered, "The Holy Spirit will come on you, and the power of the Most High will overshadow you. So the holy one to be born will be called the Son of God. Even Elizabeth your relative is going to have a child in her old age, and she who was said to be unable to conceive is in her sixth month. For no word from God will ever fail."

"I am the Lord's servant," Mary answered. "May your word to me be fulfilled." Then the angel left her.

At that time Mary got ready and hurried to a town in the hill country of Judea, where she entered Zechariah's home and greeted Elizabeth. When Elizabeth heard Mary's greeting, the baby leaped in her womb, and Elizabeth was filled with the Holy Spirit. In a loud voice she exclaimed: "Blessed are you among women, and blessed is the child you will bear! But why am I so favored, that the mother of my Lord should come to me? As soon as the sound of your greeting reached my ears, the baby in my womb leaped for joy. Blessed is she who has believed that the Lord would fulfill his promises to her!"

And Mary said:

> "My soul glorifies the Lord
>> and my spirit rejoices in God my Savior,
> for he has been mindful
>> of the humble state of his servant.
> From now on all generations will call me blessed,
>> for the Mighty One has done great things for me —
>> holy is his name.
> His mercy extends to those who fear him,
>> from generation to generation.
> He has performed mighty deeds with his arm;
>> he has scattered those who are proud in their inmost
>>> thoughts.
> He has brought down rulers from their thrones
>> but has lifted up the humble.
> He has filled the hungry with good things
>> but has sent the rich away empty.

He has helped his servant Israel,
    remembering to be merciful
to Abraham and his descendants forever,
    just as he promised our ancestors."

Mary stayed with Elizabeth for about three months and then returned home.   LUKE 1:26–56

Mary committed herself, as "the Lord's servant," to be faithful to God's plan, and she extolled God's faithfulness. After visiting her relative Elizabeth, Mary—now about three months pregnant—returned to her home in Nazareth. But Nazareth was at least a three-day trip from Bethlehem. How then was the prophecy that the Messiah would come from the town of Bethlehem going to be fulfilled?

In those days Caesar Augustus issued a decree that a census should be taken of the entire Roman world. (This was the first census that took place while Quirinius was governor of Syria.) And everyone went to their own town to register.

So Joseph also went up from the town of Nazareth in Galilee to Judea, to Bethlehem the town of David, because he belonged to the house and line of David. He went there to register with Mary, who was pledged to be married to him and was expecting a child. While they were there, the time came for the baby to be born, and she gave birth to her firstborn, a son. She wrapped him in cloths and placed him in a manger, because there was no guest room available for them.

And there were shepherds living out in the fields nearby, keeping watch over their flocks at night. An angel of the Lord appeared to them, and the glory of the Lord shone around them, and they were terrified. But the angel said to them, "Do not be afraid. I bring you good news that will cause great joy for all the people. Today in the town of David a Savior has been born to you; he is the Messiah, the Lord. This will be a sign to you: You will find a baby wrapped in cloths and lying in a manger."

Suddenly a great company of the heavenly host appeared with the angel, praising God and saying,

"Glory to God in the highest heaven,
    and on earth peace to those on whom his favor rests."

When the angels had left them and gone into heaven, the shepherds said to one another, "Let's go to Bethlehem and see this thing that has happened, which the Lord has told us about."

So they hurried off and found Mary and Joseph, and the baby, who was lying in the manger. When they had seen him, they spread the word concerning what had been told them about this child, and all who heard it were amazed at what the shepherds said to them. But Mary treasured up all these things and pondered them in her heart. The shepherds returned, glorifying and praising God for all the things they had heard and seen, which were just as they had been told.

On the eighth day, when it was time to circumcise the child, he was named Jesus, the name the angel had given him before he was conceived.   LUKE 2:1–21

Throughout the Bible, God called believers to be faithful to his assignment for them, no matter how difficult. In fact, it was often amid the difficult seasons that they most discovered the trustworthiness of God. When they aligned their lives to God's story, he was with them and accomplished great things through them. All believers have the opportunity to open their lives to God's will and demonstrate their faithfulness. The results of such faithfulness can be both great and beautiful as God works through those who believe.

CHAPTER

29

Gentleness

KEY IDEA

I am thoughtful, considerate and calm
in my dealings with others.

KEY VERSE

Let your gentleness be evident to all.
The Lord is near.
Philippians 4:5

Nothing kills a family, a friendship, a neighborhood or even a church like pride, arrogance, anger, closed ears and raised voices. Since God is all about community, he calls his followers to be gentle. Of course, he teaches us by modeling this virtue right in our midst.

GENTLE JESUS

Throughout the Bible we find stories and people who reinforce the fact that gentleness is a character trait that God has intended for us. Jesus, of course, is our greatest example of someone who displayed gentleness in his dealings with others. This is particularly true in his relationship with Peter. At the Last Supper the night before Jesus was crucified, Peter told Jesus he would die for him. Jesus, predicting Peter's future betrayal, corrected him. Jesus had already predicted the betrayal of Judas, who had just stepped out of the room.

When [Judas] was gone, Jesus said, "Now the Son of Man is glorified and God is glorified in him. If God is glorified in him, God will glorify the Son in himself, and will glorify him at once.

"My children, I will be with you only a little longer. You will look for me, and just as I told the Jews, so I tell you now: Where I am going, you cannot come.

"A new command I give you: Love one another. As I have loved you, so you must love one another. By this everyone will know that you are my disciples, if you love one another."

Simon Peter asked him, "Lord, where are you going?"

Jesus replied, "Where I am going, you cannot follow now, but you will follow later."

Peter asked, "Lord, why can't I follow you now? I will lay down my life for you."

Then Jesus answered, "Will you really lay down your life for me? Very truly I tell you, before the rooster crows, you will disown me three times!"   JOHN 13:31–38

Peter could not imagine betraying his master. He had left everything to follow Jesus. However, when Jesus was arrested later that evening the stakes increased beyond the fisherman's allegiance.

Then the detachment of soldiers with its commander and the Jewish officials arrested Jesus. They bound him and brought him first to Annas, who was the father-in-law of Caiaphas, the high priest that year. Caiaphas was the one who had advised the Jewish leaders that it would be good if one man died for the people.

Simon Peter and another disciple were following Jesus. Because this disciple was known to the high priest, he went with Jesus into the high priest's courtyard, but Peter had to wait outside at the door. The other disciple, who was known to the high priest, came back, spoke to the servant girl on duty there and brought Peter in.

"You aren't one of this man's disciples too, are you?" she asked Peter.

He replied, "I am not."

It was cold, and the servants and officials stood around a fire they had made to keep warm. Peter also was standing with them, warming himself.

Meanwhile, the high priest questioned Jesus about his disciples and his teaching.

"I have spoken openly to the world," Jesus replied. "I always taught in synagogues or at the temple, where all the Jews come together. I said nothing in secret. Why question me? Ask those who heard me. Surely they know what I said."

When Jesus said this, one of the officials nearby slapped him in the face. "Is this the way you answer the high priest?" he demanded.

"If I said something wrong," Jesus replied, "testify as to what is wrong. But if I spoke the truth, why did you strike me?" Then Annas sent him bound to Caiaphas the high priest.

Meanwhile, Simon Peter was still standing there warming himself. So they asked him, "You aren't one of his disciples too, are you?"

He denied it, saying, "I am not."

One of the high priest's servants, a relative of the man whose ear Peter had cut off, challenged him, "Didn't I see you with him in the garden?" Again Peter denied it, and at that moment a rooster began to crow.   JOHN 18:12–27

Sometime between Jesus' resurrection and ascension to heaven, he appeared to seven of his disciples who had gone fishing. With a heart of gentleness, Jesus restored Peter's relationship with him and reinstated Peter to a position of special responsibility in the church.

Afterward Jesus appeared again to his disciples, by the Sea of Galilee. It happened this way: Simon Peter, Thomas (also known as Didymus), Nathanael from Cana in Galilee, the sons of Zebedee, and two other disciples were together. "I'm going out to fish," Simon Peter told them, and they said, "We'll go with you." So they went out and got into the boat, but that night they caught nothing.

Early in the morning, Jesus stood on the shore, but the disciples did not realize that it was Jesus.

He called out to them, "Friends, haven't you any fish?"

"No," they answered.

He said, "Throw your net on the right side of the boat and you will find some." When they did, they were unable to haul the net in because of the large number of fish.

Then the disciple whom Jesus loved said to Peter, "It is the Lord!" As soon as Simon Peter heard him say, "It is the Lord," he wrapped his outer garment around him (for he had taken it off) and jumped into the water. The other disciples followed in the boat, towing the net full of fish, for they were not far from shore, about a hundred yards. When they landed, they saw a fire of burning coals there with fish on it, and some bread.

Jesus said to them, "Bring some of the fish you have just caught." So Simon Peter climbed back into the boat and dragged the net ashore. It was full of large fish, 153, but even with so many the net was not torn. Jesus said to them, "Come and have breakfast." None of the disciples dared ask him, "Who are you?" They knew it was the Lord. Jesus came, took the bread and gave it to them, and did the same with the fish. This was now the third time Jesus appeared to his disciples after he was raised from the dead.

When they had finished eating, Jesus said to Simon Peter, "Simon son of John, do you love me more than these?"

"Yes, Lord," he said, "you know that I love you."

Jesus said, "Feed my lambs."

Again Jesus said, "Simon son of John, do you love me?"

He answered, "Yes, Lord, you know that I love you."

Jesus said, "Take care of my sheep."

The third time he said to him, "Simon son of John, do you love me?"

Peter was hurt because Jesus asked him the third time, "Do you love me?" He said, "Lord, you know all things; you know that I love you."

Jesus said, "Feed my sheep. Very truly I tell you, when you were younger you dressed yourself and went where you wanted; but when you are old you will stretch out your hands, and someone else will dress you and lead you where you do not want to go." Jesus said this to indicate the kind of death by which Peter would glorify God. Then he said to him, "Follow me!" JOHN 21:1–19

Peter's relationship was fully restored by Jesus' gentle invitation. Peter went on to stay in a relationship with Jesus for the remainder of his life. In the end, tradition tells us Peter was martyred by being crucified upside down. Jesus invites all people to receive his gift of peace and rest.

"Come to me, all you who are weary and burdened, and I will give you rest. Take my yoke upon you and learn from me, for I am gentle and humble in heart, and you will find rest for your souls. For my yoke is easy and my burden is light." MATTHEW 11:28–30

NUGGETS ON GENTLENESS

The New Testament offers us wonderful nuggets on being thoughtful, considerate and calm. Jesus offered up powerful insights and encouragement in the Sermon on the Mount.

> "Blessed are the meek,
> for they will inherit the earth." MATTHEW 5:5

"You have heard that it was said, 'Eye for eye, and tooth for tooth.' But I tell you, do not resist an evil person. If anyone slaps you on the right cheek, turn to them the other cheek also. And if anyone wants to sue you and take your shirt, hand over your coat as well. If anyone forces you to go one mile, go with them two miles. Give to the one who asks you, and do not turn away from the one who wants to borrow from you." MATTHEW 5:38–42

"Do not judge, or you too will be judged. For in the same way you judge others, you will be judged, and with the measure you use, it will be measured to you.

"Why do you look at the speck of sawdust in your brother's eye and pay no attention to the plank in your own eye? How can you say to your brother, 'Let me take the speck out of your eye,' when all the time there is a plank in your own eye? You hypocrite, first take the plank out of your own eye, and then you will see clearly to remove the speck from your brother's eye." MATTHEW 7:1–5

Inspired by the life and teaching of Jesus and led by the Holy Spirit, the apostles offered further understanding and encouragement on the virtue of gentleness.

The fruit of the Spirit is love, joy, peace, forbearance, kindness, goodness, faithfulness, gentleness and self-control. Against such things there is no law. GALATIANS 5:22–23

Be completely humble and gentle; be patient, bearing with one another in love. EPHESIANS 4:2

"In your anger do not sin": Do not let the sun go down while you are still angry, and do not give the devil a foothold. Anyone who has been stealing must steal no longer, but must work, doing something useful with their own hands, that they may have something to share with those in need.

Do not let any unwholesome talk come out of your mouths, but only what is helpful for building others up according to their needs, that it may benefit those who listen. And do not grieve the Holy Spirit of God, with whom you were sealed for the day of redemption. Get rid of all bitterness, rage and anger, brawling and slander, along with every form of malice. Be kind and compassionate to one another, forgiving each other, just as in Christ God forgave you. EPHESIANS 4:26–32

Fathers, do not exasperate your children; instead, bring them up in the training and instruction of the Lord. EPHESIANS 6:4

Therefore, as God's chosen people, holy and dearly loved, clothe yourselves with compassion, kindness, humility, gentleness and patience. COLOSSIANS 3:12

Here is a trustworthy saying: Whoever aspires to be an overseer desires a noble task. Now the overseer is to be above reproach, faithful to his wife, temperate, self-controlled, respectable, hospitable, able to teach, not given to drunkenness, not violent but gentle, not quarrelsome, not a lover of money. He must manage his own family well and see that his children obey him, and he must do so in a manner worthy of full respect. 1 TIMOTHY 3:1–4

Do not rebuke an older man harshly, but exhort him as if he were your father. Treat younger men as brothers, older women as mothers, and younger women as sisters, with absolute purity. 1 TIMOTHY 5:1–2

The love of money is a root of all kinds of evil. Some people, eager for money, have wandered from the faith and pierced themselves with many griefs.

But you, man of God, flee from all this, and pursue righteousness, godliness, faith, love, endurance and gentleness. 1 TIMOTHY 6:10–11

The Lord's servant must not be quarrelsome but must be kind to everyone, able to teach, not resentful. Opponents must be gently instructed, in the hope that God will grant them repentance leading them to a knowledge of the truth, and that they will come to their senses and escape from the trap of the devil, who has taken them captive to do his will. 2 TIMOTHY 2:24–26

Remind the people to be subject to rulers and authorities, to be obedient, to be ready to do whatever is good, to slander no one, to be peaceable and considerate, and always to be gentle toward everyone. TITUS 3:1–2

The wisdom that comes from heaven is first of all pure; then peace-loving, considerate, submissive, full of mercy and good fruit, impartial and sincere. Peacemakers who sow in peace reap a harvest of righteousness. JAMES 3:17–18

Paul encouraged two Christian women in the church at Philippi to reconcile their differences and then urged the entire congregation to put their gentleness on public display in light of the Lord's arrival.

I plead with Euodia and I plead with Syntyche to be of the same mind in the Lord. Yes, and I ask you, my true companion, help these women since they have contended at my side in the cause of the gospel, along with Clement and the rest of my co-workers, whose names are in the book of life.

Rejoice in the Lord always. I will say it again: Rejoice! Let your gentleness be evident to all. The Lord is near. PHILIPPIANS 4:2–5

Likewise, Peter told his readers that a thoughtful, considerate and calm gentleness is key in a marriage relationship.

Wives, in the same way submit yourselves to your own husbands so that, if any of them do not believe the word, they may be won over without words by the behavior of their wives, when they see the purity and reverence of your lives. Your beauty should not come from outward adornment, such as elaborate hairstyles and the wearing of gold jewelry or fine clothes. Rather, it should be that of your inner self, the unfading beauty of a gentle and quiet spirit, which is of great worth in God's sight. 1 PETER 3:1–4

Husbands, in the same way be considerate as you live with your wives, and treat them with respect as the weaker partner and as heirs with you of the gracious gift of life, so that nothing will hinder your prayers. 1 PETER 3:7

STORIES OF GENTLENESS: ABIGAIL

Samuel anointed young David to be the next king of Israel, but the reigning King Saul hated David, causing David to flee as a fugitive. David was on the run from Saul when he encountered a couple who displayed opposite qualities—Abigail was wise and gentle, while Nabal was foolish and cruel. When David asked

Nabal for reasonable payment for the protection that he and his men had voluntarily rendered for Nabal's benefit, Nabal's response was harsh and rude. Abigail repaired the situation with gentleness and diplomacy.

Now Samuel died, and all Israel assembled and mourned for him; and they buried him at his home in Ramah. Then David moved down into the Desert of Paran.

A certain man in Maon, who had property there at Carmel, was very wealthy. He had a thousand goats and three thousand sheep, which he was shearing in Carmel. His name was Nabal and his wife's name was Abigail. She was an intelligent and beautiful woman, but her husband was surly and mean in his dealings — he was a Calebite.

While David was in the wilderness, he heard that Nabal was shearing sheep. So he sent ten young men and said to them, "Go up to Nabal at Carmel and greet him in my name. Say to him: 'Long life to you! Good health to you and your household! And good health to all that is yours!

"'Now I hear that it is sheep-shearing time. When your shepherds were with us, we did not mistreat them, and the whole time they were at Carmel nothing of theirs was missing. Ask your own servants and they will tell you. Therefore be favorable toward my men, since we come at a festive time. Please give your servants and your son David whatever you can find for them.'"

When David's men arrived, they gave Nabal this message in David's name. Then they waited.

Nabal answered David's servants, "Who is this David? Who is this son of Jesse? Many servants are breaking away from their masters these days. Why should I take my bread and water, and the meat I have slaughtered for my shearers, and give it to men coming from who knows where?"

David's men turned around and went back. When they arrived, they reported every word. David said to his men, "Each of you strap on your sword!" So they did, and David strapped his on as well. About four hundred men went up with David, while two hundred stayed with the supplies.

One of the servants told Abigail, Nabal's wife, "David sent

messengers from the wilderness to give our master his greetings, but he hurled insults at them. Yet these men were very good to us. They did not mistreat us, and the whole time we were out in the fields near them nothing was missing. Night and day they were a wall around us the whole time we were herding our sheep near them. Now think it over and see what you can do, because disaster is hanging over our master and his whole household. He is such a wicked man that no one can talk to him."

Abigail acted quickly. She took two hundred loaves of bread, two skins of wine, five dressed sheep, five seahs of roasted grain, a hundred cakes of raisins and two hundred cakes of pressed figs, and loaded them on donkeys. Then she told her servants, "Go on ahead; I'll follow you." But she did not tell her husband Nabal.

As she came riding her donkey into a mountain ravine, there were David and his men descending toward her, and she met them. David had just said, "It's been useless — all my watching over this fellow's property in the wilderness so that nothing of his was missing. He has paid me back evil for good. May God deal with David, be it ever so severely, if by morning I leave alive one male of all who belong to him!"

When Abigail saw David, she quickly got off her donkey and bowed down before David with her face to the ground. She fell at his feet and said: "Pardon your servant, my lord, and let me speak to you; hear what your servant has to say. Please pay no attention, my lord, to that wicked man Nabal. He is just like his name — his name means Fool, and folly goes with him. And as for me, your servant, I did not see the men my lord sent. And now, my lord, as surely as the LORD your God lives and as you live, since the LORD has kept you from bloodshed and from avenging yourself with your own hands, may your enemies and all who are intent on harming my lord be like Nabal. And let this gift, which your servant has brought to my lord, be given to the men who follow you.

"Please forgive your servant's presumption. The LORD your God will certainly make a lasting dynasty for my lord, because you fight the LORD's battles, and no wrongdoing will be found in you as long as you live. Even though someone is pursuing you to take your life, the life of my lord will be bound securely in the bundle of the living by the LORD your God, but the lives of your enemies he will hurl away as from the pocket of a sling. When the LORD has fulfilled for my lord every good thing he promised concerning him and has appointed him ruler over Israel, my lord will not have on his conscience the staggering burden of needless bloodshed or of having avenged himself. And when the LORD your God has brought my lord success, remember your servant."

David said to Abigail, "Praise be to the LORD, the God of Israel, who has sent you today to meet me. May you be blessed for your good judgment and for keeping me from bloodshed this day and from avenging myself with my own hands. Otherwise, as surely as the LORD, the God of Israel, lives, who has kept me from harming you, if you had not come quickly to meet me, not one male belonging to Nabal would have been left alive by daybreak."

Then David accepted from her hand what she had brought him and said, "Go home in peace. I have heard your words and granted your request."

When Abigail went to Nabal, he was in the house holding a banquet like that of a king. He was in high spirits and very drunk. So she told him nothing at all until daybreak. Then in the morning, when Nabal was sober, his wife told him all these things, and his heart failed him and he became like a stone. About ten days later, the LORD struck Nabal and he died.

When David heard that Nabal was dead, he said, "Praise be to the LORD, who has upheld my cause against Nabal for treating me with contempt. He has kept his servant from doing wrong and has brought Nabal's wrongdoing down on his own head."

Then David sent word to Abigail, asking her to become his wife. His servants went to Carmel and said to Abigail, "David has sent us to you to take you to become his wife."

She bowed down with her face to the ground and said, "I am your servant and am ready to serve you and wash the feet of my lord's servants." Abigail quickly got on a donkey and, attended by her five female servants, went with David's messengers and became his wife.

1 SAMUEL 25:1–42

STORIES OF GENTLENESS: DAVID

Our gentleness toward others is tested most when things are not going well for us—when we are frustrated, tired or discouraged.

David was now king of Israel, but his son Absalom had con-
spired against him to take the throne. Uncertain of the extent of
Absalom's support, David feared being trapped in Jerusalem
and wanted to spare the city a bloodbath. So he fled as a fugi-
tive once again. On his way out of Jerusalem, David experienced
a situation that was nearly unbearable. How would he respond?

As King David approached Bahurim, a man from the same clan
as Saul's family came out from there. His name was Shimei son of
Gera, and he cursed as he came out. He pelted David and all the
king's officials with stones, though all the troops and the special
guard were on David's right and left. As he cursed, Shimei said,
"Get out, get out, you murderer, you scoundrel! The LORD has repaid you for all the blood you shed in the household of Saul, in
whose place you have reigned. The LORD has given the kingdom
into the hands of your son Absalom. You have come to ruin because you are a murderer!"

Then Abishai son of Zeruiah said to the king, "Why should this
dead dog curse my lord the king? Let me go over and cut off his
head."

But the king said, "What does this have to do with you, you
sons of Zeruiah? If he is cursing because the LORD said to him,
'Curse David,' who can ask, 'Why do you do this?'"

David then said to Abishai and all his officials, "My son, my
own flesh and blood, is trying to kill me. How much more, then,
this Benjamite! Leave him alone; let him curse, for the LORD has
told him to. It may be that the LORD will look upon my misery and
restore to me his covenant blessing instead of his curse today."

So David and his men continued along the road while Shimei
was going along the hillside opposite him, cursing as he went and
throwing stones at him and showering him with dirt. The king
and all the people with him arrived at their destination exhausted.
And there he refreshed himself.   2 SAMUEL 16:5–14

STORIES OF GENTLENESS: PAUL

Like David, Paul carried great responsibility on his shoulders and
often was challenged by others and had his work undermined. It
would have been easy for Paul to lose his temper with the new

*believers he sought to encourage in Christ. But he didn't. In his
first letter to the church of Thessalonica Paul laid out his effective
approach of gentleness in ministering to them. It's an approach
we would be wise to emulate with the people God has placed in
our lives.*

You know, brothers and sisters, that our visit to you was not
without results. We had previously suffered and been treated out-
rageously in Philippi, as you know, but with the help of our God we
dared to tell you his gospel in the face of strong opposition. For the
appeal we make does not spring from error or impure motives, nor
are we trying to trick you. On the contrary, we speak as those approved by God to be entrusted with the gospel. We are not trying
to please people but God, who tests our hearts. You know we never
used flattery, nor did we put on a mask to cover up greed — God is
our witness. We were not looking for praise from people, not from
you or anyone else, even though as apostles of Christ we could
have asserted our authority. Instead, we were like young children
among you.

Just as a nursing mother cares for her children, so we cared for
you. Because we loved you so much, we were delighted to share
with you not only the gospel of God but our lives as well. Surely you remember, brothers and sisters, our toil and hardship; we
worked night and day in order not to be a burden to anyone while
we preached the gospel of God to you. You are witnesses, and so
is God, of how holy, righteous and blameless we were among you
who believed. For you know that we dealt with each of you as a
father deals with his own children, encouraging, comforting and
urging you to live lives worthy of God, who calls you into his kingdom and glory.

And we also thank God continually because, when you received the word of God, which you heard from us, you accepted it
not as a human word, but as it actually is, the word of God, which
is indeed at work in you who believe.   1 THESSALONIANS 2:1–13

CHAPTER

30

Humility

---------- KEY IDEA ----------

I choose to esteem others above myself.

---------- KEY VERSE ----------

Do nothing out of selfish ambition or vain conceit.
Rather, in humility value others above yourselves,
not looking to your own interests
but each of you to the interests of the others.
Philippians 2:3 – 4

Humility is a driving virtue in the Christian life and community. Choosing to esteem others above oneself encourages harmony and love. The opposite of humility is pride. Prideful people typically believe they are better than others. They strive to get their way at the expense of others or boast as a way of boosting low self-esteem. When a person possesses Biblical humility they draw from internal "God-esteem." They have received God's unconditional love and embraced their inherent worth as God's child. From this belief they are capable of lifting others up.

CHRIST AS OUR EXAMPLE

Jesus is our supreme example of humility. The God of the universe could have ridden into our world on a white horse with a serious entourage and fanfare. Instead he came to us as a baby born in a stable to poor parents.

In those days Caesar Augustus issued a decree that a census should be taken of the entire Roman world. (This was the first census that took place while Quirinius was governor of Syria.) And everyone went to their own town to register.

So Joseph also went up from the town of Nazareth in Galilee to Judea, to Bethlehem the town of David, because he belonged to the house and line of David. He went there to register with Mary, who was pledged to be married to him and was expecting a child. While they were there, the time came for the baby to be born, and she gave birth to her firstborn, a son. She wrapped him in cloths and placed him in a manger, because there was no guest room available for them.

And there were shepherds living out in the fields nearby, keeping watch over their flocks at night. An angel of the Lord appeared to them, and the glory of the Lord shone around them, and they were terrified. But the angel said to them, "Do not be afraid. I bring you good news that will cause great joy for all the people. Today in the town of David a Savior has been born to you; he is the Messiah, the Lord. This will be a sign to you: You will find a baby wrapped in cloths and lying in a manger."

Suddenly a great company of the heavenly host appeared with the angel, praising God and saying,

"Glory to God in the highest heaven,
> and on earth peace to those on whom his favor rests."

When the angels had left them and gone into heaven, the shepherds said to one another, "Let's go to Bethlehem and see this thing that has happened, which the Lord has told us about."

So they hurried off and found Mary and Joseph, and the baby, who was lying in the manger. When they had seen him, they spread the word concerning what had been told them about this child, and all who heard it were amazed at what the shepherds said to them. But Mary treasured up all these things and pondered them in her heart. The shepherds returned, glorifying and praising God for all the things they had heard and seen, which were just as they had been told. LUKE 2:1–20

As Jesus was coming to the end of his time on earth, he wanted to impress upon his disciples the importance of humility. He does so in an unforgettable way.

It was just before the Passover Festival. Jesus knew that the hour had come for him to leave this world and go to the Father. Having loved his own who were in the world, he loved them to the end.

The evening meal was in progress, and the devil had already prompted Judas, the son of Simon Iscariot, to betray Jesus. Jesus knew that the Father had put all things under his power, and that he had come from God and was returning to God; so he got up from the meal, took off his outer clothing, and wrapped a towel around his waist. After that, he poured water into a basin and began to wash his disciples' feet, drying them with the towel that was wrapped around him.

He came to Simon Peter, who said to him, "Lord, are you going to wash my feet?"

Jesus replied, "You do not realize now what I am doing, but later you will understand."

"No," said Peter, "you shall never wash my feet."

Jesus answered, "Unless I wash you, you have no part with me."

"Then, Lord," Simon Peter replied, "not just my feet but my hands and my head as well!"

Jesus answered, "Those who have had a bath need only to wash their feet; their whole body is clean. And you are clean, though not every one of you." For he knew who was going to betray him, and that was why he said not every one was clean.

When he had finished washing their feet, he put on his clothes and returned to his place. "Do you understand what I have done for you?" he asked them. "You call me 'Teacher' and 'Lord,' and rightly so, for that is what I am. Now that I, your Lord and Teacher, have washed your feet, you also should wash one another's feet. I have set you an example that you should do as I have done for you. Very truly I tell you, no servant is greater than his master, nor is a messenger greater than the one who sent him. Now that you know these things, you will be blessed if you do them." JOHN 13:1–17

Following in the steps of his Savior, the apostle Paul wrote a tender letter to the church at Philippi instructing them to practice humility. He cited Jesus as the model.

Therefore if you have any encouragement from being united with Christ, if any comfort from his love, if any common sharing in the Spirit, if any tenderness and compassion, then make my joy complete by being like-minded, having the same love, being one in spirit and of one mind. Do nothing out of selfish ambition or vain conceit. Rather, in humility value others above yourselves, not looking to your own interests but each of you to the interests of the others.

In your relationships with one another, have the same mindset as Christ Jesus:

> Who, being in very nature God,
>   did not consider equality with God something
>   to be used to his own advantage;
> rather, he made himself nothing
>   by taking the very nature of a servant,
>   being made in human likeness.
> And being found in appearance as a man,
>   he humbled himself
>   by becoming obedient to death —
>   even death on a cross!

Therefore God exalted him to the highest place
    and gave him the name that is above every name,
that at the name of Jesus every knee should bow,
    in heaven and on earth and under the earth,
and every tongue acknowledge that Jesus Christ is Lord,
    to the glory of God the Father.

Therefore, my dear friends, as you have always obeyed — not only in my presence, but now much more in my absence — continue to work out your salvation with fear and trembling, for it is God who works in you to will and to act in order to fulfill his good purpose.   PHILIPPIANS 2:1–13

GOD OPPOSES THE PROUD, GRANTS FAVOR TO THE HUMBLE

Throughout the Bible we find a pattern—God opposes the proud but grants favor to the humble. The following passages from the book of Psalms and the book of Proverbs are brief, but their messages are powerful.

In his arrogance the wicked man hunts down the weak,
    who are caught in the schemes he devises.
He boasts about the cravings of his heart;
    he blesses the greedy and reviles the LORD.
In his pride the wicked man does not seek him;
    in all his thoughts there is no room for God.   PSALM 10:2–4

You save the humble
    but bring low those whose eyes are haughty.   PSALM 18:27

Good and upright is the LORD;
    therefore he instructs sinners in his ways.
He guides the humble in what is right
    and teaches them his way.   PSALM 25:8–9

The LORD sustains the humble
    but casts the wicked to the ground.   PSALM 147:6

The LORD's curse is on the house of the wicked,
    but he blesses the home of the righteous.

He mocks proud mockers
  but shows favor to the humble and oppressed.

PROVERBS 3:33–34

When pride comes, then comes disgrace,
  but with humility comes wisdom.   PROVERBS 11:2

Pride goes before destruction,
  a haughty spirit before a fall.

Better to be lowly in spirit along with the oppressed
  than to share plunder with the proud.   PROVERBS 16:18–19

Before a downfall the heart is haughty,
  but humility comes before honor.   PROVERBS 18:12

Haughty eyes and a proud heart —
  the unplowed field of the wicked — produce sin.

PROVERBS 21:4

The proud and arrogant person — "Mocker" is his name —
  behaves with insolent fury.   PROVERBS 21:24

Humility is the fear of the LORD;
  its wages are riches and honor and life.   PROVERBS 22:4

Do not exalt yourself in the king's presence,
  and do not claim a place among his great men;
it is better for him to say to you, "Come up here,"
  than for him to humiliate you before his nobles.

PROVERBS 25:6–7

Pride brings a person low,
  but the lowly in spirit gain honor.   PROVERBS 29:23

An example of God opposing the proud and granting favor to the humble can be found in the story of a young Hebrew man named Daniel who was taken captive from Jerusalem to Babylon in 605 BC. There, after three years of training, Daniel was given

*a responsible post in King Nebuchadnezzar's service. Through
divine wisdom, Daniel was able to interpret dreams, and he soon
became one of the most prominent figures in the royal court.
God used Daniel to teach Nebuchadnezzar a memorable lesson
in humility. The book of Daniel includes the following letter that
the king wrote to his subjects regarding his experience.*

King Nebuchadnezzar,

To the nations and peoples of every language, who live in all
the earth:

May you prosper greatly!

It is my pleasure to tell you about the miraculous signs and
wonders that the Most High God has performed for me.

> How great are his signs,
>   how mighty his wonders!
> His kingdom is an eternal kingdom;
>   his dominion endures from generation to generation.

I, Nebuchadnezzar, was at home in my palace, contented and
prosperous. I had a dream that made me afraid. As I was lying in
bed, the images and visions that passed through my mind terrified
me. So I commanded that all the wise men of Babylon be brought
before me to interpret the dream for me. When the magicians, enchanters, astrologers and diviners came, I told them the dream,
but they could not interpret it for me. Finally, Daniel came into my
presence and I told him the dream. (He is called Belteshazzar, after
the name of my god, and the spirit of the holy gods is in him.)

I said, "Belteshazzar, chief of the magicians, I know that the
spirit of the holy gods is in you, and no mystery is too difficult for
you. Here is my dream; interpret it for me. These are the visions I
saw while lying in bed: I looked, and there before me stood a tree
in the middle of the land. Its height was enormous. The tree grew
large and strong and its top touched the sky; it was visible to the
ends of the earth. Its leaves were beautiful, its fruit abundant, and
on it was food for all. Under it the wild animals found shelter, and
the birds lived in its branches; from it every creature was fed.

"In the visions I saw while lying in bed, I looked, and there before me was a holy one, a messenger, coming down from heaven. He called in a loud voice: 'Cut down the tree and trim off its branches; strip off its leaves and scatter its fruit. Let the animals flee from under it and the birds from its branches. But let the stump and its roots, bound with iron and bronze, remain in the ground, in the grass of the field.

" 'Let him be drenched with the dew of heaven, and let him live with the animals among the plants of the earth. Let his mind be changed from that of a man and let him be given the mind of an animal, till seven times pass by for him.

" 'The decision is announced by messengers, the holy ones declare the verdict, so that the living may know that the Most High is sovereign over all kingdoms on earth and gives them to anyone he wishes and sets over them the lowliest of people.'

"This is the dream that I, King Nebuchadnezzar, had. Now, Belteshazzar, tell me what it means, for none of the wise men in my kingdom can interpret it for me. But you can, because the spirit of the holy gods is in you."

Then Daniel (also called Belteshazzar) was greatly perplexed for a time, and his thoughts terrified him. So the king said, "Belteshazzar, do not let the dream or its meaning alarm you."

Belteshazzar answered, "My lord, if only the dream applied to your enemies and its meaning to your adversaries! The tree you saw, which grew large and strong, with its top touching the sky, visible to the whole earth, with beautiful leaves and abundant fruit, providing food for all, giving shelter to the wild animals, and having nesting places in its branches for the birds — Your Majesty, you are that tree! You have become great and strong; your greatness has grown until it reaches the sky, and your dominion extends to distant parts of the earth.

"Your Majesty saw a holy one, a messenger, coming down from heaven and saying, 'Cut down the tree and destroy it, but leave the stump, bound with iron and bronze, in the grass of the field, while its roots remain in the ground. Let him be drenched with the dew of heaven; let him live with the wild animals, until seven times pass by for him.'

"This is the interpretation, Your Majesty, and this is the decree the Most High has issued against my lord the king: You will be driven away from people and will live with the wild animals; you will eat grass like the ox and be drenched with the dew of heaven. Seven times will pass by for you until you acknowledge that the Most High is sovereign over all kingdoms on earth and gives them to anyone he wishes. The command to leave the stump of the tree with its roots means that your kingdom will be restored to you when you acknowledge that Heaven rules. Therefore, Your Majesty, be pleased to accept my advice: Renounce your sins by doing what is right, and your wickedness by being kind to the oppressed. It may be that then your prosperity will continue."

All this happened to King Nebuchadnezzar. Twelve months later, as the king was walking on the roof of the royal palace of Babylon, he said, "Is not this the great Babylon I have built as the royal residence, by my mighty power and for the glory of my majesty?"

Even as the words were on his lips, a voice came from heaven, "This is what is decreed for you, King Nebuchadnezzar: Your royal authority has been taken from you. You will be driven away from people and will live with the wild animals; you will eat grass like the ox. Seven times will pass by for you until you acknowledge that the Most High is sovereign over all kingdoms on earth and gives them to anyone he wishes."

Immediately what had been said about Nebuchadnezzar was fulfilled. He was driven away from people and ate grass like the ox. His body was drenched with the dew of heaven until his hair grew like the feathers of an eagle and his nails like the claws of a bird.

At the end of that time, I, Nebuchadnezzar, raised my eyes toward heaven, and my sanity was restored. Then I praised the Most High; I honored and glorified him who lives forever.

> His dominion is an eternal dominion;
>   his kingdom endures from generation to generation.
> All the peoples of the earth
>   are regarded as nothing.
> He does as he pleases
>   with the powers of heaven
>   and the peoples of the earth.
> No one can hold back his hand
>   or say to him: "What have you done?"

At the same time that my sanity was restored, my honor and splendor were returned to me for the glory of my kingdom. My advisers and nobles sought me out, and I was restored to my throne and became even greater than before. Now I, Nebuchadnezzar, praise and exalt and glorify the King of heaven, because everything he does is right and all his ways are just. And those who walk in pride he is able to humble.   Daniel 4:1–37

James, the brother of Jesus, wrote a practical book of application for the first followers of Jesus. Contained in the letter is a "cost-benefit" analysis between pride and humility from which all of us can learn.

What causes fights and quarrels among you? Don't they come from your desires that battle within you? You desire but do not have, so you kill. You covet but you cannot get what you want, so you quarrel and fight. You do not have because you do not ask God. When you ask, you do not receive, because you ask with wrong motives, that you may spend what you get on your pleasures.

You adulterous people, don't you know that friendship with the world means enmity against God? Therefore, anyone who chooses to be a friend of the world becomes an enemy of God. Or do you think Scripture says without reason that he jealously longs for the spirit he has caused to dwell in us? But he gives us more grace. That is why Scripture says:

> "God opposes the proud
>   but shows favor to the humble."

Submit yourselves, then, to God. Resist the devil, and he will flee from you. Come near to God and he will come near to you. Wash your hands, you sinners, and purify your hearts, you double-minded. Grieve, mourn and wail. Change your laughter to mourning and your joy to gloom. Humble yourselves before the Lord, and he will lift you up.

Brothers and sisters, do not slander one another. Anyone who speaks against a brother or sister or judges them speaks against the law and judges it. When you judge the law, you are not keeping it, but sitting in judgment on it. There is only one Lawgiver and

Judge, the one who is able to save and destroy. But you — who are you to judge your neighbor?

Now listen, you who say, "Today or tomorrow we will go to this or that city, spend a year there, carry on business and make money." Why, you do not even know what will happen tomorrow. What is your life? You are a mist that appears for a little while and then vanishes. Instead, you ought to say, "If it is the Lord's will, we will live and do this or that." As it is, you boast in your arrogant schemes. All such boasting is evil. If anyone, then, knows the good they ought to do and doesn't do it, it is sin for them.   JAMES 4:1–17

In Peter's first letter to the growing group of Christians in Asia Minor he instructed believers of all ages to practice the virtue of humility.

To the elders among you, I appeal as a fellow elder and a witness of Christ's sufferings who also will share in the glory to be revealed: Be shepherds of God's flock that is under your care, watching over them — not because you must, but because you are willing, as God wants you to be; not pursuing dishonest gain, but eager to serve; not lording it over those entrusted to you, but being examples to the flock. And when the Chief Shepherd appears, you will receive the crown of glory that will never fade away.

In the same way, you who are younger, submit yourselves to your elders. All of you, clothe yourselves with humility toward one another, because,

"God opposes the proud
but shows favor to the humble."

Humble yourselves, therefore, under God's mighty hand, that he may lift you up in due time.   1 PETER 5:1–6

THE PARADOX OF HUMILITY

Some might believe that a humble person always loses out, gets overlooked and comes in dead last, while someone with less humility always wins, gets noticed and comes in first. The Bible teaches that regardless of circumstances or the world's perspective, Christians experience true joy and contentment in this life and anticipate the full blessings of God's kingdom in the next life. Read carefully Jesus' opening words in the Sermon on the Mount.

Now when Jesus saw the crowds, he went up on a mountainside and sat down. His disciples came to him, and he began to teach them.

He said:

> "Blessed are the poor in spirit,
>   for theirs is the kingdom of heaven.
> Blessed are those who mourn,
>   for they will be comforted.
> Blessed are the meek,
>   for they will inherit the earth.
> Blessed are those who hunger and thirst for
>   righteousness,
>   for they will be filled.
> Blessed are the merciful,
>   for they will be shown mercy.
> Blessed are the pure in heart,
>   for they will see God.
> Blessed are the peacemakers,
>   for they will be called children of God.
> Blessed are those who are persecuted because of
>   righteousness,
>   for theirs is the kingdom of heaven.

"Blessed are you when people insult you, persecute you and falsely say all kinds of evil against you because of me. Rejoice and be glad, because great is your reward in heaven, for in the same way they persecuted the prophets who were before you."

MATTHEW 5:1–12

It was not uncommon for large crowds of people to follow and gather around Jesus to hear him teach and watch him perform all kinds of miracles. On one such occasion, after Jesus healed a demon-possessed boy, a disagreement broke out between the disciples. Before pride got the best of them, Jesus reiterated the role of humility in a believer's life.

The next day, when they came down from the mountain, a large crowd met him. A man in the crowd called out, "Teacher, I beg you to look at my son, for he is my only child. A spirit seizes him and he suddenly screams; it throws him into convulsions so that he foams at the mouth. It scarcely ever leaves him and is destroying him. I begged your disciples to drive it out, but they could not."

"You unbelieving and perverse generation," Jesus replied, "how long shall I stay with you and put up with you? Bring your son here."

Even while the boy was coming, the demon threw him to the ground in a convulsion. But Jesus rebuked the impure spirit, healed the boy and gave him back to his father. And they were all amazed at the greatness of God.

While everyone was marveling at all that Jesus did, he said to his disciples, "Listen carefully to what I am about to tell you: The Son of Man is going to be delivered into the hands of men." But they did not understand what this meant. It was hidden from them, so that they did not grasp it, and they were afraid to ask him about it.

An argument started among the disciples as to which of them would be the greatest. Jesus, knowing their thoughts, took a little child and had him stand beside him. Then he said to them, "Whoever welcomes this little child in my name welcomes me; and whoever welcomes me welcomes the one who sent me. For it is the one who is least among you all who is the greatest."   LUKE 9:37–48

This question of which of Jesus' disciples would be the greatest arose on a number of occasions. You would think the message would have eventually sunk in, but it hadn't. As Jesus was on his way to Jerusalem for the last time, the brothers James and John—two of Jesus' inner circle of disciples—approached him with a request.

James and John, the sons of Zebedee, came to him. "Teacher," they said, "we want you to do for us whatever we ask."

"What do you want me to do for you?" he asked.

They replied, "Let one of us sit at your right and the other at your left in your glory."

"You don't know what you are asking," Jesus said. "Can you drink the cup I drink or be baptized with the baptism I am baptized with?"

"We can," they answered.

Jesus said to them, "You will drink the cup I drink and be baptized with the baptism I am baptized with, but to sit at my right or left is not for me to grant. These places belong to those for whom they have been prepared."

When the ten heard about this, they became indignant with James and John. Jesus called them together and said, "You know that those who are regarded as rulers of the Gentiles lord it over them, and their high officials exercise authority over them. Not so with you. Instead, whoever wants to become great among you must be your servant, and whoever wants to be first must be slave of all. For even the Son of Man did not come to be served, but to serve, and to give his life as a ransom for many." MARK 10:35–45

Jesus did acknowledge one individual who got it right.

"Truly I tell you, among those born of women there has not risen anyone greater than John the Baptist; yet whoever is least in the kingdom of heaven is greater than he." MATTHEW 11:11

What was John's secret to success? John gave the answer in a powerful conversation with his disciples.

Jesus and his disciples went out into the Judean countryside, where he spent some time with them, and baptized. Now John also was baptizing at Aenon near Salim, because there was plenty of water, and people were coming and being baptized. (This was before John was put in prison.) An argument developed between some of John's disciples and a certain Jew over the matter of ceremonial washing. They came to John and said to him, "Rabbi, that man who was with you on the other side of the Jordan — the one you testified about — look, he is baptizing, and everyone is going to him."

To this John replied, "A person can receive only what is given them from heaven. You yourselves can testify that I said, 'I am not the Messiah but am sent ahead of him.' The bride belongs to the bridegroom. The friend who attends the bridegroom waits and listens for him, and is full of joy when he hears the bridegroom's voice. That joy is mine, and it is now complete. He must become greater; I must become less."

The one who comes from above is above all; the one who is from the earth belongs to the earth, and speaks as one from the earth. The one who comes from heaven is above all. JOHN 3:22–31

> *People who struggle with humility are often caught boasting or bragging about themselves. In 2 Corinthians, Paul responded to criticism he received about his ministry. Using a unique style of writing, almost tongue-in-cheek, Paul introduced his readers to a proper form of boasting.*

I repeat: Let no one take me for a fool. But if you do, then tolerate me just as you would a fool, so that I may do a little boasting. In this self-confident boasting I am not talking as the Lord would, but as a fool. Since many are boasting in the way the world does, I too will boast. You gladly put up with fools since you are so wise! In fact, you even put up with anyone who enslaves you or exploits you or takes advantage of you or puts on airs or slaps you in the face. To my shame I admit that we were too weak for that!

Whatever anyone else dares to boast about — I am speaking as a fool — I also dare to boast about. Are they Hebrews? So am I. Are they Israelites? So am I. Are they Abraham's descendants? So am I. Are they servants of Christ? (I am out of my mind to talk like this.) I am more. I have worked much harder, been in prison more frequently, been flogged more severely, and been exposed to death again and again. Five times I received from the Jews the forty lashes minus one. Three times I was beaten with rods, once I was pelted with stones, three times I was shipwrecked, I spent a night and a day in the open sea, I have been constantly on the move. I have been in danger from rivers, in danger from bandits, in danger from my fellow Jews, in danger from Gentiles; in danger in the city, in danger in the country, in danger at sea; and in danger from false believers. I have labored and toiled and have often gone without sleep; I have known hunger and thirst and have often gone without food; I have been cold and naked. Besides everything else, I face daily the pressure of my concern for all the churches. Who is weak, and I do not feel weak? Who is led into sin, and I do not inwardly burn?

If I must boast, I will boast of the things that show my weakness. The God and Father of the Lord Jesus, who is to be praised forever, knows that I am not lying. In Damascus the governor under King Aretas had the city of the Damascenes guarded in order to arrest me. But I was lowered in a basket from a window in the wall and slipped through his hands.

I must go on boasting. Although there is nothing to be gained, I will go on to visions and revelations from the Lord. I know a man in Christ who fourteen years ago was caught up to the third heaven. Whether it was in the body or out of the body I do not know — God knows. And I know that this man — whether in the body or apart from the body I do not know, but God knows — was caught up to paradise and heard inexpressible things, things that no one is permitted to tell. I will boast about a man like that, but I will not boast about myself, except about my weaknesses. Even if I should choose to boast, I would not be a fool, because I would be speaking the truth. But I refrain, so no one will think more of me than is warranted by what I do or say, or because of these surpassingly great revelations. Therefore, in order to keep me from becoming conceited, I was given a thorn in my flesh, a messenger of Satan, to torment me. Three times I pleaded with the Lord to take it away from me. But he said to me, "My grace is sufficient for you, for my power is made perfect in weakness." Therefore I will boast all the more gladly about my weaknesses, so that Christ's power may rest on me. That is why, for Christ's sake, I delight in weaknesses, in insults, in hardships, in persecutions, in difficulties. For when I am weak, then I am strong.   2 CORINTHIANS 11:16—12:10

Although he eventually became one of Christ's most trusted followers, Paul was not always a humble servant of Jesus. He was once arrogant and violent, a vehement persecutor of Christians. In his first letter to Timothy, the apostle wrote honestly and openly about this amazing shift in his life.

I thank Christ Jesus our Lord, who has given me strength, that he considered me trustworthy, appointing me to his service. Even though I was once a blasphemer and a persecutor and a violent man, I was shown mercy because I acted in ignorance and unbelief. The grace of our Lord was poured out on me abundantly, along with the faith and love that are in Christ Jesus.

Here is a trustworthy saying that deserves full acceptance: Christ Jesus came into the world to save sinners — of whom I am the worst. But for that very reason I was shown mercy so that in me, the worst of sinners, Christ Jesus might display his immense patience as an example for those who would believe in him and receive eternal life. Now to the King eternal, immortal, invisible, the only God, be honor and glory for ever and ever. Amen.

1 TIMOTHY 1:12–17

GOD'S REQUIREMENT

What does God require from us? Micah, a prophet to Israel and Judah in the eighth century BC, answered this question with convicting succinctness. What God required then, he still requires of us today.

Listen to what the LORD says:

"Stand up, plead my case before the mountains;
  let the hills hear what you have to say.

"Hear, you mountains, the LORD's accusation;
  listen, you everlasting foundations of the earth.
For the LORD has a case against his people;
  he is lodging a charge against Israel.

"My people, what have I done to you?
  How have I burdened you? Answer me.
I brought you up out of Egypt
  and redeemed you from the land of slavery.
I sent Moses to lead you,
  also Aaron and Miriam.
My people, remember
  what Balak king of Moab plotted
  and what Balaam son of Beor answered.

Remember your journey from Shittim to Gilgal,
   that you may know the righteous acts of the LORD."

With what shall I come before the LORD
   and bow down before the exalted God?
Shall I come before him with burnt offerings,
   with calves a year old?
Will the LORD be pleased with thousands of rams,
   with ten thousand rivers of olive oil?
Shall I offer my firstborn for my transgression,
   the fruit of my body for the sin of my soul?
He has shown you, O mortal, what is good.
   And what does the LORD require of you?
To act justly and to love mercy
   and to walk humbly with your God.   MICAH 6:1–8

Epilogue

You have just finished reading stories of real people who lived in ancient times and encountered the one true God. They were invited to take part in the unfolding of God's Grand Love Story.

Many believed; many did not. But for all it was a journey. We see this in one particular story from the Bible. A man brought his boy to Jesus to deliver him from demon possession. Jesus asked the father how long his son had been like this. The father replied that he had been afflicted since childhood. "It has often thrown him into fire or water to kill him. But if you can do anything, take pity on us and help us."

"'If you can?' said Jesus. 'Everything is possible for one who believes.' Immediately the boy's father exclaimed, 'I do believe; help me overcome my unbelief!'" (Mark 9:22–24).

Right now, Jesus invites you to believe — to believe in him and to believe the truths taught in the pages of Scripture that guide our lives daily and into eternity. Be honest like the man who spoke with Jesus and tell Jesus about your doubts and invite him to help you with your unbelief. He will. He doesn't want you to believe these truths are the right answer. He wants you to take them in your heart where they will affect how you will live.

Here is the promise: what you once thought was impossible will now be possible. The more you believe, the more you see and discover the power of God. The more you believe, the more he changes you from the inside out to become the kind of person you have only dreamed about — filled with love, joy, peace, forbearance, kindness, goodness, faithfulness, gentleness and self-control. These virtues are displayed in your life like fruit on a tree for others to taste and enjoy.

When we *think* and *act* like Jesus, empowered by his presence within us, little by little we *become* like Jesus. This is not only the most truthful and abundant way to live, but it is truly the best gift we can give to our family and others God places sovereignly into our lives.

So, spiritual pilgrim, BELIEVE.

"Taste and see that the LORD is good" (Psalm 34:8).

Discussion Questions

CHAPTER 1: GOD

1. In what ways do you see the invisible qualities of God revealed in nature?

2. What are some of the main points of God's requirements for his people?

3. Why did God have to prove over and over that he is the One true God?

4. In what ways have you experienced God as Father? As Jesus the Son? As the Holy Spirit?

5. What do you think is meant by the phrase Paul quoted: "For in him we live and move and have our being"?

CHAPTER 2: PERSONAL GOD

1. In the story of Abraham, Sarah and Hagar, what are some ways in which God showed his goodness to them?

2. How have you experienced God's personal knowledge of you? When have you known he was searching your heart? What was the result?

3. How did God show the captives in Babylon that he still cared for them and wanted the best for them?

4. Why does Jesus want us to refrain from worry? How does freedom from worry demonstrate confidence in God's provision and care?

5. What does it mean to live according to the flesh? What does living according to the Spirit look like?

CHAPTER 3: SALVATION

1. How would you describe Adam and Eve's life in the garden with God before they disobeyed him? What was life like for them afterward?

2. How did the Lord provide a substitutionary animal for Abraham's sacrifice?

3. Recalling the details of Jesus' time on earth, what similarities do you see in prophecy of the "suffering servant" from the book of Isaiah?

4. Can you pinpoint a moment or chart a sequence of moments in time when you realized that Christ died for you? How would you describe that process?

5. Why is it important to both believe in our hearts and profess with our mouths that Jesus is Lord?

CHAPTER 4: THE BIBLE

1. How does the story of Moses and the burning bush convey the holiness of God? How did Moses respond? How would you respond in a similar situation?

2. How did Jesus help his disciples understand who he was and why he came?

3. In what ways did God, through the Scriptures, build a case for the identity and purpose of Jesus?

4. Do the Ten Commandments remain as relevant today as they were when Moses delivered them to the people of Israel? How?

5. In what ways have you experienced the Word of God as "alive and active" in your own spiritual life?

CHAPTER 5: IDENTITY IN CHRIST

1. What were the main points of God's covenant with Abraham? How did God use the circumstances of Abraham and Sarah's advanced age to validate his covenant with Abraham?

2. How did Jeremiah's prophecy define God's new covenant? What were the main points?

3. How do Jesus' words in the Gospel of John assure you of your identity as one of God's own people? Pinpoint the phrases that mean the most to you.

4. What does God require of those who find their identity in Jesus Christ?

5. Describe some of the ways in which the concept of being adopted by God the Father as his child and being welcomed into his household affect your identity and your sense of purpose.

CHAPTER 6: CHURCH

1. How did Abraham respond that resulted in God crediting "it to him as righteous"? How did Peter respond when Jesus asked Peter who Jesus was? How are these responses related?

2. How did God equip the early church to carry out their mission to spread the gospel of Jesus Christ?

3. Identify some of the ways in which persecution helped the early church in its mission to share the gospel.

4. What were some of the events that show the transformation of a small group of Jesus' Jewish followers into a universal Christian church?

5. Find some of the key phrases that define the purpose of the Christian church in the world.

CHAPTER 7: HUMANITY

1. Describe in your own words God's original intent for the human race.

2. What are some of the results of human sin reflected in these chapters?

3. What is our best defense against false teachers?

4. How does the book of Hosea show both God's discipline and punishment and his compassion and redemption?

5. How do the stories in this chapter highlight God's persistence and compassion in bringing people into a right relationship with him? Which phrases speak to you personally?

CHAPTER 8: COMPASSION

1. List some of the ways in which God showed both compassion and justice to the Israelites.

2. Moses gave the Israelites specific laws governing how the Israelites were to treat others. What are some of the principles behind those laws?

3. How did Boaz express his faith when he helped Ruth and Naomi? What was the motivation behind his acts of compassion?

4. In your own words, describe how love for God and love for others are related.

5. What are the attitudes that James advocates? How can you adopt those same attitudes?

CHAPTER 9: STEWARDSHIP

1. If God is self-sufficient, why do we have to return a portion of our wealth to him?

2. Contrast the lifestyle of someone who loves money with that of someone who loves God.

3. Why are we encouraged to practice hospitality? Why is hospitality important to God?

4. List some of the things God has entrusted to you to manage. How are you doing in each of these areas? How can you deepen your stewardship of them?

5. Does God reward good stewardship of his resources? If so, how?

CHAPTER 10: ETERNITY

1. How does what the Bible writes about heaven compare with some of the popular notions of heaven today?

2. According to Paul, why is the resurrection essential to Christian theology?

3. In the apostle Peter's passage about "the day of the Lord," what phrases encourage you? Challenge you? Frighten you?

4. How does the prospect of eternal life in heaven affect your perspective on what is going on in your life today?

5. What do you most look forward to in heaven?

CHAPTER 11: WORSHIP

1. The chapter begins with Psalm 95. What does this psalm tell us about how and why we should worship God?

2. With what behaviors and attitudes of the Pharisees did Jesus take issue?

3. Why is it important to remember what God has done in the past in order to worship him in the present?

4. Why does God desire that we worship him exuberantly and unabashedly? When was the last time you worshiped God without holding back?

5. According to the apostle Paul, what is the centerpiece of New Testament worship? What attitudes and actions constitute proper worship?

CHAPTER 12: PRAYER

1. As you read these passages, consider: What are some of the reasons we pray to God? Are any of our concerns too big or too small to bring to God's attention? Why or why not?

2. What do you learn about prayer from David's psalms?

3. What do Gideon's interactions with God teach us about God's character?

4. What are the main points of Jesus' teachings about prayer?

5. How do Paul's words about prayer encourage you? How do they challenge you?

CHAPTER 13: BIBLE STUDY

1. Study the Key Verse. As you read the passages that follow it, highlight some of the phrases that illustrate how the Word of God is like a double-edged sword. In what ways have you experienced this?

2. The psalmist expresses a profound love for the Scriptures. What emotions does the Word of God evoke in you? Explain.

3. What were some of the ways in which the Israelites were to immerse themselves in the commands of God?

4. How did the Israelites respond when they heard the Book of the Law read after their return from captivity? How would you be affected if access to the Bible was denied you? How much could you remember well enough to write down?

5. What role does the Holy Spirit have in the way we perceive the Scriptures?

CHAPTER 14: SINGLE-MINDEDNESS

1. What did God promise to the Israelites if they would put him first and keep their covenant with him?

2. What did Jesus promise to those who would seek first the kingdom of God?

3. Why is it so difficult to put God first when we have many possessions?

4. List some of the things that tend to distract you from putting God first in your life.

5. Paul tells us "whatever you do, whether in word or deed, do it all in the name of the Lord Jesus." What does that admonishment mean to you?

CHAPTER 15: TOTAL SURRENDER

1. The first three of the Ten Commandments govern our relationship with God. Why is it important to get in right relationship with God in order to keep the rest of God's commandments?

2. Reflect on the stories of Shadrach, Meshach and Abednego and Esther and Mordecai, Stephen and Paul. How might you have reacted in their places?

3. What does it mean to "take up your cross daily"?

4. Which of these stories most inspires you? Why?

5. Reflect on the Key Verse. What does it mean to offer ourselves as "living sacrifices"?

CHAPTER 16: BIBLICAL COMMUNITY

1. The passage from Ecclesiastes describes a relationship between two people. Why, then, does the Teacher say "a cord of *three* strands" is not quickly broken?

2. What is the relationship between the temple and the New Testament church? Why does Paul call Jesus Christ the cornerstone?

3. Would you have wanted to be a member of the early church after Pentecost? Why or why not? In what ways should the early church be a model for churches today?

4. Why was hospitality so important in the early church? Is it important still today? Why or why not?

5. After reading these passages, how many benefits of Biblical community can you list?

CHAPTER 17: SPIRITUAL GIFTS

1. What gift did David use in his service to Saul? What was Daniel's gift?

2. How does God give spiritual gifts to his people?

3. Why is it so important that people identify their spiritual gifts? How do people in the church work together using their spiritual gifts?

4. Why is love the greatest gift, according to Paul?

5. For what purposes did God give spiritual gifts to the church?

CHAPTER 18: OFFERING MY TIME

1. In light of what you have learned about the Old Testament temple, why did God want the returning captives to build his house before they built their own?

2. How was the woman of noble character serving God?

3. How does God reward those who do what he has asked them to?

4. How do these readings change the way you think about time and how you use it? What might you do differently?

5. Study the Key Verse. In your own words, explain what it means to you.

CHAPTER 19: GIVING MY RESOURCES

1. Why do you think the Israelites were the most generous when they were the most vulnerable?

2. In what ways is Christian giving a "flow-through" system? In other words, how do resources circulate in God's economy?

3. Is it more difficult for people to give when they are wealthy or when they have limited resources? Why do you think so?

4. Why is it important to give cheerfully?

5. How does God reward generous giving?

CHAPTER 20: SHARING MY FAITH

1. What are some ways in which we can be God's "ambassadors" to the world?

2. What might be the reasons Christians lose their "saltiness"?

3. Which of the phrases in these readings indicate that God desires for all people to hear the gospel?

4. Why is it difficult for many Christians (in a relatively free society) to share their faith verbally? What are they afraid of? How does this apply in your own situation?

5. If you have not already done so, take some time to write out your own gospel story — what Jesus has done for you and how he has affected your life and worldview.

CHAPTER 21: LOVE

1. In 1 Corinthians 13, Paul explores love's many characteristics. Make two lists. What are characteristics in the positive sense (all that love is). What characteristics does love *not* have? What does each of these characteristics mean to you?

2. Why is it impossible to simultaneously love God and hate our neighbors?

3. In what respect is love a gift we receive? In what respect is love an active choice we make? What is the relationship between the two?

4. What is the relationship between love and forgiveness?

5. Why is it easy to give lip service to love but difficult to show love? How can we increase in love?

CHAPTER 22: JOY

1. These readings include several psalms. What were the sources of the psalmists' joy? Highlight the phrases that reveal them.

2. God gave the Israelites festivals and feasts to celebrate his provision and goodness. How did people celebrate in the New Testament era?

3. According to James, why are we to be joyful in suffering, especially in persecution?

4. What is the difference between joy and happiness?

5. What aspects of your faith give you the most joy?

CHAPTER 23: PEACE

1. How do you reconcile the concept of the Prince of Peace with the portrayal of the suffering servant?

2. How does having peace with God through Jesus reveal itself in your life?

3. Describe a Biblical view of resolving conflict. What steps are we to take in settling differences with others?

4. What do Jesus' words "Peace I leave with you; my peace I give you" mean to you? How might you let them shape the way you think and feel as you go about your day?

5. What is Paul's prescription for anxiety and worry?

CHAPTER 24: SELF-CONTROL

1. What can you learn regarding self-control from the examples of these Biblical characters highlighted in this chapter?

2. To what kinds of trouble does a lack of self-control lead?

3. Why is our tongue so difficult to control?

4. Why is self-control important in living a Biblical lifestyle? How does self-control relate to other fruit of the Spirit?

5. In what areas of your life do you struggle with self-control? How do these readings challenge you? What can you do to grow in self-control?

CHAPTER 25: HOPE

1. Have you ever felt despair like Job did? What questions did you ask of God?

2. In what sorts of things do many people in our culture put their hope, albeit false?

3. Highlight some of the phrases that reveal the psalmist's doubt. Which phrases reveal his deep and passionate hope in God?

4. What promises of God can you find in these readings? Write them out.

5. According to the writer of Hebrews, what did the Biblical heroes endure because they had hope in God? What is the "race marked out" for us? How is hope dependent on faith?

CHAPTER 26: PATIENCE

1. Highlight some of the examples of God's patience in these readings.

2. How did David wait on God's timing? Why is it difficult to do so?

3. How does patience diffuse a conflict? How does impatience and rashness escalate it?

4. In what ways is waiting patiently different from merely waiting?

5. How does the idea that God is a compassionate Father help you have patience in suffering?

CHAPTER 27: KINDNESS/GOODNESS

1. To whom did Joshua credit for the kindness to Rahab? To whose kindness did Jonathon refer in asking David to be kind to him?

2. In the stories of Rahab and David, the kindness of one person was reciprocated by the receivers. But what does Jesus tell us about expecting reciprocation?

3. Find all the phrases in Paul's writing about kindness and goodness. What are three things you've learned from them?

4. Is there a difference between kindness and goodness? If so, explain.

5. Look around you. Where in your life do you see evidence of the kindness of God?

CHAPTER 28: FAITHFULNESS

1. Which phrases in these readings best reveal the faithfulness of God?

2. Which of the stories of faithful people has the most impact on you? Why?

3. How is faithfulness related to hope? To love? To trusting God?

4. In what areas has God called you to be faithful? How are you doing?

5. Based on what you have learned about faithfulness, who are some of the most faithful people you know? How have they found honor and a good name in your sight? In the sight of others?

CHAPTER 29: GENTLENESS

1. Highlight the sentences in the first four readings that most reveal the gentleness of Jesus.

2. In what ways are you weary and burdened? In what ways has Jesus given you rest? What is the yoke to which Jesus is referring? How was the yoke of Jesus different than the yoke of the law?

3. Describe the ways in which Abigail, David and Paul were gentle.

4. Why is gentleness so often likened to weakness? What is the difference?

5. Look at the Key Verse. Why do you think Paul put those two sentences together?

CHAPTER 30: HUMILITY

1. In what ways did Jesus demonstrate humility?

2. Based on these readings, how would you define humility?

3. What are some of the "rewards" of humility? What is the fate of the proud and arrogant?

4. How does Paul's "boasting" in fact reveal his humility? Highlight key phrases.

5. Micah tells us that God requires us to act justly, love mercy and walk humbly with God. How are these acts related?

Chart of References

CHAPTER 1: GOD

Genesis 1:1
Psalm 19:1–4
Romans 1:20
Deuteronomy 6:1–9
Joshua 24:1–31
1 Kings 18:16–40
Genesis 2:4–9

Genesis 2:15–24
John 1:1–5
Luke 3:1–6
Luke 3:15–18
Luke 3:21–23
Acts 17:16–34
2 Corinthians 13:1–14

CHAPTER 2: PERSONAL GOD

Genesis 16:1–16
Genesis 21:1–21
Psalm 8:1–9
Psalm 23:1–6
Psalm 139:1–24
Psalm 145:1–21

2 Kings 20:1–7
Jeremiah 1:1–19
Jeremiah 29:1–14
Matthew 6:25–34
Romans 8:12–39
James 1:1–18

CHAPTER 3: SALVATION

Genesis 2:8–9
Genesis 2:15–17
Genesis 3:1–24
Genesis 22:1–18
Exodus 11:1—12:31
Isaiah 52:13—53:12

Matthew 26:1–4
Matthew 27:27—28:10
John 3:1–21
Romans 5:12–21
Romans 10:1–13

CHAPTER 4: THE BIBLE

Exodus 3:1—4:17
Luke 24:27–49
2 Peter 1:1–21
Exodus 19:1–9
Exodus 19:16–19
Exodus 20:1–21
Matthew 4:1–11

2 Timothy 3:10–17
Isaiah 40:6–8
Isaiah 55:6–13
Hebrews 4:12–13
Deuteronomy 4:1–2
Proverbs 30:5–6
Revelation 22:18–19

CHAPTER 5: IDENTITY IN CHRIST

Genesis 17:1–7
Genesis 17:17
Genesis 17:19
Genesis 21:1–7
Jeremiah 31:31–34
John 17:1–26
John 1:9–13
Hebrews 10:1–18
Luke 19:1–9
Romans 3:10–26
Romans 5:1–2

Romans 5:6–11
Romans 6:1–7
Romans 8:1–39
Ephesians 1:1—3:21
1 Corinthians 3:16–17
1 Corinthians 6:19
1 Corinthians 12:12–14
1 Peter 1:1–5
1 Peter 1:22–23
1 Peter 2:4–10

CHAPTER 6: CHURCH

Genesis 12:1–9
Genesis 15:1–6
Genesis 15:7–21
Matthew 16:13–19
Acts 1:1–11
Acts 2:1–41
Acts 8:1–25
Acts 9:31
Acts 11:1–18

Acts 11:19–26
Acts 13:1–3
Acts 13:4–6
Acts 13:13–52
Acts 20:17—21:1
Ephesians 2:11—3:12
Ephesians 4:1–16
Revelation 2:1–7

CHAPTER 7: HUMANITY

Genesis 1:1–31
Genesis 4:1–5
Genesis 4:6–16
Jude 1–16
Romans 1:18–32
Romans 2:17–24
Romans 3:9–20
Hosea 1:1–3
Hosea 3:1–3
Hosea 11:1–11
John 1:4
John 1:7
John 1:11–12
John 3:16
John 3:36

John 4:14
John 5:24
John 6:35
John 6:37
John 6:51
John 6:54
John 7:38
John 8:12
John 8:51
John 10:9
John 11:26
John 12:31–32
Matthew 18:1–14
Luke 6:27–36
Philemon 1–25

Chapter 13: Bible Study

Deuteronomy 6:1–25
Deuteronomy 31:9–13
Joshua 1:1–9
Nehemiah 7:73—9:3
Psalm 19:7–14
Psalm 119:9–24
Psalm 119:33–40

Psalm 119:97–112
Matthew 13:1–23
John 14:15–27
1 Corinthians 2:1–16
1 Timothy 4:1–16
2 Timothy 2:14–16
Hebrews 5:11—6:3

Chapter 14: Single-Mindedness

Exodus 20:2–3
Deuteronomy 6:1–9
Matthew 6:19–33
Philippians 3:1–14
2 Chronicles 20:1–30
John 8:12–30

Matthew 14:22–36
Acts 5:12–42
Deuteronomy 29:16—30:20
Romans 12:1–2
Colossians 3:1–4
Colossians 3:15–17

Chapter 15: Total Surrender

Exodus 20:1–7
Daniel 3:1–28
Esther 3:1—4:16
Luke 9:23–26

Luke 22:7–62
Acts 6:8—7:60
Acts 21:4–14
Philippians 1:12–21

Chapter 16: Biblical Community

Genesis 2:4–25
Ecclesiastes 4:8–12
Exodus 25:1–9
Exodus 40:1–35
2 Chronicles 7:1–3
Ephesians 2:11–22
Acts 2:1–4
Acts 2:42–47
Acts 4:32–37
Hebrews 10:19–25
Nehemiah 2:11—3:32
Nehemiah 6:15
John 13:1–17
Romans 12:4–5
Romans 12:10
Romans 13:8
Romans 15:5–7

Romans 15:14
Galatians 5:13
Galatians 6:2
Ephesians 4:2
Ephesians 5:21
1 Thessalonians 5:9–11
Hebrews 13:1–3
Hebrews 13:15–16
Acts 18:1–3
Acts 18:18–19
Acts 18:24–26
1 Corinthians 16:19
Romans 16:3–4
1 John 1:1–7
1 John 2:7–11
1 John 3:16–18
1 John 4:7–21

CHAPTER 17: SPIRITUAL GIFTS

1 Samuel 16:1–23
Daniel 2:1–47
John 14:15–31
Acts 2:1–21
Romans 12:4–8

1 Corinthians 12:4—13:13
Matthew 25:14–30
1 Peter 4:7–11
Ephesians 4:1–16

CHAPTER 18: OFFERING MY TIME

Jonah 1:1—2:10
Haggai 1:1–15
Luke 2:41–52
Exodus 16:1–30
Exodus 18:5–27

Proverbs 31:10–31
John 7:1–16
Matthew 25:31–46
Ephesians 5:15–17
Galatians 6:7–10

CHAPTER 19: GIVING MY RESOURCES

Genesis 27:41—28:22
Exodus 35:4–29
Exodus 36:3–7
1 Chronicles 29:1–18
Proverbs 3:9–10
Proverbs 11:24–25
Proverbs 11:28
Ecclesiastes 5:10–20
Matthew 6:1–4

Matthew 6:19–24
Luke 12:13–21
Mark 12:41–44
Luke 6:32–36
Acts 4:32–37
2 Corinthians 8:1—9:15
Philippians 4:10–19
1 Timothy 6:17–19

CHAPTER 20: SHARING MY FAITH

Genesis 12:1–4
2 Corinthians 5:14–21
2 Kings 5:1–15
Matthew 5:13–16
Acts 2:42–47
1 Corinthians 9:19–23
Psalm 40:1–10
Acts 1:1–8

Acts 8:1–8
Acts 8:26–40
Acts 20:17–24
Ephesians 6:19–20
Colossians 4:2–6
Jonah 3:1—4:11
John 4:3–42
Romans 10:1–15

CHAPTER 21: LOVE

1 Corinthians 13:1–13
Deuteronomy 6:4–9
Leviticus 19:17–18
Mark 12:28–34
Matthew 5:43–48
Romans 13:8–10

Galatians 5:13–25
1 John 4:7–21
Matthew 18:21–35
1 Samuel 18:1–4
1 Samuel 19:1–7
1 Samuel 20:1–42

CHAPTER 22: JOY

Psalm 16:1–11
Psalm 19:8
Psalm 119:14
Psalm 119:162
John 15:1–11
James 1:2–17
Deuteronomy 16:13–17
1 Chronicles 16:7–36
Ezra 6:13–22
Habakkuk 3:2–19
John 13:1

John 16:16–24
Philippians 1:1–19
Philippians 1:27–30
Philippians 2:12–18
Philippians 3:1–21
Philippians 4:1–9
Philippians 4:10–13
1 Peter 1:3–9
1 Peter 4:12–16
1 Peter 5:6–11

CHAPTER 23: PEACE

Isaiah 9:6–7
Isaiah 53:1–12
Romans 5:1–11
2 Corinthians 5:11 — 6:2
Ephesians 2:1–22
Genesis 13:1–18
Matthew 5:21–26
Romans 14:1 — 15:13
Colossians 3:1–17
Romans 12:17–21

1 Timothy 2:1–8
Titus 3:1–11
2 Samuel 15:1–16
2 Samuel 15:23
2 Samuel 15:30
Psalm 3:1–8
Matthew 6:25–34
Mark 4:35–41
John 14:15–27
Philippians 4:4–9

CHAPTER 24: SELF-CONTROL

Proverbs 16:32
Proverbs 17:27
Proverbs 25:28
Proverbs 29:11
Titus 1:4–9
Titus 2:1–15
Judges 16:1–21
Genesis 39:1–23
Luke 15:11–32

1 Corinthians 6:12–20
1 Corinthians 10:14–22
1 Timothy 6:2–16
2 Timothy 2:22 — 3:7
James 3:1 — 4:10
1 Peter 5:8–11
1 Corinthians 7:1–9
2 Peter 1:3–11
Galatians 5:16–25

CHAPTER 25: HOPE

CHAPTER 26: PATIENCE

CHAPTER 27: KINDNESS/GOODNESS

CHAPTER 28: FAITHFULNESS

CHAPTER 29: GENTLENESS

John 13:31–38
John 18:12–27
John 21:1–19
Matthew 11:28–30
Matthew 5:5
Matthew 5:38–42
Matthew 7:1–5
Galatians 5:22–23
Ephesians 4:2
Ephesians 4:26–32
Ephesians 6:4
Colossians 3:12

1 Timothy 3:1–4
1 Timothy 5:1–2
1 Timothy 6:10–11
2 Timothy 2:24–26
Titus 3:1–2
James 3:17–18
Philippians 4:2–5
1 Peter 3:1–4
1 Peter 3:7
1 Samuel 25:1–42
2 Samuel 16:5–14
1 Thessalonians 2:1–13

CHAPTER 30: HUMILITY

Luke 2:1–20
John 13:1–17
Philippians 2:1–13
Psalm 10:2–4
Psalm 18:27
Psalm 25:8–9
Psalm 147:6
Proverbs 3:33–34
Proverbs 11:2
Proverbs 16:18–19
Proverbs 18:12
Proverbs 21:4
Proverbs 21:24
Proverbs 22:4

Proverbs 25:6–7
Proverbs 29:23
Daniel 4:1–37
James 4:1–17
1 Peter 5:1–6
Matthew 5:1–12
Luke 9:37–48
Mark 10:35–45
Matthew 11:11
John 3:22–31
2 Corinthians 11:16—12:10
1 Timothy 1:12–17
Micah 6:1–8

BELIEVE

POWERED BY ZONDERVAN®

Dear Reader,

Notable researcher George Gallup Jr. summarized his findings on the state of American Christianity with this startling revelation: "Churches face no greater challenge...than overcoming biblical illiteracy, and the prospects for doing so are formidable because **the stark fact is, many Christians don't know what they believe or why."**

The problem is not that people lack a hunger for God's Word. Research tells us that the number one thing people want from their church is for it to help them understand the Bible, and that Bible engagement is the number one catalyst for spiritual growth. Nothing else comes close.

This is why I am passionate about the book you're holding in your hands: *Believe*— a Bible engagement experience to anchor every member of your family in the key teachings of Scripture.

The *Believe* experience helps you answer three significant questions: Can you clearly articulate the essentials of the faith? Would your neighbors or coworkers identify you as a Christian based on their interactions with you and your family? Is the kingdom of God expanding in your corner of the world?

Grounded in Scripture, *Believe* is a spiritual growth experience for all ages, taking each person on a journey toward becoming more like Jesus in their beliefs, actions, and character. There is one edition for adults, one for students, and two versions for children. All four age-appropriate editions of *Believe* unpack the 10 key beliefs, 10 key practices, and 10 key virtues of a Christian, so that everyone in your family and your church can learn together to be more like Jesus.

When these timeless truths are understood, believed in the heart, and applied to our daily living, they will transform a life, a family, a church, a city, a nation, and even our world.

Imagine thousands of churches and hundreds of thousands of individuals all over the world who will finally be able to declare—**"I know what I believe and why, and in God's strength I will seek to live it out all the days of my life."** It could change the world. It has in the past; it could happen again.

In Him,

Randy Frazee
General Editor, *Believe*

LIVING THE STORY OF THE BIBLE TO BECOME LIKE JESUS

Teach your whole family how to live the story of the Bible!

- **Adults** – Unlocks the 10 key beliefs, 10 key practices, and 10 key virtues that help people live the story of the Bible. Curriculum DVD and Study Guide also available.
- ***Think, Act, Be Like Jesus*** – A companion to *Believe*, this fresh resource by pastor Randy Frazee will help readers develop a personal vision for spiritual growth and a simple plan for getting started on the *Believe* journey.
- **Students** – This edition contains the same Scriptures as the adult edition, but with transitions and fun features to engage teens and students. Curriculum DVD also available.
- **Children** – With a Kids' Edition for ages 8-12, a Storybook for ages 4-8, and three levels of curriculum for preschool, early elementary, and later elementary, children of all ages will learn how to think, act, and be like Jesus.
- **Churches** – *Believe* is flexible, affordable, and easy to use with your church, in any ministry, from nursery to adult Sunday school, small groups to youth group ... and even the whole church.
- **Spanish** – All *Believe* resources are also available in Spanish.

FOR ADULTS

9780310433583

9780310250173

FOR STUDENTS

9780310745617
(Available May 2015)

FOR CHILDREN

9780310746010
(Available May 2015)

9780310745907
(Available May 2015)

FOR CHURCHES

Campaign Kit 9780310681717
(Available June 2015)

THE STORY

POWERED BY **ZONDERVAN**

READ THE STORY. EXPERIENCE THE BIBLE.

Here I am, 50 years old. I have been to college, seminary, engaged in ministry my whole life, my dad is in ministry, my grandfather was in ministry, and **The Story has been one of the most unique experiences of my life**. The Bible has been made fresh for me. It has made God's redemptive plan come alive for me once again.
—Seth Buckley, Youth Pastor, Spartanburg Baptist Church, Spartanburg, SC

As my family and I went through *The Story* together, the more I began to believe and the more real [the Bible] became to me, and **it rubbed off on my children and helped them with their walk with the Lord**. *The Story* inspired conversations we might not normally have had.
—Kelly Leonard, Parent, Shepherd of the Hills Christian Church, Porter Ranch, CA

We have people reading *The Story*—**some devour it and can't wait for the next week**. Some have never really read the Bible much, so it's exciting to see a lot of adults reading the Word of God for the first time. I've heard wonderful things from people who are long-time readers of Scripture. They're excited about how it's all being tied together for them. It just seems to make more sense.
—Lynnette Schulz, Director of Worship Peace Lutheran Church, Eau Claire, WI

FOR ADULTS

9780310950974

FOR TEENS

9780310722809

FOR KIDS

9780310719250

TheStory.com

Dive into the Bible in a whole new way!

The Story is changing lives, making it easy for any person, regardless of age or biblical literacy level, to understand the Bible.

The Story comes in five editions, one for each age group from toddlers to adults. All five editions are organized chronologically into 31 chapters with selected Scripture from Genesis to Revelation. The additional resources create an engaging group Bible-reading experience, whether you read *The Story* with your whole church, in small groups, or with your family.

- **Adults** – Read the Bible as one compelling story, from Genesis to Revelation. Available in NIV, KJV, NKJV, large print, imitation leather, and audio editions. Curriculum DVD and Participant's Guide also available.
- **Teens** – Teen edition of *The Story*, with special study helps and features designed with teens in mind. Curriculum DVD also available.
- **Children** – With a Kids' Edition for ages 8-12, a Storybook Bible for ages 4-8, a Storybook Bible for toddlers, fun trading cards, and three levels of curriculum for preschool, early elementary, and later elementary, children of all ages will learn how their story fits into God's story.
- **Churches** – *The Story* is flexible, affordable, and easy to use with your church, in any ministry, from nursery to adult Sunday school, small groups to youth group…and even the whole church.
- **Spanish** – *The Story* resources are also available in Spanish.

FOR CHILDREN

FOR CHURCHES

9780310719755

9780310719274

Campaign Kit 9780310941538

THE STORY

POWERED BY **ZONDERVAN**